VOICES OF FIRE

Voices of Fire

Reweaving the Literary Lei of Pele and Hiʻiaka

kuʻualoha hoʻomanawanui

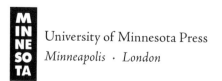

University of Minnesota Press
Minneapolis · London

Publication of this book was made possible, in part, with a grant from the Andrew W. Mellon Foundation.

Portions of the Introduction were previously published as "Ke Ha'a Lā Puna i ka Makani (Puna Dances in the Breeze): Pele and Hi'iaka Mo'olelo and the Possibilities for Hawaiian Literary Analysis," *Educational Perspectives* 45, nos. 1–2 (2013): 42–51.

Published by the University of Minnesota Press
111 Third Avenue South, Suite 290
Minneapolis, MN 55401-2520
http://www.upress.umn.edu

Library of Congress Cataloging-in-Publication Data

ho'omanawanui, ku'ualoha.
    Voices of fire : reweaving the literary lei of Pele and Hi'iaka / ku'ualoha ho'omanawanui. (First peoples: new directions in indigenous studies)
    Includes bibliographical references and index.
    ISBN 978-0-8166-7921-8 (hc : alk. paper) —
    ISBN 978-0-8166-7922-5 (pb : alk. paper)
1. Hawaiian literature—History and criticism. 2. Publishers and publishing—Hawaii—History. 3. Literature and folklore—Hawaii. 4. Hawaiian mythology. 5. Hawaii—Folklore. 6. Pele (Hawaiian deity). I. Title.
    PL6448.H66   2014
    899'.4209—dc23
                                                                    2013028377

Printed in the United States of America on acid-free paper

The University of Minnesota is an equal-opportunity educator and employer.

20 19 18 17 16 15 14   10 9 8 7 6 5 4 3 2 1

If Pele is not real to you, you cannot comprehend the quality of relationship that exists between persons related to and through Pele, and of these persons to the land and phenomena, not "created by" but which are, Pele and her clan. A rosy dawn is not merely a lovely "natural phenomenon": it is that beloved Person named "The-rosy-glow-of-heavens," who is "Hiiaka-in-the-bosom-of-Pele," the youngest and most beloved sister of that greater (and loved though awe-inspiring) Person, Pele-honua-mea . . . whose passions expressed themselves in the upheavals of volcanism, whose "family" or "clan" are the terrestrial and meteorological phenomena related to vulcanism and the land created by vulcanism, as actively known in Ka-'u. The stories that we are about to review are not archaic "legends" to a true native of Ka-'u: they are living, dynamic realities, parts of an orderly and rational philosophy, now obscured and superseded by the new dynamics and the chaotic values of the sugar plantation, with its mechanical and industrial modernism and concomitant ethnic, social, economic, political, religious, and other "new ways." These "new ways" are not a New Order for the country Hawaiian, and never will be: for they have exterminated him. He was engulfed and drowned in the tidal wave of Progress which inundated his land, his folks, his life, and his spirit.

E. S. Craighill Handy and Mary Kawena Pukui,
The Polynesian Family System in Ka-'u, Hawai'i

Papa Kuhikuhi / Contents

Ka Pule Wehe

Kūnihi ka mauna i ka la'i ē
'O Wai'ale'ale lā i Wailua
Huki a'ela i luna ka pōpō ua o Kawaikini
Ālai 'ia a'ela e Nounou
Nalowale Kaipuha'a
Ka laulā ma uka o Kapa'a ē
Ha'a i ka laulā
Ha'a ka ipu, ha'a ma kai o Kapa'a ē
Ha'a ka ipu, ha'a ma uka o Kapa'a ē
Mai pa'a i ka leo—
He 'ole kāhea mai
E hea mai ka leo—ē.

The Opening Prayer

Steep stands the mountain in the calm
Waiʻaleʻale there at Wailua
The rain bundles of Kawaikini are drawn up
Hidden above by Nounou
Kaipuhaʻa disappears
The expansive plain between the mountains above Kapaʻa
Dancing across the broad plain
The ipu gourd is dancing, dancing below at the seaside of Kapaʻa
The ipu gourd, is dancing, dancing in the uplands above Kapaʻa
Don't withhold the voice—
No reply comes;
Let the voice call forth.[1]

Ka Pane

Eia a'e e ka lā ma ka hikina
Ka hiki mai aloha, kūpuna ē
Kū ka hali'a i ka li'a Kawaikini
Wai'ale'ale, molale ē
Eia a'e nā pua lei mokihana
Kamāwaelualani ua wehi ē
E wehi kēia aloha ē
Aloha ku'u one hānau ē
Aloha nō, aloha ē
Manokalanipō, aloha ē.

The Response

The sun rises in the east
The affection of the ancestors arrives
Fondly recalled is Kawaikini
Wai'ale'ale is unobstructed
Here are the mokihana blossoms
Kamāwaelualani is embellished
With the adornment of love
Love for my beloved birth sands
Greetings, greetings
We greet you with affection, Manokalanipō,
Kaua'i's esteemed chief![1]

'Ōlelo Ha'i Mua / Preface

Kanaka 'Ōiwi (Native Hawaiian)[1] nationalist, scholar, and poet Haunani-Kay Trask begins her landmark essay "From a Native Daughter" by stating, "When I was young the story of my people was told twice: once by my parents, then again by my school teachers."[2] What Trask succinctly describes is how Kanaka 'Ōiwi exist between stories—those told by our kūpuna (elders, ancestors), and those told about us by our colonizers.

Without knowing it as a child, my life has been profoundly influenced by the stories of my Maoli ancestors, most particularly those associated with Pele and Hi'iaka. I say without knowing because they were absent from the curriculum of the public and private school education I received. When discussed in the public sphere, stories about Pele and Hi'iaka, like other Hawaiian traditions, were interpreted via a settler colonial lens, presented as cute myths meant to entertain or scare children and tourists, quaint folktales of an ancient past, fabrications of a simple, "savage" people who sustained superstitions of dubious origin and no historical significance.

At home, the stories I heard about Hawaiian anything primarily came from my paternal tūtū wahine (grandmother), Sarah Poni'ala Kakelaka. She was a pious Christian woman who spoke Hawaiian as her first language. She was born in Honolulu and lived in Kalihi, but spent much time throughout her youth on our family lands of Poupou and Kapa'ahu in Puna, Hawai'i, where her mother, Louise Akeao Apo, was born, and Wanini, Kaua'i, where uncle Enoka Kāwika's side of the 'ohana (family) fished the ample reef fronting the hale (house), and planted lo'i kalo (irrigated taro gardens) on the hillside fed by freshwater springs behind it. This 'āina (land) was land passed down to my tūtū's oldest sister, Kaui, who helped raise (hānai) my dad, 'āina that sustained our 'ohana for generations. Despite my tūtū's urban upbringing and fierce adherence to a Christian worldview, there were always the mo'olelo (stories and history) of our 'āina, lovingly told, stories of our kūpuna, stories that were told so that we would remember them so they would continue to live within us, stories that wove the genealogy, experiences, and history of our 'ohana with that of the 'āina, our culture, and our traditions, including those of Pele, Hi'iaka, Ka'ahupāhau, and more.

Born into a Hawai'i colonized and occupied by the United States, stories of American imperialism, conquest, and settler colonialism from George Washington to Pearl Harbor, from American Calvinist missionary letters and journals to the story lines of the revised television series *Hawaii Five-O* are inescapable. Yet born into a Hawai'i-based Maoli family, the stories of our akua (gods), kūpuna, and our 'āina have been woven through my life in deep and profound ways.

I was born in Kailua, O'ahu, at a hospital named for the American Board of Commissioners for Foreign Missions (ABCFM) missionary descendant Harold K. L. Castle, who had purchased nearly ten thousand acres of this ahupua'a (traditional land district) in 1917. It was built on the edge of the eight hundred–acre Kawainui Marsh, home of the great mo'o (reptilian) goddess Hau[mea]wahine, whom Hi'iaka encounters in her travels through the region. I spent the first few years of my life in the Oneawa and Keolu Hills areas of Kailua; Oneawa, the sandbar that separates Kawainui from Kailua Bay, on which most of Kailua town is built; Keolu, the dry hilly area dividing Kailua from Waimānalo, the home of Kanahau, the taro farmer with whom Hi'iaka falls in love, lands famous for the abundance of lo'i kalo, which thrived because of the wealth of freshwater caught by the verdant Ko'olau mountain range.

I was raised in Kaipuha'a in the mountainous region of Wailuanui-aho'āno, the most sacred area of Kaua'i, the 'āina to which Hi'iaka must pay homage and ask permission to enter the island on her quest to fetch her sister Pele's lover, Lohi'au; Wailua, the name of the large, deep river and its resident mo'o, which Hi'iaka must negotiate to continue on her journey to Hā'ena. The main road to our home, Kuamo'o, is named for the great dragon-like gods of the region, and Pilikua, the street I grew up on, for the enormous "Sleeping Giant," Nounou, who guarded our backyard. Pilikua, a giant, or one living in the country; Nounou, the mountain separating the ocean lands of Kapa'a from the uplands of Kaipuha'a as indicated in the opening chant "Kūnihi ka Mauna."

In her work on research and indigenous peoples, Māori scholar Linda Tuhiwai Smith points out that academic research is a site of contestation and struggle between the West and indigenous people, and lays the groundwork for indigenous researchers to write from a cultural perspective that serves the home community. Hawaiian cultural protocols serve as guidelines for research, particularly the value of kuleana (right, responsibility). In academic inquiry, kuleana is applicable to the concept of one's right to information or to share information, as well as one's responsibilities in this knowledge and sharing. Indigenous scholars must be cognizant of what and how we have a right to know and share; as kahu (caretakers) of knowledge, we are responsible in differing degrees to our disciplines, colleagues, and the institutions we work in, but we have equal responsibility to our kūpuna, ʻāina, and lāhui Hawaiʻi (Hawaiian nation).

When I am asked how I came to choose to study and write about Pele and Hiʻiaka literature, my answer is always the same: I did not choose it, it chose me. There are many fortuitous events that have occurred far too often over the years of studying these moʻolelo to be considered mere accidents. Rather, I strongly believe I am guided by my kūpuna on this path of discovery and scholarship. What this kuleana means to me, my ʻohana, and the greater lāhui is deeply imbedded within, and guides this study.

Nā Mahalo / Acknowledgments

Many kumu (teachers), mentors, and friends throughout my life have shaped me as an indigenous practitioner and intellectual. Some are living treasures who have committed themselves to upholding our language and cultural traditions; others have passed into Pō (the realm of the ancestors). My work could not have been accomplished without their aloha (love), support, and insistence that I travel this path.

The librarians and archivists who assisted me in my research were invaluable, especially Stu Dawrs, Joan Hori, Jodie Mattos, and Dore Minatodani of the Hawai'i-Pacific Collection, Hamilton Library, University of Hawai'i at Mānoa, DeSoto Brown and the staff of the Bishop Museum Archives, and the staff of the Mission House Museum Library.

Professors and colleagues at the University of Hawai'i at Mānoa who have generously shared their time, knowledge, and insights with me include Hōkūlani Aikau, Carlos Andrade, Noelani Arista, Cristina Bacchilega, Leilani Basham, John Charlot, Candace Fujikane, Noelani Goodyear-Ka'ōpua, Pualani Hopkins, Paul Lyons, Brandy Nālani McDougall, Puakea Nogelmeier, Georganne Nordstrom, Kapā Oliveira, Noenoe Silva, Alice Te Punga Somerville, Ty Kāwika Tengan, and Haunani-Kay Trask.

Others who have generously shared information and ideas, and encouraged me in my work include Marie Alohalani Brown, Vicky Creed, E. Kalani Flores, Kekuhi Kanaka'ole Frias, T. Ilihia Gionson, Ioane Ho'omanawanui, Daniel Heath Justice, Ka'imipono Kahumoku, Walter Kahumoku III, John Ka'imikaua, Kalani Kalima, Lopaka Kapanui, Kalei Nu'uhiwa, Yan Peirsegaele, Hiapo Perreira, Manuwai Peters, Michael Puleloa, Malia "Alohilani" Kuala Rogers, Leslie Keli'ilauahi Stewart, and Steve Winduo. I am particularly grateful to Makana Garma, who allowed me to include his oli (chant) as a pule pane (prayer response) that invites readers into this mo'olelo, and Noenoe Silva and Ty Kāwika Tengan, who provided invaluable assistance with Hawaiian language, including thorough and careful reading and critique of the manuscript, which was indispensible. Together, everyone's support and suggestions were invaluable throughout the process of deconstructing and reweaving this "lei palapala" (literary lei) into something much more beautiful.

I am particularly grateful to the Mellon-Hawai'i Doctoral and Post-doctoral Fellowship Program for awarding me a postdoctoral fellowship for 2009–2010 to complete this work, and the Andrew W. Mellon Foundation, Kamehameha Schools, the Kahiau Foundation, and the Kohala Center, who support this program. Mahalo a nui loa (much thanks) to Matt Hamabata and the Kohala Center staff for their support, and to co-fellows and friends Kauanoe Kamanā and Karin Ingersoll for the many conversations that helped to clarify my thinking on parts of this project.

Mahalo nui to Jason Weidemann, Danielle Kasprzak, and everyone on the University of Minnesota Press team for their support and enthusiasm for this project, and for their patience and professionalism as well.

The Hawaiian editors and writers who had the foresight to record our precious mo'olelo on paper left us a priceless cultural treasure, an intellectual and cultural legacy of unfathomable depth and beauty to which we are greatly appreciative and indebted. I have much mahalo to the collectors, editors, and publishers of the Pele and Hi'iaka mo'olelo for their commitment to our language and culture in a time of great adversity; as we embark on a journey of rediscovery, may we learn from and enjoy these mo'olelo as they intended.

The best of what everyone has offered me is contained within these pages and reflected within this work, but all errors and omissions are my own. I have spent over a decade of my life researching, reading, writing, analyzing, thinking, reflecting, and talking about these mo'olelo. I have dreamed them. I have visited the 'āina from Pele's home at Kīlauea, Hawai'i, Lohi'au's hula pā (dance platform) at Kē'ē, Kaua'i, and our ancestral homeland, Tahiti. Much time, thought, and aloha has gone into these pages. In the words of esteemed scholar Mary Kawena Pukui:

Pa'i ana nā pahu a ka hula le'a;
'O ka'u hula nō kēia.

Let more famous chanters beat their own drums
This hula is indeed mine.[1]

ʻŌlelo Mua / Introduction

Ke Haʻa lā Puna i ka Makani (Puna Dances in the Breeze)

Ke haʻa lā Puna i ka makani
Haʻa ka ulu hala i Keaʻau
Haʻa Hāʻena me Hōpoe
Haʻa ka wahine
ʻAmi i kai o Nānāhuki lā
Hula leʻa wale
I kai o Nānāhuki ē
ʻO Puna kai ʻkua [kai kuwā] i ka hala[1]
Paʻē ka leo o ke kai
Ke lū lā i nā pua lehua
Nānā i kai o Hōpoe
Aloha wale nō hoʻi ʻo Hōpoe
Ka wahine ʻami i kai o Nānāhuki lā
Hula leʻa wale
I kai o Nānāhuki ē.[2]

Puna dances in the breeze
The hala groves dance at Kea'au
Hā'ena and Hōpoe dance
The woman dances
A graceful 'ami step at the sea of Nānāhuki
A perfect, pleasing dance
At the sea of Nānāhuki
Puna's sea resounds in the hala
The voice of the sea strikes the ear
The lehua blossoms are scattered
Look toward the sea of Hōpoe
Hōpoe is indeed beloved
The dancing woman at the sea of Nānāhuki
A perfect, pleasing dance
At the sea of Nānāhuki.

IT IS MID-JULY, 1990, and I am in my second year of Hawaiian language at the University of Hawaiʻi at Mānoa. A group of Hawaiian-language classes from the Oʻahu-based campus has just arrived at Kalanihonua in ʻOpihikao, a remote area of Puna, Hawaiʻi, for a weeklong Hawaiian-language immersion camp. As our caravan of rented vehicles descends the last long slope of highway toward Kaimū, the latest eruption of the Kupaianaha vent is clearly visible in the distance. Roiling pillars of silvery steam clouds form where the lava meets the sea, billowing high into the atmosphere, extending far above Puna's brilliant blue ocean. It is a spectacular, awe-inspiring sight, one that plunges our van of fifteen excited and bubbly college students into reverent silence.

The main rule for the week is No English Allowed. When we arrive at Kalanihonua, my roommates Kanani, Mapuana, and I pledge an oath, right hands resting over our hearts, left hands solemnly placed on a frayed copy of Elbert and Pukui's *Hawaiian Dictionary*, that we will speak only Hawaiian for the rest of the week, "pau Pele, pau manō" (lest we be overrun by lava or consumed by a shark).

That afternoon, our kumu reminds us that we are responsible for a short haʻi ʻōlelo (speech) on a topic of our choice at one of several wahi pana (legendary places) we would visit, including Kaimū where the lava was active. And one more thing, she said, almost as an afterthought—the entire speech would be ma ka ʻōlelo Hawaiʻi wale nō (only in Hawaiian). As we visited each place over the following days, I wondered and worried what I would talk about; nothing inspired me. On the last day of our visit we met with Piʻilani Kaʻawaloa, a cultural practitioner and kamaʻāina (native born of a place) with deep roots in Kaimū. She would escort us to where the lava was flowing into the sea. It was even more exciting because we would go at night. With Piʻilani as our guide, we were allowed to enter the restricted areas beyond the guarded barricades erected to keep curious tourists far from danger. Uncle Kaipo Roberts (my grandmother's cousin) and other kūpuna from Puna recounted the significance of this ʻāina, of how Pele, the Hawaiian volcano goddess, was alive, her lava kino lau (body form) flowing and creeping relentlessly toward the sea. The regeneration of Hawaiʻi island, commonly referred to as the "Big Island," is clearly visible, its eminent size the result of regular lava flows steadily expanding its dimensions long after volcanoes across the rest of the Hawaiian archipelago have become dormant.

We stood in a semicircle near the sea, the famous hala (pandanus) groves of Puna surrounding us. As the kūpuna spoke, we could hear the crackling of dried hala leaves on the ground nearby; the lava slowly advanced, haukamumu (crunching sound of footsteps), sounding like someone was walking with measured deliberation through the undergrowth. Periodically, a hala tree burst spontaneously into flames, a giant lamakū (torch) ignited by the intense heat of lava creeping over its aerial roots. At that moment, I recalled the lines of a hula Pele (dance for Pele) I had learned that described her godly presence:

Aia lā 'o Pele i Hawai'i, 'eā
Ke ha'a maila i Maukele, 'eā
'Ūhī 'ūhā mai ana, 'eā
Ke nome a'ela iā Puna, 'eā
'Oaka e ka lani nokenoke
E Pele ē, Pele ē.

Pele is there at Hawai'i
Dancing at Maukele
Rumbling, puffing, and blowing this way
Devouring the land of Puna bit by bit
The heavens flash repeatedly
It is Pele, it is indeed Pele.

I knew it was time to present my ha'i 'ōlelo to the group, here in Kaimū in the middle of the night under a bright Māhealani moon illuminating the shimmering sea misted by Pele's steam billowing off the ocean before us; the rumble of the ocean and the relentless hiss of lava pouring into it were deafening. I recalled the stories of my kūpuna who were kama'āina to this place, their land just beyond Kaimū in Kapa'ahu and Poupou, areas already reclaimed by Tūtū Pele. I remembered visiting Punalu'u, a freshwater pond renamed "Queen's Bath" by settlers in the twentieth century. I retold the stories my tūtū told to me, about going upland on a donkey to the Poupou lands, a place renamed "Royal Gardens" by developers, where her tūtū pā (grandfather) tended their mala kalo (dryland taro gardens), and her tūtū mā (grandmother) sat beneath the shade of the hala trees and wove hats, "double-piko style" (with two centers on the crown), from the hala leaves she gathered there. I recounted the genealogical connections to other lines of her 'ohana (family). I told how it took them two days to walk to Hilo, first traveling ma uka (inland and uphill) to 'Ōla'a, where they spent the night with cousins, before walking to Hilo town on the sea the following morning.

When I was pau (done), I felt a slight stirring of the cool breeze wafting the scent of limu (seaweed) and salt inland from the undulating sea, causing the leaves of the hala groves around us to chatter. Ke ha'a lā Puna i ka makani—Puna was dancing in the breeze. A soft light rain sprinkled my arms and face, as one of my classmates exclaimed with awe, "E nānā a'e!" (Look up!). We all looked up. The Māhealani moon was full and bright, the stars sparkled and glistened, a shimmering night rainbow arched across the deep aubergine sky, and not a single cloud was anywhere in sight.

The following day we said good-bye to Hawai'i island; the day after that, Kaimū was consumed by Tūtū Pele. Two months later, Kaimū Bay was no more.

Mai ka Pō mai (From the Ancient Past): The Pele and Hi'iaka Mo'olelo

Over the course of Hawaiian history, no figure has captivated the imagination more than Pele, the Hawaiian akua associated with volcanic activity, land formation, and hula. *Pele* means lava, eruption. Epithets ascribed to her include Pele-'Ailā'au (forest-eating Pele), Pele-'Aihonua (Earth-eating, land-ruling Pele), and Pelehonuamea (red-earth Pele). Born in the primordial past, Pele is a living ancestor for Kanaka Maoli *mai ka pō mai* (from the beginning of time to now), and *mai nā kūpuna mai* (from the ancestors to us),[3] the vast record of chants, songs, and narratives composed and passed down over centuries.

Pele has inspired Kanaka 'Ōiwi for countless generations, and we continue to honor her through aloha 'āina (nationalism, environmental) practices, such as anti-geothermal development activism as much as through cultural traditions like the performance of mele (chant),[4] hula (dance), ha'i mo'olelo (storytelling), and haku mele and haku mo'olelo (poetic and literary composition). Her many adventures are vividly described in the vast repository of mele and mo'olelo. Distinct poetic genres such as hula Pele and hulihia (overturning) chants are directly associated with her.

A notable quantity of mele and mo'olelo are dedicated to Pele's favored youngest sister, Hi'iakaikapoliopele (commonly referred to as Hi'iaka), a primary hula deity. Over five hundred mele dedicated to them are listed in the Bishop Museum Archives (BMA) Mele Index, the largest publicly available repository of Hawaiian texts. Others, how many we cannot know, are held in private collections. Within the cultural practice of hula, new compositions continue. Thus, Pele- and Hi'iaka-related Hawaiian-language compositions number in the hundreds, if not thousands. Combined, these texts significantly outnumber mo'olelo for all other akua, including male deities.

At least thirteen separate and extensive epic-length Hawaiian-language

Kīlauea volcano has been active for decades. Puʻu ʻŌʻō crater is part of the most recent eruption; this photograph, showing the lava lake within, was taken in April 2011. Courtesy of Kalei Nuʻuhiwa.

moʻolelo published between 1860 and 1928 have been rediscovered in recent years. The majority were serialized and printed in the Hawaiian-language newspapers, ranging in length (from a few hundred to over three hundred thousand words) and content (discussed in later chapters). Several hand-written manuscript copies of these epic moʻolelo are also found in the BMA. Yet despite the immense repository of Hawaiian-language literature dedicated to them, Pele and Hiʻiaka are still sisters whom "we do not know much about."[5] One reason is that traditions associated with them, including the performance of the ubiquitous, beloved hula, were suppressed by settler colonialism in the nineteenth century.[6] Hula is a physical and spiritual embodiment of these sister akua, integrally connected to hula through Hiʻiaka, a founder of the art in one tradition, and their sisters Kewelani (Laka) and Kapōʻulakīnaʻu in another. Additionally, the repository of information about Pele and Hiʻiaka is recorded primarily in the Hawaiian language, which relatively few (several thousand) people speak or comprehend today, the result of an 1896 ban on the Hawaiian language as a medium of instruction in the public schools imposed by missionary descendant, haole (Amer-European)[7] settlers. Combined with other anti-Native laws and intense pressure on Kanaka Maoli to assimilate and Americanize and forget all things Hawaiian, generations of Kanaka were effectively cut off from our heritage language and many cultural practices of our kūpuna. While the move toward cultural and linguistic genocide against Kanaka Maoli was never completely success-ful, immense damage was done through these settler colonial efforts, from which Kanaka Maoli are still trying to recover. One strategy of healing and revitalization has been to delve into the literary legacy left by our kūpuna and rediscover our Indigenous intellectual history.

He Hoʻokupu Kēia i ka Lāhui (An Offering to the Hawaiian Nation): Contributions of the Project

This book examines Pele and Hiʻiaka moʻolelo published between 1860 and 1928 from an Indigenous perspective, with a focus on Kanaka Maoli agency rather than displacement. Much of what has previously been writ-ten about the literature, particularly in the nineteenth and early twenti-eth centuries, has been framed within the context of folklore studies and ethnography written by haole, resulting in violent translation practices of language and culture that disparage Native people and substantiate colonialism (both imperial and settler) and their misuse (or neglect) of Hawaiian cultural and literary resources.[8] Such practices resulted in woefully inadequate summaries, often poorly translated English, and inaccurately interpreted conclusions based on what Hawaiian-language professor Puakea Nogelmeier has identified as a "discourse of suffi-ciency."[9] One example is folklorist Martha Warren Beckwith's *Hawaiian Mythology*. Considered a seminal text of Hawaiian literary study, Beck-with devotes three chapters to Pele and Hiʻiaka moʻolelo. However, she relies solely on three secondary English-language summaries without mentioning the numerous primary Hawaiian-language accounts.

Beckwith is certainly not alone, as settler scholars—folklorists, an-thropologists, ethnographers, literary critics, and others—continue to rely on inadequate secondary-source English translations of varying quality, as Nogelmeier argues, as sufficient substitutions of primary Hawaiian-language sources. Language always plays a crucial role in the identity of a people because it "carry[s] with it centuries of shared ex-perience, literature, history, traditions reinforce[ed] . . . through daily use."[10] Thus the violence of translation resonates throughout Hawaiian and scholarly communities, the misinterpretation of literature, history, and ultimately the people themselves a tool justifying colonization (past) and occupation (present).

Abenaki scholar Lisa Brooks identifies Native language as one of the three important sites in investigating sources of Native intellectual tradi-tion and what they reveal about practicing an ethical criticism. She cites

.ationship signifies a foundational tenet of Hawaiian ontology, which is discussed later in the introduction and throughout subsequent chapters.

Grounded in Indigenous epistemology, this work seeks to kahuli (counter, overturn) settler colonial scholarship that has intentionally ignored, romanticized, infantilized, or vilified Kanaka Maoli intellectual history and cultural practices. It also seeks to encourage ʻŌiwi agency in our continuing rediscovery and reevaluation of our kūpuna (ancestral, source) texts in culturally relevant ways, approaching and discussing these cultural treasures from within the paradigm of ʻŌiwi perspectives and analysis. This is an important step for the larger Lāhui, as we continue to assert a nationalist voice of political sovereignty and cultural dignity, rebuilding an indigenous identity outside the touristic gaze, and in opposition to increasing American occupation and militarization. It is my hope that this work contributes in a positive way to the ongoing efforts of the Lāhui that Kanahele aptly describes as "unveil[ing] the knowledge of our ancestors" in a process whereby we "interpret for ourselves who our ancestors are, how they thought, and why they made certain decisions," because "in this process, we treat them with honor, dignity, love and respect . . . because they are our ʻohana."[15] In honoring our ancestors, we honor ourselves as we continue to build a healthy, thriving Lāhui.

Ka Laulā a ka Palena o Kēia Moʻolelo (Scope and Limitations of the Project)

As the first book-length study of Hawaiian literature that engages the discourse of Indigenous literary nationalism interwoven with indigenous Pacific-based literary theory, this work tackles many challenges and opportunities. When nineteenth-century ʻŌiwi writers first captured oral traditions on paper, they were faced with the physical limitations of the page. In 1861, M. J. Kapihenui, the first Kanaka to publish an epic-length Pele and Hiʻiaka moʻolelo, complained that the newspaper editors were censoring the lengthier chants. One reason is that they simply ran out of space and cut the story off when it reached the bottom of the page. There are similar limitations to what can be discussed within the pages of a book. Thus, this is not an exhaustive study of all Pele and Hiʻiaka literature covering every aspect of the moʻolelo, nor should it be. Rather, I highlight specific themes within the corpus of the moʻolelo and discuss how they relate to the broader context surrounding their publication—the politics of the polytexts, so to speak—and how those themes are present and relevant in contemporary ʻŌiwi culture and activism. In this way, I argue, their publication formed a strand of Hawaiian literary nationalism meant to uphold Hawaiian identity as a Lāhui prior to the overthrow of the Hawaiian kingdom in 1893, evoking and thus reminding Kanaka Maoli to remember their long-standing intellectual traditions, meant to counter missionary-led settler rhetoric that they were incapable of self-governance. After the overthrow, the continued publication of Pele and Hiʻiaka moʻolelo asserted what I identify as a hulihia discourse of ʻŌiwi agency, one that continued to counter settler rhetoric claiming Hawaiʻi for the United States and Hawaiians as Americans. The political nature of the moʻolelo was recognized by Kanaka writer Moses Manu in his 1899 version of the moʻolelo, who referenced Kapihenuiʻs earlier version, identifying it as a "moʻolelo kālaiʻāina" (political narrative).[16] Such literary activism reminded Kanaka Maoli of their intellectual history, to hāliʻaliʻa (positively remember) their identity as a Lāhui, one rooted in ʻōlelo Hawaiʻi (Hawaiian language), moʻokūʻauhau (genealogy), and aloha ʻāina, and to resist Americanization. Read this way, the Pele and Hiʻiaka moʻolelo of 1860–1928 inform Hawaiian nationalism and literary production today, which continues to weave new moʻolelo of the poʻe aloha ʻāina (cultural and political nationalists, *lit.* people who love the land) into our intellectual moʻokūʻauhau handed down mai ka pō mai, mai nā kūpuna mai.

This book is neither a translation of the Pele and Hiʻiaka moʻolelo, nor a retelling of it. Rather, it is a culturally centered literary analysis inspired by the larger discussions of Indigenous literary nationalism by Native American scholars in the United States and Canada, including Lisa Brooks, Daniel Heath Justice, Robert Warrior, Jace Weaver, and Craig Womack, among others, adding a Kanaka ʻŌiwi voice to the ongoing conversation.

I draw from Daniel Heath Justiceʻs overview of Indigenous literary nationalism as a philosophy that places Indigenous intellectual and cultural values at the center of analysis, rather than the margins, one that operates with the understanding that Native nations have powerful and sophisticated intellectual foundations, that these are ideally suited to the study of Indigenous literatures. As an avowedly political movement, it asserts the active presence of Indigenous values in the study of the literatures of Indigenous people, seeking transformative possibilities in studying nation-specific literatures through the critical lenses of their source cultures.[17]

As Kristina Fagan and colleagues argue in the context of Canadian Indian literary nationalism, it also examines how stories work within communities, calling on literary scholars to consider culturally specific contexts and aesthetics of native literary production.[18] In privileging Native voices, knowledge, and experience, Robert Warrior argues, Native people are not just treated as storytellers or "informants." Rather, they are intellectuals with abilities to articulate and devise dynamic, complex, and sustaining philosophies, theories, and approaches to their own lives and literatures.[19]

Indigenous nationalism is rooted in community values, histories, and traditions, as Justice argues, that "asserts a sense of active sociopolitical agency," and its inherent kinship responsibility and rights—what Kanaka Maoli call kuleana—rather than a "nation-state" model, which depends on unifying patriotisms, coercive policing of perceived deviance, and hegemonic allegiance to the structures of the state at the expense of kinship and other loyalties.[20]

It is more than simple political independence or the exercise of distinctive cultural identity; it is also an understanding of a common social interdependence within the community, the tribal web of kinship rights and responsibilities that link the People, the land, and the cosmos together in an ongoing and dynamic system of mutually affecting relationships.[21] Indigenous literary nationalism offers a way to shift the focus of research away from postcolonialism studies and the effects of colonization to the contributions and potential of Indigenous worldviews.[22]

The book is also grounded in Oceania (the Pacific) and our continuing efforts within our own disciplines, such as Pacific literary studies, as we negotiate our own experiences and histories with settler colonialism and the misappropriations of our literature that are too often relegated to the realms of folklore, mythology, ethnography, and the postcolonial. Inspired by the academic and creative writing of Indigenous Pacific scholars such as Vilsoni Hereniko, Noenoe Silva, Alice Te Punga Somerville, Konai Helu Thaman, Haunani-Kay Trask, Linda Tuhiwai Smith, Albert Wendt, and Steven Winduo, among others, this work also seeks to "unwrite Oceania," as Winduo proposes, and reweave the literary foundation of Hawaiian traditions with the voices of our kūpuna, unburdened by the often demeaning rhetoric of settler colonialism.

This study takes up Warrior's call in Tribal Secrets to recover our own intellectual histories, and to assert what Brooks calls "a move toward a deeper analysis of and sovereignty over Native literature, with a focus that is more tribally [nation] specific and much more entrenched in the study of our own systems of knowledge," one that is specific to Kanaka Maoli.[23] 'Ōiwi literature reflects the knowledge system of our Lāhui, one that contributes to the study of Indigenous, Pacific, and Hawaiian studies.

Traditional Kanaka Maoli ethics dictate a strong protocol of kapu (sacred, restricted, private) and noa (open, public). The publication of Pele and Hiʻiaka moʻolelo in public forums such as newspapers are noa because they were meant to be shared with everyone. Other traditions passed down, collected, and held within private entities (ʻohana, hālau) are kapu to them. It is not my kuleana to represent kapu traditions or to argue that the traditions I am writing about have a particular hierarchical order, value, or importance over one another or over other versions. Western scholarship often demands a singular, authoritative text be established. However, the presence of multiple writers and narratives of the Pele and Hiʻiaka moʻolelo demonstrates the cultural value of makawalu (multiple perspectives); Kanaka ʻŌiwi accept and even appreciate multiple and sometimes conflicting accounts, reflected in the ʻōlelo noʻeau (proverb) ʻaʻole pau ka ʻike i ka hālau hoʻokahi (not all knowledge is contained in one school). This philosophy is embodied by the myriad Pele and Hiʻiaka moʻolelo, which enrich the breadth and depth of Kanaka ʻŌiwi intellectual wisdom and artistry reflected in their diverse expression. There is also something to be said about the "friendly" rivalries between competing perspectives—many narratives tease the Kauaʻi aliʻi (chief) Lohiʻau, because his name means *dimwitted*, yet the Kauaʻi account portrays him as handsome, smart, and beloved by his people. A makawalu approach also facilitates the cultural concept of ka ʻimi loa, long-standing (life-long), in-depth research and exploration of knowledge with a goal of mastery for preservation and education of others with an eye on future generations.

Technology is constantly improving, and research possibilities continue to expand. Since I first began this work scrolling through endless spools of archived microfilm over a decade ago, many Hawaiian-language newspapers have been digitized, are keyword-searchable, and are now available on the World Wide Web (e.g., http://www.nupepa.org/). The possibility of an even greater number of Pele and Hiʻiaka source materials awaits discovery.

Questions that underlie this study include: What is a Hawaiian literary tradition? How does the corpus of Pele and Hiʻiaka moʻolelo represent one? What can an Indigenous-centered analysis of traditional literature look like? How is it different from writing framed within folklore studies, ethnography, or anthropology, for example, disciplines closely associated with settler colonialism? How does it fit within literary studies? What impact can the recovery of our Indigenous intellectual heritage have in understanding Hawaiian nationalism of the past? How is it applicable for Hawaiian nationalism into the future, including areas of education (e.g., Indigenous language immersion, culturally centered charter schools), language revitalization, and politics (e.g., sovereignty movement, de-occupation)?

In exploring these questions, this study engages Kanaka Maoli epistemological frameworks for analyzing Pele and Hiʻiaka moʻolelo, discussing moʻolelo as moʻo ʻōlelo (a succession of words), words being the foundational elements of moʻolelo, and the cultural ideas reflected in and embodied by them. Such an approach contextualizes and historicizes moʻolelo as not only being mai ka pō mai and mai nā kūpuna mai but also mai Kahiki mai (coming from the homeland), flourishing as our culture blossomed with new influences (such as those exchanged with other Polynesian cultures through a rich history of voyaging across the Pacific in the centuries before Western invasion). These concepts counter the haole discourse of "authentic," fixed (stagnant), precontact societies. They also expand the production of moʻolelo as being part of a long, extensive intellectual heritage, not simply one newly developed and dependent on Western literacy practices introduced in the nineteenth century, or an emerging field of world (or multicultural) literature in the twentieth.

Such an approach also allows me to position this work—my moʻolelo— within a moʻokūʻauhau of Indigenous intellectual kinship relations. As Brooks argues, our indigenous perspectives and educational grounding puts us in unique positions to approach texts, as claims to Indigenous perspective are not based in identity politics, but from perspectives embedded in long-standing sources of knowledge, and thus our work is part of ongoing cultural and philosophical conversations.[24] For ʻŌiwi scholars, kuleana to our families and Lāhui and the cultural knowledge we possess and study is as important as (if not more so) than the kuleana we have to (or through) our institutions and disciplines. It also contributes to laying a foundation of what Chadwick Allen (Chickasaw) calls "transindigenous" methodologies for a global study of Indigenous literatures.[25]

Similarly, ʻŌiwi scholars such as Kanahele and Amy Kuʻuleialoha Stillman assert ancestral and cultural memory as both kuleana and valid epistemologies in the study and practice of cultural traditions in their own separate projects. Maoli anthropologist Ty Kāwika Tengan similarly stresses the value of ancestral knowledge for ʻŌiwi as "a powerful tool for addressing contemporary problems."[26]

As Brooks reminds us, what is at stake is the recognition of the validity of our knowledge, and the sustenance of indigenous epistemologies.[27] Therefore, such an interconnected and culturally rooted approach to moʻolelo studies is one strategy in recovering, reclaiming, and reviving them as an integral part of our living Lāhui. Each chapter addresses a specific way in which to do this.

Mokuna (chapter) 1 provides a general overview of Hawaiian history and discussion of the larger historical and political context from which the Pele and Hiʻiaka moʻolelo evolved. It also provides points of reference for later discussions about the moʻolelo and their publication history in subsequent chapters. A synopsis of the moʻolelo is provided to help familiarize readers with the narrative. Cultural metaphors drawn from traditional objects and concepts integral to this study include moʻokūʻauhau, makawalu, waʻa (canoe), and lei (garland), which ground the literary analysis of these moʻolelo within the parameters of Hawaiian epistemology, and are appropriate ways to approach, study, and understand these texts.

Mokuna 2 introduces the concept of meiwi (traditional poetic devices), and discusses the interweaving of oral and literary traditions. It focuses on moʻokūʻauhau as an important cultural concept, and how it is an appropriate indigenous approach to the study of literature.

Mokuna 3 considers Pele and Hiʻiaka moʻolelo as ʻŌiwi intellectual history. It centers on Kapihenui's "He Moolelo no Hiiakaikapoliopele" as a transitional text weaving written literature into the oral tradition. Specific meiwi (pīnaʻi, ʻēkoʻa, and kaona) are explored as examples reflecting Kanaka Maoli worldviews and poetics. Mokuna 4 continues the exploration of Pele and Hiʻiaka moʻolelo as intellectual history, using specific cultural values as examples. Mokuna 5 addresses mana wahine (women's knowledge and power) within the context of the moʻolelo.

Mokuna 6 explores the development of Kanaka Maoli literature and the cultural and political value of the Pele and Hiʻiaka moʻolelo within the context of Hawaiian literary nationalism during the historical period the narratives were published, focusing on selected cultural themes that illustrate this point. Recovering Hawaiian intellectual knowledge counters (kahuli) the violence of settler mistranslation and misappropriation of our intellectual history to benefit the colonial project.

Mokuna 7 considers Pele and Hiʻiaka moʻolelo as a foundation of Hawaiian literary nationalism today, and how it continues to inspire Kanaka nationalism via the continuity of our literary and performative arts. I suggest that understanding Hawaiian literary nationalism in its earlier formation (1860–1928) can help us better comprehend our intellectual history, our relationship to it, and how it is a part of the contemporary Hawaiian identity and nationalist movement. As we continue our creative and intellectual traditions through literary production today, we honor the past and strengthen its foundation for the future.

Writing Back to the Empire: A Note on Nathaniel B. Emerson's
Pele and Hiiaka: A Myth from Hawaii

Nathaniel B. Emerson's *Pele and Hiiaka: A Myth from Hawaii* is often considered *the* Pele and Hiʻiaka literary text, and has sometimes been referred to by those unaware of the deeper, richer Hawaiian language moʻolelo as the "Bible" of Pele and Hiʻiaka literature. In print for nearly a century, most of what is popularly known (and taught) about Pele and Hiʻiaka over the past century often comes from this book, a great tragedy, considering the depth of Kanaka Maoli thought and literary expression it suppresses. Emerson's moʻolelo draws heavily from the Hawaiian-language newspaper sources, which he mentions in his preface. Upon closer examination it is clear that Emerson drew the bulk of his text from Kapihenui, whom he neither credits or names, a point previously noted by other scholars.[28]

Remaining in print and widely available since it was first published, *Pele and Hiiaka* is often viewed as an important source text of the Pele and Hiʻiaka moʻolelo.[29] This is probably due to several factors that derive from colonialism and the expanding American empire, including the seizing of lands to create the Volcanoes National Park in 1916, the year after *Pele and Hiiaka* was published. As Emerson was a Western-educated missionary son and thus part of the U.S. empire, these factors include but are not limited to related issues of authority, format, language, and the reframing of the moʻolelo to fit a Western paradigm that reinforced the overall colonial project.

Other than for brief comparative purposes, Emerson's text will not be discussed in this study. Likewise, his *Unwritten Literature of Hawaii: The Sacred Songs of the Hula* is not referenced. It is my sincere hope and desire that the recovery, reclaiming, retelling, and revitalization of the more culturally rendered Hawaiian-language moʻolelo published before and after Emerson's book, the ones discussed in this study, will gain a larger audience who will come to appreciate the depth and breadth of the culturally significant knowledge they contain, and acknowledge the Hawaiians who collected, wrote, and published them as true intellectuals, literary scholars, and ka poʻe aloha ʻāina (the people who fiercely love our land and nation).

I ka ʻŌlelo ke Ola (In the Language Is Life): A Note on Hawaiian Language and Terminology

ʻŌlelo Hawaiʻi is a living language, with diverse views on translation and orthography held by scholars and practitioners. Cursory translations and a glossary of key terms are provided for the general reader. No language thoroughly translates the gradations of meanings of the original language into the "target" language (here, English). Thus, in translations of ʻōlelo Hawaiʻi to English, particularly of poetic passages, subtle but important nuances of meaning will inevitably be lost. This is the challenge of working between languages and cultures. Supplemental definitions and explanations are provided for selected terms.

There are differing schools of thought in regard to the use of diacritical marks for Hawaiian language, in part because myriad Hawaiian words contain multiple meanings. The writers and editors of the original moʻolelo did not use the orthography system in place today, and words were not marked consistently in publication; in many cases, the writers may have been intentionally ambiguous. However, the absence of diacritical marks has since been recognized as essential to understanding the meaning or possible multiple meanings of Hawaiian terms. Thus, I do not use modern orthography when I quote from the Hawaiian source texts; in my own writing, I do. Unless otherwise noted, all translations of Hawaiian text into English are my own.

There are other issues in the spelling and typesetting of ʻōlelo Hawaiʻi in the older orthography of Hawaiian source texts, including hyphenation and the combination and separation of compound words that are considered incorrect by modern standards.[30] While it is not possible to correct the spelling and punctuation of published works, I would be remiss not to point out that many older titles of Hawaiian source texts, including Pele and Hiʻiaka moʻolelo, contain punctuation such as dashes and hyphens that reflect an imposition of Western syntactic structure and understanding of sentence formation, which traditionally does not account for single (compounded) words that consist of multiple words (including personal names, such as Hiʻiakaikapoliopele). To follow the haphazard presentation of the original is to impose a Western epistemological frame on Hawaiian that is inappropriate. Therefore, I use modern Hawaiian orthography throughout this book, and will include the original orthography only when quoting from sources.

Because Hawaiian language is not foreign to Hawaiians, Hawaiian words are not italicized except for specific emphasis. Hawaiian vocabulary with multiple, nuanced meanings are contextualized, resulting in English glosses provided more than once as needed. Such a culturally centered practice supports language advocacy in my own Indigenous community, in the discipline of literary studies, and in the academy overall toward respect for Hawaiian as a language of culture and scholarship.

An emphasis on Hawaiian language terms allows for a deeper

understanding of the manaʻo (concept, thought) embodied in Hawaiian in ways English cannot. As Hawaiian-language professor Larry Kauanoe Kimura writes:

> In discussing the role of the Hawaiian language in Hawaiian culture, it is also well to remember that American English is a vehicle of its own culture and that English words carry their own connotations and history. Whenever Hawaiian is translated into English, the English words used add cultural connotations to the idea conveyed, while eliminating intended connotations and meanings of the original Hawaiian. An example . . . are the words *aliʻi* and *makaʻāinana*. The usual translations of these words in English are "king" and "commoner" respectively. In American fairy tales, an English king carries the connotation of the European feudal system, the American historical rebellion against King George (American law still forbids titles), royal decadence, and a fascination with royalty . . . the word "common" . . . connotes . . . strong social stratification and distance, and even some of the economic and racial separation that exists in America. . . . The Hawaiian terms *aliʻi* and *makaʻāinana* have completely different connotations and even meanings. From the traditional Hawaiian viewpoint, the *aliʻi* and *makaʻāinana* are the same people and one family . . . descended from Papa and Wākea.[31]

Likewise, Kanaka Maoli (real people) and ʻŌiwi (of the bones) do not mean the same as "Hawaiian," which is falsely expanded in colonial discourse to include anything or anyone "of Hawaiʻi" (i.e., the addition of pineapple, a cash crop introduced in 1900 that benefited settlers and disenfranchised Kanaka Maoli from land and culture, to a pizza does not make it "Hawaiian" pizza). Similarly, "Hawaiian literature" (often referred to in Hawaiʻi as "Local" literature) is not the same as moʻolelo Hawaiʻi (a general category for literature written by Kanaka Maoli). As treasured "hi/stories" (histories + stories) mai ka pō mai, mai nā kūpuna mai, moʻolelo kuʻuna are traditional stories that are one strand of moʻolelo Hawaiʻi; moʻolelo kuʻuna have a genealogy and history that precedes (and supersedes) written, contemporary literature, in part because it informs (as least) or is the foundation (at best) of it.

I purposefully utilize Hawaiian-language terms as a strategy of reasserting an indigenous authority over our oral and literary traditions. Ngũgĩ wa Thiongʻo reminds us that language is a carrier of culture, and Kimura writes extensively about this within a Hawaiian context.[32] Craig

Womack argues that evocation is an important part of indigenous expression,[33] and the use of Hawaiian words and phrases intentionally evoke the mana of the words and language, as well as the Hawaiian worldview that underpins such ideas. Many of the terms express key ideas in other areas of cultural practice that I hānai or adopt as appropriate to analyze the moʻolelo. A fundamental ʻōlelo noʻeau, "i ka ʻōlelo ke ola, i ka ʻōlelo ka make" (in words is the power of life and death) supports this practice. I elucidate a few of the most important terms here; others will be explained throughout the chapters.

Kanaka ʻŌiwi, Kanaka Maoli, Kanaka, ʻŌiwi, Maoli, Hawaiian, and Native Hawaiian are all synonymous terms meaning the inhabitants of the Hawaiian islands at the time of Western invasion (1778), their ancestors, and their descendants, and are used interchangeably throughout this text. U.S. federal and Hawaiʻi state laws delineate between "Native" and "part" Hawaiian status based on blood quantum for the purpose of specific legal and social service benefits (e.g., qualifying for the Department of Hawaiian Home Lands leasehold property program). These settler-imposed legal definitions of indigeneity do not factor into my analysis or description of Kanaka Maoli or our cultural production, including literature. Kanaka Maoli assert that our ethnic identification is based on genealogy, not on blood quantum.

Moʻolelo is a term I use throughout this book. It is a more culturally appropriate designation to interpret and analyze literature as it incorporates both history *and* story, oral traditions and literature, intertwining these disciplines in ways that are impossible to unravel, and references to history, oratory, or literature as separate practices is inadequate. Moʻolelo is increasingly used in ʻŌiwi scholarship because its meaning is multiply layered as "story, history, literature, or any kind of narrative."[34]

The integral relationship between the sister deities is fundamental to the moʻolelo and understanding it. John Charlot writes that "single stories along with chants [were] gathered into complexes" and that "The Story of Pele" and "The Story of Hiʻiaka" were two that were often told together.[35] Silva also acknowledges this connection in her writing on Kapihenui, stating, "In the story of *Hiiakaikapoliopele*, Pele the volcano goddess migrates to Hawaiʻi with her family, of whom she is the aliʻi nui (highest ranking, above all the men). Later, in Hawaiʻi nei, the focus is on Hiʻiakaikapoliopele, a young woman who comes of age through traveling the island chain, fighting moʻo, sharks, and rapacious men, with two other young women as companions."[36] Identified as separate narratives in other contexts, I refer to them throughout this book as a single interwoven entity, the Pele and Hiʻiaka moʻolelo.

Moʻokūʻauhau is the Hawaiian term for genealogy, or a genealogical relationship that is applied to people and living things, "the genealogical starting point of all things Hawaiian."[37] One meaning of the root word *moʻo* is "series or succession"; *kū* has myriad meanings, including to stand, resemble, reveal, transform and rule the land, while one definition of *ʻauhau* references the leg bones.[38] One way of understanding moʻokūʻauhau is the succession of generations standing on the bones of the ancestors. I use moʻokūʻauhau to describe the relationship between texts with the intentional connotation of a genealogical succession. This relationship is multidimensional—the texts simultaneously represent the writers, editors, and islands they are from. Collectively they kept the moʻolelo alive and at the forefront of the Hawaiian national consciousness, successfully transforming the vibrant oral narrative to a robust literary form. Thus, a relationship of cultural and historical production and reception is also implied; moʻokūʻauhau suggests a level of kuleana inherent in Hawaiian practice, a Hawaiian expression of what Warrior calls an intellectual tradition, discussed more in mokuna 1.

Similarly, a *waʻa* is a canoe; more generally, a vessel of transportation. Pele and her ʻohana travel to Hawaiʻi from Kahiki (ancient homeland) in a waʻa. Hiʻiaka and her companions must travel between islands in waʻa; for centuries, the waʻa was the most important vehicle of transportation for people to travel across the vast expanse of Te Tai Moana Nui (Oceania). Metaphorically, the moʻolelo are waʻa that transport the oral tradition, and the literary tradition is a waʻa that carries cultural tradition, carrying readers on a journey of cultural enlightenment. Collectively, they carry the voices of our ancestors and ancestral knowledge across time and space, as they continue to enlighten and inspire us, reminding us who they were, and by extension, who we are as a Lāhui. More important, each moʻolelo is a waʻa carrying the thoughts and intentions of each writer, metaphorically serving as a vehicle for their familial genealogies as well.[39] Likewise, this book is a waʻa that carries the Pele and Hiʻiaka moʻolelo, navigating across a sea of Indigenous literary discourse.

Figuratively, waʻa is both a woman and "a moving mass of liquid lava, so-called because of similarity to a moving canoe."[40] The kaona (hidden, metaphorical, or underlying meaning) carries additional depth when applied to Pele who also has a molten lava form, making it an even more appropriate Hawaiian metaphor.

In the article "He Lei Hoʻoheno no nā Kau a Kau: Language, Performance and Form in Contemporary Hawaiian Poetry" I discuss the composition of contemporary Hawaiian poetry as a haku (braided) lei that weaves together Hawaiian and Western literary elements, drawing strength and beauty from each.[41] The lei metaphor describes Pele and Hi'iaka mo'olelo as well, a "lei mo'olelo" (lei of stories) or "lei palapala" (literary lei), oral and written stories and histories woven together. The lei metaphor suggests another dimension of textual genealogy between the texts. Much more than a garland of flowers, lei metaphorically represent someone beloved.[42] As the regenerative power of the forest, a healer, and a hula practitioner, Hi'iaka is intimately connected to the art of lei making, and is the most beloved of Pele's siblings, hence her name, Hi'i (carried [like a beloved child]) aka (reflection) i ka poli o Pele ([held] in the heart [and arms] of Pele).

Kanaka Maoli writing in the nineteenth century often referred to traditional knowledge of ka wā kahiko (the ancient past), the time before Christianity and Westernization. The practice of mai ka pō mai and mai nā kūpuna mai visibly connect the oral tradition to the written, demonstrating the longevity of the mo'olelo and how far back in time they stretch. Mai nā kūpuna mai is a synonym for *traditional*; while kūpuna is commonly understood as "grandparent" or "ancestor," it is also "starting point, source, growth."[43]

Mai ka pō mai and *mai nā kūpuna mai* express the long historical context of mo'olelo ku'una, and are woven throughout the writers' and editors' own indigenous readings of their own texts. In this way, they are intellectual frameworks modeling how 'Ōiwi narrated their literary history. Reflecting mo'okū'auhau, they are different models of presenting Kanaka Maoli literary history rather than settler ones. *Mai Kahiki mai* incorporates new traditional knowledge during the precolonial past, demonstrating that Kanaka Maoli intellectual traditions were not stagnant. It provided a model for incorporating new knowledge after Western intrusion, including comparative literary analysis between Hawaiian and foreign literary traditions.

Kuleana consciousness is a specific recognition of responsibility and call to act (ma ka hana ka 'ike—in action is knowledge—demonstrates empowerment or agency), a concept that extends to everyone. Settler colonialism benefits settlers, and is bent on, as Patrick Wolfe argues, the elimination of the Native.[44] Yet kuleana-conscious settlers can interrogate themselves and others and ask what their kuleana to Hawai'i and to Kanaka Maoli is, can, or should be. As Kanaka Maoli, our kuleana is to continue the fight for and revitalize our culture, 'āina, nation, and identity, and to follow the path so clearly set by our kūpuna. Tengan expresses this mana'o in his explanation of the word '*ōiwi*, that "literally roots indigeneity in the iwi (bones) by identifying the people with the kulāiwi ('bone plain' or native land) where they bury the iwi of their ancestors, the same land that feeds their families and waits for their bones to be replanted by their descendants"; thus, "as an 'ōiwi I have a special kuleana . . . to nurture and maintain the genealogical connections between place, people, and gods."[45]

Makawalu literally means "eight eyes." It refers to a culturally based concept of analysis from multiple perspectives or dimensions. The Pele and Hiʻiaka moʻolelo exhibits makawalu within their content and between their myriad publications. An Indigenous literary analysis utilizing a makawalu approach allows for multiple levels and new insights of understanding.

Hulihia literally means "overturned, a complete change, overthrow." Likewise, kahuli means to overturn or overthrow. "I ka ʻōlelo ke ola, i ka ʻōlelo ka make" encapsulates the culturally important concept of word power, found throughout the Pele and Hiʻiaka moʻolelo, including canonized vocabulary for Pele. The hulihia chants are an integral part of the Pele and Hiʻiaka moʻolelo and are the climax of the narrative. They refer to the destruction and regeneration of ʻāina through volcanic eruption, "overturning" the established order on the land and building something new. Pele and Hiʻiaka moʻolelo (1860–1928) express a "hulihia discourse" of Hawaiian literary nationalism in the time they were published. Nationalist messages to kahuli or resist settler colonialism are embedded in the moʻolelo, employing kaona or metaphors of resistance that spoke to Kanaka ʻŌiwi of that time period; this message of Hawaiian nationalism continues to speak to us today.

This hulihia discourse is expressed in the epithet for Pele, "noho Pele i ka ʻāhiu" (Pele stays in the wild), an ʻōlelo noʻeau that recognizes Pele's powerful female nature and her godly stature with the right (kuleana) and power (mana) to kahuli the order or sovereignty over the land established by Kāne and other male gods, without the fear of retribution. Metaphorically, this study seeks to kahuli the authority of Western scholarship, and reestablish the kuleana and mana of Kanaka ʻŌiwi intellectual and academic kuleana.

Structure and Methodology

The core of the Pele and Hiʻiaka moʻolelo are the highly poetic collection of mele. Mele are performative, simultaneously reflecting performance through the motion, activity, and action inherent in the words, embodying performance through the chanter, singer, dancer, or storyteller. The corpus of written moʻolelo is perhaps best exemplified by the title of this introduction, "Ke haʻa lā Puna i ka makani," recognized by Noenoe Silva as "dancing on the page."[46] Silva's description has always struck me as the most culturally succinct way to interpret the written moʻolelo.

An indigenous framework of book design developed by Māori in Aotearoa (New Zealand) over a decade ago adapts oral, performative cultural practices and applies them to the wahi kapu (sacred space) of a book. Such an approach was undertaken by Kanaka Maoli graphic designer ʻAlika McNicoll for *ʻŌiwi: A Native Hawaiian Journal*. In his "Graphic Artist's Note," McNicoll discussed how existing frameworks of Maoli cultural practice, including cosmogonic genealogies, the protocol of asking permission to enter a sacred space, like a heiau (temple) or a hālau hula (traditional dance academy), and the use of ʻōlelo noʻeau can and should be incorporated into Kanaka Maoli book design.[47] My analysis of Pele and Hiʻiaka moʻolelo aligns with this manaʻo, beginning and ending with pule (prayer). It also utilizes mele from the Pele and Hiʻiaka moʻolelo to frame arguments within each chapter.

The first and last words are pule that ask for permission to wehe (open), komo (enter), and pani (close) the book, framing the sanctity of the space between and allowing one to enter and exit the ritual space. "Kūnihi ka mauna" (steep stands the mountain) is commonly used as an oli komo (chant asking permission to enter) for hālau hula; it is performed within multiple Pele and Hiʻiaka moʻolelo in different contexts, including Hiʻiaka asking for permission to enter the Kauaʻi lands where Lohiʻau lives. While we are accustomed to American ideals of individual freedom that allow one to freely traverse "public" space, such cultural protocol of *asking permission* is embedded in the moʻolelo through this oli—Hiʻiaka is "Hawaiian" and a deity no less, but still she must humble herself and ask permission to enter a space that is not hers.

Permission to enter a wahi kapu is not guaranteed, but when permission is granted, a pane (response) welcoming the visitor ensues. The pane, "E aʻe e ka lā ma ka hikina" (The sun rises in the east) is a contemporary mele composed by Kauaʻi native Makana Garma. The pule pani (closing prayer) at the end of the book, "He Pule no Hiʻiakaikapoliopele" (a prayer of Hiʻiakaikapoliopele) is from Hoʻoulumāhiehie. When Hiʻiaka is hosted by Wahineʻōmao's family, she instructs them in the importance of memorizing this pule to use when trouble comes, to avoid misfortune. Thus, it functions as a blessing of sorts to those exiting the wahi kapu of the moʻolelo, on behalf of the writer as much as the reader.

The opening epigraph comes from Kaʻū native and highly respected cultural practitioner and scholar Mary Kawena Pukui. Despite her Christian background, Pukui acknowledged and wrote about her kinship connections with Pele, as evidenced by the opening epigraph, which further orients the reader to the 'Ōiwi perspective celebrated through-out this book. Pukui was born just after the overthrow of the Hawaiian kingdom; she lived and worked at a time when Hawaiian traditions and knowledge were strongly discouraged in the name of Americanization and "progress." Yet she tirelessly contributed her time and knowledge to many scholars and publications in multiple fields, keeping such knowl-edge alive; many foundational books in Hawaiian research and scholar-ship would not have been possible without her.

I evoke her words as evidence of Hawaiian literary nationalism at a time when settler colonialism (the New Order she refers to in the open-ing epigraph) decimated Kanaka Maoli, and a dearth of Hawaiian publi-cations pointed toward the demise of 'Ōiwi intellectual history. Pukui's work is even more impressive considering she was the primary source for many important publications, but was always given second billing to the haole anthropologists, ethnographers, linguists, folklorists, and others she worked with, if she was credited at all. Read her words carefully here. Her voice may have been an almost singular whisper in the time she was writing, but it is a voice that continued asserting 'Ōiwi agency, one that refused to remain silent. There are many mele Hiʻiaka chants that end "He leo wale" (It is *just* a voice). Yet, as Hiʻiaka exemplifies, the voice is the most precious, "mana-full" gift and resource. Pukui's manaʻo on Pele and Hiʻiaka expressed in the epigraph, and their relationship to Kanaka Maoli in the context of expanding settler colonialism, is a strand in the lei palapala that weaves the voices of the past with the voices of the present.

The focus of each chapter is framed by a mele from the Pele and Hiʻiaka moʻolelo, which foregrounds the importance of indigenous meth-ods of literary analysis. Because they provide a nuanced and profound depth of thought beyond the prose narrative, the mele are an integral part of the moʻolelo. It is difficult to comprehend the politics and poetics of the larger narratives without a deeper exploration of key mele associated with them. The title of each chapter, named for the mele, thus grounds the narrative, arguments, and examples presented in that chapter within the parameters of 'Ōiwi intellectual traditions.

Because mele often did not have formal titles, they are primarily ref-erenced by first line. The Pele and Hiʻiaka moʻolelo, which have similar titles, are therefore referenced by author's last name.

Ke Haʻa lā Puna i ka Makani (Puna Dances in the Breeze)

Hawaiian literary nationalism was established in 1860 through the pub-lication of important traditional oral narratives such as Pele and Hiʻiaka.

Kanaka Maoli writers and editors published Hawaiian moʻolelo as a strategy asserting political agency in an effort to first strengthen Hawaiian nationalism prior to the overthrow of the Hawaiian kingdom, and later as a strategy to help regain it. These moʻolelo kuʻuna were kept at the forefront of ʻŌiwi public discourse to remind Kanaka of our long intellectual history, of the importance of the words, thoughts, and actions of our ancestors, and as a source of cultural and national pride. Throughout the nineteenth and early twentieth centuries, Kanaka Maoli writers and editors displayed a high degree of agency, vigorously (and peacefully) resisting colonization by such powerful and purposeful acts as publishing traditional moʻolelo that countered and disrupted the settler colonial discourse of the "dying, ignorant, inept Native." Their efforts and courage continue to inspire Kanaka in our current efforts to recover our oral and literary traditions of the past, as they collectively form the foundation of our contemporary cultural practices, including literary and performance-based arts.

Kanaka ʻŌiwi continue to weave a literary lei of resistance to colonization through the continued practice of our literary and performing arts. We continue to assert cultural and political nationalism by continuing to remember, recover, and revitalize our mele and moʻolelo, of which Pele and Hiʻiaka is but one example. We also continue to assert kinship to our ʻāina as well, ʻāina formed from the body of our ancestral deities—Pele and Hiʻiaka—upon which we are still sustained as a Lāhui.

Brooks reminds us that identity is always relational, and grounded in particular places and particular histories.[48] "Ke haʻa lā Puna i ka makani" is the first hula, performed for Pele by her beloved younger sister Hiʻiaka. The genesis of this hula occurs at a specific location—the beach of Nānāhuki, in the ʻili (small land section) of Hāʻena, in the ahupuaʻa (land division) of Keaʻau, in the moku (district) of Puna, on the mokupuni (island) of Hawaiʻi—all of which are remembered and recorded in the lines of the mele. Thus, it grounds us (as performers and audience, including a reading audience) in a specific wahi pana made famous through the presence and actions of Pele and Hiʻiaka, Hōpoe and Hāʻena, a place particularly important to recall—memorialized in the words of the mele, historicized in the words of the moʻolelo—because it is the birthplace of hula. Ethnomusicologist Amy Kuʻuleialoha Stillman describes the performance of hula as not only being a means of communication, but also constituting "over time, recollection and commemoration."[49] I discuss this more in mokuna 1, but would add that written moʻolelo are a complementary practice that also commemorate and transmit cultural knowledge and "memories of people and events that endure long after they have passed."[50] Hence, in remembering the ancestors, ancestral places where knowledge is born and nurtured through the performance and recording of mo'olelo, we also re-member (Stillman, Tengan) the Lāhui that was dis-membered (Osorio) through settler colonialism.[51] Such 'āina-based epistemology has emerged as a foundation of more recent indigenous education efforts as 'ike 'āina, meaning both learning *about* the land and learning *from* the land.[52]

Kumu hula Pualani Kanaka'ole Kanahele's foundational knowledge of hula has been passed down within her 'ohana for generations; her expertise in the performative aspect of mele and hula is unparalleled. She describes the performance of "Ke ha'a lā Puna" as an act of blessing that 'āina.[53] Her groundbreaking text on Pele and Hi'iaka mo'olelo, *Ka Honua Ola*, stresses the integral intertwining of hula and nature, represented by Pele, Hi'iaka, and their 'ohana. She writes, "Hula begins with the movement of the sun, the wind, the sounds, the growth on land, and the ocean. Hula is ritualized as it personifies nature. Like nature, hula is rhythmic, inclusive, transformative, physical, spiritual, healing."[54] More specifically, "Ke ha'a lā Puna" is a chant that focuses on "movement as it appears in certain places, with particular weather phenomena, motivated by the wind portraying the natural imagery of dance through the trees, upon the grass, and in the ocean . . . Puna is the source of regenerative energy."[55]

Puna is a freshwater spring, and districts bearing the name (on Kaua'i and Hawai'i) are located on the eastern side of the islands, and associated with the rising sun, symbolic of cosmic energy, a source of life and regeneration. The easternmost 'āina in the Hawaiian archipelago, Puna, Hawai'i, is particularly significant. Davianna Pomaika'i McGregor writes:

> The northeast tradewinds, with their rain-infused cloud formations and rainfall, first reach Hawai'i in Puna. A Hawaiian proverb, "Ka makani hali 'ala o Puna" (The fragrance-bearing wind of Puna), speaks of how these winds grow fragrant as they travel over Puna, luxuriant with *maile, lehua,* and *hala.*
>
> The name . . . derives from observations by Native Hawaiian ancestors of how the forests of Puna attract clouds to drench the district with its many rains . . . [that] refresh and enrich the Puna water table and sustain the life cycle of all living things in Puna and the entire island of Hawai'i.[56]

McGregor names three of the most important plants associated with Puna and with the practice of hula. Maile and lehua are endemic flora to the region, and hala is so abundant that an 'ōlelo no'eau for Puna describes it as "Puna paia 'ala i ka hala" (Puna's forest are scented with the fragrance of hala). All are associated with hula and Hiʻiaka, and two of the three are explicitly named in the mele (maile is named in numerous other chants associated with Pele and Hiʻiaka). Each is considered beautiful in appearance and fragrance, and are common adornments worn on the body in hula and other contexts. Maile and lehua are poetic references for beauty (usually youthful, applicable to males or females). Hiʻiaka adorns herself with a fragrant lei of strung hala on her trip to Kauaʻi. The word *hala* also means "to pass by, to pass away," and a lei hala symbolizes an important rite of passage (such as the journey Hiʻiaka is about to undertake), transitioning from one stage of life to another. There are numerous positive connotations of 'ala, which is also a figurative reference to one who is esteemed, chiefly, or beloved.

The wind McGregor describes is likely Moaniʻala (wafted fragrance), characterized by its fragrance-bearing quality, one of several winds of the district personified with person names (others include Puʻulena, ʻAwa, and Ulumano).[57] Each wind name of Puna is related to a quality of the environment personified as well by Pele and Hiʻiaka—Puʻulena (yellow hill), colored by the smoke of volcanic eruption, and 'Awa, a cold mountain rain or fog, figuratively associated with misfortune. In defining the word 'awa, Pukui and Elbert also note that in Pele and Hiʻiaka moʻolelo, "this word . . . may refer to volcanic eruption"; the two examples they provide are from Emerson's *Pele and Hiiaka*, "Uwē au, puni ʻā i ke 'awa (PH 193), I weep, surrounded by lava in the downpour," and "ʻO ka uahi noe lehua, 'o ke 'awa nui i ka mauna (PH 205), the lehua mist smoke, the great outburst on the mountain."[58] The wind name also connotes āwā, "noisy, or to talk loudly," which is suggested in the oli as well, as the motion of the elements of the land, sea, and sky—blowing wind, crashing waves, wind-blown forest, leaves aflutter, volcanic eruption bursting and lava creaking and groaning as it creeps across the land—are suggested in the kinesthetic and auditory imagery of the oli, contained in the lines, "ʻO Puna kai *kuwā* i ka hala / Paʻē ka leo o ke kai" (Puna's sea *resounds* in the hala groves / The voice of the sea strikes the ear). The 'āina is personified with movement, dancing, a voice. The 'āina is alive.

Another kaona reference in the wind name is to 'awa (kava, *Piper methysticum*), the intoxicating drink made from the pulverized root of the 'awa plant that grows abundant in Puna, offered to Pele, and profuse in poetic references to Puna. Ulumano can refer to lush growth and regeneration, associated with Hiʻiaka and the dense native forests of Puna. This manaʻo is replicated in line 2, "Haʻa ka ulu hala i Keaʻau" (The hala groves at Keaʻau dance). Keaʻau (rippling current) locates the hula near the sea, the ever-present pathway that connects the islands of Oceania, as discussed by Tongan scholar 'Epeli Hau'ofa in "Our Sea of Islands"—the ocean links us in kinship across Oceania, "a sea of islands" rather than "islands in a far sea."[59]

Winds and rains are important metaphoric references in Hawaiian poetic expression, and the quality, strength, or association with specific places imbue them with positive or negative references. Silva discusses winds as literary devices in Hawaiian mo'olelo, one particularly associated with Pele and Hi'iaka mo'olelo.[60]

Kanahele provides a comprehensive, line-by-line analysis of this mele in *Ka Honua Ola*, which I will not replicate here. But there are particular aspects of it I would like to discuss as they complement other arguments made in this study about the importance of Hawaiian language, understanding culturally based aesthetics, metaphors, and epistemologies, and how they inform and embody indigenous literary studies and/as cultural practice.

Various kinship relationships are also present in the mele. Aside from Pele and Hi'iaka's symbiotic sister connection is their association with other family members. For example, there is a clear link with Kāne, a male akua associated with the sun and fertility of the land; Kāne is another regenerative force that is complementary to that of Pele and Hi'iaka. Puna is poetically referenced as the land "I ka houpo a Kāne" (In the heart of Kāne). Connections between other representations of nature are also present—Hā'ena and Hōpoe are Hi'iaka's companions and hula teachers, and specific 'āina are named for these ancestral figures. Hā'ena (fiery breath) is both the origin of hula in Puna, Hawai'i, and the place where hula is perpetuated and where Lohi'au lives on Kaua'i. Between them, Hā'ena is where "the day begins and ends," as at "Hā'ena . . . Kaua'i, on the summer solstice, the sun's rising and setting are in full view from that one location."[61]

Hōpoe is described as an aikāne to Hi'iaka, an "intimate friend" and love(r). Hōpoe is the lehua in full bloom, intimating sexual maturity, attraction, and desire. Lei made from lehua hōpoe are "worn with the hula as part of the celebration."[62] Lehua also "connotes the dome of the sun's path rising on the island of Hawai'i—renowned for its lehua—and setting on the island of Lehua in the west," an 'ēko'a metaphorically connecting one end of the Hawaiian archipelago to the other.[63] The interrelationship between Pele, Hi'iaka, and Hōpoe is not just metaphorical. As Kanahele argues, it is also functional: "Pele is land growth, the production of fresh lava. Hi'iakaikapoliopele is new growth, the natural movement on the land. Hōpoe is the physical essence of both deities.

Lehua mamo hōpoe, yellow lehua in full bloom, represents Hiʻiaka's ipo (sweetheart) and aikāne Hōpoe. Photograph by author, 2010.

She is the kiʻi, or recipient of the natural movement inspired by the gods, which developed into the haʻa, or the dance. The imitation of these move-ments is an act of recognizing, praising, and honoring these sources [acts of remembering], which are Pele and Hiʻiaka."[64]

Hiʻiaka reflects Pele; Hōpoe embodies Hiʻiaka and Pele. Similarly, in the cosmogonic genealogy Kumulipo (discussed more thoroughly in mokuna 1), the woman Laʻilaʻi paired with Kāne, a god, whose name means "male," and then with Kiʻi, a male whose name means "image." Kanaka are born from these pairings, linking godly ancestors (Laʻilaʻi, Kāne, Kiʻi) with human ones. In both chants, Kāne is associated with the sun and the dawning of day. Both establish genesis, regeneration, and birth (genealogical succession) as a means of creation, regrowth, and sustainability. Each suggests the process of such regeneration is in the imitation of nature. Such reflection is present in "Ke haʻa lā Puna" and the practice of hula, Kanahele explains, where "one must be ingenious to create the dance by imitating things found in nature. Imitation of nature gives praise to the elemental deity reflected. Just as Hiʻiaka is a reflection of natural phenomena, the movement of hula is a natural process that reflects nature itself."[65]

The lines "[Haʻa] ka wahine / ʻAmi i kai o Nānāhuki lā / Hula leʻa wale / I kai o Nānāhuki ē" (The woman dances / A graceful ʻami step at the sea of Nānāhuki / A perfect, pleasing dance / At the sea of Nānāhuki) are presented twice in the oli, like a chorus or refrain. The repetition of the lines emphasizes the dance (hula), the category of dance (haʻa), a specific dance step (ʻami), its incredibly pleasing quality (leʻa wale), and the location of its performance and origin (Nānāhuki). Haʻa is an older name for hula (a term that came to prominence in the nineteenth century), reminding us of how such narratives imbed important cultural information in the heritage language, as discussed by Kimura, Basso, Shanley, and Brooks.[66] Haʻa is also a specific type of hula, one often associated with ritual rather than entertainment. Kanahele explains that "the haʻa is a ritual to maintain the saga of Pele and Hiʻiaka in dance form."[67] Haʻa means "low" and connotes a humble demeanor. When the entire environment from the land to the sea is dancing in the haʻa style in the opening for lines of the chant, a sense of humility is suggested. The dance form requires a deeper bend of the knee than other hula, intimating a closer connection to the earth. In the video *Kumu Hula: Keepers of a Culture*, Kanahele describes haʻa as both a vigorous, bombastic dance, and one in which the dancers retain a body position lower to the ground because that ʻāina (Pele) is the source of mana.[68]

Puna connotes the presence of freshwater, which counterbalances (ʻēkoʻa) the name Keaʻau and Nānāhuki. Both Keaʻau and Nānāhuki convey the sound and motion of the sea. Nānāhuki where the hula occurs also embodies the back-and-forth swaying of the sea currents famous along this rugged coastline, imitated in the swaying motion of the hula. Nānāhuki alternately means "to pull away; contrary" and "to attract the eyes." The first connotes the movement of the sea, the second Hōpoe's mesmerizing beauty and hula that draws Hiʻiaka's attention, and by extension that of the audience/reader.

Upon seeing her hula performance, Pele remarks on Hiʻiaka's skill in dance and chant. Her recognition of Hiʻiaka's talent demonstrates the emphasis on skill (ʻaʻapo, akamai, ʻeleu) and knowledge (ʻike) being important, culturally recognized qualities. This recognition and value reflects other contexts, such as Queen Kapiʻolani's motto, "Kūlia i ka nuʻu" (strive for the summit), and counters the Amer-European discourse of lazy, careless, inept Natives. Pele also recognizes Hiʻiaka's ʻike pāpā lua (foresight), her intuition and vision, as the mele plays with a double reference to where they are in Hāʻena, Puna, as well as the ahupuaʻa of Hāʻena, where Lohiʻau lives on Kauaʻi. Kanahele writes, "[Pele said to Hiʻiaka,] ʻI admire the chant you just delivered, especially the line, "Hāʻena dances in the calm." This Hāʻena which you speak of is not here in Puna, but on Kauaʻi. You have great knowledge. You understand the revelation of our dream . . . because of [your] skill in interpreting dreams, [you shall] be the one to fetch my lover, Lohiʻau.'"[69] Thus, it is Hiʻiakaʻs kuleana to journey to Kauaʻi and fetch Lohiʻau for Pele. Hiʻiaka accepts this kuleana and all it entails, allowing her to both use and increase her knowledge and mana.

Finally, Kanahele emphasizes the cultural specificity of hula, saying, "Above all, it is Hawaiian."[70] Asserting a specifically Hawaiian art, performed and recorded in the Hawaiian language, the practice, performance, remembrance, and transmission of such texts is inherently political and nationalistic. Thus, while hula is viewed within settler colonial discourses as entertainment women do for men and Natives do for tourists as part of capitalist exchange, hula is also political as it inherently resists and challenges settler colonialism; hula represents ʻŌiwi philosophies and paradigms as much as ballet, for example, represents specific European ones.[71] Performing hula is *not* the same as performing ballet; speaking, chanting, writing, reading, understanding, or internalizing ʻōlelo Hawaiʻi creates a worldview that is *not* the same as one formed in English.

As we begin this exploration of Pele and Hiʻiaka moʻolelo, the lines of "Ke haʻa lā Puna i ka makani"—Puna, the wellspring, dances, animated into life by the wind, a powerful natural invisible element made visible through the motion of other actors within the environment. In this way it becomes life-giving. It reminds us that in Hawaiian epistemology, movement or action is evoked by ʻōlelo (language, words), and the power of words mai ka pō mai, mai nā kūpuna mai, mai Kahiki mai—from the ancient past to the present, from the ancestors to us, from the ancient homeland to here is the continuity of a long, flourishing intellectual, cultural, poetic, and embodied moʻokūʻauhau.

Mai Kahiki Mai ka Wahine, ʻo Pele
(From Kahiki Came the Woman, Pele)

Historicizing the Pele and Hiʻiaka Moʻolelo

Mai Kahiki mai ka wahine ʻo Pele
Mai ka ʻāina i Polapola
Mai ka pūnohu a Kāne
Mai ke ao lalapa i ka lani
Mai ka ʻōpū lā i Kahiki
Lapakū i Hawaiʻi ka wahine ʻo Pele
Kālai ka waʻa ʻo *Honuaiākea*
Kō waʻa, e Kamohoaliʻi
Hoa mai ka moku a paʻa
Ua oki ka waʻa o ke akua
Ka waʻa o Kālaihonuamea
Holo mai ke au, hele ʻaeʻaʻe Pele
ʻAeʻaʻe ka lani, ʻai puni i ka moku
ʻAeʻaʻe kini o ke akua
Iā wai ka uli, ka hope o ka waʻa?
Iā Kamohoaliʻi
Iā ʻEhuamenehune
Kā ʻia ka liu o ka waʻa
Hoʻohoa kai hoe o luna
ʻO Kū mā lāua ʻo Lono
Holo i ka honua ʻāina moku
Kau aku i ka hoʻolewa
ʻO Nuʻakea noʻiau ke akua
Hele aʻe a komo i ka hale o Pele
Huahuaʻi i Kahiki, lapa ʻulaʻula
ʻO Pele ke kumu o Kahiki
Nāna i hoʻolele ka pōhaku kē
Kani kē, kuʻi kē Kahiki
Ka moku newa ʻula
I laila hoʻi ka pili kua, ka pili alo
Ka pili, ka hoene ʻana a Kahoāliʻi (nā hoa aliʻi)
Kawewe i ka lani, nehe i ka honua
Kōhia e Kāne ka moku
ʻOhi, ʻoeke ka lani
Nehe i ka honua
Na Pele ia ahi, ke ʻā lā i Kīlauea
Wakawaka ka niho o ke akua
ʻAi pōhaku ʻo Haumea, ke akua
Hele aʻe a komo i ka hale o Pele
Huahuaʻi Kahiki, lapa uila
E Pele ē
Huaʻina hoʻi ē!ʻ

From Kahiki came the woman, Pele
From the lands of Polapola
From the rising red mist of Kāne
From the flashing clouds in the heavens
From the center there in Kahiki
The woman, Pele, is afire for Hawai'i
Carve the canoe, *Honuaiākea*
Your canoe, Kamohoali'i
Lash it to the island to be held fast
The canoe of the goddess is complete
The canoe of Kālaihonuamea
The current rushes as Pelehonuamea comes aboard
The heavenly one steps aboard, and rules the isle
The host of gods step aboard
For whom is the stern, the rear of the canoe?
For Kamohoali'i
For 'Ehuamenehune
The bilge of the canoe is bailed
As though paddling the sea above
Kū and Lono
Sail a world of islands
Boarding as familiars
Nu'akea, deity of wisdom
Goes to enter the abode of Pele
Kahiki erupts, blazing redness
Pele is Kahiki's own source
Who causes rumbling stones to fly
Sounding with a crash, Kahiki booms
The isle is red as a warclub
The dear ones, distant and near, are there
The close ones, the murmurings of Kahoāli'i (the royal companions)
Clattering in the heavens, rustling on the earth
The island is held back by Kāne
The heavens gush with chatter, opening forth
Murmuring on the earth
The fire is Pele's, blazing at Kīlauea
Like flashing teeth of the goddess
The goddess Haumea devours stones
Trekking up to enter the domain of Pele
Kahiki erupts, flashing and blazing
O Pele
An erupting flow indeed![2]

ON A MERRIE MONARCH[3] STAGE, a hālau dances with rhythmic precision to the resonant bass tones of the pahu (wooden) drum. The kumu hula chants, the ʻōlapa (dancers) dance, red pāʻū (skirts) sway, the audience cheers its appreciation. Such is the scene multiplied dancer by dancer, hālau by hālau, an ancient story transcending time, passed down for myriad generations, recalling, remembering, retelling a primeval story of creation, migration, history, cultural values, practices of our ancestors, lessons of aloha ʻāina and mālama ʻāina (love and caring for the land); of love, passion, betrayal, forgiveness; instructions of origin, migration, environmental kinship, memorialized and perpetuated through a performance of drum beats and verbalized chant, embodied in swaying hips and precise hand movements—and Ka Palapala (written literature).

ʻO ke Au i Kahuli Wela ka Honua (When Time Turned, the Earth Became Hot): A Maoli Accounting of History

But what should we know about the larger cultural, historical, and political environment that the Pele and Hiʻiaka moʻolelo reflects? How do the cultural and political changes that occur before, during, and after 1860–1928 influence and affect how it developed as literature and contributed to the development of Hawaiian literary nationalism? An overview of Kanaka Maoli history that contextualizes the production of Pele and Hiʻiaka moʻolelo helps us better understand and appreciate this cultural treasure.

Like Pele herself, the Hawaiian islands were born in fire millennia ago. Hawaiian moʻolelo detail the origins and history of our archipelago of islands and our ancestors that extend back in time to pō (night), the dark, chaotic time of akua. Kumulipo (source of deep darkness), a pre-eminent koʻihonua (cosmogonic genealogy) recounting the birthing of the Hawaiian universe from pō, sets a foundational tenet of Maoli culture—moʻokūʻauhau, genealogical succession. The Maoli universe is not created from the divine breath of a singular male god, but through a birthing process beginning with Kumulipo and Pōʻele (black night), paired (ʻēkoʻa) male and female entities of the cosmos. Sixteen wā (epochs) span eons of time, recounting the birth of the heavens, the earth, and all known things held within their cosmic embrace. The first eight wā occur in pō, the time of the gods, where corals, earth, and numerous aquatic and land plants and animals appear, enumerated in specific ʻēkoʻa pairings, birthed within a framework of kinship and evolution. Kumulipo begins:

'O ke au i kahuli wela ka honua
'O ke au i kahuli lole ka lani
'O ke au i kuka'iaka ka lā
E ho'omālamalama i ka malama
'O ke au o Makali'i ka pō
'O ka walewale ho'okumu honua ia
'O ke kumu o ka lipo, i lipo ai
'O ke kumu o ka pō, i pō ai
'O ka lipolipo, o ka lipolipo
'O ka lipo o ka lā, o ka lipo o ka pō
Pō wale ho'i
Hānau ka pō
Hānau Kumulipo i ka pō, he kāne
Hānau Pō'ele i ka pō, he wahine
Hānau ka 'Ukuko'ako'a
Hānau kāna, he 'Āko'ako'a, puka . . .

When time turned, the earth became hot
When time turned, the heavens turned inside out
When time turned, the sun was darkened
Causing the moon to shine
This is the time the Pleiades rose in the night
The slime was the source of the earth
The source of the darkness that made darkness
The source of the night that made night
The intense darkness, the deep darkness
Darkness of the sun, darkness of the night
Nothing but night
The night gave birth
Born was Kumulipo in the night, a male
Born was Pō'ele in the night, a female
Born was the coral polyp,
Born was the coral, it emerged . . .

At the conclusion of wā 8, dawn breaks. Ao, the time of light and order emerges from pō; the naissance of star constellations and the birth of kanaka continues the mo'okū'auhau through several hundred generations, mo'okū'auhau of akua and ali'i intertwined. The descent of kanaka from Papahānaumoku (foundation birthing islands), Earth Mother, and Wākea (broad expanse), Sky Father through their kalo child, Hāloanakalaukapalili (long breath fluttering leaf), and his younger sibling Hāloa, the first aliʻi are also detailed.[4]

At 2,108 lines long, Kumulipo culminates with the birth of the aliʻi Kalaninuiʻīamamao (The great supreme chief from afar) in the late seventeenth century. It establishes moʻokūʻauhau as a foundation of ʻŌiwi culture, identity, and worldview.

Hawaiian nationalist and scholar Haunani-Kay Trask explains that "who we are is determined by our connection to our lands and to our families. Therefore, our bloodlines and birthplace tell our identity."[5] Hawaiian historian Kanalu Young argues, "Far more than a 'who-begat-whom' structure of linear descent, moʻokūʻauhau functioned as an identity cohesive and role determining force which brought different subgroups of aliʻi together in a system that, at its height, operated to the benefit of all in ʻŌiwi Maoli society."[6] In writing about the pig kupua (demigod) Kamapuaʻa, historian Lilikalā Kameʻeleihiwa emphasizes that the moʻolelo "begins with the hero's genealogy, for his lineage defines his character."[7]

The ʻŌiwi concept of birth (hānau) and succession (moʻo) is similar to other Indigenous moʻolelo and even haole theories of evolution. It contrasts the biblical account of creation, where a single male god's thought and speech is the genesis for the formation of the universe and all life within it. In the Hawaiian view, akua are *born* within a genealogical context; while Hawaiian akua can have shape-shifting kino lau (body forms) that are often elements of nature (wind, clouds, rain, specific plant forms, etc.), some also have human kino lau and travel as humans do.

Consequently, Kanaka Maoli are genealogically related to our ʻāina, literally born from the land. Kumulipo establishes Kanaka Maoli as the younger siblings of the ʻāina (represented as gods); embodied as aliʻi, they were intermediaries between the people and the divine. Within this framework of cosmological kinship, a sense of pono—balance, harmony, dualism—is an integral part of Kanaka Maoli worldview. Christianity, a patriarchal, monotheistic religion, cannot conceive of life beginning with a female goddess or more than one deity; in polytheistic religions, such as traditional Hawaiian hoʻomana (spirituality), beginning with less than two is unconceivable, as both are necessary for birth and succession. The philosophy of moʻokūʻauhau is deeply embedded in ʻŌiwi Maoli culture, and reflected in multiple ways. Kanaka ʻŌiwi maintain pono with our environment through mālama and aloha ʻāina, demonstrating care of and respect for our ʻāina and ancestors. It is reflected in our moʻolelo, and is prevalent throughout the Pele and Hiʻiaka moʻolelo, exhibited in numerous ways.

He Hōʻuluʻulu Pōkole o ka Wā o ka Poʻe Kahiko (A Synopsis of the Times of the People of Old): Traditional Religion, Politics, and Arts

Like other Polynesian cultures, traditional Hawaiian religion was polytheistic and highly spiritual. An ʻōlelo noʻeau references "ke kini o ke akua, ka lehu o ke akua, ka mano o ke akua" (the 400, 4,000, 40,000 Hawaiian gods). This vast pantheon of akua oversaw every aspect of Hawaiian life. Within traditional society, Kameʻeleihiwa notes, "the people and the land prospered as a sophisticated civilization was developed, including the largest network of wet land taro fields and hundred acre fishponds, ever found anywhere in the world. Living in harmony with the land developed into an exquisite art form and generosity in all things, especially in the sharing of food, was considered the highest mark of civilized behavior."[8] Another ʻōlelo noʻeau describes the importance of genealogies and the familial relationship between aliʻi and makaʻāinana: "Kūneki nā kūʻauhau liʻiliʻi, noho mai i lalo; hoʻokahi nō, ʻo ko ke aliʻi ke piʻi i ka ʻiʻo (Let the lesser genealogies sit below; that of the aliʻi alone should be raised up towards significance)."[9]

Before the onslaught of Western invasion, traditional ʻŌiwi society was organized around moʻokūʻauhau and the kinship between the ʻāina, akua, aliʻi, and makaʻāinana (the working class). Aliʻi held different titles that came with specific kuleana (aliʻi ʻaimoku, for example, were the high chiefs who controlled islands, while kaukau aliʻi were junior-ranked chiefs who were supervisors and administrators). Kahuna (spiritual leaders, experts in various fields) and koa (the warrior class) also served the aliʻi and assisted in governmental affairs. Ea (political control of the ʻāina) was established through the ʻAikapu (separate or sacred eating) at the time of Papahānaumoku and Wākea. The pono aliʻi was a spiritual one.[10] The primary male akua of the state—Kāne (male), Kū (erect), Lono (messenger), and Kanaloa (unconquerable)—represented political control, the fertility of the land and sea (fishing, farming, hunting, gathering), and societal practices (medicine, war, arts, horticulture). The male akua were balanced by numerous powerful female counterparts, including Haumea (sacred ruler), Hina (woman), Pele, and Hiʻiaka, who were important female deities of medicine, war, and arts such as kapa production and hula.[11]

Some kuleana were divided by gender (in the ʻAikapu, for example, men and women ate in separate eating houses, and certain foods were restricted to men only because of their association with the masculine prowess of the four major male deities),[12] but the arts were enjoyed by all;

men and women excelled in the performance of mele and hula and other leisure activities, such as heʻe nalu (surfing).

Prior to the Amer-European invasion in the eighteenth century, Kanaka Maoli had created and sustained a highly organized, self-sufficient sociopolitical system that included a highly sophisticated language, culture, and religion, as well as a system of land and ocean resource management that maintained the abundance of resources through a strictly regulated practice of kapu and aloha ʻāina.

Ka Hopena Luku Komoʻiʻiʻi ʻole (The Devastating Outcome): Effects of Western Imperialism and Settler Colonialism

British Captain James Cook accidentally stumbled on the Hawaiian islands in 1778, the first Western intruder to arrive in the islands and change Hawaiian life forever. It is estimated that as many as one million Kanaka Maoli thrived in the island when Cook first arrived.[13] Yet by the first missionary census in 1823, a scant 134,000 Hawaiians remained, reflecting a population collapse of up to 80 percent in the first four decades of Western contact, the consequence of the deadly agent of haole imperialism—disease. Cook's men were the first to infect Kanaka men and women with highly transmittable venereal diseases such as syphilis and gonorrhea that began the genocide of the Hawaiian people. At least a dozen epidemics occurred throughout the nineteenth century that decimated the Native population: bubonic plague (1804), influenza (1826), whooping cough (1832), mumps (1839), leprosy (1840), measles, whooping cough, and influenza (1848), smallpox (1853), whooping cough (1888), diphtheria (1890), cholera and smallpox (1895), and bubonic plague (1899).[14] By the time the overthrow of the Hawaiian kingdom occurred in 1893, only forty thousand Kanaka Maoli remained.[15]

Merchants and traders followed, pressing Hawaiians into consumer capitalism. Traditional society had been one of subsistence and active trade, mai kō uka, mai kō kai, goods from the uplands exchanged with those from the seaside. A portion of one's livelihood was given as an annual hoʻokupu (offering), collected by the aliʻi ʻaimoku and reapportioned to the kaukau aliʻi and their retainers in exchange for their service. By the 1820s, new economic industries such as the sandalwood trade and whaling emerged, controlled by foreigners who saw fortunes to be made, as Hawaiʻi had no internationally recognized government and no tax system. Businessmen and opportunists gleefully bought and sold commodities through the aliʻi, who soon acquired phenomenal amounts of debt.

Hawaiian historian Jonathan Kamakawiwoʻole Osorio argues that the introduction of Western capitalism (including private property), Christianity, and other aspects of settler colonialism in the early nineteenth century, eroded and eventually severed the symbiotic kinship relationship between aliʻi and makaʻāinana.[16] Exposure to such radically different ways of living and the continued rapid collapse of Kanaka ʻŌiwi by the mid-nineteenth century caused many to question the traditional political and religious power structure in place for generations. Kameʻeleihiwa writes, "In traditional times, the society was pono, or in harmony, when the Aliʻi Nui, konohiki, and commoner worshipped the Akua and cared for the land. The sign of the divine pleasure was a prosperous people and fertile land. Conversely, there could be no pono, or harmony, with such great death. As a result of the changes brought by Western contact, Hawaiians began to search for a new convention for pono, one that would control the new world in which they found themselves."[17]

In 1810, the Hawaiian political structure was transformed by Kamehameha I from the traditional ʻAikapu to a monarchy; with the advantage of Western weaponry, Kamehameha I was the first aliʻi nui to successfully unify all of the Hawaiian islands under one ruler. While considered the first mōʻī (king) who incorporated Western representation into his government—including a national flag and a military equipped with foreign weaponry—he maintained a traditional style of governance. Upon his death in 1819, the ʻAikapu was forever abolished by his son and successor, Liholiho (Kamehameha II), with the participation of his mother, Keōpūolani (Kamehameha's most sacred wife), and the kuhina nui (regent) Kaʻahumanu (Kamehameha's favorite wife). The period after Kamehameha I's death was declared ʻAinoa (unrestricted eating). Kaʻahumanu ordered the destruction of the traditional heiau, and Kanaka ʻŌiwi began searching for a new way of governance and spiritual leadership.

The first group of American settlers in the islands were Calvinist missionaries sent by the Boston-based ABCFM. The first wave of these missionaries arrived in 1820, determined to bring Christianity and Western civilization to the "heathen" Natives. While Cook had commented on "a handsome people and a beautiful land," missionary Hiram Bingham, leader of the first mission, saw only degradation:

> The appearance of destitution, degradation, and barbarism, among the chattering, and almost naked savages, whose heads and feet and much of their sunburnt skins, were bare, was appalling. Some of our number, with gushing tears, turned away from the spectacle. Others with firmer nerve continued their gaze, but were ready to exclaim, "Can these be human beings! How dark

and comfortless their state of mind and heart! How imminent the danger to the immortal soul, shrouded in this deep pagan gloom! Can such beings be civilized? Can they be Christianized?"[18]

Fellow ABCFM missionary Charles Samuel Steward similarly commented:

> Their rapid and unintelligible exclamations, and whole exhibition of uncivilized character, gave to them the appearance of being half-man and half-beast, and irresistibly pressed on the thoughts the query—"Can they be men—can they be women? Do they not form a link in creation, connecting man with the brute?" The officer heading the boat ... exclaimed ... "Well, if I never before saw brutes in the shape of men, I have seen them this morning," [adding] "You can never live among such a people as this, we shall be obliged to take you back with us!"[19]

Perhaps seeing an opportunity to fill the spiritual void left by the abolition of the 'Aikapu, Kamehameha I's most politically astute widow, Ka'ahumanu, and other ali'i allowed the Calvinists to stay and preach. The missionaries were appalled not only by the "heathen" Hawaiians, but by the lawlessness of Hawaiian society, particularly in the port towns of Honolulu and Lāhainā that serviced the burgeoning whaling industry, and how foreign opportunists were eagerly duping Kanaka.

Kame'eleihiwa argues that the price to be paid by the Hawaiian ali'i for their alliance with the puritanical missionaries was quite high, because American missionary "protection" meant complete obedience and the rejection of everything Hawaiian, and that "under the American missionaries, Hawaiians fell from being the divine descendants of the Akua Papahānaumoku and Wākea to a pseudo-scientific version of the 'missing link' between brute and man."[20]

The missionaries set out to teach Western literacy (reading and writing), what Hawaiians called Ka Palapala (*lit.* the writing) for the purpose of converting Hawaiians to Christianity, because it was impossible to successfully convert Kanaka if they could not read ka Paipala (the Bible). They also concerned themselves with establishing a civil society based on Western social, religious, cultural, and legal practices. Simultaneously, they frowned on any Kanaka practice that violated their severe brand of Christian morality. Hula, 'awa drinking, he'e nalu, and other traditional practices were discouraged. Regarding hula, Silva writes, "the missionaries sought to silence this rather obvious public demonstration of sexuality on the grounds that it was vulgar, savage, and a violation of their Christian morals"; such views were "no doubt part of the civilizing process."[21]

Paul Burlin argues that "their efforts sought nothing less than the complete transformation of the Hawaiian people and culture into something resembling Pacific Island New Englanders."[22] Clifton Jackson Philips describes how the instructions to the first company of missionaries "encompassed much more than simply the conversion of the natives to a new faith and their adoption of what the missionaries termed 'civilized' standards of dress, habitation, and moral behavior," writing, "You are to aim at nothing short of covering those islands with fruitful fields and pleasant dwellings, and schools and churches; of raising up the whole people to an elevated state of Christian civilization; of bringing, or preparing the means of bringing, thousands and millions of the present and succeeding generations to the mansions of blessedness."[23] Instructions to the fifth company over a decade later were similar:

> Your mission . . . aims at nothing less than making every Sandwich islander intelligent, holy, and happy. Its appropriate work will not, therefore, be fully accomplished, until every town and village is blessed with a school house and church, and these . . . well furnished with competent native masters . . . and . . . native preachers—until every inhabitant is taught to read, and is furnished with a Bible in the *native tongue*; . . . [not] until christianity [sic] is fully established as the religion of the island, and its benign influence has become paramount in every rank and class of people.[24]

Under their influence, Kanaka Maoli society began transforming to haole ideals of "civilized modernity"—in 1821 the first Christian church was built, in 1822 the first Hawaiian-language lesson primer was published, and in 1823 Keōpūolani, Liholiho's mother and a high-ranking aliʻi, converted to Christianity.

Liholiho died in 1824, and his younger brother Kauikeaouli (Kamehameha III) came to power at the young age of eleven; Kaʻahumanu was named regent. The first civil laws of the aupuni (government) were soon established; in 1826 the first general tax law was enacted, and in 1827 kānāwai (laws) against murder, theft, rum selling, prostitution, and gambling went into effect. Hula, ʻawa drinking, and other traditional (and pleasurable) practices the missionaries had frowned on were outlawed in 1830.

In 1831 the first school, Lāhaināluna Seminary, was opened; the first printing press was set up by 1834, which soon after published the first Hawaiian-language newspaper, *Ka Lama* (The Luminary). In 1839 the first Paipala was published, as was He Kumu Kānāwai a me ke Kānāwai Hoʻoponopono Waiwai—the Declaration of Religious Rights (Rights and Laws of 1839), the predecessor to the first constitution, which soon followed in 1840.

Ke Kumukānāwai a me nā Kānāwai o ko Hawaiʻi Pae ʻĀina (The 1840 Constitution and Laws of the Kingdom of Hawaiʻi) established a constitutional monarchy with democratic principles by which everyone, including the mōʻī, was to abide. The constitution declared that the Hawaiian kingdom was based on Christian values and equality for all. Declaring the mission successful, the ABCFM soon withdrew support. Some missionaries left Hawaiʻi. But a number stayed and became involved in business and politics of the islands, including Lorrin Andrews, Richard Armstrong, Gerrit P. Judd, and William Richards. They advised the aliʻi nui that Western forms of government would ensure Hawaiʻi a place among civilized nations, and would bring foreign respect for the independent nation. Kauikeaouli also proclaimed, "He aupuni palapala koʻu"—mine will be a nation of literacy. The Department of Public Instruction was established, and Kanaka Maoli achieved one of the highest literacy rates in the world.[25]

While the missionaries are praised by some for modernizing Hawaiʻi and guiding Kanaka Maoli along the path of becoming one of the internationally recognized "family of nations," Kanaka Maoli were not unanimously keen on such "accomplishments." They mistrusted haole participation in kingdom affairs. Between 1840 and 1845 numerous petitions from the makaʻāinana to the aliʻi nui protested foreign participation in Maoli government, the privatization of lands, and foreigners swearing an oath of allegiance to the kingdom.[26] A petition against foreign citizenship in 1845 states in part, "Good foreigners will become no better by taking the oath of allegiance under our Chiefs. Good people are not opposed to us; they do not evade the laws of the Chiefs; they do not wish this kingdom to be sold to others."[27]

On July 10, 1839, the first international crisis occurred, when French Naval Captain Laplace arrived in Hawaiʻi on behalf of the French government, threatening military action if the Hawaiian government did not stop the persecution of French Catholics by the established Protestant population.[28]

Still reeling from narrowly averting war with the French in 1839, the first occupation of Hawaiʻi followed soon after, when British Lord George Paulet arrived in Honolulu on February 10, 1843, and demanded that the ruling mōʻī Kamehameha III cede the Hawaiian islands to Great Britain. Hawaiian Minister of Foreign Affairs Judd dispatched envoys to the United States, France, and Britain. The protest was forwarded to British Rear Admiral Richard Thomas, who arrived in Honolulu on July 26. On July 31, Thomas declared Hawaiʻi free from British claims; upon the restoration of Hawaiian sovereignty, Kauikeaouli declared, "Ua mau ke ea o ka ʻāina i ka pono" (The life or sovereignty of the land is perpetuated in just action).[29]

The crisis sparked renewed pressure on the mōʻī to privatize lands. Traditionally no one owned land; the ʻāina was administered by the ruling chiefs, and when a new aliʻi came to power via warfare or inheritance, a kālaiʻāina (political redistribution of land rights) was held. The lands in question were reapportioned to other aliʻi, administered by konohiki (supervisors) and worked by the makaʻāinana. But no one, not even the aliʻi, owned the land.

Judd and Richards, among other haole, insisted that privately held lands could not be legally taken by foreign nations. Thus, not only would the makaʻāinana be protected, but the sovereignty and economic prosperity of the kingdom as well, as another Paulet affair could not occur under such circumstances. Moreover, American missionaries had long argued that Hawaiians were dying because they were lazy and licentious, and the only avenue to salvation was private ownership of land, which they believed would inspire Kanaka to work and be responsible for their own fate.

The call for privatization of land caused much concern and trepidation for Kanaka Maoli, aliʻi and makaʻāinana alike. Foreigners, on the other hand, including the former missionaries, lusted at the possibility of owning Hawaiian ʻāina. Under intense pressure from his haole advisers, Kauikeaouli reluctantly agreed to privatize Hawaiian land. On December 10, 1845, a land commission was established for the purpose of overseeing land transactions of what has become known as the Māhele, or division of lands, which occurred between January and March 1848. Under the land commission, Hawaiian land was divided into thirds between the government (Crown or public lands), the aliʻi nui (lands privately held by the chiefs for their own use and benefit), and lands for the working-class makaʻāinana. For various reasons, only 8,200 makaʻāinana, or roughly 1 percent of the total Kanaka Maoli population at the time, received land awards, with an average lot size of three acres. In contrast, missionaries received 560 acres each.[30] The genesis of modern multinational corporations bearing the names of their missionary ancestors, such as Castle and Cooke, and Alexander and Baldwin, began prior to these awards of Hawaiian land, but having a stake in the land solidified their capital enterprise and facilitated their growing economic and political power. Government lands were sold off to foreigners to support capitalism by means of foreign investment. By 1893, even most of the aliʻi nui lands were controlled by foreigners, if not by outright sale or mortgage default, then as trustees on the boards of the aliʻi nui estates.[31]

By 1848, the depopulation crisis was so severe that tax breaks were offered to any makaʻāinana willing to cultivate undeveloped lands.[32] Sugar planters, well established in the islands, demanded sources of cheap labor, and the first contract labor system went into effect in 1850.

The Kuleana Act, which allowed makaʻāinana to claim lands after the aliʻi and konohiki had completed land transactions, also went into effect in 1850. Perhaps more significant is the Disabilities of Aliens Act that followed shortly thereafter, as it allowed anyone to own land, even foreigners. Land ownership automatically conferred suffrage on male citizens and denizens alike.[33] A few weeks later (July 30), the legislature authorized haole voting and office holding as well, regardless of citizenship.

By 1853, Hawaiʻi sugar planters were frustrated by U.S. duty on all imported sugar. Discussions began on annexing Hawaiʻi to the United States for economic reasons, regardless of what Kanaka Maoli thought. A smallpox epidemic further reduced the Native population from eighty-eight thousand to eighty thousand. Kauikeaouli considered the demands for annexation, but only if Hawaiʻi would be admitted as a state, which the U.S. Congress was not willing to consider, as Hawaiʻi was a nation of nonwhites.

When Kauikeaouli died the following year, his nephew Alexander Liholiho ʻIolani (Kamehameha IV) ascended the throne. Mistrustful of American advisers, Kamehameha IV fostered closer ties with Britain. He and his wife, Queen Emma, started the first hospital to serve Hawaiians, Queen's Hospital. They also became members of the Anglican Church, further separating their government from the American Calvinist missionary influence. Yet Kamehameha IV still contended with increasing missionary political influence as the sugar planters continued to press for a reciprocity treaty or annexation to the United States.

By 1860, ʻŌiwi society had been severed from traditional religious practices for four decades. Osorio notes that by 1853, virtually the entire native population was associated with "some Christian denomination."[34] Despite four decades of Calvinist influence that regulated every aspect of ʻŌiwi life, and two decades as a Christian nation, interest in and practice of certain cultural arts, such as hula, continued. Thus the haole community began agitating for a ban on the public performance of hula in the 1850s, which was enacted in 1860.

Silva traces the ban on hula to Hawai'i's political economy, as the plantations had encountered serious problems with Kanaka labor, blaming their "laziness" on their love of hula (not recognizing, perhaps, the Kanaka resistance to settler colonialism in their compulsion for traditional practices, and resistance to the puritanical work ethic): "The missionaries benefited from the establishment and growth of the capitalist economy in at least two ways: first, they were appointed or elected to positions of power and influence in the privy council, the cabinet, and the legislature; and, second, they were given large tracts of land, which a number of them converted to sugar plantations."[35] Silva argues that the move to ban hula was related to the labor shortage the plantations were facing, accompanied by moral judgments. She writes, "The puritan work ethic and disdain for traditional Kanaka Maoli practices dovetailed seamlessly with the attempts to exploit Kanaka Maoli labor," evoking the "'myth of the lazy native' . . . [that] also serves to 'justify compulsion and unjust practices in the mobilization of labor.'"[36]

Noel Kent summarizes the situation thus: "The missionaries' . . . response was to expunge those Hawaiian customs that seemed to undermine the grand objective of material accumulation—in effect, most of the indigenous culture: traditional art, language, dance, sexual mores, nudity, etc."[37]

While missionary- and government-run newspapers had been in circulation since the 1830s, content was strictly controlled and monitored by missionaries and former missionaries to reflect "civilized" Christian values. The Hawaiian nationalist press, independent newspapers free of missionary and government control, demonstrated 'Ōiwi agency. They were founded by Kanaka beginning in 1861 with the publication of *Ka Hoku o ka Pakipika* (The Star of the Pacific). For the first time in thirty years of literacy, Kanaka Maoli could express themselves as they wished. From the first issue of the first paper, much to the chagrin of the missionary and foreign populace, Kanaka Maoli prominently featured mo'olelo ku'una, mo'okū'auhau, mele, and other culturally important genres of poetic and historical importance, most of which were being written and published for the first time.[38] Letters to the editors, hīmeni (Christian-inspired hymns), foreign tales translated into Hawaiian, and news of the day from around the globe were also included. Thus, Hawaiian literary nationalism was born. In the span of a century (1830s–1930s), seventy-five newspapers were published, the majority of which were owned and run by Kanaka.[39]

The American Civil War (1861–1865) affected Hawai'i politics and economics. Lot Kapuāiwa (Kamehameha V) declared Hawai'i neutral in the war, and sugar prices and production boomed. The first sugar trade agreement between Hawai'i and the United States was signed in 1867. More plantations were opened and a larger labor force was needed, precipitating the mass arrival of the first plantation labor. By 1872, only fifty-one thousand Hawaiians remained, and sugar planters began importing more foreign labor. By 1890, more than fifty-five thousand immigrant workers, primarily Chinese, Japanese, and Portuguese, had been imported to work the sugar fields.

To entice the United States into a reciprocity deal, haole banker Charles Reed Bishop (who later married Kamehameha descendant Bernice Pauahi) proposed the cession of Pearl Harbor to the U.S. military. Kanaka Maoli were absolutely opposed to the idea. The general outcry was enough to halt public negotiations, although they continued in secret. Queen Emma, Liholiho's widow, remarked on Americans living in Hawai'i, "I like the *excessive* impudence of that race. What people possessed of any love of country, patriotism, identity and loyalty can calmly sit and allow foreigners to propose cession of the native born's soil, in spite of their unanimous protests? My blood boils with resentment against this insult."[40] The Kamehameha dynasty ended with the death of Kamehameha V on December 11, 1872. William Charles Lunalilo was the first elected mō'ī. He was voted into office on January 8, 1873, with unanimous support by the House of Nobles and House of Representatives (over rival David Kalākaua) because of his genealogical connection to the Kamehamehas, as mo'okū'auhau continued to be an important factor for Kanaka Maoli.[41] Unfortunately, Lunalilo's reign was cut short as he died unexpectedly the year following his election at the age of thirty-eight.

Lunalilo's death precipitated another election, a highly contested race between Kamehameha IV's widow, Queen Emma, and Kalākaua. While Emma was far more popular than Kalākaua, who was viewed by some Kanaka as maha'oi (rude) with an inferior genealogy, Kalākaua won the election.

After a tumultuous election process, which spawned a riot, Kalākaua was elected to the throne in 1874. Friendlier to Americans (in part because of debt owed to American businessmen), Kalākaua's first act as mō'ī was to lobby Washington for a reciprocity treaty without cession of Pearl Harbor. After his success with the reciprocity treaty, Kalākaua turned his attention to the Lāhui and the dismal state of affairs with the Hawaiian people. Ravaged by foreign diseases and dispossessed from a subsistence lifestyle, Kalākaua's vision for a robust Lāhui was expressed through his motto, Ho'oulu Lāhui, to increase, reinvigorate, revitalize the Hawaiian people. Kalākaua built 'Iolani Palace as a modern symbol of the strength of the Hawaiian monarchy, a regal testament to the mana of the aupuni. But his focus was reinstating traditional practices including arts, such as the documentation of texts and the performance of hula and mele.

Kalākaua set out to revive traditional arts, beginning with the Hale Nauā, a society dedicated to fostering, collecting, and perpetuating Hawaiian traditions, such as moʻokūʻauhau aliʻi (chiefly genealogies). He reestablished the beloved practice of hula, which had been banned in 1860. Traditional hula, including hula Pele, were sanctioned in his court as the national dance, prominently featured at his poni mōʻī (coronation ceremonies) in 1883. Kalākaua also supported modern practices, such as the publication of moʻolelo. Prior to becoming mōʻī, Kalākaua was an editor associated with several independent newspapers that published moʻolelo kuʻuna, including Pele and Hiʻiaka. He lent his name to a collection of Hawaiian myths and legends published in English in 1888. In 1889, Kalākaua commissioned the Kumulipo to be written down for the first time in the Hawaiian language. Kalākaua's collective efforts at revitalizing Hawaiian pride through the culture and the arts have been discussed by more recent ʻŌiwi scholars and others as part of a cultural nationalism aimed at keeping "Hawaiʻi for Hawaiians" and affirming "the cultural distinction between Hawaiians and foreigners."[42] Silva devotes a chapter of *Aloha Betrayed* to Kalākaua's revival of traditional cultural practices such as moʻokūʻauhau, mele, and hula as "resistance strategies" to colonialism.[43] Cristina Bacchilega observes that, "like the Brothers Grimm in early 19th century Germany, Kalākaua... recognized the nation-building power of tradition or 'folklore,'" and also "saw the political currency of divulging the moʻolelo of Hawaiʻi beyond the shores of his kingdom."[44] American missionary descendants were outraged, and they soundly denounced, as they saw it, such "recrudescence of heathenism" that commenced under Kalākaua's reign, "as evinced by [Kalākaua's] encouragement of the lascivious hulahula dancers and... sorcerers."[45]

Despite Kalākaua's efforts to placate haole, they still agitated for more political and economic power. They formed a secret group, the Hawaiian League. Arms were smuggled into the kingdom with the intent of overthrowing the Hawaiian government. Lorrin Thurston, grandson of missionaries Asa and Lucy Goodale Thurston, was a ringleader.

Thurston was the primary architect of what has become known as the Bayonet Constitution, which Kalākaua was forced to sign under duress in 1887. The Bayonet Constitution effectively stripped the powers of the mōʻī, reducing him to a figurehead, transferring power instead to the Legislature and Cabinet, composed primarily of haole. Shortly thereafter,

Pearl Harbor was ceded to the United States, with the hope that once the Americans had a military stake in Hawaiʻi annexation would surely follow. Vehement protests by Kanaka Maoli were ignored.

Kanaka refused to give up fighting for their county. Aloha ʻāina, or love for the land, was described by Mary Kawena Pukui as "a very old saying."[46] In the nineteenth century, it was evoked to rally Kanaka nationalism; the poʻe aloha ʻāina, the people who loved the land, were patriots who fought for the Lāhui. Such aloha extended to the divine and human ancestors and leaders that were recorded in traditional sayings, and observed and commented on by early Western explorers and missionaries. In an 1869 installment of "Ka Moʻolelo Hawaiʻi," published in the newspaper *Ke Au Okoa*, Hawaiian historian Samuel Kamakau observed:

> The aupuni of Hawaiʻi is an aupuni that feels aloha for its aliʻi, that feels aloha for the voice with which the aliʻi speak, that feels aloha for their words, that feels aloha for the discussion between us, that honors the command that falls solely from the heights to down below. Aloha is certainly not for sale, decidedly not for rent, and by all means not for personal gain—for aloha is truly genuine. This aloha pertains to the mōʻī and the aliʻi for whom aloha is felt because they are kind to the makaʻāinana [everyday people] and the entire lāhui.[47]

Such sentiments of aloha ʻāina continued through the tumultuous 1880s and 1890s. As Silva notes, "Aloha ʻāina . . . encompasses more than nationalism and is not an exact fit with the English word 'patriotism,' the usual translation. Where nationalism and patriotism tend to exalt the virtues of a people or race, aloha ʻāina exalts the land."[48] The political organization Hui Kālaiʻāina (Hawaiian Political Party) formed after the Bayonet Constitution was enacted in 1887 with this sentiment in mind, restoring the power of governance over the land to its rightful place, the mōʻī, the modern representative of his traditional predecessors, the aliʻi ʻai moku, the one who ruled (ʻai) the land (moku). The name Hui Kālaiʻāina itself is derived from the traditional practice of politics, literally meaning the carving (kālai) of the land (ʻāina).[49]

In 1889, Robert Kalanihiapo Wilcox led a brief and unsuccessful revolt against the reformed (post-Bayonet) government. It was his first attempt to return political power to Kanaka Maoli, but it would not be his only effort.

When Kalākaua unexpectedly died in 1891, his sister, Lydia Kama-ka'eha Lili'uokalani, ascended the throne. She immediately began receiving petitions from Kanaka Maoli who wanted the political power of the kingdom returned to Hawaiian hands. The queen wrote, "Petitions poured in from every part of the Islands for a new constitution. . . . They were supported by petitions addressed to the Hui Kalaiaina, who in turn indorsed [sic] and forwarded them to me. . . . [An] estimated [6,500], or two thirds [of 9,500 registered voters] had signed these petitions. To have ignored or disregarded so general a request I must have been deaf to the voice of the people . . . no true Hawaiian chief would have done other than to promise a consideration of their wishes."[50] The queen tried to promulgate a new constitution in 1893 that would restore powers to the office of mō'ī and to Kanaka Maoli, but the majority of her cabinet was too afraid to support her. Several of her ministers betrayed her, informing Thurston of the queen's intent. Thurston used this information to justify overthrowing the kingdom, with the support of foreign (primarily American) businessmen, particularly those who had helped implement the Bayonet Constitution. In violation of established treaties between the Hawaiian and U.S. governments, U.S. Minister to Hawai'i John L. Stevens colluded with Thurston and his cohorts, ordering the landing of U.S. Marines in Honolulu. On January 17, 1893, a provisional government was declared, naming coconspirator Sanford B. Dole as president.

The queen responded by acquiescing, under protest, until an appeal could be heard by the U.S. government, declaring, "To avoid any collision of armed forces, and perhaps loss of life, I do, under this protest and impelled by said forces, yield my authority until such time as the Government of the United States shall, upon the facts being presented to it, undo . . . the action of its representative reinstate me in the authority which I claim as the constitutional sovereign of the Hawaiian Islands."[51] The queen's statement has often been misinterpreted in settler textbooks as the queen relinquishing power to the United States, which is far from her intent. In this period immediately following the overthrow of the monarchy, the Hui Aloha 'Āina (Hawaiian Patriotic League) was founded. Like the Hui Kālai'āina, its expressed purpose was restoring political power to Hawaiians. Together these hui (associations) expressed the intent of Kanaka Maoli, led by their beloved queen, to regain Hawaiian sovereignty.

Dole, Thurston, and their accomplices pressed once again for annexation to the United States. But President Grover Cleveland sent Georgia Congressman James Blount to Hawai'i to investigate. Nearly 1,500 pages in length, the "Blount Report" found that Stevens's actions had indeed contributed to the overthrow of the Hawaiian monarchy, against the will of the Hawaiian people. Referring to this illegal action as "an act of war," Cleveland directed Congress to restore Hawaiian sovereignty.

But the provisional government would not give up so easily. On July 4, 1894, they reorganized as the Republic of Hawai'i, with Sanford Dole again named president.

In 1895, Wilcox once again tried to mount a counterrevolution against the provisional government; he and other leaders were imprisoned.

The Republic carried on with business as usual, doing what they could to retain their own interests and undermine Kanaka even further. The controversial Land Act of 1895, designed by Dole, established a commissioner of public lands who was authorized to sell off public lands (the former Crown lands). The Land Act was designed to get as much public lands into private hands as possible; perhaps Dole was afraid Hawai'i would be returned to Kanaka Maoli, and that a stronger foreign presence could be retained if even more haole owned lands. This was the beginning of a multi-decade project aimed at homesteading, one that failed in part because of unscrupulous land speculation.

In 1896, the Republic banned Hawaiian language as a medium of instruction in the public schools. Combined with the mass numbers of foreign immigrants to Hawai'i in the decades prior, the move resulted in linguistic genocide.

In 1897, McKinley succeeded Cleveland as U.S. president, significant for Hawai'i because he favored annexation. The U.S. Senate, however, failed to pass it. The Hui Aloha 'Āina and Hui Kālai'āina had actively collected signatures on two anti-annexation petitions. In the introduction to a photocopied collection of the petitions, Silva writes, "The Kanaka Maoli believed that the American government was committed to their stated principles of justice and of government of the people, by the people, and for the people. They believed that once the U.S. President and members of Congress saw that the great majority of Hawaiian citizens opposed the annexation, the principles of fairness would prevail, that is, their Native government would be restored."[52] Hui Aloha 'Āina held a mass meeting on September 6, 1897, at the Palace Square to announce and garner support for the anti-annexation petition drives:

> Thousands of poe aloha aina—*patriots*—attended. [Hui Aloha 'Āina] President James Kaulia gave a rousing speech, saying "We, the nation (lahui) will never consent to the annexation of our lands, until the very last patriot lives." He said agreeing to annexation was like agreeing to be buried alive. He predicted

that annexation would open the door for many foreigners to come here, and to take jobs and resources away from the Native people. He asked, "Then where will we live?" The crowd answered, "In the mountains," which figuratively means, "we shall be homeless." He asserted that a mass refusal by the people could prevent the annexation: "If the nation remains steadfast in its protest of annexation, the Senate can continue to strive until the rock walls of Iolani Palace crumble, and never will Hawaii be annexed to America!" The annexationist newspapers had published threats that the leaders of the mass meeting would be arrested for treason, but Mr. Kaulia assured the people that their assembly was legal. He said that it was because the brains of the government could not push over the brains of the Kanaka Maoli that the government had to resort to weapons of war. . . . He told the people . . . "Do not be afraid, be steadfast in aloha for your land and be united in thought. Protest forever the annexation of Hawaii until the very last aloha ʻāina [lives]!"[53]

By October 1897, the Hui Aloha ʻĀina had gathered over twenty-one thousand signatures, and the Hui Kālaiʻāina had collected seventeen thousand more, totaling 556 pages, quite impressive numbers, given that the entire Kanaka Maoli population was about thirty-nine thousand at that time. Delegates were chosen to go to Washington, D.C., where they joined Queen Liliʻuokalani in speaking with members of Congress. Their personal appeal and petitions were successful, and annexation did not pass.

In 1898, Hawaiʻi was still a haole-controlled republic. That year, the legislature approved legislation proclaiming English as the official language of the government, replacing Hawaiian, despite Hawaiian being the most widely used and understood language in daily life. Annexation of Hawaiʻi came up again, as Spain and the United States were at war in April of that year over the Philippines, and U.S. troops were sent to Hawaiʻi. The U.S. military wanted Hawaiʻi for strategic purposes, and worked hard to convince Congress it should be a U.S. territory. On July 4, 1898, Hawaiʻi was annexed to the United States by the joint "Newlands Resolution," which required only a simple majority in the House and Senate. Research and analysis by ʻŌiwi advocates and activists in recent years have demonstrated that such a resolution was illegal by U.S. law, and grounds for continued pressure in domestic and international political arenas for the recognition of Hawaiian sovereignty. Today, Hawaiʻi is considered illegally occupied by the United States. The illegal processes and U.S. involvement in both the overthrow of the Hawaiian government in 1893 and the subsequent illegal annexation in 1898 have not usurped Hawaiian sovereignty, but only obscured it.

On February 22, 1900, the Hawaiian Organic Act passed Congress, establishing the territorial government of Hawaiʻi. Missionary descendant Sanford Dole was appointed the first governor. Kanaka Maoli continued to protest annexation through the political means available. The Hui Kālaiʻāina and the Hui Aloha ʻĀina joined to create the Home Rule Party, with the goal of electing a delegate to Congress. In 1901, the first delegate elected was Robert Kalanihiapo Wilcox.

In 1903, Jonah Kūhiō Kalanianaʻole was elected to Congress, replacing Wilcox, a position he held until his death in 1922. Kūhiō had been deeply involved with anti-annexation work for a number of years prior, but joined the Republican party in his bid for Congress because he felt it was more powerful than the Home Rule Party and could get more done. Shortly before his death, Kūhiō successfully passed the Hawaiian Homes Commission Act, which established two hundred thousand acres of land for the purpose of "rehabilitating" Kanaka Maoli through homesteading, allowing them to rebuild traditional ties to the ʻāina.[54] Noble in intent, the Department of Hawaiian Home Lands that was created to administer the lands has had a rather rocky history and uneven success in the distribution of lands, support for the program, and realization of Kūhiō's vision for the beneficiaries of the land. While it did reconnect some Kanaka families to the land, it also displaced others from their one hānau, or traditional places of birth and residence.[55]

In 1908, the U.S. Congress approved funding to build a naval station at Pearl Harbor, and in 1909, the Army established Schofield Barracks. In 1910, the first astronomy observatory was built in order to better view Halley's Comet, and in 1912 the Hawaiʻi Volcano Observatory was erected at Kīlauea volcano. In 1915, a congressional party toured Kīlauea, interested in establishing a national park there. Coincidentally (or not), Emerson's *Pele and Hiiaka: A Myth from Hawaii* was published in Honolulu that year. The following year, the Hawaiʻi Volcanoes National Park was signed into existence by Woodrow Wilson; Kīlauea National Park was created in 1921.

In 1954, a democratic revolution of the mostly nonwhite working class occurred, effectively ending the haole Republican hold on Hawaiʻi since 1893. It was a major political shift that included everyone, as Democrats advocated for more working-class rights. In 1959, Hawaiʻi statehood was put to a vote, with no option on the ballot other than to become a state or remain a territory. Under such conditions, and with the majority of the population non-Hawaiian, Hawai'i voted for statehood, moving Hawai'i one step further away from its sovereign roots.

While 'Ōiwi aloha 'āina political and cultural activism seemed to disappear in the territorial period, it never completed dissolved. Inspired by larger political and social justice actions such as the civil rights movement, a vigorous Hawaiian cultural renaissance emerged in the 1960s and 1970s, reminiscent of Kalākaua's campaign to Ho'oulu Lāhui, reinvigorate the nation, nearly a century prior. Hawaiian language, hula, mele, and other oral and performance arts reemerged in a strong reaction against the insipid hapa haole (Western-influenced) ditties popularized in the burgeoning tourist industry and Hollywood representations of Hawai'i in the early twentieth century. The Merrie Monarch Festivals, named in honor of Kalākaua as an esteemed patron of the arts, was founded in Hilo in 1963, the preeminent hula competition introduced in 1971. Envisioned by Hawaiian artist Herb Kawainui Kāne, waterman Tommy Holmes, and anthropologist Ben Finney, *Hōkūle'a* (star of joy), the first modern Polynesian voyaging canoe built using a traditional double-hulled design, was completed in the early 1970s. Her maiden voyage to Tahiti commenced in 1975, navigated by traditional means (such as the reading of star constellations), with no modern implements. The purpose of *Hōkūle'a* was to prove that long-distance voyaging between the Polynesian islands was actually possible, something haole historians and anthropologists had long refuted. Numerous voyages throughout the Pacific and to other parts of the world have since occurred, and myriad other wa'a kaulua (traditional double-hulled canoes) inspired by *Hōkūle'a* have been built in Hawai'i and around the Pacific.[56]

Political action continued as well, the most galvanizing being the formation of the Protect Kaho'olawe 'Ohana (PKO) in 1976 with the express purpose of stopping the U.S. military bombing of the sacred island. Kaho'olawe had been seized by the U.S. military on December 8, 1941, one day after the Japanese attack on Pearl Harbor that propelled the United States to enter World War II. The island was used for live fire training. PKO filed suit in U.S. federal court to stop it and to require compliance with environmental law to ensure that cultural resources would be protected. When the courts allowed the training to continue, two PKO members, George Jarrett Helm of Moloka'i and Kimo Mitchell of Hāna, Maui, occupied the island on March 9, 1977. Modern po'e aloha 'āina, they were determined to stop the military bombing and protect numerous cultural sites, many of which had not been documented. They were never seen again.

Significantly, Kaho'olawe was important to traditional navigation, which had just been reborn with *Hōkūleʻa*. After a long battle, Kahoʻolawe was added to the National Register of Historic Places in 1981, and in 1990, U.S. President George W. Bush ended live fire training on the island. In 1993, a century after the overthrow of the Hawaiian government, Title X of the 1994 Department of Defense Appropriations Act authorized that jurisdiction of Kahoʻolawe be conveyed to the state; the Kahoʻolawe Island Reserve Commission, which now administers access to the island, was established in 1994; by state law, commercial use of the island and surrounding waters is prohibited, which can be used only for Hawaiian cultural, subsistence, or spiritual purposes, or environmental restoration, historic preservation, and education.[57]

In 1984, the first Pūnana Leo (language nest) Hawaiian-language immersion preschool was established in Honolulu by parents and educators concerned with the dismal state of Hawaiian language. The last generations of native Hawaiian-language speakers were quickly passing on, and a very small number of native Hawaiian-language speakers remained. Pūnana Leo preschools and the Kula Kaiāpuni Hawaiian-language immersion schools that serve grades K–12 are now instituted throughout the islands. The links between land, language, cultural practice, and political activism within ʻŌiwi communities have thus continued.

In 1993, Kanaka Maoli commemorated the centennial of the overthrow of our nation. That year, President Bill Clinton signed Public Law 103-150, the "Apology Bill," that admitted the United States played a role in the overthrow of the Hawaiian government and "suppression of the inherent sovereignty of the Native Hawaiian people."[58] In 1998, Kanaka Maoli observed the centennial of annexation, and in 2009 held our own counter-commemoration (against the backdrop of state-sanctioned celebrations) of fifty years of statehood for the "fake state" of Hawaiʻi.

Upon the restoration of Hawaiian sovereignty in 1843, Kamehameha III declared, Ua mau ke ea o ka ʻāina i ka pono (The life of the land is perpetuated in just action). While Paulet's seizure of Hawaiian sovereignty in 1843 was the first of many such incidents, it certainly was not the last. Throughout the period of Western contact, Kanaka Maoli have suffered great and tragic losses; however, "He oia mau nō," we continue on.[59] Throughout periods of great physical, spiritual, emotional, and psychological devastation, we have persevered, upholding our traditional mele, hula, and other beloved cultural practices. We continued to recite and remember moʻokūʻauhau, and moʻolelo, looking to the past, to the kūpuna for direction and inspiration as we always have. In the words of Kauʻi Goodhue, "we are who we were."[60] Silva writes, "Kanaka Maoli continue to protest today. We have never relinquished our national sovereignty.

Kanaka Maoli are working on state, national, and international levels to have our existence as a nation recognized. Kanaka Maoli also continue to resist and protest every encroachment upon our inherent rights to this land, our ocean and fresh waters, and all the other natural resources of Hawaii. We are insisting as well on our rights to keep our language and cultural traditions, and the land itself, alive."[61]

Since Captain Cook's journals first introduced the haole world to Hawai'i two centuries ago, what Hawai'i signifies to many people is framed between settler colonial discourses of dying pagan Natives and Christian-derived civilized enlightenment; paradise and adventure; tourism and militarism. Yet Kanaka 'Ōiwi have had a long history of cultural practice, politics, and nationalism on multiple fronts, mai ka pō mai—as outlined by the great cosmogonic genealogy, Kumulipo, and mai nā kūpuna mai, in the mo'olelo passed down from our ancestors. Where do the Pele and Hi'iaka mo'olelo fit in, and what role do they play? Who are Pele and Hi'iakaikapoliopele? Where do they come from, and what do they represent to Kanaka Maoli that their mo'olelo would be remembered and retold, over and over, in countless formats and versions, mai ka pō mai?

Mai Kahiki Mai (From Tahiti Forth): Voyaging Traditions

Numerous mo'olelo document the long history of oceanic voyage, discovery, and settlement by 'Ōiwi ancestors who traversed thousands of miles across the vast Pacific on wa'a kaulua, generations ago, navigating by stars, winds, swells, and experience. These narratives are new strands of history and genealogies woven into the lei mo'olelo of Hawaiian origins, identity, and tradition. There is no agreement on precisely when 'Ōiwi ancestors first settled Hawai'i, but current archaeological evidence supports multiple contacts between Polynesian island groups between 800 BCE to 1200 CE.[62]

Pele is a malihini (foreigner, newcomer) who voyaged, like countless generations of Kanaka, mai Kahiki mai—from the ancient homeland to Hawai'i with a vast entourage of family members who populated the islands centuries ago. Mele such as "Holo mai Pele" (Pele comes [to Hawai'i]) and "Mai Kahiki ka wahine 'o Pele" (The woman Pele comes from Kahiki) intimately detail the preparations for travel, record the names of the entourage who accompanied her, their status and roles, and a possible motivation for departing Kahiki—a series of volcanic eruptions. Kahiki represents Tahiti, or any foreign land outside of Hawai'i. But hiki has related possible meanings, including possibility, to arrive at a destination, and "to fetch" or "to carry back and forth," all suggesting the multiple (and successful) voyages across the vast Pacific.[63] Through the arrival and settlement of voyaging akua and kanaka, new moʻokūʻauhau were woven into existing ones.

Once the Pele family arrived in Hawaiʻi, the myriad adventures of both Pele and Hiʻiaka unfold. One of the longest, richest moʻolelo is Hiʻiaka's epic journey from the crater of Halemaʻumaʻu on Hawaiʻi island 1,500 miles across the pae ʻāina (archipelago) to Hāʻena, Kauaʻi to fetch Pele's dream lover Lohiʻau, most often referred to as "Ka Moʻolelo o Hiʻiakaikapoliopele" (The epic of Hiʻiakaikapoliopele).

A basic synopsis is helpful in understanding the core strands of the narrative, particularly when reading comparatively across multiple texts. As I discuss in subsequent chapters, not all of the Pele and Hiʻiaka moʻolelo contain all of the same episodes, including the migration of the Pele ʻohana to Hawaiʻi. Nor do they present the narrative in the same way. Some have more episodes in common than others. But the one referent they share is the inclusion of Pele as a character and the volcano as her place of residence.

He Hōʻuluʻulu Pōkole o ka Moʻolelo mai nā Kūpuna mai (A Synopsis of the Epic from the Ancestors): The Pele and Hiʻiaka Moʻolelo

Pele is the daughter of Kūwahailo (maggot-mouth Kū, a war god) and Haumea; Rice says her father is Moemoeaʻaliʻi (creeping rootlets).[64] *Ilo* also means "to germinate, sprout," and refers to a shoot as well, suggesting underground movement of roots, or magma, as does *moe* (horizontal) and *aʻa* (rootlets).[65] Haumea is another name for both Papahānaumoku and Pele; one meaning of hau is a kind of porous stone, and a definition of mea is reddish-brown, thus, one way to interpret her name is "red rock."[66]

Pele departs from her homeland of Kahiki (more specifically the island of Polapola)[67] with an entourage comprising different family members aboard the canoe *Honuaiākea* (earth explorer).

The Pele ʻohana arrives in the Hawaiian archipelago starting in the northwest. They make their way down the island chain in search of a suitable home. Members of the entourage are left (or choose to stay) at island locations along the way, such as Nihoa, Kaʻula, Niʻihau, Lehua, Kauaʻi, Oʻahu, Molokaʻi, Lānaʻi, Kahoʻolawe, Maui, and finally Hawaiʻi island, populating the islands with Pele's people. Along the way, Pele creates specific geographic formations as she digs in the earth with her ʻōʻō (digging stick) Pāoa searching for a home. She finally settles at Halemaʻumaʻu on Kīlauea, the volcanic lands between the borders of the districts of Kaʻū and Puna on the island of Hawaiʻi.

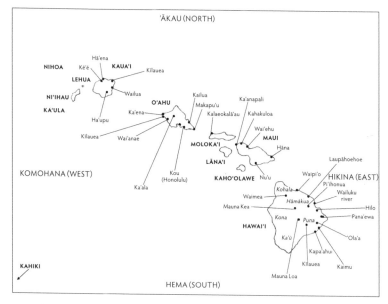

Nā wahi a Pele a me Hiʻiakaikapoliopele e holoholo ai (Places Pele and Hiʻiaka visited on their journeys).

One day, Pele desires to go down to the ocean and invites her siblings to accompany her. There, Pele witnesses Hōpoe and Hāʻena, kamaʻāina of the area, dancing at the sea of Nānāhuki. She is so taken with their hula performance that she asks all her younger sisters if they know how to hula, and they each say no. But Pele's youngest and favorite sister, Hiʻiakaikapoliopele, says she knows how. "Ke haʻa lā Puna i ka makani" (Puna dances in the breeze) is the hula Hiʻiaka learns from Hōpoe and dances for Pele, much to her delight; this is the origin of hula. As the sisters gather seafood, surf, and enjoy their time at the beach, Pele falls asleep at a place called Kapaʻahu (kapa cloak). Her spirit hears the sound of pahu drumming and follows it. Ending up across the archipelago at Hāʻena on the island of Kauaʻi, Pele's spirit meets the chief of that land, Lohiʻau. The handsome, athletic aliʻi is in the midst of participating in his favorite activity, hula. Bedecked in the fragrant flora of Puna (maile, lehua, hala, etc.), Pele presents a young and beautiful human version of herself. The two are immediately attracted to each other.

They stay together for several days, forgetting all other activity. Yet Pele knows she must return to the crater soon, and cannot stay with Lohiʻau in her spirit form. She tells him she must leave, but promises him she will send someone to fetch him. Lohiʻau is so distraught by the sudden

Our family lands at Kapaʻahu, Puna, Hawaiʻi, circa 1985. This is where Pele wrapped herself in an ʻahu (cloak) of kapa to sleep after a day at the seashore; it is a wahi pana (place celebrated through story), as the etiology of the place name Kapaʻahu (kapa cloak) is embedded in the moʻolelo. A finger of lava from the on-going eruption is visible in the distance. The land and bay have since been covered, reclaimed by Pele's lava flows shortly after this photograph was taken. Sarah P. Meyer collection; courtesy of the author.

departure of his new love that he withers away (or commits suicide). In the meantime, Pele returns to the crater, where she asks each Hiʻiaka sister in turn to undertake the long and arduous journey to Kauaʻi to fetch her new love. One by one they refuse, familiar with their older sister's fickle nature and unpredictable temperament. Hiʻiakaikapoliopele is the only one who will attempt it, and only if Pele promises to care for her beloved lehua groves of Puna and her love, Hōpoe. Pele agrees. Arming Hiʻiaka with the powers of Kīlauea, a smiting hand; ʻĀwihikalani, a critical eye; and a pāʻū ʻuila, or lightning skirt, Pele orders Pāʻūopalaʻe (in some versions, Pāʻūopalaʻā)[68] to accompany Hiʻiaka on the long and dangerous journey. Pele reminds Hiʻiaka that Lohiʻau is kapu (off-limits) to Hiʻiaka and any other woman, and any infraction of the kaiʻokia kānāwai (*lit.* separating sea law) will result in severe punishment. Hiʻiaka agrees.

Along the way, they meet Wahineʻōmaʻo (*lit.* green woman), a young woman from the Hāmākua area en route to the volcano to sacrifice a black pig to Pele. After Hiʻiaka assists Wahineʻōmaʻo in her task, Wahineʻōmaʻo joins the traveling party. The three encounter many dangerous obstacles as they make their way to Kauaʻi, including manō (sharks), moʻo, and kanaka. Hiʻiaka is also presented with opportunities to heal sick kanaka and to defend hapless ones, all the while sharpening the healing skills she will need to revive the deceased Lohi'au, the ultimate demonstration of her mana, once she reaches Kaua'i. As she travels the archipelago, she encounters family members left behind on the original voyage from Kahiki; her trip to Kaua'i provides many opportunities to reunite with 'ohana members, rekindling their familial ties and receiving their assistance when needed.

When they reach Kaua'i, the traveling women are offered hospitality by the disabled fisherman, Malaeha'akoa, a devotee of Pele. In exchange for his kind hospitality, Hi'iaka heals him. Once they realize Lohi'au is dead, Hi'iaka must rescue his body from the clutches of two mo'o women, Kili'oeikapua and Kalamainu'u, and restore his life. After Lohi'au is healed, the entourage head home to the crater.

On their return trip, they once again encounter kanaka in need of Hi'iaka's assistance, who offer hospitality, or who are hostile toward them. Along the way, Hōpoe's death and the destruction of the lehua groves of Puna are revealed to Hi'iaka—Pele has broken her promise to care for them in Hi'iaka's absence, and she must now decide how she will confront her sister upon her return to Halema'uma'u. When they arrive at the rim of the crater, Hi'iaka defies the kānāwai kai'okia. Wreathing Lohi'au with lei lehua, sacred symbols of the Pele 'ohana, she "kisses" him. Outraged at the blatant betrayal, Pele orders Lohi'au killed by covering him in lava. Hurt and angry, Hi'iaka threatens to destroy the volcano by digging deep into the earth to flood the caldera with seawater and quench the volcanic fires.

Kahuaka'iapaoa (the fragrant journey),[69] Lohi'au's beloved companion, learns of his friend's second death at the volcano and vows to kill Pele. He travels to Halema'uma'u to confront her, performing a series of hulihia chants on Lohi'au's behalf. True to her temperamental but seductive nature, Pele charms him. She then discovers that Hi'iaka had been faithful all along, and learns that the delay in their return is because of the many tribulations encountered, including the revivification of Lohi'au. Pele's jealousy and rage subsides, and she seeks Hi'iaka's return to the crater. Pele retains her position as the haku (leader) of the 'ohana, but she has gained new respect for her powerful younger sister, resulting in peaceful coexistence between them.

Mai Kahiki Mai ka Wahine, 'o Pele
(From Tahiti Comes the Woman, Pele)

It is July 2006, and I am preparing for my first trip to Tahiti. The night before my departure I have a dream. I see a verdant, majestic mountain enshrouded in mist and steady, moderate rain. I do not recognize the mountain, but it feels familiar. Raised near Waiʻaleʻale on the island of Kauaʻi, rain is comforting. Waiʻaleʻale accumulates enough annual rainfall to be designated "the wettest spot on earth." For Hawaiians, rain symbolizes wealth, abundance, and mālama ʻāina—uē ka lani, ola ka honua, the heavens weep, the earth lives. It was a good sign.

The next day we depart and arrive safely in Papeʻete. Amer-Europeans describe Tahiti as "exotic." But for me, it resonates of home—the dramatic volcanic peaks rising sharply out of the sea to embrace the clouds and touch the heavens, the brightly colored pareu prints and ubiquitous rubber slippers worn by everyone, everywhere; the friendly Māʻohi (indigenous Tahitian) families who host us, offering smiles, kisses, and always more food, like the aunties and uncles and cousins back home; the familiar staples of niu (coconut), ʻulu (breadfruit), papaya, and mangoes from the ʻāina, fresh fish caught off the coral reefs from the sea, with a twist—lime and coconut marinated *poisson cru*, instead of poke (cubed and seasoned raw fish) and meals with *pain* instead of poi—it is like visiting older, respected family members who know your history, who share your roots. What is exotic to me is *la langue française*, and the stern-faced French *gendarmes* with assault rifles who patrol the international airport in Papeʻete, confiscating jars of monoʻi (coconut oil) scented with tiare blossoms—gifts from friends or fresh bought—from surprised *les touristes français et américains*, the result of the post-9/11 enhanced airport security environment. My only sadness is that we don't have time for the trip to Porapora (Bora Bora to the rest of the world, but our mispronunciation is corrected by our Māʻohi friends); I want to visit the ancestral home of Hale Polapola, one of my kūpuna. Of Pele.

On our final day in Tahiti, my friend Nālani and I visit the Musée de Tahiti et des Îles (Museum of Tahiti and the Islands) in Punaʻauia on the west side of the island, down the road from the *pension* we have rented for the week. I've heard there is a book in the gift shop that contains chants of Pele's time in Porapora (Kahiki) and possibly recounts her travels to Hawaiʻi. A Māʻohi elder greets us, and asks, "Tahitiennes?" (Tahitian?). Nālani responds, "Non, Hawaiennes" (No, Hawaiians). He smiles broadly and waves us in, refusing to accept the Polynesian francs waiting in our hands to pay the admission fee. We take our time going through the exhibit before going to the gift shop. We locate it in another building near the back. I find the book and purchase it. On our way out, Nālani and I stop and talk story with the elder Māʻohi gentleman at the door. A few minutes turn into an hour, then two, as we work our way between French, Tahitian, and Hawaiian; English is useless here. We discover his name is Teissier Teraitua, and he is from Puna'auia. He recounts for us the ariki (chiefly) heritage of Tautu, the true ariki of Porapora, scoffing at the last ruling Tahitian family line, the Pōmare, whose history is told within the museum's exhibits. Mā'ohi to Maoli, sharing mo'okū'auhau and mo'olelo, connections to 'āina and history. He points to the large mountain behind us, 'Orohena, towering seven thousand feet above. I get excited, trying to convey, ua hānai 'ia au i Olohena, that I grew up in Olohena on Kaua'i, with deep lush valleys that look similar; we are awed at how our people, cultures, and places connect two thousand miles across the Pacific.

He asks about the package I am holding, and I show him the book. I try to explain that my ancestors are from Porapora; on a document showing our family's Royal Patent Grant issued during the 1848 Māhele, for the Kī and Poupou lands in Puna, the name Hale Polapola (Porapora house) is prominent in our family mo'okū'auhau. He smiles and nods. "You look like them [the Porapora people]." It is something I have heard throughout our week here.

That evening, we swim one last time in the turquoise lagoon overlooking Mo'orea, a dark silhouette against the horizon, the setting sun a blazing backlight, illuminating its spiring peaks from behind, a golden glowing crown. I peer into the sunlight, trying to visualize Porapora to the west, four islands and 140 miles past Mo'orea. I wonder what it was like for my ancestor who sailed to Hawai'i generations before on a wa'a, carrying the name and the memory of his 'āina with him. I try to imagine the Pele 'ohana preparing for their voyage east, readying the wa'a *Honua-iākea*, a name announcing their intention of world exploration. Perhaps a voyage across two thousand miles of open ocean seemed like an exploration of the globe; perhaps it was meant only as a first step.

It had been a glorious, sun-filled week, perfect July weather. We wake up early on our last morning in Tahiti to a heavy steady rain. On the drive to the airport in Pape'ete, we pass the museum. I look up toward 'Orohena, shrouded in mist and rain, and instantly recognize the mountain I had dreamt of the night before our arrival.

The chant "Mai Kahiki mai" tells us that Pele arrived from Polapola, a specific island. She is a foreigner, not from just "any place outside of Hawai'i," another interpretation of Kahiki. The flashes of lightning in the cloud-filled skies suggest a storm, a hō'ailona (sign) of activity. The canoe *Honuaiākea* is carved, an endeavor that takes months, suggesting a long period of planning and preparation for the trip. It is Kamohoali'i's, Pele's brother with a shark kino lau, suggesting the canoe follows a migratory path of manō. It is a metaphor poetically describing the electromagnetic sensors sharks use to follow the magma (pele) hotspots across the Pacific plate, something now confirmed by Western science.[70] The waʻa is steered by Kū and Lono, two of the four major male deities in the ruling pantheon of the ʻAikapu. Perhaps they had to leave Porapora because of violent volcanic activity suggested in the chant, which contains images of earthquakes, atmospheric disturbances, and flowing lava. These lava flows are connected to Pele's fires at Kīlauea (*lit.* bubbling, spreading), justifying her arrival in Hawaiʻi.

Mele are meant to be performed. Kimura stresses the importance of the vocalization of words, because "from a traditional Hawaiian viewpoint, the Western concept of silent prayer denies the god-given human privilege of using words . . . [chanting the prayer] makes the words purposefully more subtle, thus very personal."[71] Under the missionary surveillance of nineteenth-century Hawaiʻi, writing became a kind of performance, a dance across the pages of journals, manuscripts, and newspapers. Writing represented the fiery voices of Pele and Hiʻiaka, mea kākau (writers) and haku mele (composers), at a time when actual hula and mele were publicly silenced. In this environment, Ka Palapala spoke on behalf of performance, keeping the memory of integral cultural practices mai ka pō mai, mai nā kūpuna mai, alive through a new media.

There are many aspects of the Pele and Hiʻiaka moʻolelo that invite further inquiry. The next chapter examines some of the early written sources of Pele and Hiʻiaka moʻolelo, and the relationship between oral and written traditions. Indeed, Pele has arrived mai Kahiki mai, firmly established in ʻŌiwi memory, culture, and literature.

'O nā Lehua Wale i Kāʻana
(The Lehua Blossoms Alone at Kāʻana):
Weaving the Moʻokūʻauhau of Oral and
Literary Traditions

'O nā lehua wale i Kā'ana
Ke kui 'ia a'ela ua lawa
He lei no ka wahine
'O Kapō ali'i nui o ia moku
Ki'eki'e, ha'aha'a
Ka lā o ka 'ike e 'ike ai
He 'ike kumu, he 'ike lono
He 'ike pū'awahiwa ka 'ike ke akua ē
E lono.

A kānikani'ā'ula ka leo o ka wahine
O Kani'ā'ula, 'o Maheanu
O ka wahine e noho ana i ka ulu a ka makani
Noho ana Kapō i ka uluwehiwehi
Kū aku i luna o Ma'ohelāia
'Ōhi'a kū i Maunaloa
Aloha mai Kaulana'ula ia'u
Eia ka 'ula lā he 'ula leo
He mōhai na'u iā 'oe e Kapō
'O Kapōkūlani, 'o Moehaunaiki
E hea au ē, e ō 'oe.[1]

The lehua blossoms alone at Kāʻana
Are being strung into a complete lei
A lei for the woman
Kapō great chiefess of the forest
High, humbled
The day whereby knowledge is obtained
Knowledge from the source, knowledge by hearing
Like a flourishing dark ʻawa plant is the knowledge from the gods
O hear me.

Mournfully chanting is the voice of the woman
Of Kaniaʻula, of Maheanu
The woman who lives where the wind rises.
Kapō lives in a beautiful grove
Standing up on Maʻohelāia
An ʻōhiʻa tree growing on Maunaloa.
Have compassion on us, o Kaulanaʻula
Here is a gift, an offering of the voice
An offering from me to you, Kapō
Kapōkūlani, Moehaunaiki
I call to you—answer me.

IT IS 2 A.M. ON A WARM MAY NIGHT IN 1991, and hālau Kukunaokalā has been up for hours preparing our lei, pāʻū skirts and kīkepa (for women), and malo and ti-leaf capes (for men) for the trek up the slopes of Maunaloa (long mountain), the most prominent hill in the west Molokaʻi mountains, for the inaugural Molokaʻi ka Hula Piko celebration. We make our way west from the Kaluakoʻi resort down Maunaloa Highway. It is a dark, moonless night; there are no streetlights, no other vehicles on the road. The only sound is the hum of tires and rustling of the dried ti-leaf capes and the kukui leaves in our lei. As the two-lane highway winds through the night-darkened hills of Maunaloa, I am surprised to see lines of vehicles parked along the way in the middle of nowhere. The people waiting patiently for our arrival are other hālau invited by Kumu to participate and a few Molokaʻi residents; word travels fast and far on an island. We lead the procession through the just-unlocked gates of Molokaʻi Ranch up to Kāʻana, the birthplace of hula in Kumu Kaʻimikauaʻs Molokaʻi tradition.

Kumu has received special permission from the ranch for this occasion. The sacred spot had been forgotten, abandoned and overrun by cattle and introduced plant life for over a century, ever since a group of haole ranchers purchased seventy thousand acres from Bishop Estate (land inherited by Bernice Pauahi Bishop from Kamehameha V) four years after the overthrow of the Hawaiian kingdom; leasing another thirty thousand from the Republic of Hawaiʻi for their cattle operation, Kanaka Maoli were displaced from this ʻāina. Between 1923 and 1985, large portions of the ranch were leased out to James Dole, the "pineapple king," to develop pineapple plantations, a new agricultural crop that would be synonymously linked to Hawaiʻi thereafter.

Kumu Kaʻimikaua has single-handedly reclaimed this wahi pana. This is no small feat, given the tight grip the ranch has had on this small island with the highest concentration of Kanaka Maoli in the state. Many are poʻe aloha ʻāina who are not shy about expressing themselves as aloha ʻāina warriors (Molokaʻi kamaʻāina Walter Ritteʻs term). Kumu Kaʻimikaua is the only one in recent memory whose hula tradition is connected to Molokaʻi, and some of the Hiʻiaka and Hōpoe followers scoff at his practice, claiming he "just made it all up," a perspective that discounts the validity of makawalu and oral tradition.

In 1994 I discover Moses Manuʻs "Pelekeahiʻāloa" moʻolelo establishing Kāʻana as the birthplace of hula, published in a Hawaiian-language newspaper in 1899.[2] Manuʻs publication demonstrates another strand of intellectual history and cultural knowledge of this hula tradition that was public knowledge some seven decades before Kumuʻs hālau was founded; Kumu Kaʻimikaua's tradition is not a modern invention. Rather, it demonstrates the interweaving of oral and written traditions, each validating and supporting the other.

We proceed slowly up the dusty track in the dark, the dust of the ʻāina a swirling red mist around us. Up and up the long mountain we drive. The darkness stunts our depth perception; we don't know yet that when we stop at the summit, we are 1,300 feet above sea level, the highest elevation on this end of the island.

A kuahu has already been constructed; the headlights illuminate the four thick ʻōhiʻa lehua posts reaching up ten feet into the sky; a lele (platform) to receive hoʻokupu connects the posts, and is about head height off the ground. We gather our lei adornments and prepare for our hula—lei poʻo for the head to inspire our thoughts, lei ʻāʻī for the neck draping over our chests to inspire our hearts, kūpeʻe for our wrists and ankles to inspire precise motion in our dance. Kukui is symbolic of light, knowledge, and the island of Molokaʻi. Creating our lei haku the night before, weaving the thick but pliable stems of the lau kukui in and out and between each other, carefully folding each leaf to fit into the other the way Kumu taught us, as a reminder of how our moʻokūʻauhau as ʻōlapa are woven into that of our Kumu, rooting us back to this ʻāina through our hula, mai ka pō mai, mai nā kūpuna mai. Wearing our lei honors the hula deities Laka and Kapō, hula passed down for generations from them at the place it was born in the Molokaʻi tradition, reminds us of the symbolism of these adornments of the ʻāina, of the akua, and how they help to strengthen and inspire us as individuals, as a hālau, as members of a Lāhui.

We pick our way over rocks and clumps of grass to the place we will sit and wait for Kumu's signal to dance. Soon everyone is settled in the dark, and a hush descends on us. We wait patiently for kumu to lead us in a ceremony completely unfamiliar to us all, as forgotten as the kapu of this place, both equally eroded from our ancestral memories by the pressures of settler colonialism to forget. But Kumu Kaʻimikaua remembers, and he will initiate this place, this practice, into our experience, into our memories. Kumu is not in a rush to speak; it is pō, the time of the gods, the time of inspiration. After a period of quiet meditation, kumu begins a series of oli. My spine tingles, and I wonder when the last time these oli dedicated to Kāʻana, to Kapōʻulakīnaʻu and Laka, Pele's other hula sisters, were heard here at the place they were born in hula.

As the sky lightens, I see the shadowy silhouettes of people sitting and standing in a circle around us. It is about forty to fifty feet in diameter surrounding a relatively flat, grassy area at the top of the hill that will be our stage. Kumu's chanting is pulling the light out of the darkness; hiki mai, hiki mai e ka lā ē, the sun is indeed rising. There is not a single cloud in the sky, and the stars that had been shining brilliantly down on us begin to fade in the pale pink–orange light of dawn. Kumu gives us the signal that it is time to dance; the hālau stands up and we make our way to the open space.

I notice the hillside we are standing on drops away to our north, sweeping down a sheer cliff to the deep blue sea 1,300 feet below. Later Kumu will point out Pu'u Nānā (observation hill), the next highest summit, where prospective students who sought entrance to Laka's hālau would oli kāhea, asking permission to enter. As a light breeze buffets the cliff, I wonder—how could I have seen the silhouette shapes of people forming a circle around us, when all this time we were sitting on a precipice?

He Mo'o 'Ōlelo (A Succession of Words)

In her scholarship, Hawaiian studies professor Leilani Basham argues that *Lāhui* is defined by mo'okū'auhau, mo'olelo, mele, 'āina, loina, and ea, not because we possess them, but because we embody them—we are who we were because we still are our genealogies, songs, hi/stories, land, cultural practices, and sovereignty.[3] In the interweaving of each is the foundation of literary nationalism in nineteenth-century Hawai'i. In mokuna I, I discussed the establishment of Ka Palapala. But where did the mo'olelo ku'una that were published come from? This chapter explores the relationship between mo'olelo ha'i waha—oral traditions, mo'olelo palapala, written literature, and the larger historical–cultural context they reflect.

The root word of mo'olelo is mo'o, "a succession, to follow after," and 'ōlelo, "to speak, to say, speech," ideas that clearly anchor the term in oral traditions; indeed, in the centuries before haole literacy was introduced, all stories were oral.

Storytelling surrounds us every day. Traditional stories of akua and ancestors such as Pele and Hi'iaka are regularly performed in homes, schools, churches, and the tourist industry; at special functions such as weddings or community celebrations; and at sanctioned events such as exhibitions and competitions. Singers, storytellers, spoken word poets, visual artists, educators, cultural practitioners, and everyday people also perpetuate the legacy of our mo'olelo ku'una. In Hawai'i, "talk story" is a specific term for more casual storytelling. These days, it is possible to access Web sites such as 'ōiwi TV or YouTube and watch any number of oral performances of every caliber from just about any location on the planet.

But how do we know about the history of 'Ōiwi oral traditions and their

influence on written ones? Oral transmission of moʻolelo and other elements of cultural practice still occurs in a variety of settings, and both
inform and are informed by Ka Palapala, the written literature. What
can be known about oral traditions mai ka pō mai, mai nā kūpuna mai
through Ka Palapala?

Ka Hoʻopaʻa ʻana a Ka Palapala i Hawaiʻi
(The Establishment of Written Literature in Hawaiʻi)

Once a printing press was established in 1819, reading and teaching
materials were published and distributed. But these were missionary-
controlled and strictly monitored to promote Christian morality and
Western practices and information on such topics as agriculture and
farming. The first missionary-printed newspaper, *Ka Lama Hawaii*, appeared in 1834. By many accounts, Kanaka ʻŌiwi took quickly to reading and writing, becoming one of the most literate populations on the
planet.[4] Kameʻeleihiwa writes, "Once Hawaiians learned the miracle of
writing, a literary tradition arose that reflected their traditional love of
orature. People from every class and background, and with varying degrees of eloquence, seemed compelled to write down what they knew, and
often challenged the opinions of fellow Hawaiians in heated letter-writ-
ing debates."[5] During this historically documented period of the Native
population collapse due to foreign diseases, chaos, and despair, Kanaka
ʻŌiwi viewed writing as an important method of cultural preservation
for themselves and for future generations. While the missionaries envisioned Kanaka literacy as an important part of their successful Christian conversion, Kanaka Maoli saw Ka Palapala as a new technology that
could save moʻolelo previously recorded only in memory—traditions, histories, genealogies, and related manaʻo—from extinction. A new way to
paʻa moʻolelo (memorize, *lit.* hold fast the traditions), Ka Palapala became
a site of knowledge and power.

Haku Moʻolelo (Composing Narratives):
Weaving Oral and Written Aesthetics

Throughout the publication of moʻolelo kuʻuna, Maoli writers made con-
tinuous reference to the moʻolelo being mai ka pō mai, mai nā kūpuna
mai, and mai ka waha, from the mouths of the ancients. In different
projects, Kanahele and Stillman have described the oral traditions as
exemplifying collective ancestral memory.

The transformation of moʻolelo kuʻuna from oral traditions to literary ones transcended a single person and a single generation, demonstrating how culture is constantly reinvigorated and never stagnant. Such dynamism is evident in the older oral traditions, as Kanaka ʻŌiwi incorporated new religious and social practices over time, new knowledge woven in with the old, as additional mele and moʻolelo were composed. The oli "Mai Kahiki mai," detailing Peleʻs migration from Kahiki and becoming an akua in Hawaiʻi, is just one example. The continued insistence of settler scholarship to describe Kanaka Maoli moʻolelo as fixed and only oral is discussed by Silva as part of the continuing settler colonial project to silence Native voices and intellectual history:

> Our moʻolelo are most often characterized as springing from the oral tradition, which is true to an extent. However, moʻolelo (and mele, moʻokūʻauhau, etc.) have been written down since the advent of writing in the 1820s. Literature in Hawaiian was consistently produced well into the 1930s. Why then should we characterize moʻolelo as oral when our access to it is through the written and printed word? It could be argued that the skipping over, the invisibilizing of moʻolelo and other genres of writing, is part of a discourse of savagery and primitivism that represents "true" Kānaka Hawaiʻi as only existing in the past. Writing is a part of modernity forever withheld from the "real" native.[6]

In nineteenth-century Hawaiʻi, the act of writing represents such cultural adaptation, one embraced with enthusiasm. Kanaka ʻŌiwi viewed this practice as a new avenue of expression for their own purpose, adapting it to their own style. The publication of oral traditions precipitated new ways of thinking about and engaging with moʻolelo. Looking back from a twenty-first-century perspective, one comfortable and familiar with print culture, we can imagine that it must have been strange and exciting to see moʻolelo kuʻuna in print for the first time—strange because it was new and different, exciting because of the potential print technology created for distribution and transmission of moʻolelo in ways not previously possible. I imagine the strangeness and excitement at that time would be analogous to the first generation who experienced television, personal computing, or the Internet. While these new technologies have not replaced other forms of communication and performance, they have forever altered how we interact with, record, and transmit all kinds of information, including moʻolelo.

The similarities and differences between oral and written forms of moʻolelo (including poetic texts, such as mele), demonstrating what

Moʻolelo Haʻi Waha Orature	Ka Palapala Literature
• Performance-based • Performance "texts" recorded in the collective memory of the people • Performance of text contextualized by place, occasion; "edited" by performer as appropriate, more fluidity in how text is presented/received • Heavy use of songs, prayers, and chant (and in extension, music and dance), power of vocalization • Live (direct) interaction between audience and performers • Text interpreted by the performer • Strong use of repetitive phrases and formulaic language • Performative elements important part of textual interpretation • Ambiguity and word play emphasized in performance aspect of poetry	• Text-based (print) • Text recorded on paper by an individual author • Printing fixed the text in a particular way; moʻolelo decontextualized to a degree, no fluidity once printed; text edited to satisfy literary standards (i.e. to fit on the page) • Songs, prayers, and chants printed; but function is minimized, vocalization silenced • Limited or non-existent interaction between author and reader, no opportunity for immediate feedback • Text interpreted by the reader • Repetition and formulaic language discouraged; viewed as "boring" or redundant • Performative elements minimized or non-existent • Ambiguity and word play more one dimensional; emphasis on clarity through single meaning, particularly when diacritical marks are employed

Moʻolelo kuʻuna, traditional narratives.

factors writers needed to consider when publishing them, are listed in the box. Moʻolelo haʻi waha were dependent on memorization and performance. It was common for lengthy compositions, or those related to moʻokūʻauhau such as Kumulipo, to be memorized by a hui (collective).[7] Such practices of collective or ancestral memory helped ensure the composition would be remembered and transmitted. Meiwi are "traditional elements of Hawaiian poetry, story telling, oratory and narration."[8] Moreover, they are literary devices that supported the memorization and transmission of moʻolelo haʻi waha. Furthermore, they were important in the transition of moʻolelo kuʻuna from oral to literary forms.

Meiwi were an integral part of oral tradition that were embodied in memory and performance. As Ka Palapala developed, it represented these performative practices on the page, and expanded to include literary and oral devices of recording, memorizing, and transmitting knowledge.

In his work on Hawaiian oratory, Hiapo Perreira identified twenty-four meiwi or "ethno-poetic devices" in fifteen categories specific to Kanaka Maoli oral and literary expression.

Meiwi Moʻokalaleo (Traditional Hawaiian Poetic Devices)

- moʻokūʻauhau (genealogy)
- pīnaʻi (repetition of words, actions)
- helu (list, sequence)
- kuʻi, kuʻina hoʻi (join together, redaction)
- kōkua (asides)
- kīkahō kualehelehe (interjection that imposes writer's thought or further explanation)
- puanaʻī, kuhia (quote, note)
- mele (songs)
- akapili (apposition)
- hoʻomakili (flash-forward)
- hoʻokanaka (personification)
- hoʻokalakupua (magical elements)
- ʻikioma (idioms)
- ʻōlelo noʻeau (proverbs)
- hoʻokaʻau (humor)
- kaona (veiled, poetic meaning)
- nane (riddling)
- ʻēkoʻa (opposites)
- kohu (imagery)
- inoa kanaka (personal names)
- inoa ʻāina/pana (place names)
- inoa kapakapa (nicknames)
- hopena (consequence, etiological)[9]

Perreira's identified meiwi aligns with work by other scholars in this area, some of whom use synonymous or additional terms. For example, welina, ʻōlelo mua, and ʻōlelo hoʻākaka are synonymous with hoʻolauna. Although ʻōlelo mua and ʻōlelo hoʻākaka are specific to writing, hoʻolauna and welina are used in oral and writing practices. Oli and hula are relatively synonymous with mele and all include subgenres, such as kau (a type of chant), hīmeni (hymns), and so forth. Wahi pana, places made famous through stories told about them, is similar to inoa ʻāina or pana.

Another example is pīnaʻi (repetition) and helu (listing), which linguist Samuel H. Elbert identifies as a process of cataloging information that provided "aesthetic satisfaction" and another layering of repetition; this repetition of similar sounds, sequences of words, thoughts, or actions, was due in part to the structure of Hawaiian language, which contains few consonants, and a frequency of doubled words (e.g., hoihoi, laulau).[10] Such repetition was "a favorite poetic device" that superseded rhyme.[11] Such listing is important within oli, or oli helu (listing chants), which Rubellite Kawena Johnson calls "papa helu." Charlot identifies them as "list chants" that "were of obvious importance in Hawaiian education as devices for learning and memorization."[12] Silva discusses the "wind chants" (oli makani) that function in the same way, using Joseph Poepoe's term, "kūlana pānoʻonoʻo," or a repetitive memory device.[13]

Hoʻokaʻau or ʻōlelo hoʻokaʻau is described by Pukui as figurative speech, and by Elbert as metaphor.[14] Elbert, Kameʻeleihiwa, and Silva emphasize the nuances of sex and sexuality within the wordplay, metaphor, symbolism, and allusion of hoʻokaʻau, particularly in moʻolelo such as Kamapuaʻa, Pele's pig–god lover and rival, and Pele and Hiʻiaka.[15] Related terms described in Pukui include hūʻeu and hoʻohūʻeu, meaning witty, rascal, comical, mischievous, playing with the language and the situation at hand.[16] Hoʻomake ʻaka is another related term that references humorous figurative language, metaphor, pun, and wordplay.[17] The emphasis on sexuality, humor, and wordplay speak to ʻŌiwi society and a worldview that not only emphasized poetic aesthetics, but also a healthy enjoyment of life, one that depended on a keen mind and intellectual understanding expressed through poetry.

Meiwi are an integral part of oral traditions, which then informed literary ones. Ka Palapala thus reflects poetic aesthetics that are as rooted in traditional culture and performance mai ka pō mai, mai nā kūpuna mai as much, if not even more so, than Western literary ones. As mea kīnohinohi (aesthetic devices), meiwi were incorporated into Ka Palapala in every genre of writing, including moʻolelo kuʻuna. Understanding meiwi is important to understanding Hawaiian poetics and the composition practice, and to better appreciate the tremendous amount of intellectual and creative skill in composing epic moʻolelo such as Pele and Hiʻiaka.

Haku Meiwi (Composing Traditional Elements of Hawaiian Poetry): Weaving Literary Devices from the Oral, or Moʻokūʻauhau Revisited

Inoa or personal names are often capsules of moʻolelo. This is true of kanaka and ʻāina. Under missionary insistence, Kanaka Maoli were pressured into adapting Christian names, forsaking traditional Hawaiian ones, a requirement for baptism into the Christian church, codified into law in 1860 (not repealed until 1967). A law banning the public perfor-mance of hula (also enacted in 1860), though the ABCFM missionaries had already been suppressing the practice since the 1830s, further eroded Kanaka Maoli abilities to transmit traditional knowledge through only traditional means—oral performance of haʻi moʻolelo and mele, and the implementation of an important aspect of moʻokūʻauhau—the naming of children. Therefore, it is important to emphasize this aspect of Hawaiian interest in literacy.

So while an important moʻokūʻauhau like Kumulipo was successfully preserved in the memories of the composers and those who inherited it for at least 150 years from when it was composed, a waʻa carrying the names of hundreds of ʻŌiwi ancestors with it, this koʻihonua probably would not have survived (at least not intact) if the mōʻī Kalākaua did not have the foresight to commission its recording on paper in the 1870s. Ka Palapala facilitated the preservation and transmission of culturally important in-formation, a point that cannot be stressed enough, as it shows ʻŌiwi under-standing of the "power of the pen" and their determination to inaugurate their own intellectual traditions in print from the beginning, establishing their own Indigenous literary nationalism that grew with the develop-ment of their Lāhui. Kimura writes, "Early Hawaiian writers recorded many long Hawaiian prose stories, some of the more famous are sagas of Pele and Hiʻiaka, Kawelo, Kamapuaʻa, and Lāʻieikawai. . . . Through their writings, these people preserved and created a body of written Hawaiian literature within approximately a one hundred–year span."[18]

Consequently, the missionaries found, much to their dismay, that they could assert only so much influence and control over what Kanaka wanted to read and write. In 1861, Kanaka established their own inde-pendent national press, wherein they published mele, moʻokūʻauhau, and moʻolelo passed down mai ka pō mai, mai nā kūpuna mai. Kimura writes, "Hawaiian writers generally chose traditional topics, shown not only in their great interest in recording old chants, but also in their own com-positions. . . . The introduction of writing . . . led to a strengthening of Hawaiʻi's culture through Hawaiian documentation of practices disap-proved by the American Calvinists."[19] These topics were published along-side more modern genres already in place since the 1830s, such as biog-raphies and autobiographies, hīmeni, and news and stories from abroad, all of which contributed to their ever-expanding literary repertoire and intellectual breadth.

As the nineteenth century progressed, literacy expanded and pub-lished material flourished so much so that by the 1860s several differ-ent sources of literature had developed. For example, mele were gath-ered together as part of buke mele (song books) or "souvenir books."[20]

Collections in the Bishop Museum Archives are attributed to ali'i such as Kalaniana'ole and Lili'uokalani. Some mele were published individually in newspapers and as sheet music. Great epics for the Pele and Hi'iaka included mele gathered together and combined with prose narratives, transformed on paper into substantial literary epics.

Haole settlers such as Nathaniel B. Emerson, Abraham Fornander, William D. Westervelt, and Thomas G. Thrum also collected and published mo'olelo ku'una (under the rubric of folklore) with the aid of Native "informants." Publishing Hawaiian legends, myths, and folklore under their own names, they claimed an authority (kuleana) over the mo'olelo they did not have, and reframed the mo'olelo to forward settler agendas. But by far the most extensive collection of Hawaiian mo'olelo is found in the Hawaiian-language newspapers.

Ka Waiwai o nā Nūpepa Hawai'i
(The Value of the Hawaiian-Language Newspapers)

Helen Chapin identifies the Hawaiian nationalist press as opposition papers that countered establishment papers run by missionaries through the church or the government.[21] The newspapers that published Pele and Hi'iaka mo'olelo were primarily opposition papers that "challenged and resisted American political and economic domination ... [and which] articulated the arguments for autonomy and sovereignty."[22] Hawaiian-language newspapers (such as *Kuokoa Home Rula*) maintained the purpose and philosophy of the Hawaiian nationalist press well into the post-annexation (1898) period, continuing to publish mo'olelo ku'una, including Pele and Hi'iaka.

Esther Mookini explains Hawaiian-language newspapers were "not only reflections of politics and culture in its many dimensions[,] but primary instruments of movements and individuals, and influences on events, trends and attitudes. Hawaiian newspapers are, therefore, indispensable sources for every aspect of our history."[23] Silva describes the newspapers as important sites of discursive struggle, the main battleground for competing discourses:

> For 40 years the mission controlled the power of the printed word in Hawai'i ... not just to save souls but to assist in the progress of ... capitalism, to control public education, to mold government into western forms and to control it, and to domesticate Kanaka women. Then, in 1861, to the shock and outrage of the missionary establishment, a group of Kanaka Maoli ... transformed themselves into speaking subjects proud of their Kanaka ways

of life and traditions and unafraid to rebel. Their medium was
a Hawaiian-language newspaper called *Ka Hoku o ka Pakipika*
[that] . . . began a long tradition of nationalist, anti-colonial resistance through the print media.[24]

The newspapers are important because they were vehicles of knowledge
preservation. Because Kanaka were trained in newspaper printing early
on, "they quickly realized that their knowledge, which was disappearing with the many people dying in the severe population collapse of the
time, could be preserved for future generations—in print. They began to
write it all down."[25] This outpouring of traditional knowledge, including
moʻolelo, is part of what made the newspaper such a site of struggle, as
the missionaries "represented traditional moʻolelo as part of what was
naʻaupō, or uncivilized and ignorant, and needed to be stopped."[26]

The Hawaiian-language newspapers were an important repository of
moʻolelo kuʻuna, collectively forming the largest and most accessible body
of written material documenting Kanaka ʻŌiwi thought, tradition, and
society. An estimated one to one and a half million pages of writing in the
Hawaiian-language newspapers still exists today.[27]

The Hawaiian-language newspapers published every traditional genre
of moʻolelo, including kaʻao (stories), mele pana (place songs), mele inoa
(name songs), kanikau (laments), and mele aloha ʻāina (patriotic songs).
Moʻolelo kuʻuna such as the legend of the pig–god Kamapuaʻa were sometimes described as kaʻao, and new fictional stories were also composed.
Mele pana and mele inoa celebrated significant places and people of the
past and present. Kanikau took on new meaning as the massive depopulation of Kanaka Maoli in the islands continued, as ruling Mōʻī or their
family members died young and unexpectedly. Mele aloha ʻāina also came
to prominence in the 1890s as the Hawaiian nation was dealt one blow
after another, with the forced implementation of the Bayonet Constitution in 1887, the overthrow of the monarchy in 1893, the establishment
of a haole-run republic in 1894, and the illegal annexation of Hawaiʻi to
the United States in 1898. The nineteenth century also saw the creation
of new genres of Hawaiian moʻolelo and mele, as Kanaka ʻŌiwi adapted
Western genres to Hawaiian language, such as Christian hīmeni, mele
poema (poems, including sonnets and anagrams), nowela (novels), and
nowela pōkole (short stories, novellas).

Three broad categories of moʻolelo were published in the Hawaiian-language newspapers from the 1860s to the 1930s: moʻolelo kuʻuna (e.g.,
legends concerning Hiʻiakaikapoliopele, Kūapākaʻa, Kamehameha,
Kawelo), moʻolelo kaʻao (e.g., *Mokulehua*, *Lāʻieikawai*, and the heavily
Christianized *Kumuhonua Legends*), contemporary Hawaiian moʻolelo

or Hawaiian moʻolelo influenced by Western genres or themes, and moʻolelo no nā ʻāina ʻē, foreign stories translated from other languages, which included the moʻolelo *The Arabian Nights* and nowela such as *The Count of Monte Cristo*, *Tarzan*, and *20,000 Leagues under the Sea*). These foreign stories came from myriad continents and cultures, including Europe, Asia, North America, and the Middle East. Notably, there are few stories from the United States.[28]

Huli i ke Ao (Transitioning to the Modern Era): Translating Moʻolelo to Myth

Western concepts of stories of godly beings are also rooted in the spoken word. Myths are oral stories "about divine beings, generally arranged in a coherent system; they are revered as true and sacred; they are endorsed by rulers and priests; and closely linked to religion."[29] The word *myth* comes from the Greek *muthos*, meaning to speak or say; speech; it also implies story, including stories of gods.[30] By their nature, myths serve as a foundation reflecting the worldview of a people. The popularized use of the term as "false or untrue" stems from a modern Western perspective that elevates knowledge based on science, technology, writing, and empirical research, and devalues knowledge based on orality, traditions, and intuition. Bacchilega writes:

> From early on, Native Hawaiian moʻolelo were for the most part identified by haole as "legends," "myths" and "folktales" interchangeably, and thus seen as "folklore," a newly formed category in European and American nineteenth-century thought. Because "folklore" was and is often viewed in the science-centered West as an outmoded or "false" way of knowing, this classification has unfortunately also provided an opening to view the *moʻolelo* as "untrue." As belief narratives, legends and myths maintain a relationship with history for scholars, but more generally "legend" is interpreted as fanciful or undocumented history. This has resulted in erasing the meaning of "history" carried in the Hawaiian word and genre, with *moʻolelo* being translated and understood only or primarily as "story."[31]

The erasure of multiple meanings of moʻolelo by haole collectors played out in different ways. The emphasis on "story" transformed how moʻolelo were presented to English speaking (primarily haole) audiences. For example, Kanaka discussed and compared the Pele and Hiʻiaka moʻolelo and the mele and moʻokūʻauhau within them. In comparison, English "translations" did not often include moʻokūʻauhau or mele. When poetic texts were included, they were highly summarized and their importance to the narrative diminished. For instance, ABCFM missionary descendant William Hyde Rice published "Pele ame Kona Kaikaina Hiiaka i ka Poli o Pele" (Pele and Her Younger Sister Hiʻiakaikapoliopele) in Hawaiian in the newspaper *Ka Hoku o Hawaii*. Forty thousand words in length, it begins with a moʻokūʻauhau for Pele, and contains forty-six poetic texts (mele, ʻōlelo noʻeau). In contrast, "The Goddess Pele," a "translation" (more accurately, a highly edited summary) published in his English language collection *Hawaiian Legends* is a scant five thousand words, with no moʻokūʻauhau or poetic texts included. Anyone who relies on the English text would get the gist of the story but not the richness of the Hawaiian text that contains multiple levels of kaona, cultural information and numerous meiwi any literary scholar would relish.

The "translation" and decontextualization of Hawaiian moʻolelo, as Bacchilega points out, devalues Kanaka Maoli and contributes to the ongoing settler colonial discourse of the "Vanishing Native" and "inevitable progress towards civilization (Americanization, globalization)" that began in the nineteenth century. Writing about how this occurred in a Native American context, Janice Acoose argues, "Taken out of context, or retold without some relevant understanding of our history, beliefs, language, traditions, spiritual practices, and values, the stories simply become legendary references to so-called vanished Indians."[32] Put another way, ignoring the moʻokūʻauhau—the genealogy and context of the stories, steals the mana of the moʻolelo and their ability to empower Kanaka Maoli, enlighten others, and transform the world.

Despite constant pressure to "forget"—a crucial part of settler colonial assimilation, Kanaka Maoli steadfastly hold on to ancestral and cultural memory. Stillman argues one way this occurs is through hula, an important site of cultural memory.[33] The performance of hula has indeed endured throughout different time periods—from the traditional (pre-Western contact), through the post-contact period of colonization and settler colonialism (nineteenth to mid-twentieth century), to the post-statehood settler nation (later twentieth century to the present). Beginning in the nineteenth century, Ka Palapala became an alternate strand of cultural memory. At first, it was a way to record and transmit moʻolelo; over time, it has become a treasured storehouse of knowledge that might not otherwise be known today. Of hula, Stillman writes,

> Performances . . . constitute not only instances of communication, but also, over time, recollection and commemoration. . . .

The corpus of poetic texts for hula constitutes a storehouse of cultural memories that are collectively celebrated by performers and audiences alike. Through hula dances and songs, memories of people and events endure long after they have passed. Performances are moments in which remembrances are sounded and gestured.[34]

The publication of so many Pele and Hi'iaka mo'olelo reflect the recollection and commemoration of their writers about the collective past, and include numerous mele that are part of the larger repertoire Stillman is discussing. Within the mo'olelo, the writers expanded the concept of stored cultural memories by discussing meanings of hundreds of words, place names, practices, and other cultural information being lost, addressing readers and evoking their participation in collective remembering, asking rhetorical questions such as "'A'ole anei?" (Isn't that so?). In this way, Kanaka Maoli writers transformed the original intent of Ka Palapala from one meant to aid Western assimilation (what Scott Richard Lyons refers to as "the colonized scene of writing")[35] to a site of Native agency. Ka Palapala became a way for Kanaka Maoli to assert their silenced voices and reclaim Native space through writing.

Discussing the role of William Apess and the Mashpees of the U.S. Northeast, Brooks states, "While American authors were writing the story of the vanishing Indian, Apess imagined regeneration and used writing to bring the reconstruction of Algonquian New England into being."[36] Citing Cheryl Suzack's work on the potential for literature to be "an imaginative site of social reconstruction," Brooks emphasizes that such an approach for Native people is "not of individual empowerment and healing but of communal regeneration and sustenance."[37] In a Hawaiian context, such imagined regeneration was figuratively embodied via Pele and Hi'iaka mo'olelo and carried out on behalf of the Lāhui. The insistence of remembering and disseminating mo'olelo ku'una through creating and publishing literary versions was a strategy of resisting settler colonialism and asserting Native mana.

He Mo'o 'Ōlelo (A Succession of Words): Establishing a Hawaiian Literary Tradition

Mo'olelo ku'una were composed and preserved in memory and orally transmitted for generations. It is these mo'o 'ōlelo, successions of words organized into narratives, from which the written literature of the nineteenth and twentieth centuries are woven.

The metaphor of a lei haku (braided lei) is useful in understanding the relationship between the oral and written traditions. The following chart demonstrates a moʻokūʻauahu of Pele and Hiʻiaka moʻolelo. The primary known written traditions are represented on separate strands of the lei moʻokūʻauhau. Each originates in the piko (navel, center; connotes origin) of oral tradition mai nā kūpuna mai. Moʻolelo that demonstrate a close connection are listed on the same "genealogical" strand. While it is tempting to "close" or complete the lei by bringing all the "open" strands together, I suggest the lei is still being formed, as new compositions are continually being woven into this lei moʻokūʻauhau. "Closing" the lei also might incorrectly suggest that all variants are merging into a single master narrative, which would go against the very nature of Hawaiian moʻolelo composition, and the practice of makawalu.

Each strand is moʻo ʻōlelo, literary or textual successions that represent different Pele and Hiʻiaka moʻolelo. Kanahele suggests that one reason multiple moʻokūʻauhau are provided for Pele is because each emphasizes different philosophies of creation and perhaps time periods of geological events.[38] Kimura suggests that early Hawaiian writers were simply "not satisfied with a single version . . . [writing] down regional or period variants."[39] In my own work I argue that they represent different island perspectives and genealogies of knowledge. In discussing why moʻolelo have mana that make them powerful, Bryan Kamaoli Kuwada discusses the moʻokūʻauhau or "lineal and generational" aspect of stories:

> In the Hawaiian understanding of moʻolelo, the lineal and generational qualities of stories along with their capacity to carry culture really helps to explain how mana, the spiritual power and reverence that can be accumulated in all things, accrues to these stories as they are passed from person to person. Storytellers imbue their stories with breath and mana through the act of telling and their listeners inhale this mana and then have the chance to retell the story and add their breath to it as well. A further indication of the way mana accrues to stories is that each variation and variant of a story is itself called a mana. This recognizes that the diversity and variation among our stories is the very thing that gives them their mana, or power. This means that in order to re-empower our moʻolelo, we have to insure that they exist in various versions, styles, and forms, both elite and mundane.[40]

Thus, the more mana (versions) a moʻolelo has, the more mana (power) it has as well—living, surviving, adapting, and thriving with the Lāhui.

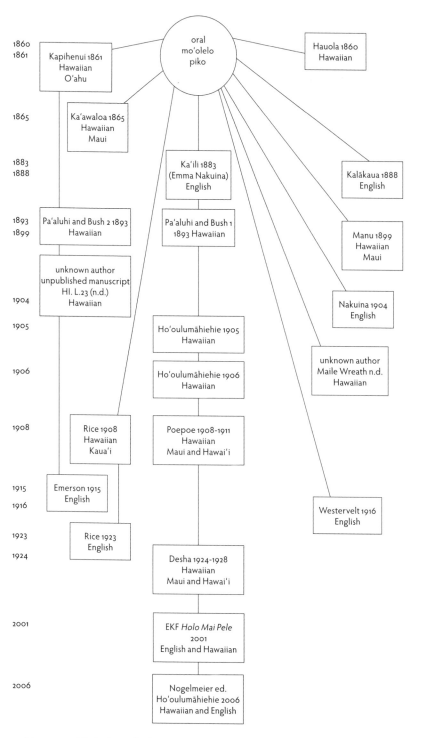

Literary moʻokūʻauhau of Pele and Hiʻiaka moʻolelo.

A makawalu discourse suggests all of these, and perhaps many more reasons explain the rich, complex source of narratives to draw from. As Kimura aptly concludes, "The great enthusiasm of the nineteenth and twentieth century Hawaiians for written literature in their own language has left today's Hawaiian people with a tremendous gift."[41]

A weaving of strands or intertextuality between the various publications is also noticeable. Later writers referred to previously published and unpublished versions they were aware of or consulting. For example, Joseph Poepoe mentions manuscripts borrowed from J. W. Naihe and D. K. Waiʻaleʻale that contained "a section that hasn't been seen in the stories of Hiʻiaka published before now."[42] Moses Manu refers to Kapihenui's 1861 publication.[43]

Once the independent nationalist press was established, a great number of moʻolelo kuʻuna appeared in Hawaiian between 1860 and 1940. The following chart shows a sampling of those published between 1860 and 1900. Pele- and Hiʻiaka-related moʻolelo are shown in boxes, other moʻolelo are shown in ovals by name and year published. Some moʻolelo were unsigned, such as "ʻAʻāhoaka." Some writers who published Pele and Hiʻiaka moʻolelo, such as Manu, also published other moʻolelo ("Keaomelemele," "Kihaapiʻilani"). The outpouring of literary and intellectual production that occurred in this period contributed to Hawaiian nation-building. In the final chapter, I offer a few examples of contemporary ʻŌiwi writing about Pele and Hiʻiaka that draw from this literary moʻokūʻauhau, and how these writers and texts are now intertwined into this lei palapala, contributing to Hawaiian literary nationalism today.

Mapping the relationships between the oral traditions and the written ones, and between the ancient and the historical past, helps us visualize the foundation of ʻŌiwi literary traditions. In her essay on locating an ethical, native criticism, Brooks identifies traditional stories as one of three sites imperative to understanding the source of the Native intellectual traditions she studies, arguing that "these oral traditions, for me, are inextricably intertwined with the written traditions that have taken root and grown up alongside them over the past few hundred years . . . where writing is informed and infused by oral tradition, and the continuance of oral tradition is aided by the tool of literacy."[44]

So what is a Kanaka Maoli literary tradition? What can we deduce about the oral traditions of the past from ka moʻolelo palapala? How do Pele and Hiʻiaka moʻolelo both reflect and carry it?

Moʻolelo kuʻuna have a genealogy. Kumulipo is a cosmogonic genealogy that establishes the foundation of Kanaka Maoli culture as one generated through succession of birth that originates with the birth of the universe.

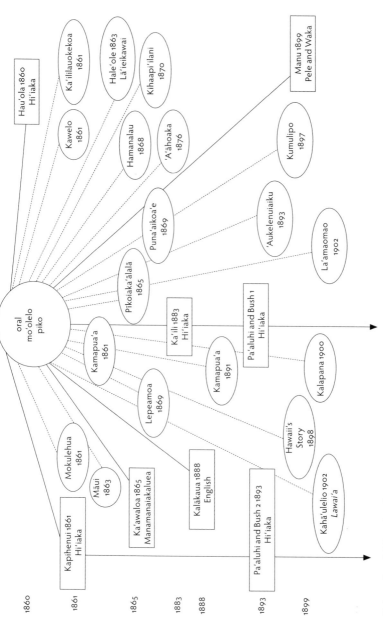

Selected moʻolelo palapala, 1860–1900.

Ka Palapala begins in pō. Written and published literature—Ka Palapala—originates in pō, the ancient past, with the moʻolelo haʻi waha, the purely oral stories of the kūpuna. The oral traditions themselves are kūpuna—the ancestors, starting point, and source—mai ka pō mai, mai nā kūpuna mai—of Ka Palapala, the written, "literary" traditions; they are the genesis of growth for the written traditions of the nineteenth century, and for the expansion of haʻi moʻolelo through new media and technology (CDs, DVDs, Internet) today. The recording and transmission of traditions through memory and performance of mele, hula, moʻokūʻauhau, and moʻolelo kept them alive for countless generations before writing was integrated. When foreign diseases caused massive population collapse, Ka Palapala became a crucial method of preserving knowledge. From that time forward, publishing became an important avenue of perpetuating and disseminating the mana and manaʻo of the ancestors.

Ka Palapala as kūpuna (source) texts. Ka Palapala allowed for the preservation of traditional stories and the mana and manaʻo contained within them. Writers and audiences familiar with moʻokūʻauhau used them as literary allusion, referring to other moʻolelo kuʻuna, and to one another's publications. Ka Palapala continues to be a rich resource of research, knowledge, inspiration, and entertainment.

Moʻolelo haʻi waha and Ka Palapala are intertwined. As much as Ka Palapala draws from the oral, once the moʻolelo were paʻa (fixed) on paper, Ka Palapala became a source to draw from for the oral performance, including hula. The oral and written traditions are lei haku moʻolelo, braided garlands of stories that inform each other. Writing is built from and built upon oral tradition. Rather than *replace* oral tradition (as a "progressive" Western timeline would suggest), writing is an *addition* to Kanaka Maoli cultural expression, another perspective on the makawalu spiral, the two strands comfortably coexisting and complementing each other.

The oral nature of moʻolelo contributes to makawalu. Because oral traditions were handed down verbally and through performance, multiple versions, sometimes told from different perspectives, sometimes highlighting different aspects of the narrative, are common. Rather than demonstrate a chaotic, fragmented, carelessly preserved history, a makawalu perspective reveals a vibrant, widespread tradition. Writers of the Pele and Hiʻiaka moʻolelo discussed versions from different islands, some of which contradicted one another in sequence of events, or where events occurred. Other Kanaka sometimes challenged writers in letters to the newspapers or offered their own versions, marking another layer of intertextuality, revealing a robust intellectual tradition that countered the settler colonial discourse of the lazy, stupid Native. Applying a makawalu approach automatically implies that multiple narratives are acceptable. Drawing from the same piko of oral traditions, Ka Palapala offer not competing versions, but ones exhibiting culturally guided kinship and succession.

Moreover, multiple versions were expected and preferred. The range of differences demonstrated within a tradition also contests the predominant colonial-inspired perspective that protocol on *exactness* was so strict (under punishment of death) that *any* variation of word or thought, however slight under any circumstance, would invalidate it.

Ka Moʻolelo Palapala aʻo Pele a me Hiʻiaka (Pele and Hiʻiaka as a Literary Tradition)

So how does the Pele and Hiʻiaka moʻolelo reflect a Hawaiian literary tradition? First, many begin with moʻokūʻauhau. On their own, moʻokūʻauhau are narrative, history, events, and story encapsulated within names of characters (kanaka, akua, ʻāina), places, and things. Pele's name triggers association with specific wahi pana associated with her, including Puna, Kīlauea, Halemaʻumaʻu, and Kahiki. "Mai Kahiki mai" recounts her journey from the homeland, naming the significant places Pele is associated with, her family members and the waʻa, names that reflect the purpose of the trip and a strand of Hawaiian history. Kimura emphasizes the importance of the evocative power of place names in Hawaiian poetic composition: "To traditional Hawaiians, place names are considered kupa (natives) themselves . . . [they] are like esteemed grandparents linking people to their home, personal past, and their history."[45] Moreover, personal names are similarly connected, because they "often incorporate ancestral place names and contain references to family history."[46]

Place names (inoa ʻāina) are also meiwi, poetic devices that contain history and story. Whereas haole saw empty, desolate lands, inoa ʻāina are sites of cultural memory. The names Kīlauea, Halemaʻumaʻu, Puna, Kapaʻahu, Kaimū, and Hāʻena, for example, immediately recall the presence of Pele and Hiʻiaka and their adventures; Hāʻena, Kēʻē, and Makana resonate with the moʻolelo of Lohiʻau, his love for hula, and tragic love affair with Pele; Kāʻana recalls Kapōʻulakīnaʻu, Kewelani, and the birthplace of hula. For myself, these places are personal sites of memory recalling family history and experiences: Kapaʻahu, Puna, is the ʻāina of my ancestors, the surrounding areas places we've visited; Hāʻena, Kēʻē, and Makana, Kauaʻi, are places they frequented, near other family lands at Wanini; Kāʻana is a place I have danced hula in tribute to Laka and Kapōʻulakīnaʻu with my hālau family, Halemaʻumaʻu is a site I have danced hula in tribute to Pele and Hiʻiaka as well, Kīlauea is a location where I have offered ho'okupu in respect to Pele. Each is a wahi pana, a place renowned and remembered through mo'olelo that carries important cultural knowledge. Moreover, each has been sparsely inhabited after Western contact, in part due to Native population collapse, in part for economic reasons, in part because they are rugged rural environments. But it is also in part because they are controlled by settler colonial entities: the larger area surrounding Kīlauea is a national park, the area surrounding Lohi'au's home in Hā'ena is partially state park, partially owned by wealthy haole, and Kā'ana is still Moloka'i Ranch land. Even though Kanaka Maoli no longer inhabit these 'āina, their history is remembered and passed on in their names and the mo'olelo they embody.

Pele's mo'okū'auhau is strongly matrilineal, connecting mana wahine (female power) and origin through birthing—her mother, Haumea, is always named. It alludes to earth mother Papahānaumoku; papa means foundation, thus mother (not father) is the foundation, exhibiting a "matriotistic," female-centered worldview that is inherently different from patriotism. Her father is either not named, or is inconsistent—Moemoe'a'ali'i, Kūwahailo (alternately Kūahailo) are different names given. Such inconsistency suggests that her father (represented through his name) or the male foundation is not as important as the female; in each case, the male element is supported by—and literally rooted in—the female foundation.

Within mo'olelo, mo'okū'auhau function as a prologue. The mo'okū'auhau of the main character (such as Pele) is often provided at the beginning of the mo'olelo, establishing who the mo'olelo is about. This in turn creates (to a knowledgeable audience) certain expectations of the kind of story (comedy, tragedy, romance, adventure) to expect, and its entertainment, educational, or cultural value.

There are different ways to recount mo'okū'auhau aside from simply listing one's ancestors. Pele's parents are not always named, but her myriad siblings usually are. In recounting the names of the siblings, Pele is often named first because she is the hiapo, the eldest child, and Polynesian cultural protocol dictates certain kuleana (rank, rights, and responsibilities) to the first-born. In this role, she is also the haku, as birth order establishes leadership. Significantly, she is female. She has a number of venerable godly brothers, but there is no gender bias that dictates sons or brothers must lead. Pele's status as hiapo and haku is never questioned by the siblings (or anyone else for that matter).

Hi'iakaikapoliopele is the youngest, another special rank in birth order. Usually the most favored, the term pōki'i is applied to the muli loa (last born) in the generation; pōki'i are often spoken of and regarded with the highest level of endearment. Pukui cites an ʻōlelo noʻeau that reflects this thought, "Pōkiʻi ka ua, ua i ka lehua" (Rain is the youngest sibling, falling on the lehua blossoms), meaning the rain and lehua are dear to each other.[47]

The genealogical ranking of Pele and Hiʻiaka demonstrate ʻēkoʻa and pono between the oldest and youngest sisters who are also opposites—Pele is temperamental, Hiʻiaka is the calming healer. Yet these qualities are dependent upon each other via an eternal opposing binary that is also complementary. Together they have the most power of the siblings, play the most important roles (which are well supported by the others), and are primarily responsible for the generation and regeneration of ʻāina.

In her analysis of the Kamapuaʻa literature, Kameʻeleihiwa discusses how one reason Kamapuaʻa's moʻokūʻauhau is important is because the names in his genealogy reflect nature, as well as the nature and temperament of the pig–god and his ʻohana (and function, which alludes back to Kumulipo).[48] This is reflected in the names of siblings, particularly the epithets applied to each of the Hiʻiaka sisters (as many as forty), their various functions and symbols described in later versions of the moʻolelo.[49]

The names are more embedded than we see at first, because each represents a larger set of images or reference points and not just one thing. For example, when "iʻa" (fish) are born in the Kumulipo (l. 123), it doesn't just refer to a fish, but to all the varieties of fish that are named in subsequent lines (manō, moano, etc.). In Pele and Hiʻiaka moʻolelo, they similarly represent more than themselves: their names embody genesis (Pele, lava, new geographic formation) and re-genesis (Hiʻiaka, reflection, reforestation of new lands created by Pele). They simultaneously evoke the idea of pono, a sense of balance, of being born from two elements (Kumulipo and Pōʻele, Haumea and Moemoeʻaʻauliʻi). Therefore, the moʻolelo carries these cultural values through the characters as much as through the story, and is thus a reminder of such values. It is a kind of synecdoche, where one word, name, image, or symbol signifies something much larger, what Shanley identifies as the "key" to the "metalanguage," a "hypertext link" that when clicked unlocks different levels of understanding and layers of meaning that connect to other words, ideas, concepts, values, moʻolelo, and so forth.[50]

The intertwining of oral and written traditions is expected in moʻolelo such as Pele and Hiʻiaka, because of the performative aspect associated with it—not just through story*telling*, but through story *performance* (hula). As Stillman argues, the practice of hula is both a practice of memory and the embodiment of tradition.[51]

Pele and Hiʻiaka moʻolelo survived orally for countless generations before being written down which speaks to the power, appeal, and tenacity of ʻŌiwi intellectualism. Their exploits, deeds, and associations were kept alive in print during a century of rapid cultural and political change, and they are popularized today because their publication extended their longevity for a culture that has become more dependent on writing and print.

The collection and publication of moʻolelo kuʻuna throughout the nineteenth century was significant because it helped preserve and perpetuate such vital cultural knowledge of the past for present and future generations. In an open letter to the newspaper *Ka Hoku o ka Pakipika* in 1865, J. H. Kānepuʻu, an Oʻahu school teacher, criticized the shortening (and misrepresentation) of moʻolelo kuʻuna being published in the Hawaiian newspapers:

> It is my desire that the stories be printed with all of the writers' knowledge and that none of the details of the story be left out, and that the editors of *Ka Hoku o ka Pakipika* actually publish everything in each story without interruption. I know that the story of Hiʻiakaikapoliopele has been edited, her songs regarding the hula have been cut short, and because of this how indeed will our generations come to know what has been left out? They will want to know, and it won't be there, because we are causing it to disappear.[52]

The continued publication of moʻolelo kuʻuna is significant as the history of "pagan" gods were carried forward into the modern, civilized, Christian era, even more meaningful considering the ban on hula at the time. As the century progressed, many oral traditions were transformed from being solely memorized to include written literature. At a time when enjoyment of hula as a living cultural practice was forced underground, the hula and exploits of Pele and Hiʻiaka continued to live on paper. Moʻokūʻauhau is critical to understanding a literary tradition (and literary nationalism) in a Hawaiian context. The moʻolelo have genealogies, the writers have genealogies, the newspapers have genealogies, the editors and publishers have genealogies. There is also an intertextuality between moʻolelo that is part of kaona and literary aesthetics coming from oral tradition and cultural practice, all of which are contextualized within a specific history of Hawaiʻi in traditional, pre-nation (ʻAikapu) governance, during the period as an independent nation (mōʻī, constitutional monarchy), after the overthrow (provisional government, republic, annexed territory of the United States), until today (statehood, U.S. occupation). The resurgence of culturally based nationalism has equaled a resurgence in cultural knowledge, practice, and Hawaiian identity.

These written moʻolelo are cultural touchstones treasured by Kanaka Maoli today. They are foundational texts for cultural knowledge and are used in a variety of contexts as such, from hālau hula to ethnobotany and mālama ʻāina sustainability to political and environmental activism that seeks to halt geothermal development by multinational corporations in Puna, Hawaiʻi, Pele and Hiʻiakaʻs home.

ʻO Nā Lehua Wale i Kāʻana (The Lehua Blossoms Alone at Kāʻana)

In 1899, Maui native Moses Manu published a Pele-related moʻolelo, "He Moolelo Kaao Hawaii no ke Kaua Nui Weliweli ma Waena o Pelekeahi-aloa a me Wakakeakaikawai" ("Pelekeahiʻāloa") in the Honolulu-based Hawaiian-language newspaper *Ka Loea Kalaiaina* (The Political Expert). "Pelekeahiʻāloa" included lengthy sections of Pele's sister Kapōʻulakīnaʻu's voyage to Hawaiʻi from Kahiki before Pele, and her establishment as an akua of ʻanāʻanā (life affirming and death dealing practices) at Hāna, Maui. It also details how their other sister, Kewelani (alternately known as Nāwāhineliʻiliʻi), became the hula deity at Kāʻana on the windswept slopes of Maunaloa, Molokaʻi; in this moʻolelo, Kāʻana is thus established as ka hula piko, the birthplace of hula. In the moʻolelo, the kamaʻāina of Maunaloa ask Kapō to teach them the art of hula. Kapō says, "This can easily be taught, but it has to be learned by observing my kapu and doing the things that will help my teaching. There are many kapu pertaining to this art, and one can only learn through strict adherence. If the desire to learn is strong, it will not take long to graduate."[53] The Maunaloa kamaʻāina agree to follow Kapō's direction. Kapō appoints her sister Kewelani to teach hula at Kāʻana, initiating her as a kumu hula because of her expertise in dancing:

> Because of their strong desire to learn, Kapōʻulakīnaʻu appointed her vivacious sister, Nāwāhineliʻiliʻi, who was also called Kewelani, to help her. She was the same sister who first danced the hula kiʻi on the island of Niʻihau, as described earlier in the narrative. When Kapōʻulakīnaʻu chose her to instruct and to chant, she placed a conspicuous brown mark on her right cheek so that the people would not confuse the two of them. She then called her Laea, Ulunui, and Laka. The art of hula was taught by her using these three names.[54]

The moʻolelo then provides detailed protocol for learning hula. First, an offering to Laka of a pig and ʻawa uli (dark-skinned kava, *Piper methysticum*);

next, Laka taught the chant for giving the offering, "ʻO na lehua wale i Kaana" (The lehua blossoms of Kāʻana). Dancers then went into the mountains to gather greenery to build and adorn the hula kuahu, evoking the names of the forest gods through the chant. Next, a piece of lehua root, symbolizing Kapōʻulakīnaʻu and her brothers, was cut, and another specific oli offered. When all materials gathered from the forest were prepared, the gatherer returned home and built the kuahu hula, chanting "A kanikaniaula ka leo o ka wahine" (Mournfully chanting is the voice of the woman) while the greenery was placed.

Both mele reference lei making as part of the offering protocol for Kapōʻulakīnaʻu, an akua ʻanāʻanā, appealing to her as a hula deity. Nature imagery emphasizes the high value placed on knowledge handed down mai ka pō mai, mai nā kūpuna mai. Pūʻawahiwa is a clump of dark-skinned ʻawa. Pū also means to come together, and hiwa also means sacred. Similarly, knowledge from the source (ʻike kumu) and knowledge that is heard and distributed through oral means (ʻike lono) refer to oral traditions passed down mai ka pō mai, mai nā kūpuna mai. Kaona references to lei and lehua connotes expertise and fearlessness—Kamehameha's fierce warriors were called lehua—and also connects Kāʻana and Kapō to Pele's ʻāina (Puna, Hawaiʻi) and the rest of the Pele ʻohana. An ʻōlelo noʻeau, Ka lehua neneʻe o Kāʻana (The creeping lehua of Kāʻana) describes the low-growing lehua, possibly unique to this place, influenced by the dry, windswept environment.[55] Pukui explains that the lehua of Kāʻana are often referenced in mele and were beloved by Kapō;[56] they were destroyed by grazing animals, such as cattle and deer, introduced by settlers in the late eighteenth and early nineteenth centuries.

The second mele stresses the chanting quality of the voice; kanikaniʻāʻula is a particular mournful quality of chant. It suggests the power and constancy of the wind at this place, mentioned in the third line, "O ka wahine e noho ana i ka ulu a ka makani" (The woman sitting where the wind rises). "Ka wahine" (the woman) is a common, understated metaphor for Pele, although here it is applied to her sisters who belong to this ʻāina, Laka and Kapō (mentioned in the following line). Maʻohelāia is Kapō's verdant ʻōhiʻa groves on Maunaloa, a name not recorded on modern maps, but known to Hawaiians into the late nineteenth century. Kamakau describes it as a desolate plain (kula anoano) where spirits wandered.[57] Kapō does not just live in the grove of lehua trees, she *is* a lehua, described as an "ʻōhiʻa kū o Maunaloa," an upright ʻōhia tree of Maunaloa, indicating power and strength. Manu writes that lehua is a symbol of Kapōʻulakīnaʻu and her brother, Kauilaokalani, who accompanies her to Molokaʻi.[58]

The chant is an appeal to Laka, poetically referred to as Kaulanaʻula (sacred one), and the chant delivered through vocalization is the mohai (offering). Kaulana means famous, and Laka was renowned for her skill at hula; ʻula evokes multiple kaona, including the color red, sacredness, and ghost or spirit. The vocalization of oli requires hā (breath), a manifestation of one's personal mana, making it an appropriate offering. There is an implied spiritual association between wind and breath, and between chanter and nature mediated through the forms of nature (such as the ʻōhiʻa tree) being evoked. There is an expectation of a reply in the last line of the chant, "E hea au ē, e ō ʻoe" (I call to you—answer me) that "the woman" (Kapō, Laka) will respond positively to the request. Offered with reverence, it is difficult to imagine the akua would not listen and respond to the call of her people.

It is through protocol and discipline and knowing one's kuleana that Kapō is established as an akua hula with the kānāwai called Piʻikuahu (altar ascending) and Mokulehua (cut section of lehua).[59] The importance of asking for knowledge, recognizing traditional cultural protocols, and understanding that knowledge comes through practice and discipline, are all exemplified in the words and chanting of the oli.

The moʻolelo is a reminder to Kanaka six years after the overthrow, within a year of annexation to the United States, and two years after the massive land sale that transferred seventy thousand acres of land surrounding Kāʻana from the Kamehamehas (through Charles Reed Bishop) to the private hands of haole businessmen, that discipline and practice of protocol are important to establish kuleana. If not an outright political message, it was an encoded one; if it was not possible to regain political sovereignty, it was possible to reestablish culture protocol, and chastise the machinations of the new government through kaona-encoded moʻolelo. Nearly a century after Christianity was implanted in Hawaiian hearts and minds, an ʻŌiwi writer presented traditional religious and spiritual protocol carried through moʻolelo kuʻuna. It is an expression of literary nationalism based in Hawaiian values mai ka pō mai, mai nā kūpuna mai—moʻokūʻauhau and kuleana through cultural practice. Similarly, it offers guidance for Kanaka Maoli today, providing a traditional answer to ongoing problems with settler colonialism.

Kāʻana i ke Ao Hou (Kāʻana Today)

I have not had the privilege of dancing with the hālau for some years now, or the opportunity to return to Kāʻana since 1995. In 1997, at the request of Kumu Kaʻimikaua, a dryland reforestation project began on Kāʻana. Supported by Molokaʻi Ranch at the time, the Hawaiʻi Forestry

Association, the Natural Resource Conservation Service, the University of Hawaiʻi Cooperative Extension Service, Moanalua Gardens, the Nature Conservancy, and even the Department of Education (who allowed Molokaʻi schoolchildren to participate by growing native plants and replanting them at Kāʻana), the goals of the project were to revegetate Kāʻana with native plants, preserve the land around the "hula piko" site, sustain cultural practice, involve the Molokaʻi community, and instill mālama ʻāina—pride, appreciation, and responsibility in the stewardship of Native land.[60] Fences were erected to keep our grazing animals, and dripline irrigation installed.

In 2000, a pā hula (performance platform) made from stones of the area was dedicated by Kumu Kaʻimikaua. However, Molokaʻi Ranch has since pulled its support of the restoration, and the fences have fallen into disrepair, allowing cattle and other ungulates once again to roam the wahi kapu at will, destroying native vegetation. Despite efforts to educate others about the importance of such sites to cultural practices, settler colonialism and transnational global capitalism, of which the foreign-owned ranch is a part, still view land as a commodity, and still control Native access to ʻāina and our ability to mālama and utilize our wahi pana for traditional cultural purposes. In response to strong community pressures against luxury home and resort development at nearby Lāʻau Point, and the development of wind farm technology to export power to electricity-hungry Oʻahu, the ranch abruptly ceased operations in 2008, firing all but a few employees. Withdrawing from the island, the ranch has left in its wake a fragile economy and way of life even more vulnerable to exploitation. Access to ranch lands are just as restricted as they've ever been.[61]

The importance of wind and our intimate relationships with it are documented throughout Hawaiian mele and moʻolelo.[62] Manu's "Pelekeahiʻāloa" describes the kino lau makani (wind bodies) of Kapōʻulakīnaʻu and her sisters, which they embody to travel throughout the islands. "A kanikaniʻāʻula ka leo o ka wahine" describes places on and elements associated with Kāʻana. The wind of this ʻāina is described in the line "O ka wahine e noho ana i ka ulu a ka makani" (The woman sitting where the wind rises). In 2000, a small plane crash below Kāʻana was attributed to the strong winds associated with this place.

Maunaloa is currently under a serious threat from wind energy development projects, and a proposed undersea cable will transfer electricity to the island of Oʻahu. Up to seventy massive wind turbines are planned for Maunaloa, generating a proposed two hundred megawatts of electricity, projected to supply 10 percent of Oʻahu's needs. Poʻe aloha ʻāina, the people who love the land, are adamantly opposed to the development of wind farms on Molokaʻi because of cultural and environmental destruction. Once more, Kanaka Maoli face an uphill battle of social, cultural, and environmental justice to aloha and mālama ʻāina—to preserve our lands, culture, and lifestyle under constant threat of destruction by government and big business. Despite vigorous, ongoing protests against it, on June 27, 2012, Hawaiʻi Governor Neil Abercrombie signed the Inter-Island Cable Bill (Act 165) into law, which creates a regulatory structure to install and implement a high-voltage electric transmission cable system connecting the Hawaiian islands. Proponents tout the development of wind (Molokaʻi, Lānaʻi) and geothermal (Puna, Hawaiʻi) energy as beneficial for everyone in the islands. Not everyone is fooled: such a project will benefit urban Oʻahu, which boasts over 70 percent of the population of the islands, including the highest concentration of military installations and tourism destinations in the state and in the Pacific region. The fight of ka poʻe aloha ʻāina continues.

The scientific and economic discourses of settler colonialism scoff at indigenous relationships with nature. In public hearings throughout the islands, the visible sneers of politicians and developers are barely contained as culture and aloha ʻāina are evoked to argue against development. Yet as such cultural practices as long-distance voyaging remind us, there is also a practical side to knowledge about wind, one from which metaphoric references in Hawaiian moʻolelo are woven. In an article about wind chants as a literary device in Poepoe's Pele and Hiʻiaka moʻolelo, Silva discusses Sydney Iaukea's argument for a makani discourse:

Iaukea [argues], "If you knew the name of the *makani* (wind) that blew through a particular area, you were never lost, both geographically and . . . epistemologically." . . . She explained further, "To know the winds of a particular place was to know one's precise location, to understand the deities that existed therein, and to be sensitive to the differences in the landscape and seascape in that space." . . .

Iaukea's . . . *makani* discourse invites us to consider "reorienting ourselves ideologically" toward "a Hawaiian sense of place" through recuperating the worldview of our kūpuna, for whom "there is no separation between nature and self." . . . She asserted that we are now "separated from the natural environment, both physically and ideologically, through contemporary spatial orders," and she wondered "how can something like *knowing the wind* close this gap by recovering a sense of place and well-being?"[63]

How can studying the knowledge of our kūpuna through our moʻolelo help us know the winds of our ʻāina? How can we use this knowledge to weave the knowledge and experiences of the past with the present? We can educate ourselves and others about our wahi kapu and the necessity of preserving and protecting them. It is not just a reorientation to a Hawaiian *sense* of place that is urgently needed, but an understanding of culturally based environmental ethics that can guide us toward making better, more sustainable decisions about ʻāina.

Kumu Kaʻimikaua passed away in 2006; Hālau Kukunaokalā continues to mālama Kāʻana and educate people about this important wahi pana. The public predawn ceremonies ended some years ago. Kumu's vision of Kāʻana once again being restored to how it is described in mele— lush ʻōhia lehua forests covering the "long mountain" of west Molokaʻi— has yet to be fully realized. Wind energy development on the slopes of Maunaloa remains a looming threat. But the inspiration of knowledge and ʻike ʻāina passed down mai ka pō mai, mai nā kūpuna mai in oral traditions and hālau practice, fixed in nineteenth-century moʻolelo published in Hawaiian-language newspapers, is sure to help this and future generations work toward the goals of mālama ʻāina. It is our cultural kuleana, an integral part of rebuilding our Lāhui. E hea mau mākou ē. Our call continues.

Lele ana ʻo Kaʻena i ka Mālie
(Kaʻena Soars Like a Bird in the Calm):
Pele and Hiʻiaka Moʻolelo as Intellectual History

Lele ana 'o Ka'ena
Me he manu lā i ka mālie
Me he kaha na ka 'ua'u lā
Nā pali 'o Nēnēle'a
Me he 'upa'i na ke koa'e lā
Ka 'ale i waho o Ka'ie'ie
Me he kanaka ho'onu'u lā i ka mālie
Ka papākea i ke alo o ka 'alā
Ua ku'ia e ke kai
A uli, a nono, a 'ula
Ka maka o ka 'alā
E nonoho ana i ke kai 'o Kāpeku
Kāpeku ka leo o ke kai
'O Ho'oilo ka malama
Ke kū maila ka pāuli i kai
Ka hō'ailona kai o ka 'āina
'Ae kai o Kahulumanu
Kai a moana ka 'āina
Ahuwale ka pae ki'i
Ka pae newenewe
Ka pae manu'u a Kanaloa
A he hoa a 'o ia
Ho'ohaehae ana Kalaeokalā'au
I kīhae 'ia e ke kai o Wawalu
Nā 'ōwaewae pali o Unulau,
Inu aku i ka wai o Koheiki i ka pali
I ka pali ka wai
Kau pū me ka lā'au
Hō'ole ke kupa, hūnā i ka wai
'Ehā ka muliwai, wai o Ka'ena
'Ena ihola e ka lā o ka Makali'i
'Oi'o mai ana ke 'ā me he kanaka koa lā
Mā'alo ana i ku'u maka
Me he huaka'i lā o ia kalana pali
Kuamo'oloa, pali o Leihonua
Hiki iho nei nō ka hau'oli
I ka hiki 'ana mai a nei makani
He aha lā ka'u makana?
I ku'u hilahila
'O ka'u wale ihola nō ia
'O ka leo ē.'

Ka'ena soars
Like a bird in the calm
Like an 'ua'u bird soaring
Above the Nēnēle'a cliffs
Like the flapping wings of koa'e birds
And the billowing waves of Ka'ie'ie channel
Like a heap of people in the calm
The sea spray flies in the face of the basalt stones on the shore
Pounded by the sea
Until the dark night turns pink, then red with dawn
In the face of the volcanic stones
Clustered together in the sea of Kāpeku
The raging voice of the sea is frightening
Ho'oilo is the season[2]
The gloomy darkness at sea has arrived
An ocean-born sign for the land
The rising tide of Kahulumanu
At the water's edge where land becomes sea
The row of godly images is exposed
The undulating figures move along in the billowing current
The multitudinous forms of Kanaloa
All fitting companions
Kalaeokalā'au initiates the movement
Torn apart by the sea of Wawalu[3]
To the furrowed cliffs of Unulau
I partake of the fresh water from the cliff of Koheiki
The water hidden in the cliffs
Also placed in the foliage
The native denies it, the water is concealed
There are four estuaries that provide water for Ka'ena
Abundant in the days of Makali'i[4]
The jagged lava rock are like a legion of warriors
Passing right before my eyes
This cliffed land is itself like a procession
The ridges of Leihonua's cliffs reach out
Happiness has arrived here
Arriving upon this breeze wafting forth
What gift indeed can I share in return?
In my embarrassment
This all I have to offer—
Just my voice.

IT IS 3:30 P.M. ON A THURSDAY AFTERNOON, and my friend Alohilani and I are rushing to leave UH Mānoa and make our way to hula practice in Makakilo, twenty-three miles away. During the hour-long drive in afternoon H-1 'Ewa-bound traffic, we practice our mele for class—"Kūnihi Ka'ena holo i ka mālie," steep stands Ka'ena, gliding in the calm.

We cruise through Kalihi, 'Aiea, and the Wai- lands that make up Pearl City (Waimalu, Waiau, Waimano, Waiawa, Waipi'o), gliding swiftly along the freeway in our four-wheeled wa'a, past Waipahu, Waikele, and Kunia; Pu'u o Kapōlei, the hill that rises up from the 'Ewa plains, named for Pele's sister, looms ahead, the visible geographic marker signaling we are approaching the Makakilo suburb built on its flanks.

Our kumu hula, John Ka'imikaua, is a practitioner of the Moloka'i hula tradition. Like many Kanaka Maoli displaced from traditional homelands, Kumu's family lives in Makakilo, where our hula practices are held. We enter the cafeteria of Makakilo Elementary School as the sun sets behind us, casting long shadows across the smooth cement floor, cool under our bare feet despite the warmth of the day. Kumu sits on the raised wooden stage at the front of the room, and we greet him and our hālau 'ohana with honi and aloha. Kumu thumps the 'ipu heke twice on the wooden floor. We straighten ourselves into lines facing him. "Ho'omākaukau!" he calls in a serious voice. Ready! "'Ae, kūnihi Ka'ena holo i ka mālie." Yes, we respond with the first line of the oli, steep stands Ka'ena, gliding in the calm.

Our feet kāholo, two steps right then two steps left, gliding like Ka'ena. They point in unison right hela, left hela, right and left leg and foot alternately extended, the balls of our feet firmly planted on the floor. We create cliffs and plains carved from the air with our hands, conjure the Kaiāulu and Koholālele winds of that 'āina as our arms sweep gracefully above our heads, our hips sway left then right then left again to the resonant tones of the ipu heke, 'ū tē tē, 'ū tē tē, and Kumu's chanting voice echoing in the cavernous space.

When our hula is finished, we inhale deeply to catch our breaths, sweat glistening on our foreheads. It takes physical strength to re-create Hi'iaka's journey in the blazing heat along the Wai'anae coast of O'ahu through our hula, remembering her homeward journey the oli describes as she walks along the shoreline, so struck by its beauty she abandons the wa'a, tells her aikāne Wahine'ōma'o and her sister's lover Lohi'au that she will rejoin them down the coast at Pu'uloa (now Pearl Harbor), over twenty miles away. She travels along the shoreline, naming each place as she encounters it—Ka'ena, Keawa'ula, Mākua, 'Ōhikilolo, Kea'au, Mākaha, Kūmanomano, Kahuanananiho, Alio, Kuaiwa, Wai'anae, Kānepūniu, Lualualei, Puʻuliʻiliʻi, Pahalono, Waikonenene, Kamoaʻula, all wahi pana mapped through the mele, only half of which appear on any modern record. The first six named are major ahupuaʻa of the Waiʻanae district. Kaʻena, Mākua, and Lualualei are now major U.S. military installations. Almost every line references the intense heat of the sun, not surprising as this moku is on the dry, Kona (leeward) side of the island, a place of long blistering days. The only refreshment the ʻāina offers is provided by the Kaiāulu and Koholālele winds and the fresh water of Lualualei.

In this oli, Hiʻiaka learns of the destruction of her beloved Hōpoe and lehua groves of Puna when she hikes to the summit of Pohākea above Nānākuli valley, which provides a clear view all the way to Puna. This is a pivotal plot point, where Hiʻiaka grieves for her beloved aikāne and forests. It gives her time to consider the consequences Pele will pay upon her return.

Despite our efforts, we have not performed up to Kumu's expectations. "Feel the sweltering heat of Kaʻena surrounding you!" he commands. "Feel the teeth of the sun! Embody the words of the oli! Feel the hot sand burning under your bare feet! If you can't imagine that, we'll go to Kaʻena and dance on the sand there in the middle of the day!" Alohilani and I look at each other. I know she is recalling our last trip to Keawaʻula, the sandy beach just before Kaʻena; the distance across the sand to the sea is short, but traversing it seems to take longer because of the sun-scorched sand burning beneath our feet. The ipu thumps the ground twice again. "Hoʻomākaukau!" he commands. We straighten our lines, resolute. "ʻAe, Kūnihi Kaʻena holo i ka mālie!" we respond, prepared to travel once more under the fiery heat of the Waiʻanae coast, re-creating this scene from Hiʻiaka's journey, our history, once more. As I kāwelu to the left, pivoting on my left foot, tap stepping lightly with my right, I have a split second to glance out the open louvered windows to the sea of ʻEwa in the distance; there, Wahineʻōmaʻo and Lohiʻau watch us from their waʻa bobbing in the calm seas just off the coastline, waiting for Hiʻiaka to come down from the heights of Pōhākea above us, the mountain ridge dividing the ahupuaʻa of Waiʻanae and ʻEwa.

The next few chapters focus on specific published Pele and Hiʻiaka moʻolelo as mediators of ʻŌiwi intellectual tradition, and address the following questions: What is an indigenous intellectual tradition? How does the corpus of Pele and Hiʻiaka moʻolelo represent such a thing? How does writing about Pele and Hiʻiaka moʻolelo as an intellectual tradition differ from how it is represented within (for example) folklore studies, ethnography, or anthropology, disciplines closely associated with settler

Kūnihi Ka'ena holo i ka mālie, the upright cliffs of Ka'ena stretch out to the point in calm seas on the northwest side of O'ahu. Hi'iaka departs O'ahu for Kaua'i from here. To the left is the northeast side of the island looking toward Mokulē'ia. To the right is the Wai'anae coast that Hi'iaka traverses on foot on her way back from Kaua'i; Wahine'ōma'o and Lohi'au paddle their canoe along the coast, and meet Hi'iaka twenty miles down the coast at Pu'uloa, known today as Pearl Harbor. The mountainous area above Ka'ena point is an Air Force Satellite Tracking Station. The large valley on the right is Mākua, a U.S. Army live fire training ground. Photograph by Keith Marrero. Courtesy of Roland Harvey and Leslie Keli'ilauahi Stewart, Harry K. Stewart collection.

colonialism? Here, let us "lele ana me he manu lā i ka mālie, me he kaha na ka 'ua'u lā," and soar, gliding like an 'ua'u (petrel) bird over the resolute sea cliffs of Ka'ena extending out into the sky-reflecting sea, and explore the 'āina of Pele and Hi'iaka mo'olelo in an indigenous context, from an indigenous perspective.

Toward an Indigenous Literary Analysis

In 1976, Samoan author and scholar Albert Wendt published a landmark essay that has since become a foundational text of Pacific literary scholarship. "Towards a New Oceania" began with a simple but profound declaration: "I belong to Oceania."[5] In saying this, Wendt roots himself—and by extension, his writing, his scholarship, Pacific literary studies, and perhaps all Pacific research—to a geographic region and Indigenous homeland, highlighting Indigenous perspectives. It is a viewpoint that has resonated far and wide throughout Oceania. Wendt calls for the people of Oceania to remember our ancestors: "Our dead are woven into our souls like the hypnotic music of bone flutes: we can never escape them. If we let them, they can help illuminate us to ourselves and to one another. They can be the source of new-found pride, self-respect, and wisdom."[6] It is a metaphor of mo'okū'auhau, reiterating respect for our kūpuna and the knowledge they embody. It is a way of understanding and expressing our genealogy of oral and written intellectual traditions.

Mo'okū'auhau is an important concept in Polynesian culture, and special attention is paid and respect given to the first born or eldest members in a family. This cultural concept also relates to literature.[7] Applying mo'okū'auhau to Hawaiian literature reveals the intentionality behind the publication of traditional mo'olelo, as these mythical and historical narratives hold an important place in Hawaiian culture.

This chapter focuses on the earliest publications of Pele and Hi'iaka mo'olelo: two oli, a wahi mo'olelo (fragment of story), and the first strand of the Pele and Hi'iaka literary genealogy outlined in mokuna 1.[8] Here we consider the questions, what was it like to take an oral tradition and transform it into a literary one?

S. M. Kamakau, H. K. Kalama, B. R. Kalama, B. K. Hauola, and *Ka Hae Hawaii*

Kapihenui was the first to publish a complete, epic-length Pele and Hi'iaka mo'olelo, but it was preceded in print by several mele and highly condensed wahi mo'olelo published the previous year. Four hulihia chants appeared in the newspaper *Ka Hae Hawaii* (The Hawaiian Flag) in 1860. The first, "He Mele i Kilauea" (A Song at Kīlauea), was published on March 21, 1860; it is attributed to the venerable historian Samuel Kamakau.[9] The oli begins, "Hulihia ka mauna wela i ke ahi" (The mountain is overturned, hot in the fire). This hulihia chant is the first poetic text associated with Pele and Hi'iaka to appear in print. A second hulihia, "Hulihia kulia mai ka moku o Kahiki" (Overturned is the island of Tahiti), was published a week later on March 28, and is also credited to Kamakau.[10]

On May 23, *Ka Hae Hawaii* published two more hulihia chants. "He Mele na Kauakahiapoiwa [Kahuaka'iapaoa], i Kilauea" (Kahuaka'iapaoa's Song, at Kīlauea) was signed by H. K. Kalama from Wai'aha, North Kona. It begins, "Hulihia ke au nee ilalo ia Kea" (The current beneath the strata of [Wākea] churns). The second, "He Mele na Lohiau, i Kilauea" (Lohi'au's Song, at Kīlauea), was signed by B. R. Kalama, also of Wai'aha, North Kona. The first line begins, "Huli aku ana ke ahi a Lono makua" (The fires of Lonomakua churn). Variations of these hulihia chants are included in the multiple published versions of the Pele and Hi'iaka mo'olelo. These hulihia chants are rather lengthy, averaging around fifty lines each. The haole editors say they were interested in publishing these mele because they contained "many names of the foreign lands."[11] It seems they were unaware of the political and cultural significance of the hulihia chants.

A few weeks later, B. Kala'iohauola of Wailua, Kaua'i, published two installments of a highly summarized Pele and Hi'iaka mo'olelo under the title "He Wahi Kaao a me Kekahi Mele Pu" (A little story and some songs, too). The first installment of the mo'olelo (July 4) begins with Lohi'au and Kaleiopaoa (an alternate name for Kahuaka'iapaoa) at Hā'ena and a brief description of Pele's arrival. The terms of agreement between Pele and Hi'iaka are outlined (called a "berita" or covenant, often used in this time period in the context of Christian marriage), and Hi'iaka departs. In the span of twelve short paragraphs, Hi'iaka revives Lohi'au, they depart for O'ahu, are hosted by Pele'ula in Māmala (an old name for Honolulu), travel to Moloka'i, and then arrive on Maui where Hi'iaka battles Waihīnalo (Waihīnano) over 'Olepau's life. The second installment (August 15) doesn't continue the previous narrative, but recaps the mo'olelo, covering Hi'iaka's journey from Hawai'i to Kaua'i, and her return with Lohi'au and Wahine'ōma'o to O'ahu. The mo'olelo ends with Hi'iaka atop the summit of Pōhākea, gazing across the archipelago to Hawai'i, where she sees the destruction of Hōpoe. A final chant she offers while playing kilu (quoits, a matchmaking game played by the ali'i class) at the home of the ali'i wahine Pele'ula in Māmala foretells Lohi'au's impending fate at the crater because of Pele's anger.

Collectively, these publications in *Ka Hae Hawaii* focus on the hulihia chants that appear chronologically near the end of the Pele and Hi'iaka mo'olelo. As such, they evoke the memory of the entire saga in a very concentrated way. It is impossible to know if these fragments of mo'olelo hinted at Kapihenui's forthcoming epic, if his lengthy publication was a response to these wahi mo'olelo (as Kala'iohauola describes them), or if it was a coincidence that four 'Ōiwi writers from four islands (Maui, Hawai'i, Kaua'i, and O'ahu) were publishing Pele and Hi'iaka mo'olelo at the same time. It may be an 'Ōiwi response to the recently enacted 1860 law banning the public performance of hula, an assertion of 'Ōiwi voices refusing to be silenced. It may have been a response to the editors' call soliciting such information, their attempt to boost newspaper sales.

Ka Hae Hawaii (1856–1861), the newspaper that carried this cluster of poetic texts, was founded by former missionary Richard Armstrong and his son Samuel. Richard Armstrong resigned from the ABCFM in 1848 and became the first minister of public instruction for the Hawaiian government (the predecessor to the current State of Hawai'i Department of Education). The paper was founded "as a way to advance literacy and Christian-American morality."[12] It was associated with the Department of Public Instruction and not part of the independent nationalist press that began in 1861, around the time Armstrong published Kala'iohauola's "He Wahi Moolelo."

While the missionary-run newspapers heavily frowned on traditional Hawaiian mo'olelo, the Armstrongs may have made an exception and published these Pele- and Hi'iaka-related texts because their newspapers "shifted . . . as the times required, from establishment to opposition and back again," and because *Ka Hae Hawaii's* primary purpose was to encourage reading among Native Hawaiians."[13] The Armstrongs' shifting political views and goals for the papers might have opened up a new opportunity for 'Ōiwi writers to publish mo'olelo ku'una. In a paragraph introducing Kamakau's first hulihia chant titled "No na Mele" (Pertaining to the songs), the editors explain their desire to publish "na mele o ka wa kahiko" (songs of the ancient times) because they had almost disappeared.[14] Their ambivalent politics are also clear in their call. On one hand, they praise the mele because they contain knowledge of the traditional culture and knowledge of earlier generations and bemoan the fact that few Hawaiians were left who understood such knowledge. On the other hand, they write that publishing such information could help the newer generations see the errors of their ancestors' thinking so that the new generations that come after can read and think carefully about this and not follow in their footsteps gone astray (hiki no i na hanauna hou aku ke heluhelu a e kawiliwili iloko o ka manao a ike i na kuhihewa o ko lakou mau kupuna, me ka ukali ole ma ko lakou meheu paee).[15] Yet that is what Kanaka Maoli wanted to read, mele and mo'olelo mai ka pō mai, mai nā kūpuna mai. Perhaps the missionaries acquiesced to market demands in order to fulfill their goal of building Kanaka literacy (and making money). Shortly after these wahi mo'olelo were published, *Ka Hae Hawaii* published the first lengthy epic of Pele's nemesis, the pig–god Kamapua'a.[16]

Together, the cluster of Pele- and Hi'iaka-related mele and wahi mo'olelo in *Ka Hae Hawaii* also suggest a more oral presentation style, one in which the performance of mele or mo'olelo through hula or storytelling would not have been contextualized with much (if any) explanation. Within Hawaiian poetry, an economy of words is preferred, in part because of kaona, wherein multiple meanings packed into a single, carefully chosen word are conveyed, or as Kimura explains, Hawaiians "value getting their own thoughts across with the least number of words, thus making an understanding of their personality a matter of subtlety and personal sensitivity on the part of the listener."[17] It places kuleana on the audience not just to make their own meaning from a text, but also to extract the layers of intended meaning; there is an expectation on the writer's part that context and meaning can be constructed by their audience with minimal explanation. In real life, such meaning can be conveyed without words altogether through a look, gesture, body posture, or even the opening beats of a musical composition.

Kapihenui and *Ka Hoku o ka Pakipika*

On December 26, 1861, *Ka Hoku o ka Pakipika*, the first independent nationalist newspaper, began printing "He Moolelo no Hiiakaikapoliopele" (A Story of Hi'iakaikapoliopele), signed by M. J. Kapihenui of Kailua, O'ahu. The first comprehensive Pele and Hi'iaka mo'olelo ever published, it had the greatest impact on the subsequent publications by Pa'aluhi and Bush and Emerson, and was copied into a "souvenir book" (an undated BMA manuscript).[18] It was mentioned in Manu's "Pelekeahi'āloa" as "the greatest legend of Hawai'i."[19]

While Hawaiian-language newspapers were founded as early as the 1830s, they were run by the ABCFM missionaries who had their own ideas of what Kanaka should be reading, and it was not mo'olelo ku'una. By 1860, Kanaka Maoli were highly literate, skilled in publishing, and tired of Calvinist control over reading materials. *Ka Hoku o ka Pakipika*, the first newspaper free from direct missionary control, was born from within this evolving cultural and political environment. Chapin describes it as "a most significant event . . . a remarkable achievement that within three short decades of acquiring literacy and a newspaper technology Native Hawaiians set up and controlled their own press."[20] The establishment of an independent press was particularly important for the preservation and distribution of mo'olelo, and by extension, for the important traditional cultural knowledge they contained.

Chapin argues that while the nationalist newspapers were diverse in viewpoint, they were united on several key points: they knew what was best for the Lāhui, they understood the seriousness of the Native population collapse, they firmly insisted that Hawaiian independence should continue, and they retained a strong sense of aloha 'āina.[21] These points were reflected in the content of the newspapers, and were perhaps most visible in the consistent inclusion of mo'olelo ku'una. The Hawaiian independent press purposely sought to revive and preserve these mo'olelo in print, which were often prominently featured on the front pages. Thus, mo'olelo ku'una as written, published, and accessible expressions of Hawaiian culture and art, and the independent, nationalist Hawaiian press, simultaneously emerged.

While future mō'ī Kalākaua was involved in founding the news-paper, it was primarily edited by J. W. H. Kauwahi and George Mila (Mills).[22] The paper was based in Honolulu, and ran from September 26, 1861, to May 14, 1863.[23] From its inception, mo'olelo ku'una were fea-tured; "Mooolelo no Kawelo" (Legend of Kawelo), contributed by S. K. Kawaili'ulā, was the first one published (September 26–December 5, 1861), and many others soon followed.[24] Mo'olelo were so prominently featured in *Ka Hoku o ka Pakipika* that they appeared in every issue save one (May 22, 1862).

Little is known about Kapihenui, the writer who contributed "Hi'i-akaikapoliopele" to the newspaper.[25] It is presumed that Kapihenui was a man, but it is just as possible that Kapihenui was a woman. The mo'olelo and other letters Kapihenui sent to various newspapers were all signed from Kailua, Ko'olaupoko, O'ahu. In an Interior Department letter dated January 11, 1858, a man named Kapihenui was responsible for the capture of stray cattle owned by John Cummins of the neighboring moku of Waimānalo.[26]

Kapihenui's "He Moolelo no Hiiakaikapoliopele" (The Epic of Hi'iakaikapoliopele)

In exploring Kapihenui's mo'olelo, some key questions that guide the discussion include the following: What kind of kuleana did Kapihenui have to "translate" this treasured mo'olelo from the oral tradition to the printed page? What does it mean to take an oral tradition to writing? In doing so, how can it be evaluated as literature? What kuleana does the mo'olelo itself carry as a kahua (foundation) for subsequent publications?

The publication of Kapihenui's mo'olelo established Pele and Hi'iaka mo'olelo as a literary tradition. For literary scholars, it offers a glimpse into the oral roots of mo'olelo ku'una in its style. This transition is ex-plored through specific examples of literary elements and devices within it. I reiterate here four important points relevant to the development of this literature:

(1) As the earliest published Pele and Hi'iaka epic, Kapihenui's relied more on oral tradition. As a transitional (oral to written) text, it is an example of how the two were woven together.

(2) Kanaka 'Ōiwi literary production adapted, incorporated, and merged oral and written elements; 'Ōiwi authors infused Western-influenced literary traditions with Hawaiian poetic

devices born in the oral traditions and considered important markers of good poetic expression.

(3) As Hawaiians became more adept at understanding the nuances of written *literature*, literary productions flourished, embracing and adapting (and not necessarily adapting *to*) the Western style.

(4) At the political level, Pele and Hi'iaka mo'olelo resisted Western colonialism, asserted cultural identity and pride, and expressed Hawaiian creativity. As such, this mo'olelo demonstrated a deft interweaving of the old and new, the oral and written, the native and Western, and created a new, dynamic lei mo'olelo that carried Kanaka 'Ōiwi cultural thought, belief, and practice forward. In this way it was an integral part of the literary nationalism that flourished in the Hawaiian kingdom between 1860 and 1893, one that affirmed a culturally based nationalism after the overthrow of the government, which had the return of Hawaiian sovereignty as its primary goal. While that goal has not yet been met, these mo'olelo remain a part of contemporary cultural practices and the assertion of Hawaiian nationalism today.

This chapter focuses on the first two points, exploring how Kapihenui wove a literary tradition from an oral one. The next two points are addressed in mokuna 6.

Kapihenui: Weaving Orature and Literature

Kapihenui's mo'olelo is a foundational text of early Hawaiian literature. Adapted from oral tradition going back countless generations, Kapihenui has been criticized by Charlot as "less desirable" than later versions because of its "mechanical" style.[27] However, what Charlot views as "mechanical" is pīna'i (formulaic repetition), a traditional oral and literary rhetorical device considered a highly desirable quality in oral storytelling, a stylistic element linking the mo'olelo to its oral roots.

In the previous chapter I discussed how orature (oral literature) and written mo'olelo were interwoven and informed each other. Kapihenui's mo'olelo is an example of how that occurred. A "transitional" writer, he wove the written tradition into the oral tradition, from the oral tradition. Later publications were more literary in their inclusion of additional prose description and kōkua (authorial asides) contextualizing the narrative. Kapihenui, however, presented a more performance-based account on paper using oral devices such as repetition and oli.

Kapihenui incorporated oratory practices that over time were adopted to print. These meiwi functioned somewhat differently from the oral tradition because they weren't spoken, sung, or danced before a live audience, although they represented these performative practices on the page.

Pīna'i is common in oral tradition and early epic narratives from other cultures, such as *Beowulf* and Homer's *Iliad*. Kapihenui relies on pīna'i to introduce oli and mele, other forms of meiwi, throughout the narrative with a standard phrase, "ua oli 'o ia penei" (she chanted thus), or a few minor variations, such as "ua oli *mai* 'o ia penei" (she chanted forth this way) or "ua oli *hou* 'o ia penei" (she chanted again like this).

These formulaic lines have a mnemonic function that helps the performer recall and the audience remember the mo'olelo. What is boring to one culture (or one time period) is not in another; the repetitive nature of pīna'i creates its own rhythm and beat, and it is part of Hawaiian verbal artistry.

Pīna'i occur in specific contexts throughout the narrative, such as the action sequences describing kilu. The player chanted a composition and tossed the kilu (usually made from a coconut shell) aimed at a post; points were acquired by hitting the target, and winners claimed a romantic encounter with a designated member of the opposite sex. Lohi'au was a skilled kilu player, as was Hi'iaka, and they were often invited to play when hosted by ali'i along their journey back to Halema'uma'u. In Kapihenui's kilu scenes, for example, the phrase "'A'ohe he pā, ua hala" (There was no strike, it missed) or a variation occurs over and over again to describe game play, as does the phrase "Ho'opuka mai 'o [Hi'iaka/Lohi'au] i kāna mele penei" ([Hi'iaka/Lohi'au] chanted her/his song, like this). Such use of repetition built up to a climax on paper in a way that replicates the excitement of the actual "performance" of the game.

Elsewhere in the mo'olelo, Hi'iaka has a verbal duel of chants with Waihīnano, the wife of Maui chief 'Olepau, battling over his life. The phrases "Hō'ole nō lāua nei ma ke mele penei" (The two of them disagreed [with Hi'iaka] in a song, like this) and "'Iliki hou aku ana nō kēia i ua ma'i o 'Olepau" (She [Hi'iaka] struck 'Olepau again with an illness) are used back and forth multiple times in their verbal sparring.[28]

As Hi'iaka and her companions travel across the pae 'āina, they call out to greet people, or are greeted by them, a common practice in Hawaiian culture. "Kāhea mai kēia ma ke mele penei" (This one [Hi'iaka] called out in a song, like this) is used when Hi'iaka is greeting characters such as Mo'olau or Punaho'olapa; Hau[mea]wahine also uses this phrase to greet Hi'iaka as she and her companions travel through her home at Kawainui in Kailua.[29]

When a closer relationship between the chanter (typically Hi'iaka) and the recipient of the chant is demonstrated, the phrase used is "'Uē aku kēia ma ke mele penei" (This one [Hi'iaka] wept [with heartfelt affection], demonstrating her fondness in a song like this). This phrase is used when Hi'iaka greets her relatives Makapu'u and Mālei on O'ahu, and when she parts company with the hospitable kalo farmer of Kailua, Kanahau. It is also chanted by Lohi'au's spirit, who calls out to Hi'iaka when she arrives on Kaua'i to retrieve him.[30]

Pīna'i introducing and concluding mele in relation to hula performances is still practiced. For example, when 'ōlapa are brought on stage for a performance, a ka'i (entrance chant) is often one of several well-known oli reserved for such a purpose. The ka'i is followed by the featured hula or set of hula. The main hula itself may end with a standardized formulaic phrase such as "He inoa no—" (In the name of [individual]). At the conclusion of the performance, a ho'i (exit chant) transitions the dancers off stage. As with early Greek drama, the audience is familiar with what to expect because of this form of repetition.[31]

Pīna'i or repetition is also prevalent within the paragraph structure of the mo'olelo. One example is found in the passage relating to Lohi'au's death:

> After Lohi'au *died* [make] and a few days passed, his sister came and opened the door of the house, entered inside, and saw what had happened: her brother was *dead*. His sister *wailed* [uē]. The people outside heard her *wailing* and came to see for themselves if Lohi'au was truly *dead*. When they saw that he was *dead*, they all *wailed* over him because of their great *love* [aloha] for him, the hula teacher [Mapuana], the companion who *loved* him [Paoa], great indeed was their *love* for Lohi'au. The best friend in particular was the one who *loved* him the most and was most affected by Lohi'au's *death*. Paoa let go of any sense of shame and stripped himself of his malo, and Paoa *vowed* [ho'ohiki] not to put on a malo until he saw Pele face to face and promised not to forsake his *oath* to eat the eyeball of Pele; that is what he *swore* to do.[32]

This passage clearly illustrates the repetitive quality of the oral tradition, stressing the four main points (italicized): Lohi'au died, he was beloved, everyone grieved, Paoa swore revenge and would not rest until he got it.

Such repetition is an important oral device in performances such as hula, where multiple senses are simultaneously engaged—the color, pattern, and texture of the clothing, the movement of the dance, the sound of the sung or chanted words and musical rhythms, the smell of lei and fresh foliage adornments. The repetition in Kapihenui's mo'olelo reflected oral performance, demonstrating another way oral and written traditions were woven together.

Another example of pīna'i occurs near the end of the mo'olelo, when Lohi'au's friend Kahuaka'iapaoa arrives at the crater to grieve for Lohi'au and enact his vow to get revenge. A series of oli and discussions between Paoa and Pele ensue, referencing Puna. Kaona is also employed in this exchange, Puna referring to both the important chiefly district on the eastern side of Kaua'i where Lohi'au and Paoa are from, and Puna, Hawai'i, home of Pele. It hints at Paoa and Lohi'au's aikāne relationship, as puna is also a freshwater spring, a figurative expression for a spouse or lover.

When Paoa arrives at Kīlauea, he is shocked to see Lohi'au's physical body entombed in lava; he stands at Lohi'au's head and weeps, beginning a series of eight chants in which he grieves for his beloved friend. "'O Kohala makani 'Āpa'apa'a e pā nei" (The 'Āpa'apa'a wind of Kohala is blowing) is the first chant.[33] It names various places on Hawai'i island starting with Kohala, naming the specific geographical features associated with each 'āina, such as the wind ('Āpa'apa'a), heiau (Mo'okini), and the twin hills Pili and Kalāhikiola. It then recalls the rain of Waimea (Kīpu'upu'u) and the mountains belonging to Ka'ū, before concluding with a reference to Puna, "Ike wale oe e ka uahi lehua / O Puna la, ike wale oe" (You are easily known by the gray smoke / Puna there, you are easily known).

Pele chastises Paoa, saying, "That's what Lohi'au gets for not listening."[34] This time, Paoa chants, "Ma Puna kahuli mai ana ka ua makalii noe" (At Puna the fine mist swirls). Pele calls to him again, repeating her warning, and once more, Paoa does not listen. Here he begins chanting the first of six hulihia chants, "Hulihia Kukeeilani, nei akula i ka pili o Hooilo" (Kūke'eilani is overturned, rumbling in the winter season of Ho'oilo).[35]

Pele repeats herself. Paoa then chants "Hulihia ke au ka papa honua o kona moku" (Overturned is the current, the foundation of the island). At this point, the author explains that "the nature of his chant is known," revealing Paoa's desire to die with Lohi'au, his grief is so intense. While Paoa is still inconsolable, Pele calls to Nonomakua (Lonomakua) to light the volcanic fires. Paoa then chants "Hulihia Kilauea po i ka uahi" (Kīlauea is overturned, darkened by smoke), detailing Pele's arrival from

Kahiki. This chant contains five direct references to Puna, concluding with the line "A o ko Puna kuahiwi no ke ahi" (The fire belongs to Puna's mountain). When Paoa finishes chanting, he sees the fires of Pele and Nonomakua rising up to consume him; the crater is darkened with smoke. Paoa chants, "Hulihia ka mauna wela i ke ahi" (The mountain is overturned, scorched by the fire). This hulihia contains five references to Puna, concluding with the lines "Kahuli Kilauea me he ama la / Kunia Puna, mo'a Puna e / Mo'a Puna" (Kīlauea is overturned as if it were a canoe outrigger / Puna is burned, Puna is indeed charred / Puna is scorched).[36] At this point, the narrator interjects:

> A pau no ia mele a ia nei, kulou ihola no keia honi i ka ihu o ke aikane, ku no keia *ue*. A pau aela no ka *ue* ana a ia nei kani no ke oli a ia nei, no ka hu ana mai o ke *aloha* i ka *aina* hanau i ka waiho ae o ke aikane, *aloha* ae keia i ko laua nei *Puna i ka paia a ala i ka hala*. No ke aikane ke *aloha*, *aloha* mai na mea a pau o ka *aina*, me he mea la i ulua mai a akoakoa ke *aloha* i kahi hookahi; oli no keia, penei.[37]

When this chant was finished, Paoa bent down and kissed [honi] Lohi'au on his nose, stood up, and *cried*. When he finished *weeping*, a chant rang out that demonstrated the *love* for the *land* of his birth which had been abandoned by his friend, in which he expressed his *love* for the *Puna* "*fragrant in the walls of hala*" of their homeland. For his friend he *loved*, *love* for everything of the *land*, as if all the *love* was assembled into one place.[38]

Paoa then chants, "Hulihia ke au pee i lalo, nei nakolo i ka honua" (Churning is the current hidden below, in the trembling earth). There are several more references to Puna within the chant, which concludes with the lines "Haohia ke ['ā] i kai o Puna e / No Puna au, no ka aina aloha" (The fire burns with great force to the sea of Puna / I am from Puna, the beloved land)."[39] The scene continues:

> When this chant of Kahuaka'iapaoa was finished, he *wept* for his friend [Lohi'au] with words of *love* for him, "*Puna is beloved* indeed, the *land of fragrance*, the *land* where sweet *fragrance* dwells, the two of us will stay in our *Puna*, we two will see Hulā'ia [River], we two will see the troubled [lumaluma'i] waters of our *land*, we two will see our surf Kalehuawehe." He turned his face and looked *inland* at the *lehua blossoms* of

Kawaikini, the *lehua blossoms* of Wai'ale'ale, at the *hala* nibbled at with the teeth, the *hala* eaten by the kīna'u eel. "The cold is calm in the *uplands, crushed down* are the *hau* blossoms, and the *ko'olau blossoms*, crushed down by the water bubbling down to the sea at Wailua. Greetings to the two swirling waters of our *land* there at Makaweli."

While Kahuaka'iapaoa was speaking like that, Pele replied, "You should give your *love* to *Puna*. You are in *Puna* and know the *fragrance*, and know the *scent* of this *Puna* here; *love* to *Puna*."

At these words of Pele, Hi'iakaikapoliopele spoke. "Your *land* is indeed *Puna*, but it is not the *Puna* of their *land*, perhaps your *Puna* is stormy ['ino] because of you, their *Puna* is beautiful, *Puna* in the *fragrant walls of hala*; perhaps it is of their *Puna* [on Kaua'i] that these words are said, it is not said on behalf of your stormy land [Puna, Hawai'i]."[40]

Paoa then chants the last hulihia, concluding the mo'olelo, "Hulihia ke au nee i lalo i Akea" (Overturned is the current creeping below [the plains of Wākea]).[41]

This example, which incorporates eight mele, six of which are signature chants specifically associated with the Pele and Hi'iaka mo'olelo, is most illustrative of how the repetition of words, phrases, images, and sounds (assonance) emphasizes the emotional and performative aspect of the mo'olelo.

Other ways that Kapihenui's text demonstrates its closeness to the oral tradition is the lack of section titles, titles, or captions for chants, or numbering chants or lines in chants, which are utilized in later, more literary narratives.

Weaving Performance and Literature

The reproduction of oral meiwi such as mele, oli, and hula in print was quite daring for the newly emerging literature in the Hawaiian nationalist press, considering that the public performance of hula had recently been banned. Hula would not be publicly reclaimed for another twenty years with Mō'ī Kalākaua's coronation ceremonies in 1883.[42]

The performance of mele holds a key place in the action of Kapihenui's narrative, superseding other aspects of more developed written literature such as character development and internal conflict/dialogue. One way this occurs is through the minimization of prose narrative between episodes. Rather than provide the reading audience with lengthy paragraphs of exposition between hula or mele "performances," the bulk of Kapihenui's text is poetic, either chanted as oli, sung as mele, recited as pule, or danced as hula. One example is when Hiʻiaka, Wahineʻōmaʻo, and Pāʻūopalaʻe are trying to cross the bridge at the Wailuku River in Hilo en route to Kauaʻi; Kapihenui is the only writer who provides the extensive and exciting scene. The bridge is guarded by two moʻo relatives of Hiʻiaka, Piliamoʻo and Nohoamoʻo.[43] The moʻo demand "payment" of all who use the bridge to cross the deep and dangerous river. Hiʻiaka performs a series of "Kāhulihuli" chants seeking permission to cross the bridge without paying a toll. Each time, the moʻo refuse. She chants again, asking for a different item:

> The eyes of the people—the men, the women, and the children—watched Hiʻiakaikapoliopele. . . . [She] approached the crowd of people assembled there. In those days, travelers on that road were required to pay a toll to cross the bridge and continue on their way. Food, fish, kapa, malo, sugarcane, salt, and other miscellaneous things were the price of passage across the bridge. Thereafter the people could continue along the road.
>
> Hiʻiakaikapoliopele called out to the heads of the road in this chant:
>
> Kāhulihuli ē!
> Ka papa o Wailuku,
> Kahuli ʻo ʻĀpua,
> Haʻa mai ʻo Maukele,
> He ʻole Kekaha,
> Kūʻai ʻai ē,
> Hō mai ka ʻai,
> Hō mai hoʻi ka ʻai ē,
> I ʻaina aku hoʻi ē.
>
> Unstable indeed
> The bridge of Wailuku
> ʻĀpua is overturned
> Maukele is humbled
> Kekaha is lacking
> Bargaining for food
> Give us food
> Please give us food
> So we may eat.

When she was finished chanting, the two mo'o replied, "Hah! We won't give you anything—you are supposed to give us something! If you travel on our road, we will not help you unless you do."

So Hi'iaka made another request, this time asking for fish, in this chant:

> Kāhulihuli ē,
> Ka papa o Wailuku,
> He 'ole Kekaha,
> Kū'ai i'a ē,
> Hō mai ka i'a ā,
> Hō mai ana ho'i ka i'a,
> I 'aina aku ho'i ē.

> Unstable indeed
> The bridge of Wailuku
> Kekaha is lacking
> The price is fish
> Grant us fish
> Please grant us fish
> So we may eat.

When her chant was finished, they both denied her request again, just as they had done before. So she asked again in song, like this:

> Kāhulihuli ē,
> Ka papa o Wailuku,
> He 'ole Kekaha,
> Kū'ai pa'akai ē,
> Hō mai ana ho'i ka pa'akai,
> I 'aina aku ho'i ē.

> Unstable indeed
> The bridge of Wailuku
> Kekaha is lacking
> The price is sea salt
> Grant us sea salt
> So we may eat.

The two mo'o denied Hi'iaka's request, just as they had done before. Then they said wickedly, "The pathway will not be had by you! You are supposed to pay the two of us! Then you can travel on our road." So Hi'iaka chanted another request, like this:

> Kāhulihuli ē,
> Ka papa o Wailuku,
> He 'ole Kekaha kū'ai kō,
> He 'ole Kekaha,
> Kū'ai kō ē,
> Hō mai ke kō,
> I 'aina a'e ho'i ē.

> Unstable indeed
> The bridge of Wailuku
> Kekaha is lacking; we barter for sugar
> Kekaha is lacking
> The price is sugar
> Grant us sugar
> So we may eat.

Because they both denied her request again, Hi'iaka asked once more, chanting like this:

> Kāhulihuli ē,
> Ka papa o Wailuku,
> He 'ole Kekaha,
> Kū'ai kapa ē,
> Hō mai ke kapa,
> I 'a'ahu 'ia aku ho'i ē.

> Unstable indeed
> The bridge of Wailuku
> Kekaha is lacking
> The price is kapa cloth
> Grant us kapa cloth
> So we may be clothed.

The two of them denied her request just as they did before. So Hi'iaka asked again, chanting like this:

> Kāhulihuli ē,
> Ka papa o Wailuku,

He ʻole Kekaha,
Kūʻai wai ē,
Hō mai hoʻi ka wai,
Hō mai hoʻi ka wai ē,
I inu ʻia aku hoʻi ē.

Unstable indeed
The bridge of Wailuku
Kekaha is lacking
The price is freshwater
Grant us freshwater
Please grant us freshwater
So we may drink.

When her chant was completed, Hiʻiakaikapoliopele said to the people there, "Look at the price they charge the people traveling to and fro on the road." One of them replied, "Ah! If perhaps you ask them and they are human, they will give it. But they will deny the request if they are spirits, they will not heed you."[44]

Pīnaʻi and performance of oli are combined in this passage, demonstrating how the performative aspect of oral tradition highlights the poetic text. In this section of the moʻolelo, the prose paragraphs are minimal and function as transitional links connecting one oli to the next, reminiscent of the construction of a lei: the pua (blossoms) are strung together on a cord, which binds them together sequentially. Likewise, the prose paragraphs function as a string that link the oli together as a "lei mele" (lei of poetry).

This particular grouping of oli is similarly constructed. Each opens with the same lines, "Kāhulihuli ē / Ka papa o Wailuku." The final three lines vary slightly, with the same basic idea expressed, "Hō mai [mea (noun)] / Hō mai [mea] ē / I [verb] aku hoʻi ē [Grant me (noun) / Grant me (noun) / So I may (verb related to noun)]." The middle lines heighten the expectation, reinforced through the repetition of the request (hō mai); "hoʻi" (indeed), an emphatic term, adds more weight to the original request. This prescribed configuration is reminiscent of the Kumulipo, where individual plants and animals are named in order of their birth, inserted into a formulaic line structure, as discussed in mokuna 1. As Hiʻiaka's series of oli progress, the addition of the emphatic "hoʻi" builds tension in the scene and anticipation in the audience, who see the destruction of the insolent moʻo as not only inevitable, but justified (pono).

This exchange also exemplifies wordplay, important in oral tradition and valued in Hawaiian poetics as ho'opāpā, a contest of wits that often depends on such verbal dexterity. In this example, there is a particular relationship to the wahi pana, or renowned places named in the mo'olelo. In the series of oli, four are mentioned: Wailuku, 'Āpua, Maukele, and Kekaha. The first, Wailuku, is the river on the edge of Hilo where this scene is located. The name literally means "water of destruction." Wailuku is the largest river in the Hilo area and is quite treacherous, prone to frequent flash floods; it is one of two main rivers that open into Hilo Bay. The kaona of the name Wailuku, however, is the pending destruction of the mo'o who do not recognize Hi'iaka's godly mana and who are rude to her, offering no hospitality or concessions. As the climax of the scene builds and the mo'o are ultimately destroyed, their demise is justified, foreshadowed by the continually referenced image of the unstable path over the highly destructive waters of Wailuku.

The next two place names, 'Āpua and Maukele, are typically paired as 'ēko'a. They correspond with each other in other parts of Kapihenui's mo'olelo and balance each other in an 'ōlelo no'eau, "Kahuli 'o 'Āpua, ha'a mai 'o Maukele" ('Āpua was overturned, Maukele is humbled).[45] 'Āpua (fish trap or basket) is a land division located in the Puna district on the island of Hawai'i; a village by the same name in the area was destroyed by a tsunami in 1868.[46] 'Āpua Point is the boundary marker between the districts of Puna and Ka'ū. 'Āpua is also referenced in other mele in the mo'olelo. Overall, there are seven mele found in different versions of the mo'olelo that include 'Āpua as a place named within oli, including two hulihia chants, "Hulihia ka mauna, wela i ke ahi" (The mountain is overturned, hot in the fire) and "Hulihia Kīlauea po i ka uahi" (Kīlauea is overturned, black as night in the smoke).[47] The third significant oli is "'O Pele lā ko'u akua" (Pele is my god).[48] The kaona of the name 'Āpua refers to the insolent nature of the mo'o, as 'āpua means "disloyal, disobedient, rebellious; such a person."[49] Hi'iaka's series of oli allude to the disobedient and rebellious demeanor of the mo'o toward her, again foreshadowing their destruction as they refuse to comply with her requests.

Both Maukele and 'Āpua are land areas in Waipi'o, Hawai'i, Maukele being a "wet mountain area" and 'Āpua being a "land division."[50] Maukele is also a "place name in Puna" alternately known as Ma'ukele, a generic name for a rainforest.[51] The pairing of the names is not coincidental, as both appear in the same two areas of the same island, albeit on opposite sides. Waipi'o is one of the farthest points on the northernmost side of the island along the Hāmākua coast, while Puna-Ka'ū is farther south, closest to the center of Pele's domain at the volcano. Perhaps this is

Wailuku River, Hilo, Hawai'i, on a relatively calm day. This is where Hi'iaka battles the mo'o Piliamo'o and Nohoamo'o, who refuse to allow Hi'iaka passage across the bridge they guard unless she pays a toll. Hi'iaka vanquishes the mo'o, allowing safe passage for all ever after. Photograph by author, 2009.

referencing a sense of 'ēko'a or pono, balance extending from one end of the island to the other (north–south).

The final place name in the chant, Kekaha (the strand), is found in a number of sources and described as an area of Kona 'Ākau (North Kona) that extends "from Keahuolu to Pu'u Anahulu characterized by recent lava flows and little precipitation."[52] An 'ōlelo no'eau refers to this area as "ka 'āina kaha" (the kaha lands).[53] Kamakau notes that Kamehameha had land here, although it was most known as lands held by the kahuna class.[54] Kekaha literally means "the place." Kaha also connotes "a hot, dry shore" and "to desolate, plunder; proud, haughty."[55] Through the kaona or metaphorical wordplay with the use of Hawai'i island place names that have alternate and applicable meanings—wailuku (utter devastation), 'āpua (disobedient), maukele (allusion to drowning or flight), and kekaha (haughty)—Hi'iaka's warning to the mo'o that their behavior is inappropriate is stressed, and their pending demise is thus imminent. There is a sense of 'ēko'a and pono in the use of the four Hawai'i island place names: Kekaha (Kona) is on the opposite (west) end of the island from Wailuku (Hilo, east side), while 'Āpua and Maukele reference both north (Waipi'o) and south (Puna/Kaʻū), as well as the wet rainforest (Maʻukele, Waipiʻo area) and dry regions (rocky Puna coast, Kaʻū desert) simultaneously. Thus paired, the references can be interpreted as Hiʻiaka boasting of her ability and right to assert her female, godly mana from one end of the island to the other. So thoroughly forewarned, Hiʻiakaʻs destruction of the moʻo who exhibit such blatant stupidity in their rebellious and insolent attitude toward her is that much more satisfying.

Kimura discusses how the philosophy of word power culminates in hoʻopāpā where "poetic references, partial homonyms, and vocabulary knowledge are used in chant form between two contestants to increase their individual powers and decrease the powers of the opponent. The loser of such a contest can theoretically submit his life to the winner . . . this Hawaiian use of the examination of words to strengthen a thought is often misinterpreted by Westerners who think that the description of the word itself is the point rather than how the word is used to make a point [or] give a feeling."[56]

The reliance on chant is expected within oral tradition because it is performative. In "How Legends Were Taught," Pukui states that moʻolelo were often "partly told and partly chanted," with specific genres of chant associated with specific moʻolelo, such as the "kau" chants in Pele and Hiʻiaka.[57] Kau are "sacred chants" performed by Hiʻiaka, her "affectionate greeting to persons, hills, and landmarks," a chant used in making a sacrifice to an akua, and a style of chant.[58] Pukuiʻs insights into the oration of traditional moʻolelo support the performative aspect of early print versions of moʻolelo kuʻuna, such as Kapihenuiʻs Pele and Hiʻiaka, as "no long legend was complete without the recitation of chants."[59] Kimura concurs, concluding that "Hawaiian chants are very long and can contain hundreds of lines. There are also sagas [i.e., Pele and Hiʻiaka] with chanted dialogues . . . and of course many songs."[60]

Lele ana Kaʻena i ka Mālie (Kaʻena Soars Like a Bird in the Calm)

It is 1996 and I am sitting in the third row of the Blaisdell Concert Hall in Honolulu, excited with anticipation. Hiloʻs Hālau o Kekuhi is about to premiere *Holo Mai Pele*, a live stage performance of hula from the Pele and Hiʻiaka moʻolelo. While hula dedicated to these sister deities are well-known and often part of the hula repertoire of many hālau, this is the first time in modern memory the hula will be performed in a narrative sequence. The production is divided into five sets of hula performances. It includes two important non-hula scenes from the moʻolelo—Hiʻiakaʻs revival of Lohiʻau from the dead, and a playful, sexually charged kilu game at the court of Pele'ula on O'ahu. A narrator takes the stage between each scene, offering a short synopsis of what the audience is about to see. Once the lights are dimmed, a hush descends over the crowd. The red velvet curtains are drawn back to reveal the large dark stage. In a moment, the authoritative resonance of several pahu drums resounds, and the stage comes to life in a whirlwind of rhythmic hula beats. As kumu Pualani Kanaka'ole Kanahele and Nalani Kanaka'ole Zane chant, the 'ōlapa move forcefully, gracefully across the stage with precise hula steps and body movements; the intense reds and yellows of pā'ū and malo, the vivid greens of palapalai fern braided into lei adornments dip and spin in a mesmerizing performance of Pele and Hi'iaka's mo'olelo brought to life.

This live performance, like the DVD production it inspired, is reminiscent of what nineteenth-century audiences might have experienced at Kalākaua's coronation in 1883, which featured hula Pele. It suggested what hula performance in traditional times might have looked like as well—the pahu drums, the chanting, the hula steps, the choreography, the colors and adornments, all traditional. It also suggested Kapihenui's written mo'olelo—a focus on performance, with minimal exposition. It is the first time a modern audience has experienced such an enactment.

The chant "Lele ana o Ka'ena" evokes two things at once: on the one hand, Hi'iaka praises the beauty of the Ka'ena area, the opening line comparing Ka'ena point stretched out in the sea, pointing to the island of Kaua'i, to a graceful 'ua'u, a seabird that nests in its cliffs, in flight, gliding across the sky. On the other hand, Hi'iaka is asking her kūpunakāne (grandfather) Pōhakuokaua'i (Rock of Kaua'i) for a canoe to sail to Kaua'i in her quest to fetch Lohi'au, suggesting in this chant that she would like to "lele" (fly, leap, jump).

"Kūnihi Ka'ena holo i ka mālie" suggests the same kind of imagery—Ka'ena gliding in calm seas. But utilizing kaona, it, too, contains two simultaneous lines of thought. Vertical imagery (kūnihi, steep standing) is embedded into the same line, at the same location, where horizontal imagery (holo i ka mālie) is also used. Lele implies vertical movement, holo implies horizontal movement, such as canoe sailing from Kahiki to Hawai'i ("Mai Kahiki mai ka wahine 'o Pele," "Holo mai Pele"), or from Ka'ena to Kaua'i. Both are integral to the first wā (2–3) of the Kumulipo, where fish are born to "holo" in the sea and birds to "lele" overhead, both able to traverse ocean and sky, navigating from island to island without human aid or interference, as Pele mā also travel.

How might these ideas of makawalu apply to Indigenous literary criticism? How does it inform a Hawaiian literary criticism of Pele and Hi'iaka mo'olelo? First, an 'Ōiwi intellectual tradition comes mai ka pō mai, mai nā kūpuna mai, mai ka waha mai. It is old and lengthy, oral and written. It is all these things and more woven together in a way that continues to inform us, providing a bridge between the past and the present, a foundation for analysis and interpretation. It can represent specific 'āina and genealogies associated with that 'āina. Thus, it invites us to approach it a way that doesn't privilege one mode over another, or look for a singular, "authoritative" or master narrative.

Second, Pele and Hi'iaka mo'olelo represent an 'Ōiwi intellectual tradition because they are mai ka pō mai, mai nā kūpuna mai. They are oral and written, performed and read. At each level—epic mo'olelo, poetic chant or hula text, proverb, vocabulary word, or metaphoric image—it conveys Kanaka Maoli culture, ethics, values, and aesthetics that are recorded in myriad ways within the mo'olelo. When viewed across traditions, the breadth of diversity and depth of knowledge contained within them are astounding.

Writing about Pele and Hi'iaka mo'olelo as an Indigenous intellectual tradition differs from how it is represented in other disciplines (or in tourist rhetoric) because such an approach takes into consideration cultural concepts that inform the mo'olelo. Recognition of an intellectual tradition is first and foremost. The mo'olelo have a genealogy; they have a relationship to each other, to the social and historical contexts in which they were created, performed, and transformed from oral to written and back again. They embody history and aesthetics, and contain many values and lessons still relevant for Kanaka Maoli and others today, values of aloha and mālama 'āina, the importance of caring for the land because it is family, because it is sacred, because it is life, not just because "going green" is in vogue.

What kind of kuleana did Kapihenui have to "translate" this treasured mo'olelo from oral tradition to the printed page? We may never know who Kapihenui was, and how that knowledge of Kapihenui's personal background could shape the way this mo'olelo is understood. Some Christian-minded Hawaiians of the time were upset at the publication of mo'olelo ku'una in general, viewing it as a step backward for the Lāhui. But Kapihenui and others felt differently, and established mo'olelo ku'una in writing as a national literature, using the newspapers as a publicly available repository of cultural and traditional knowledge. Whoever Kapihenui was, he or she certainly felt kuleana to publish this mo'olelo. Kapihenui's publication of the mo'olelo was supported. In searching through *Ka Hoku o ka Pakipika* and other newspapers in print at the time, it is clear that Kanaka (including Kapihenui) were concerned that the mo'olelo was being edited down and chants cut short, and letters to the editor encouraged them to publish the mele in their entirety.[61]

What did it mean to take an oral tradition to writing? In doing so, how can it be evaluated as literature? Transitioning an oral tradition such as Pele and Hi'iaka to a literary one allowed more people to access the mo'olelo. The newspapers became repositories of knowledge that people collected and thus treasured, which allowed for the transmission of information across generations, for the sharing (and debating) of intellectual and cultural knowledge. It was also a way to enjoy hula and cultural performance (kilu, nane, ho'opāpā) at a time when they had fallen out of practice (e.g., kilu), or were outlawed and otherwise suppressed by law (e.g., hula).

What kuleana does the mo'olelo itself carry as a kahua for subsequent publications? We will probably never know what Kapihenui thought about the possible longevity of his or her Pele and Hi'iaka mo'olelo, as he or she never did publicly state, as later writers did, that intention. However, it is certain that agreeing to publish the mo'olelo meant a desire to share, and thus perpetuate and preserve it. In Hawaiian culture, kuleana is not just taken, it is given. As the first (hiapo) text, it provides a foundation for later mo'olelo, from those published in the 1880s until today. Later writers were certainly aware of it and referred to it. It provides an early glimpse into the tradition, as well as into a way of understanding the orality of it.

For the Kanaka Maoli writers and editors associated with the Hawaiian-language newspapers, the establishment and continuity of a strong Indigenous literary nationalism supported and enhanced political endeavors and community activism, while the collection of "folklore" by haole writers forwarded the goals of settler colonialism.

Hi'iaka's mele concludes, "O ka'u wale ihola nō ia / 'o ka leo ē" (This is all I have to offer, my voice). Hi'iaka humbly states that her voice is no gift, which could metaphorically be read as oral traditions having no validity, or no mana. But is that what she is *really* saying? Kanaka Maoli ethics demands ha'aha'a, humility, a highly desirable quality and mark of civil behavior. By stating that her leo is all she can give, she is framing her chant within the cultural parameter of ha'aha'a. In actuality, oli—as performed poetry—is one of the highest gifts one could offer. First, because it contains words, which have the power of life and death (i ka 'ōlelo ke ola, i ka 'ōlelo ka make). But also in their performance, hā, breath, the essence of life, is required, carrying her mana in its delivery. Therefore, through the verbalized performance of poetry, Hi'iaka is offering the greatest gift she has, her own life spirit.

Her understanding of cultural protocol and recognition of the 'āina is what allows her safe and friendly passage along the Wai'anae lands on foot. In some mo'olelo she is well hosted by the ali'i wahine (chiefly women) Mailelauli'i, Ko'iahi, and Halakaipo. They engage in kilu and help a male chief from Moloka'i solve a riddle. Hi'iaka destroys the dangerous rock kupua at Kīlauea, a small cove along the rocky shores of Keawa'ula.

Today, ka po'e aloha 'āina continually fight the U.S. military, which has controlled Mākua valley for live-fire training for decades. The U.S. Air Force runs a satellite tracking station above Ka'ena, and access to the mountain is strictly controlled. Pu'uloa, where Lohi'au and Wahine'ōma'o waited for Hi'iaka, is better known to the world as Pearl Harbor, an Environmental Protection Agency Superfund site spanning twelve thousand acres of land and water.[62] As the war in Afghanistan winds down, the United States is shifting its focus to the Asia–Pacific region, the late Hawai'i Senator Dan Inouye announcing in 2012 an increase in U.S. military forces in Hawai'i, in part because Okinawa, another indigenous homeland in the Pacific, has had enough. As documented in Anne Keala Kelly's *Noho Hewa: The Wrongful Occupation of Hawai'i*, despite assurances of ecological sensitivity, the military training in Hawai'i continues to destroy the 'āina and desecrate wahi kapu, in Mākua and elsewhere. The state of Hawai'i continues to evict homeless camps along the Wai'anae coast Hi'iaka lovingly addressed in her mele. The majority of these homeless are Native Hawaiians. 'O ka leo wale ē—it is "just" a voice. Like Hi'iaka, perhaps all ka po'e aloha 'āina have to fight with is a voice. But it is one that speaks with knowledge and aloha for our 'āina, one that refuses to remain silent.

Ke Lei maila ʻo Kaʻula i ke Kai ē
(Kaʻula Is Wreathed by the Sea):
Pele and Hiʻiaka Moʻolelo and
Kanaka Maoli Culture

Ke lei maila 'o Ka'ula i ke kai ē
Ke mālamalama 'o Ni'ihau ua mālie
A mālie pā ka Inuwai lā
Ke inu maila nā hala o Naue i ke kai
No Naue ka hala, no Puna ka wahine
No ka lua nō i Kīlauea.

'O Kalalau pali 'a'ala ho'i
Ke ako 'ia a'ela e ka wahine
'A'ala ka pali i ka laua'e
'O Honopū i Waialoha
Aloha 'oe lā ē.'

Ka'ula is wreathed by the sea
Ni'ihau glows in the calm
The Inuwai breeze gently blows
The hala groves of Naue drink in the sea
The hala is from Naue, the woman is from Puna
From the very crater of Kīlauea.

Kalalau is indeed a fragrant cliff
Plucked by the woman [Hi'iaka]
The cliffs are fragrant in laua'e
Honopū at Waialoha
Greetings with affection to you.

IT IS SUMMER 1994 AND I AM HOME on Kaua'i. My friend Puna is visiting from Hawai'i island, and we decide to drive to Hā'ena at the end of road on Kaua'i's north shore. We will hike the short distance to Ke Ahu a Laka (the altar of Laka), the hula pā at Kē'ē on the north side of Makana (gift), the prominent mountain of Hā'ena marketed to the world as "Bali Hai," a made-up name popularized globally from the 1958 American movie *South Pacific*.[2] As a wahi pana, Makana signifies Lohi'au's home, where the pahu drumbeats lured Pele's spirit across the pae 'āina to where she met and fell in love with him.

We stop near the freshwater-filled "wet cave" of Waiakapala'e (lace fern water) to pick the sweet-smelling laua'e fern for which Makana is famous. It is one of three caves in the area associated with Pele's coming to Hawai'i from Kahiki, landing on Kaua'i in search of a suitable volcanic home; the other two are the "dry caves" of Maniniholo (swimming manini fish) and Waikanaloa (Kanaloa's water), the other "wet" cave nearby.[3]

We will haku lei as a ho'okupu, a traditional offering, a simple gesture of our aloha for this 'āina; in Hawaiian culture, one never arrives empty-handed. At the end of the road we enter the crowded parking area of Hā'ena State Park, then pick our way through the throngs of tourists who flock here to snorkel in the picturesque bay or hike the rugged Kalalau trail. We sit on the grass near the base of the steep slope that ascends to the hula pā to haku our lei laua'e. Curious tourists point at us and whisper, snapping pictures without asking. They try to be unobtrusive, but we know they are there. This time, we just ignore them. We don't always mind answering questions and educating others, but sometimes it is tiring. For Kanaka Maoli in Hawai'i, and perhaps for Indigenous people everywhere, even when we aren't "performing" on stage, every cultural act, no matter how simple, can feel like a show, especially when tourists are acculturated to think everything we do is for their benefit, and our cultural value of aloha (an exchange of love, affection, compassion) is a marketing tool of the Hawai'i tourism industry.

Our lei complete, we make our way slowly up the steep hill, climbing over and around massive boulders along the way. At the top of the hillside we stop to catch our breath and take in the view—the lichen-adorned rocks show their age, the lofty heights of Makana's perpendicular cliffs soar high above. The murmuring waves roll across the turquoise-blue seas stretched out below. We wait several minutes as two tourists finish taking pictures and leave. We are alone at this special place and begin our oli, "Ke lei maila 'o Ka'ula i ke kai ē . . ."

When we are done, we place our lei on a large pōhaku (rock) along the

Kē'ē, the pā hula where Pele first encounters Lohi'au at Hā'ena, Kaua'i. Hālau hula Keali'ika'apunihinua Ke'ena a'o Hula performs a hula, utilizing the hula pā as it was intended. Photograph by Manuwai Peters, 1990.

base of the cliff where other lei ho'okupu rustle in the light breeze. There are a few baseball-sized pōhaku wrapped in ti leaf as well, sarcastically dubbed by some locals "tourist laulau." I quietly dismantle these faked offerings, encouraged by New Age spiritual practices and the tourist industry, institutions of settler colonialism that mock Hawaiian cultural practice and desecrate our 'āina.

It would be easy to just blame tourists for such disrespect, but it isn't that simple. Soon a family arrives with three large dogs that they allow to run wild across this wahi kapu. The family plops a plastic grocery bag on another pōhaku and begin unpacking their meal. A paper napkin is snatched away in the breeze, unnoticed by them. The dogs mark "their" territory. It would be simple if they were the only ones who are careless. But there are discarded beer bottles and soda cans strewn along the hillside, ribbons of decaying plastic bags stuck in the foliage. All these we pick up to properly dispose of. This is one consequence when culturally significant sites are enfolded into government-run park systems created through settler colonialism. Indigenous sacred sites become picnic spots, a vantage point to snap souvenir photos, to drink a beer and toast the sunset; aloha or mālama 'āina practices respecting the sanctity of the land are not taught, learned, or valued in the daily discourse and practice of settler colonialism or its institutions.

We make our way down to the beach and jump into the cool, cleansing salt water. The later afternoon sun turns the water and imposing cliffs golden. From here the sheer fluted cliffs of the Nāpali coast are visible. Puna begins to sing, "'O Kalalau pali 'a'ala . . ." and I join in. Even though Kalalau is eleven miles down the coast, we imagine we can see it from here. We imagine what it was like living here in Lohi'au's time, how exciting the hula performances were, what the resonant tones of pahu drums echoing off the sheer volcanic cliffs of Hā'ena sounded like.

A silver sedan pulls up by the lifeguard stand, and three young women get out. They are tourists. One whips off her sundress, revealing her skimpy bikini beneath, shaking her long blonde hair free from a ponytail. "Oh geez . . . ," I groan under my breath. "What?" Puna says. "Watch," I reply. The tourist begins a slow run down the sloped beach to the water, Pamela Anderson–*Baywatch* style; I already know what's coming, I've seen this many times before. As she reaches the shoreline, her bare foot hits the sea-slicked sandstone at the water's edge and she slips quickly, scraping her backside on the hardened sand. Puna and I turn away and watch Kānehoalani's giant sun orb body slip into the sea; we suppress a giggle. Our impulse to laugh is because we witness this all the time—Hawai'i is marketed as a paradise and playground, a completely safe and benign place free of danger. Respect for the 'āina is nonexistent in the discourse of tourism. Far too often there are deadly consequences. We understand aloha 'āina, a knowledge of and respect for our 'āina. 'Ike 'āina, aloha 'āina, mālama 'āina—observe the environment before engaging with it no matter where we go, respect the land and it will take care of you.

'Ike 'Āina (Learning from the Land)

In *Decolonizing Methodologies*, Linda Tuhiwai Smith (Māori) discusses the difference between Native and Western discourse, writing, "Indigenous peoples across the world have other stories to tell which not only question the assumed nature of those [Western] ideals and the practices that they generate, but also serve to tell an alternative story."[4]

The Pele and Hi'iaka mo'olelo published between 1860 and 1928 were an alternative story to Amer-European colonialism. During this period Kanaka Maoli continued to assert counter-narratives to the colonial discourse that insisted they were dying, noble, but primitive savages with silly or superstitious worldviews and cultural practices that did not belong in the "modern" world. Their insistence in affirming Hawaiian intellectual traditions and cultural practices contained in mo'olelo ku'una like Pele and Hi'iaka throughout such a tumultuous period of political and social upheaval was one strategy of what the Mō'ī Kalākaua called Ho'oulu Lāhui, increasing, perpetuating, invigorating the Hawaiian people, and by extension, the nation. After the overthrow of the Hawaiian kingdom in 1893, it became a political strategy supporting the aloha 'āina movement and restoration of political independence, a movement that continues today.

'Ōiwi writers and editors of that time were concerned with the erosion of Hawaiian language and cultural knowledge overall, and openly stated these as reasons for publishing mo'olelo, to keep such knowledge alive for the purpose of invigorating the Lāhui. The consequences of such ignorance—and revitalization—are visible every day.

This chapter focuses on selected themes in the mo'olelo that exemplify important skills, practices, and cultural values that resonate throughout it, the cultural knowledge 'Ōiwi writers and editors were so concerned about losing under the pressures of colonization. These include:

+ adeptness and skill ('ike, 'a'apo, 'eleu, akamai)
+ he'e nalu or surfing (recreation, competition, healing)
+ hula and kilu (enjoyment, ritual, expression, skill)
+ oli and mele
+ ho'okipa (hospitality) and mea 'ai (food; including preparation, kānāwai, ritual, abundance, type)

These cultural values and practices are found throughout other mo'olelo ku'una. Read intertextually across the mo'olelo, they form the basis of early Hawaiian literary nationalism that refused to accept Western settler discourse of Hawaiian identity as inferior, with no intellectual history or value, and 'Ōiwi cultural practices and knowledge as inferior to Western ones.

Nā Kāhua 'Ike a Mākau (Foundations of Knowledge and Skills)

Knowledge and intelligence ('ike) were highly valued within traditional Hawaiian culture, and reflected within the Pele and Hi'iaka mo'olelo in a variety of ways. 'Ike (knowledge, recognition), 'a'apo (to learn or grasp quickly), 'eleu (alert, nimble, quick, dexterous, agile, prompt), akamai (clever, expert, skill, wit), and maka'ala (alert, vigilant) are all rather synonymous and are emphasized again and again as valuable and attractive attributes. This is demonstrated in numerous ways throughout the mo'olelo. One way is in the appreciation for someone's skill, such as when Pele and Hi'iaka admire Lohi'au's expertise in hula.

The valuing of 'ike is also demonstrated in the appreciation for people who exhibit quick thinking without having to be told what to do or how to act. The following example demonstrates both the reciprocal nature of generosity and Wahine'ōma'o's quick grasp ('eleu) of the situation:

> They met a man returning from Hilo loaded with fish and Hiiaka asked if he couldn't spare them some, to which he quickly answered[,] "Why not, when I have so much?" and he gave them four. All these were given to the old woman by the goddess [Hi'iaka] on the condition that she ate one whole fish there and then, throwing away or leaving no edible portion. This she did, and was further cautioned to do the same when she ate the remaining fish and was sent back rejoicing. This was one of Hiiaka's kanawais [nā kānāwai, or rules of etiquette] and all her devotees were supposed to always do so. . . . By this time Wahineomao had become aware of the supernatural character of her companions, but she was a model friend and asked no embarrassing questions.[5]

In discussing the particular cultural details within the Pele and Hi'iaka mo'olelo, of particular note is "A Hawaiian Legend by a Hawaiian Native," published in English in the settler newspaper *Pacific Commercial Advertiser* in 1883 by "Kaili," a pen name for Maoli writer Emma Ka'ilikapuolono Metcalf Beckley Nakuina (1847–1929). Nakuina is the only identifiable writer who was a woman, and the only 'Ōiwi writer who was publishing extensively in English at the time. Nakuina was the daughter of American businessman Theophilus Metcalf and Ka'ilikapuolono of Kūkaniloko, O'ahu, an ali'i woman of O'ahu and Hawai'i lineages. In writing about Nakuina and her collection of mo'olelo, *Hawaii: Its People, Their Legends*, Cristina Bacchilega notes that Nakuina was well educated, attending Sacred Hearts Academy and Punahou School in Honolulu, and Mills Seminary in California. Nakuina "is reported to have been fluent in English, Hawaiian, French and German," and while her "education was bicultural, and her social standing high in both Euro-American and Hawaiian society," she strongly identified with her Hawaiian background.[6]

It may or may not be important to consider that the description of cultural etiquette and social standing within the mo'olelo is being explained by a woman descended from chiefly rank herself. But it is interesting to consider, who was Nakuina's audience? When the mo'olelo was published, Hawai'i was still under kingdom rule, and Hawaiian was the dominant language of the populace. Did Nakuina write in English

Emma Ka'ili Metcalf Beckley Nakuina, who wrote under the pen name "Kaili," was the only Kanaka Maoli to publish a Pele and Hi'iaka mo'olelo in English during the kingdom period. Date and photographer unknown. Courtesy of Bishop Museum Archives.

because she envisioned her audience as other Kanaka Maoli of higher social status, who were bi- or multilingual like her? Or was her interest in describing such important cultural protocols designed to educate haole settlers, who continued to denigrate Kanaka Maoli as uncivilized and unfit to rule their own country? It is difficult to know exactly what Nakuina was thinking at the time, but she offers insights into the mo'olelo that add important details and nuances to the larger body of Pele and Hi'iaka mo'olelo.

This insight is evident later in the mo'olelo, when Hi'iaka admires Wahine'ōma'o's observance of her kānāwai to eat a fish "from head to tail." Hi'iaka is pleased she does not need to explain the kānāwai to Wahine'ōma'o; she is 'eleu enough to understand and follow it without being told. She learns through observing Hi'iaka's behavior and instruction to others: "Hiiaka watched her when eating and saw that she ate the whole fish up, and she was more pleased than ever with her friend, who, she was convinced, was entirely devoted to her. Wahineomao had observed Hiiaka's commands to the old woman to eat the fish all up, and without asking the reason had applied the command to herself."[7] These episodes within the mo'olelo dispel the colonial, post-missionary rhetoric of Kanaka being stupid, lazy, and inept.

'Ike is knowledge, and also recognition—alertness is important and is emphasized in different ways. Throughout the mo'olelo, those who exhibit rude, lazy, or inept behavior (such as the mo'o Piliamo'o and Nohoamo'o of the Wailuku River in Hilo) are punished for their unsavory behavior, demonstrating little tolerance for such unacceptable actions.

He'e Nalu (Surfing) as Pleasure, Competition, and Healing Ritual

While hula is the cultural activity most closely associated with the Pele and Hi'iaka mo'olelo, other cultural pursuits are highlighted in different texts, including he'e nalu. The mo'olelo reflect the role of surfing in Hawaiian culture: it is a form of recreation and enjoyment, competition, and even healing. Kapihenui begins with the Pele sisters departing the crater for the sea to surf, swim, and gather food from the sea, an overall enjoyable time. When the other sisters return to the uplands, Hi'iaka stays at the beach with Hōpoe, where the two enjoy each other's company and continue surfing the waves of Kaimū.[8] Ka'ili's description includes specific vocabulary describing the waves: "They were out to sea during this conversation waiting for a favorable wave on which to place their surf boards. As Hiiaka ceased speaking, a round wave like a little hillock and known to surf riders as an aleopuu ['ale'ōpu'u, or budding wave], arose right behind, so they poised their surf boards and rode in on it, or rather just before it."[9]

Here, the ocean becomes a place of knowledge, because here Hi'iaka learns about Pele's desire for her to go to Kaua'i to fetch Lohi'au. It is also a place to exhibit knowledge. In *Waves of Resistance*, Isaiah Helekunihi Walker identifies ka po'ina nalu, the surf zone, as an extremely significant indigenous space.[10] In Pele and Hi'iaka, ka po'ina nalu is a place of empowerment for Kanaka Maoli women. It is also a place of empowerment for readers who learn that surfing is a normal activity for Kanaka Maoli women (countering those who erroneously suggest it was a sport of "kings" or a purely masculine domain). They also learn vocabulary specific to the kind of wave the women were riding during a time when the Hawaiian language was being eroded by English. Moreover, while the ABCFM missionaries had severely and consistently condemned Hawaiian activities that were physically, spiritually, and emotionally fulfilling, such as hula and he'e nalu, depictions of surfing within the mo'olelo portrayed it as le'ale'a, pleasurable, and was a subtle way to encourage Kanaka to take up traditional cultural practices as another form of resistance to settler colonialism.

There are several examples in different versions of the mo'olelo where surfing competitions between Kanaka, or between Kanaka and the Pele sisters, are described. In some instances, the competition is not one of surfing prowess, but of 'ike (recognition) and 'eleu (adeptness) at recognizing Hi'iaka as a deity, with dire consequences for those who fail to do so and offer her hospitality, a hallmark of Kanaka civility. Two examples are Hi'iaka's encounter with Punahoa, an ali'i wahine from the Hilo-Hāmākua region of Hawai'i island, and with Palani, an ali'i kāne (male chief) of Kahana, O'ahu.

In Ka'ili, Punahoa is the name of the 'āina, as well as the ali'i wahine whose father is the ruling chief. This mo'olelo is etiological, connecting the naming of the 'āina to the kanaka. When Hi'iaka mā arrive at Punahoa, they notice a large crowd at the beach watching Punahoa surfing:

> They were admiring her as she was the best surf-rider of the bay and the people were loud in praise of her skill.
>
> Hi'iaka asked some of the people the reason of such a crowd and was told they were admiring the feats of the young lady on the surf-board. The mischievous goddess said[,] "Oh, she doesn't understand surf-riding; she will be drawn under." At that, all those who could hear her, indignantly protested, such a thing had never happened to Punahoa and never could. But Hi'iaka irritated them by looking incredulous and saying, "[W]ait and see." As Punahoa rode in on a wave at that moment, they all cried, "[Y]ou see." But just as she had got half-way from the starting place and the shore, she lost her balance, was drawn under, and turned over in plain view of the crowd, to her great mortification.[11]

This episode is included in multiple versions of the mo'olelo, demonstrating its importance in the tradition. The scene describes Punahoa's 'eleu at surfing and the people's admiration of her prowess. Yet it is also about the consequences of not being 'a'apo, because the people do not grasp who Hi'iaka is. Even worse, they exhibit maha'oi behavior toward Hi'iaka. As an akua, Hi'iaka has the foresight ('ike pāpālua) to predict Punahoa's fall; she has the ability to cause Punahoa to lose her balance and wipe out in the surf. As an ali'i, Punahoa has kuleana for her people (or the people living under the leadership of her father). In this context, she must suffer the consequences of the wipeout because she is their leader; as such, her kuleana is not only her right to rule over the people, but responsibility to protect them as well.

In another episode (also described in Walker's *Waves of Resistance*), as Hiʻiaka mā are passing through the region of Kahana, Koʻolauloa, Oʻahu, en route to Kauaʻi, they encounter Palani, the aliʻi kāne of Kahana, and his wahine, ʻIewale. When they arrive at Kahana, the chiefly pair is surfing in the bay:

> The two of them [Hiʻiaka and Wahineʻōmaʻo] came upon Kahana and took in the view. The wind of Kahana is called the ʻĀhiu [Wild]. The chief of Kahana, Palani was his name, was surfing with his wahine, ʻIewale. They were quite fond of surfing the waves brought by the ʻĀhiu wind, and that is the name of this wind that blows only when the surf breaks there.
>
> When Hiʻiaka saw the two of them surfing there, she chanted to them, like this:

> The wild ʻĀhui wind blows cold at Kahana,
> Gusting along the twisting Koʻolau coast
> Loʻikeʻe is hunched up, shivering in the cold
> The great forests of the uplands above Kalehualoa
> Traveling the long road to Huilua
> You are Palani, the surfing chief of Kahana

> Palani rudely responded to Hiʻiakaikapoliopele, "Yes, I am Palani, the surfing chief of this land, Kahana. Who indeed are you haughty women coming here and calling to me? This sport is my passion; perhaps you saw me surfing with my wahine; you are a woman who doesn't know me—who indeed are you?"
>
> At these impudent words of Palani, an angry thought entered Hiʻiakaikapoliopele. So when Palani tried to catch another wave, he wiped out in the surf. He was unable to get his bearings before the waves rose once more. He tried again to come ashore, but couldn't right himself before the waves rose up again. Palani tried again, but he was pulled under by the waves and drowned in the surf. Palani died there along with his wahine, ʻIewale, both of them died together.[12]

Both episodes illustrate Hiʻiaka's power over the elements of the ʻāina, as well as the consequences for rude behavior exhibited by those who do not recognize her as a deity. There is also a play on language that Hawaiian-speaking audiences recognize; pālani means to "skim lightly," and may reflect the ali'i's adept surfing skills, and palani is a reef sturgeon fish (*Acanthurus dussumieri*) known for a strong odor.[13] It also refers to a stinking odor or a detested person, a not so subtle reflection of Palani's rude or "stink" personality.[14] I'e is a kapa beater; kapa work is associated with chiefly women in the Pele and Hi'iaka mo'olelo. 'Ie is a vine used to make chiefly items, such as the base of the mahiole (feathered helmet). It is also used to weave baskets to trap fish, 'ie palani being a recognized type; wale is an intensifier and a word for slime. 'Iewale is also translated as "Slimy-basket."[15] Thus, 'Iewale is alluded to in negative terms as well, an 'ēko'a to Palani.[16]

It is not coincidental that the two kanaka involved are ali'i, representatives of the highest level of Hawaiian society; if they are punished by the deity for their maha'oi behavior, what consequence for similar impudence could be meted out for kanaka of lesser status? While pono ali'i were loved and respected by the people, rude behavior was not condoned. There is also an entertainment factor for the audience or readers in ali'i being punished for bad behavior, although that is probably not as significant as the point that ali'i had more at stake than maka'āinana in lacking 'ike or offering proper ho'okipa.

Wahi pana specific and important to Kahana are also named in Hi'iaka's chant, including a beach area (Kalehualoa), mountain peak (Kekila), wind name ('Āhiu), and fishpond (Huilua).[17] As seen with references to other places in the mo'olelo, these specific places are 'ēko'a with one another: the beach area on the south side of the bay with a mountain peak on the northern side; the atmospheric element of wind ('Āhiu) with the element of water (the fishpond). Once again, Hi'iaka demonstrates her intimate knowledge of all the locations she travels through by naming such specific details of each place. Hi'iaka herself is an accomplished surfer, and well versed in paying attention to the natural environment. It is a subtle reminder to such rude kama'āina (such as Palani) that observing one's environment and internalizing cultural practice is integral to one's survival, in the ocean and beyond.

Manu presents perhaps the most interesting surfing scene, one that pits the Pele sisters against some male surfers of Wailua, Kaua'i. This episode is etiological, in that it explains the origin of the "pae ki'i o māhū" petroglyphs etched into the large boulders along the south flank of the Wailua River mouth:

They soon arrived at the sands of Alio [to scream], and it was not long before they arrived at the mouth of the great river discussed in a chant, "The hooks of the fishermen became entangled at Wailua" [Huikau nā makau o nā lawai'a i Wailua]. This place made Kapō'ulakīna'u and the others linger as they observed a number of men and women surfing there. What a large number! Some surfed on the left side, which the people of old called the lala, as in the adage, "Lilo i ka lala, ho'i i ka muku, or 'taken on the diagonal, returned on the crest.'" The audience on the beach whooped and hollered at the most skilled surfers. Surfing was a sport that brought everyone on the island together, the native youth of the region, the champions from other parts of the island, and the sweet-voiced maidens of those ancient times. . . . They had so much fun! . . .

Then, Kapō'ulakīna'u did something very odd to some of the surfers of Wailua, she turned them into stone. . . . The beautiful daughters of Haumea were invited to surf, and Kapō'ulakīna'u accepted their offer without hesitation. The sisters quickly picked up the boards and paddled out to where the waves were beginning to roll in.

As they and the men mounted their boards, waiting for a good wave, Kapō'ulakīna'u said to them, "Friends, let us ride tandem, two to a board. One of you can come here with me, and the other can ride with my sister there. Thus we can ride in pairs and after we are pau surfing, we can go to your hale, just as we have paired off here. What do you think of this idea?"

The men quickly agreed. . . . When they finished talking, the surf rose behind them, and they rode the wave in tandem. The ride to shore was mere play to the mischievous ones of Kahiki. The people on shore cheered and hollered in great admiration. When they reached the shore, some of the men and women came and bedecked them with lehua and 'ilima lei, placing them around the necks of each of these mysterious women, who wore them with great pride on their heads and around their necks. The men just laughed, but they were truly disappointed by the women the next time they paddled out.

Sitting in the water when the next set approached, the men couldn't figure out what to do. When the third set of waves approached, it was the largest and strongest. When the boards were turned shoreward, Kapō'ulakīna'u said, "This is not surf, this is a mountain! Let each one try his skill. Go ahead—ride toward the shore!"

No sooner had they begun the men sank beneath the waves

and were pummeled by the roiling surf and drowned. Their
bodies were changed into stone at the mouth of the Wailua
River, and are now known as the pae ki'i or row of images. They
are there until this day. . . . After that, Kapō'ulakīna'u named
the surf break Kalehuawehe.[18] The people on the beach fled in
terror as the huge waves rolled in. Everyone wondered about the
women and the men, as they could not be seen on the waves, but
the mysterious daughters of Haumea were "gone with the fish of
Uko'a that were blown away by the wind." They were no longer
on the waves of Kalehuawehe in Wailua, but surfing on the waves
of Makaīwa down the coast in Kapa'a. The surfers there became
confused, landing every which way. Because of that incident, the
surf there was called "Ke kua nalu o Makaīwa, or 'The surf back
of Makaīwa.'"[19]

This scene demonstrates mana wahine, the physical, intellectual, and
spiritual (intuitive) power of the godly women over the kanaka men, a
theme that resonates throughout all the Pele and Hi'iaka mo'olelo. There
is also an etiological function as several surf breaks (Makaīwa, Kalehuawehe) are named. It also explains the origins of the row of stones containing petroglyph carvings located at the mouth of the Wailua River,
called Paeki'imahūowailua (Row of petroglyph images at Wailua).[20] The
scene also exhibits the enjoyment of surfing by men and women alike.

What these three surf scenes also have in common is the importance
of 'ike—recognition and knowledge, and the dire consequences from
lacking these skills. Walker argues that "it was Palani's failure to recognize and respect Hi'iaka as an individual (and goddess) that got him
into trouble—not necessarily his claim over the territory of Kahana. In
both ancient and contemporary Hawai'i, recognition is still critical in
social settings. Recognition of one's family, community, and origins are
essential to social relationships. . . . Thus Hi'iaka, as a visitor to Kahana,
followed proper protocol by recognizing Palani's family and status before
she asked to enter. She was angered when Palani failed to reciprocate in
the social exchange."[21] Walker links this cultural practice to Oceania,
utilizing Tēvita Ka'ili's work, where "exchanges of love, respect, mutual
assistance, and nurturing sociospacial ties are core principles in maintaining healthy social relationships" in most Pacific Island cultures and
communities, where "commitment to sustain harmonious social relations
with kin and kin-like members" was crucial.[22] 'Ike is thus highly valued,
prompted by the culturally stressed desire to maintain good relationships. When recognition does not occur, social or kinship relationships

are damaged or broken. In cultures developed on islands, which are relatively small land bases, such cultural and social expectations of courtesy and acknowledgment go a long way in maintaining positive relationships among individuals and larger communities.

Finally, he'e nalu is an instrumental part of Lohi'au's healing after Hi'iaka restores his life. Once Hi'iaka completes this difficult task through rigorous healing ritual, part of his prescribed activity necessary for complete healing is time in the ocean, surfing:

> From night until day, from day until night, they went down to the shore of Hā'ena to swim in the ocean, to help Lohi'au recuperate. In no time he returned to his healthy self. . . . When they arrived at the shore below, they went until they reached their kapu [reserved] surf spot. Lohi'au's board was still in his surfboard storage area. He grabbed his board and went surfing. He surfed until the middle of the night when "The Fish" [Milky Way] turned. Dawn was soon approaching; Kahuanui awoke from sleep with a start; she went outside and came back in, and went back outside and came back in again and tried to sleep, but she could not; her thoughts kept lingering on her brother.[23]

Once Lohi'au is brought back to life, he is nursed and fed in his sister's home by day, and taken to a nearby freshwater cave at night, where he is treated by being rubbed with oil (kākelekele) for an anahulu (two-week period). He is then ready to go out surfing, which concludes Hi'iaka's course of treatment; he continues to surf for another anahulu, and is then free to return home and associate with family and friends.[24]

Ho'oulumāhiehie provides the most descriptive scene of Lohi'au's restoration through he'e nalu. When Lohi'au expresses a desire to surf, it becomes an opportunity for Hi'iaka to reveal to the people of Hā'ena (and to Lohi'au) the full extent of her power. He desires to surf the most stormy conditions, signaling that his health has been restored to the point where he can complete the healing rituals, culminating with surfing. They do not just surf—Hi'iaka carefully instructs Lohi'au in what to wear and how to respond to the appearance of the god Kāne, who assists in the restoration of his health. Hi'iaka's power revealed in this scene is not just in healing or even just in Lohi'au's compliment to her on her expertise in he'e nalu. Rather, she becomes the board on which he rides, accompanied by sharks, dolphins, and even 'iwa (frigate) birds, all hō'ailona of Lohi'au's chiefly status and Hi'iaka's godly one.

Thus the surfing scenes become an expression of Kanaka Maoli cultural practice, not just as sport or competition, but also as healing, including the restoration of the spirit through the cultural value of le'ale'a, enjoyment of life, and akamai, expertise at the activity. In Emerson's translation, these metaphorical allusions are lost. He does not include Hi'iaka's role or surfing as a healing ritual. Instead, he describes Lohi'au's singular, male desire to surf once he is revived; he simply grabs his board and paddles out into the surf, "reserved for kings," a false, gendered stereotype that also conceals his reliance on Hi'iaka's healing nature. This rhetoric of conquest continues in settler colonialism representations of surf, from Steinlager beer commercials to surf industry films. The spiritual and cultural dynamics of surfing are lost on his English-speaking readers because surfing is transformed from a shared space of healing to one of individual empowerment. In Emerson's colonialized representation, as a privileged male of chiefly status, Lohi'au has agency to make the decision to surf and reclaim what "belongs" to him—his exclusive surf spot. In this context, by surfing the waves he is metaphorically "taming" them by asserting his masculine prowess over nature, feminized in a Western paradigm. By comparison, in the Hawaiian mo'olelo it is the female goddess who prescribes the activity as part of her holistic healing method, suggesting that optimal health is achieved through pono both by ritual (her prayers) and with nature (plants used in the healing ritual, physical activity in harmony with nature). This concept is taken furthest by Ho'oulumāhiehie, as Hi'iaka has the authority and ability to command nature through the power of her voice—she causes a storm to appear with the large thunderous waves Lohi'au craves by chanting—and she restores health through the pono between herself as a female deity and Kāne, a male deity also associated with healing. This reflects Pele's ability to call winds that cause stormy weather and the surf to rise.[25]

Walker argues that fewer Kanaka were surfing in the decades after the first haole arrived because of the collapse of the Native population from foreign-introduced disease. While surfing was a necessary part of Lohi'au's revivification, it wasn't as effective against the onslaught of foreign diseases. But as Walker points out, Kanaka Maoli continued to surf, and mo'olelo about he'e nalu, or containing surfing scenes (such as Pele and Hi'iaka) were very popular in the Hawaiian nationalist press, which, he says, "not only reveals that surfing still held value in the 1860s, but also suggests that he'e nalu was heavily associated with both Hawaiian cultural pride and resistance."[26] The role of mo'olelo in Hawaiian nationalism today continues, woven into Kanaka Maoli cultural practice and new expressions of aloha 'āina, which includes the ocean. Kanaka Maoli surfers still assert their presence in ka po'ina nalu surf zone, look to mo'olelo ku'una in reclaiming traditional names for surf breaks (such as Makaīwa and Kalehuawehe, identified in "Pelekeahi'āloa" as being named by Kapō'ulakīna'u), still work to keep surf sites accessible, and protect traditional surf sites from destruction by development.

Rituals of Hula (Dance) and Kilu (Quoits)

Hula is the most prominent cultural activity featured in the Pele and Hi'iaka mo'olelo, one also connected to 'anā'anā and healing. Pele, Hi'iaka, and their sisters Kewelani (Laka) and Kapō'ulakīna'u are akua of hula.[27] Silva identifies five hula scenes in Kapihenui:

Ke ha'a lā Puna—Pele's family travels from the crater to the beach in Puna. Hōpoe and Hā'ena dance for them. The dance praises the 'āina and functions as a welcome.

Lu'ulu'u Hanalei i ka ua nui—Pele arrives at a hula festival at Hā'ena, Kaua'i. She transforms herself into a beautiful young woman adorned with the forest greenery of Puna . . . she and Lohi'au chant back and forth to each other. Lohi'au dances for his people and for his own enjoyment.

Aloha wale ka i'a lamalama o ku'u 'āina lā, ua 'ino Honokohau, Aloha wale ka pali o Pinana'i, and Ha'a ka lau o ka i'a— Manamanaiakaluea dances for Hi'iaka mā when they arrive on Maui, explaining her plight and warning of the presence of sharks.

'O kaua a Pele i haka i Kahiki and 'Oe mauna i ka ohu ka pali ("Holo mai Pele")—Malaeha'akoa and his wife dance to entertain Hi'iaka as part of the hospitality they offer. It is also to honor their deity, Pele.

Ke lei maila Ka'ula i ke kai ē, Ku'u hoa i ka 'ili hau o Mānā, Ku'u hoa i ke Kāwelu oho o Malailua, A Kalihi au i ka hala o Hanalei, Aloha wale ka nikiniki, Moe e no Waialua ke Ko'olau, and 'O Hā'upu mauna Kilohana—Lohi'au dances for Hi'iaka after he loses at kilu.[28]

Silva argues that one of the political messages of the mo'olelo is that for "nineteenth-century Kanaka readers and to the generations before, hula was profoundly spiritual but also entertaining, and, at times, sexy."[29]

Hula is a ritual connected to celebrating traditional deities and honoring spiritual practices associated with them. It was a form of le'ale'a that was culturally and spiritually based, and could be coy or blatant in any sexual messages expressed in different hula. That is the reality of hula as a practice. *Publishing* mo'olelo that featured positive portrayals of hula at a time when a ban on public performance of hula had been codified by law in 1860 not only countered the negative haole view of hula (and Kanaka Maoli), it blatantly challenged it by depicting a world that was "possibly even more dangerous to the 'civilizing' project" of American colonialism:

> In the world of Pele and Hi'iaka, women have power: They act on their desires, they travel, they kill, and they heal. Viewing hula in this context enables us to see that missionaries such as Emerson felt compelled to ban hula not only because it celebrates a rival religion and created obstacles for the colonial capitalist economy but also because a major missionary goal was to discipline female sexuality and restrict female power in order to establish patriarchy.
>
> The emergence of the mo'olelo in print was clearly in response to both legal and cultural imperialism being put into place by Puritanical and capitalist missionaries. It was a refusal on the part of Kanaka Maoli to despise their ancient culture, and was, instead, a way to celebrate the artistry of the oral traditions and of the hula itself. It was a way to keep the traditions alive during times when the public performance of hula and chant was not permitted. The mo'olelo talked back to the oppressive colonial powers in indirect yet powerful ways. As important, the mo'olelo was being read by thousands of people across the entire archipelago, bringing them together as a *lāhui*. It also, however, indirectly, reminded women that their female ancestors were powerful and that there were alternatives to being subordinated to men.[30]

Hula did not function in isolation in the text, but rather was connected to other activities, such as kilu. Kilu is a matchmaking game associated with the ali'i in which the player chanted as he or she tossed the kilu (typically a small gourd or coconut shell) toward an object placed in front of another player of the opposite sex; if they hit the goal they claimed a "kiss." *Kilu* describes both the gourd and game play. A less-known definition is "to be wet, very damp, drenched with rain."[31] Dampness, particularly when associated with rain, is a common metaphor for lovemaking, and would be an appropriate allusion in kilu. The ultimate expression of ali'i class hospitality, perhaps this is why kilu is so prevalent in the Pele and Hi'iaka mo'olelo, as it demonstrates the 'ike of ali'i who recognize Hi'iaka and Lohi'au's status as they traveled across the pae 'āina.

Many of the kilu scenes in the mo'olelo involve Pele'ula's court at Kou in Honolulu, but kilu was played in other locations. In Rice, Hi'iaka mā participate in a kilu game with Koananai, an ali'i wahine of Keālia, Kaua'i, a noted kilu player in other traditions.[32] Ho'oulumāhiehie includes a kilu scene with the ali'i wahine of Mākua, O'ahu, on the Wai'anae coast:

> That night, the kilu party of the chiefess was assembled. Lohi'au played against the chiefess of Mākua, along with some others.
>
> Lohi'au and the beauty of Mākua did the toss to choose the starter, and to the chiefess went the chance to make the first play.
>
> When she spun her kilu, it passed the mark, and it was the first time the people of Mākua had ever seen the chiefess's kilu miss, for this was the game at which she had gained great skill, but in this instance, her piece overshot on the first strike.
>
> The play went to Lohi'au. When he spun the kilu it moved straight along, touching the wooden post, but then moving right on past. Hi'iaka commented, "Ah! You are evenly matched in your losses. Try again, perhaps."
>
> She added, "Yes, this last time was a loss, but perhaps in this next play you will be lucky, like casting nets that attract the dark snake mackerel, the hāuliuli."
>
> Again, the first play went to the chiefess of Mākua. Making the toss, her piece spun and struck the wooden goal but then passed far to the left of the stake.
>
> "Chiefess, your kilu missed again!" Hi'iaka chided the ali'i of Mākua, and then turning to Lohi'au, said, "That is that! It will be up to you! Make some good use of your kilu. The land to aim for is that fuzzy hill, Pu'uohulu."
>
> Her remark made everyone there laugh, and one of them asked teasingly of Hi'iaka, "Which Pu'uohulu are you talking about as a home base for this son of Hā'ena's cliffs? Do you mean that Pu'uohulu over on the other side of Wai'anae? Which fuzzy hill are you implying?"
>
> Hi'iaka laughed as well, saying, "The Pu'uohulu I made reference to is the one that all of Wai'anae knows!"
>
> Lohi'au tossed his game piece and it almost brushed the stake, but then shot off in an arc, some distance away.
>
> "Yours has overshot the mark, O son of Kaua'i! You are both a bit blind! Well, maybe I should try against the Kaua'i boy."

"Wait, though. We have one try left. If it comes up a loss, then you give it a go," said the young lady of Mākua.

She spun her kilu again, but it missed just like her earlier attempts. The chiefess said, "This is such an unlucky night for me. This has been my game from my childhood until now when I am fully grown, and I have never experienced losses like these. Take over our spot, Hi'iaka."

Then Lohi'au twirled his kilu. As the piece moved, it stayed straight on target until touching the stake. Everyone roared about the son of Kaua'i.

The chiefess of Mākua gave up her spot to Hi'iaka, who moved over and sat where the chiefess had been, saying, "Ah! Your marker has been lucky, Chief. Now how will mine be?"

Hi'iaka took up the playing piece, but before she sent the kilu into action, she chanted this chant.

. . .

The sea spray flies
Rising over the headlands
Beloved is Ka'ena Point in the sea mist
The sea in the lee of Wai'anae
Sliding over the sand dunes
Those beloved sands of Mākua
Let not love develop, lest I be faulted
Your name it will be, O Pu'uohulu
It is known.

Hearing Hi'iaka's chant, all were delighted and filled with admiration for her fine chanting.

As Hi'iaka finished her chant, she tossed her kilu, which went directly to touch the stake and stop right at its center, whereupon a roar went up from the people.

She and Lohi'au played a second time, and again, both of their kilu hit the mark. Then Hi'iaka began this chant.

. . .

Beloved is the dew of Ka'ala
The dew which carries the scent of nēnē grass
For the people of Pu'uloa to inhale and enjoy
Long has been the search, my love
We must not get tangled in womanly wiles

> You have been made sacred, my dear
> By the word of the privileged one
> I have no privilege there
> We may stray toward Kānehili
> To satisfy desire and relinquish toil
> My toil may then be in vain, my friend
> Wait, lest you suffer!

. . . Hiʻiaka invited the chiefess of Mākua to compete again with the chief of Kauaʻi, to which she agreed. The chiefess seized the kilu and sent it spinning, hopeful that it would touch the stake, but her hopes were dashed once again.

The chiefess tried every way she could to gain a single winning kilu, but to no avail, so she gave up the game without satisfying her desires.[33]

Heʻe nalu is clearly linked to healing within the Pele and Hiʻiaka moʻolelo while kilu is not, but a connection is implied between kilu and healing when they arrive at the court of the chiefly woman Peleʻula (red Pele) in Kou (Honolulu), Oʻahu. While it's the name of the royal woman who offers them hospitality and engages them in a game of kilu, trying (unsuccessfully, as with the other women before her) to "win" Lohiʻau for herself, it is also an old name for a small section of land in Honolulu. Hawaiian historian John Papa ʻĪʻī notes that this was also the name of a healing heiau located in this area.[34] A notice in *Ka Hoku o ka Pakipika* mentions that Kalākaua's younger brother Prince William Pitt Leleiō-hoku Kalāhoʻolewa was baptized at a church there in 1863.[35]

The connection between healing and kilu is unclear at this point. However, the kilu scenes are an opportunity to demonstrate leʻaleʻa and to showcase mele and hula, with which the modern Kanaka audience may or may not have been familiar. Certainly enjoyment is a crucial part of our mental and emotional health and overall sense of well-being. Conveying such leʻaleʻa in print was an important opportunity to experience kilu through the moʻolelo, as participation in a live match would have been impossible under missionary surveillance and settler colonialism in the nineteenth century, the mechanism for such traditional pleasurable pursuits already destroyed.

Perhaps another reason kilu is so closely associated with the moʻolelo is because hula accompanies it. As hula deities, the Pele sisters would certainly preside over and be adept at hula kilu, as would their followers.

Hula kilu is a particular classification of hula, performed by Lohi'au during the kilu ritual (most notably when he loses at Pele'ula's court in Kou).[36] Hula kilu associated with Lohi'au and Pele, like other hula Pele, were performed at Kalākaua's coronation celebration in 1883.

At the very least, Kanaka Maoli could collectively read, learn, discuss, enjoy, and appreciate them as part of this new national and cultural literature being developed through the Hawaiian nationalist press, of which the Pele and Hi'iaka mo'olelo were a part.

Nā Mea Pā'ani Ho'okūkū 'ē a'e (Other Competitive Games): Pūhenehene, 'Ulu Maika, Nane

Other games that demonstrated intelligence, ability, skill, and enjoyment found in the Pele and Hi'iaka mo'olelo include pūhenehene (a guessing game), 'ulu maika (similar to bowling), and nane (riddling contests). These games were opportunities to exhibit akamai and 'eleu in the context of ho'opāpā (a contest of wit and skill) that collectively demonstrate 'Ōiwi intellectual history in another way. The most important scene found in the majority of the Pele and Hi'iaka mo'olelo is the pūhenehene game between Pi'ihonua and Pu'ueo in the Hilo–Hāmākua area of Hawai'i island. Pūhenehene is a game of skill; a no'a (stone or piece of wood) was hidden on a player. The other players took turns guessing who was hiding the no'a and where it was hidden.

When Hi'iaka comes upon Pi'ihonua in an area of Hilo named for him, he is saddened that he cannot offer them hospitality because he recently lost all his possessions in a game of pūhenehene with his nemesis, a rival ali'i named Pu'ueo:

> [Pi'ihonua] told them that the game was to be continued that day, his life being the stake, when if he lost, he was to be cooked alive in an imu (underground oven), but should he win, he was to get back all he had lost, as well as all the property of his rival, who was then to lose his life . . . the fires were already lighted in the imu by the orders of Pu'ueo, so confident was he of winning.
>
> Hi'iaka had pity on Pi'ihonua's forlorn condition and possible fate, and determined to accompany him on his next visit. She told him to cheer up and to bravely play his last game, and asked him to let her be his assistant, to which he gladly consented. . . . Pi'ihonua and his friends were greeted with scornful remarks by the partisans of the heretofore victorious Pu'ueo. The latter had

the hiding of the stone, and when the chant accompanying that had ceased, Hi'iaka asked Pi'ihonua which division he intended to take, and on his pointing to one said, "No wonder you have been so badly beaten, why you are ignorant of the very first principles of the game. That choice proves that you have not been watching the muscles of your opponents arm or of his face. Now, you do as I direct." Whereupon she took the lead in the game, whispering her commands to him and chanting the oli when it was his turn to hide the pebble.

Pu'ueo was badly beaten and lost his life, being burned alive in the imu he had himself ordered lighted. Pi'ihonua recovered all his own property and received that of his rival as well.[37]

The pūhenehene game is another opportunity for Hi'iaka to demonstrate her godly mana and to instruct the kanaka Pi'ihonua on cultural values of 'a'apo and akamai; she scolds him for not being keenly observant of his opponent's movement, which caused his embarrassing losses. With Hi'iaka's instruction he is able to defeat his opponent. Why does Hi'iaka choose to assist Pi'ihonua? Perhaps it is because she cannot resist the opportunity to teach the hapless kanaka how to excel and thus succeed. Perhaps it is another opportunity to punish a kanaka (Pu'ueo) for his bad behavior—his overconfidence is a negative trait highly frowned upon in Hawaiian culture. Perhaps it is because Pi'ihonua attempts to demonstrate aloha and ho'okipa to Hi'iaka, but cannot, so she has aloha (compassion) for him.

While not as prevalent, 'ulu maikai is also described in some of the mo'olelo. In 'ulu maika, a semi-flat, rounded stone is rolled across a field; the goal is to roll the stone between two upright stakes set parallel to each other in the ground. High skill is demonstrated when the stakes are moved closer together, thereby narrowing the target. When Hi'iaka mā travel through the Waimea region of Hawai'i island, Wahine'ōma'o takes pity on two men crying on the side of the road. Hi'iaka tells her they are spirits and beyond help, as their bones have been stripped from their bodies, leaving them "alualu" (slack; i.e., without bone structure), but Wahine'ōma'o asks Hi'iaka to intercede. Hi'iaka agrees, but enlists Wahine'ōma'o's assistance, asking her to get a bundle of 'aukī (ti leaf stalks) from a particular place a distance away. Wahine'ōma'o agrees and fetches the required items. Hi'iaka fashions "bones" for the kanaka alualu out of the ti stalks. The men are hula dancers who are so overjoyed at having their skeletal structure restored that they chant and dance all the way back to Waimea, where they encounter a number of people playing 'ulu maika:

The restored hula men kept right on dancing and chanting on
to the maika ground. The players called to them to get out of
the way but they would not pay any attention, possibly relying
on Hi'iaka to see them through all their difficulties. As a consequence some of the players getting impatient threw their maikas
which hitting them in the legs, the auki [aukī, ti stalk], which was
doing duty for their bones, was broken to pieces. When the hula
men found themselves lamed they appealed again to Hiiaka to
restore them, but she was so displeased with their arrogance, that
she would not help them.[38]

Emerson frames this scene quite differently. In his version, Wahine-
'ōma'o is silenced; it is the men who have agency and call out to Hi'iaka
in a chant for assistance. Emerson blames the Mahiki mo'o for the men's
brutal assault, and describes their physical condition in gruesome terms:

Hiiaka's march to encounter the Mahiki was interrupted for
a short time by an incident that only served to clinch her resolution. An agonizing cry of distress assailed her ear. It came
from a dismantled heap of human flesh, the remains of two men
who had been most brutally handled—by these same Mahiki,
perhaps—their leg and arm-bones plucked out and they left to
welter in their misery. It was seemingly the cruel infliction of the
Mahiki. The cry of the two wretches could not be disregarded. . . .
Hiiaka, with a skill that did credit to her surgery, splinted the
maimed limbs, inserting stems from her favorite ti plant to take
the place of the long bones that had been removed. She left them
seated in comfort at the roadside at Pololu.[39]

These episodes provide opportunities for Hi'iaka to exercise and
practice her healing powers (which she will need to restore Lohi'au's life
when she arrives on Kaua'i), and to punish those who break or disregard
cultural etiquette. In Ka'ili, the men are allowed to die because they are
maha'oi and kāpulu (careless). They do not respect Hi'iaka's orders, the
playing field, or 'ulu maika players. They are kāpulu with their newly
restored bodies, made possible through Hi'iaka's skill. They are by extension disrespectful to her as they don't mālama (care for) the gift she has
given them, and their demise is therefore inevitable.

By blaming the Mahiki, Emerson gives Hi'iaka reason to destroy
them, which is unnecessary in the other texts. Emerson recasts Hi'iaka's
role into a Christian-influenced dichotomy of "good" versus "evil"—Pele

is portrayed as mean-spirited, treating Hi'iaka unfairly, while Hi'iaka is the wholesome, innocent "good" girl who can do no wrong.

Nane (riddling) is presented in Ho'oulumāhiehie. When Hi'iaka and company are in Wai'anae, O'ahu, on their return trip to Kīlauea, they encounter Kaulanaakalā, an ali'i of Moloka'i, who is burdened by a riddle. Hi'iaka cannot resist helping the troubled chief, which presents another opportunity to share her knowledge and skills. While being hosted at Mākua, a wailing voice was heard down the road. They see a man coming from Wai'anae. He is welcomed into the home, and Hi'iaka discerns that he is burdened by a riddle. Only by answering it correctly will his life be saved. Kaulanaakalā replies:

> "Yes, actually, there is a riddle for which I must seek the answer. What incredible insight you have, my friend, to know this secret that I hold inside."
>
> "I revealed to no one the reason I wander in lament, but you already know," replied the man, his hopes rising, but still filled with uncertainty. "Could this be where my distress will end?"[40]

Hi'iaka invites him to eat first before sharing the riddle, saying, "Once the empty stomach is taken care of, then explain your riddle to us . . . my advice to you is to eat your meat and fish with gusto and enthusiasm. My premonition tells me this is a day for salvation."[41] Before Hi'iaka even helps Kaulanaakalā with his problem, she exhibits important cultural skills and etiquette—she uses her 'ike pāpālua to discern Kaulanaakalā's problem, and then she invites him to eat until he is full, a sign of hospitality, generosity, and compassion.

While Kaulanaakalā is eating, Hi'iaka turns to the ali'i women Mailelauli'i, Ko'iahi, and Halakaipo and asks them about the riddle, even though she already knows the answer. Mailelauli'i discerns that the riddle is from Waipi'o:

> I stand, one
> I stand, two
> I stand, three
> I stand, four
> I stand, five
> O sun from down below
> I shield my eyes
> Gazing down below
> The stormy days are changed

Crawling about below
I am a manini, swimming about.[42]

Hi'iaka asks each in turn if they know the answer, and they confess they don't. When Kaulanaakalā is finished with his meal, he shares the riddle, not realizing the women already know it. Hi'iaka then asks Lohi'au if he knows the answer, and he says he doesn't. Hi'iaka turns the riddle into a teachable moment for the people with her, and the reading audience, a lesson of 'ike 'āina, knowledge about land. She calls for kūkini (trained runners) to fetch manini (striped reef sturgeon) from a pond located in the cliffs of Ka'ena called Manini; they demonstrate their knowledge of the 'āina by taking a lesser-known but shorter route:

> The kūkini didn't run along the shore to reach Ka'ena, but took off on the shortest route through Keawa'ula and up over Kuao-kalā, veering across the succession of steep cliffs and gulches of Ka'ena.
>
> They descended into the gully where the water gathered into Manini Pond. When they got there and looked into the water, there was a hole where manini gathered.
>
> They laid a net around the manini hole. Selecting one fish, they seized it and immediately dashed off, climbing up over the cliff. . . . Perhaps less than a quarter of an hour was spent getting there and returning with the . . . manini . . . they gave the fish to Hi'iaka, who took it and said to Kaulanaokalā: "Here with this little fish lies the answer to your riddle. I ask you, what is the name of this fish?"
>
> To which Kaulanaokalā replied, "A manini!"
>
> "And what is the offspring of the manini?" asked Hi'iaka.
>
> "An 'ōhua!" was his intelligent response.
>
> "And where does the offspring form?" Hi'iaka asked again.
>
> "In the belly of the mother," answered Kaulanaokalā.
>
> "Now you have it. A newborn child is the answer to your riddle, and the manini is the analogy that the riddler has used. Now listen to the explanation of your puzzle. 'I stand, one': one month that the child is outside. 'I stand, two': two months of the child outside. 'I stand, four': four months of the child outside. 'I stand, five': it makes five months of the child being outside the mother.
>
> "In the sixth month, these words are added to the riddle, 'O sun from below. Shield my eyes.' The child's hands begin to clap and to make fists.

"Your puzzle goes on to say, 'Gazing down below!' The child is beginning to rise up. 'The stormy days are changed!' The child can sit up well, and begins to crawl.

"'Crawling about below!' The child is crawling and has crawled everywhere in the house. 'I am a manini swimming about.' The child has stood up, walked, and run as well. This is the explanation of your riddle, so now you know. Now you can go back . . . for the burden is relinquished."[43]

The representation of contests is an opportunity to demonstrate Hawaiian 'ike; it is also a metaphorical way to pass on these activities, practices, and skills to the modern Kanaka audiences these writers were addressing, a method that wouldn't trip the censorship radar of the "missionary police."[44] What is most indicative of mana wahine is that the women work collaboratively to solve the riddle. They are also the source of the answer that neither male ali'i knows.

Collectively, these competitions dispel colonially constructed myths about Hawaiian society being completely noncompetitive: competitions (surfing, hula, games of skill like kilu, pūhenehene, 'ulu maika, and nane) abound in the Pele and Hi'iaka mo'olelo. Moreover, they often occur with serious consequences. The pūhenehene and nane episodes are literally a matter of life and death; if successful, Pi'ihonua and Kaulanaokalā will live; if not, they will pay with their lives. When Hi'iaka challenges the mo'o Piliamo'o and Nohoamo'o at the Wailuku River bridge (discussed in the previous chapter), the kama'āina of the area wish to make a wager. They bet whether Hi'iaka can defeat the mo'o, and ask Hi'iaka to bet something. She replies, "There is only one thing to wager—the bones."[45] Word of the wager spread quickly, as the serious bet excited people. One of the ali'i urges the people to persuade Hi'iaka against it, saying, "Perhaps the one who wagered the bones doesn't realize they are truly valuable."[46] Hi'iaka is literally betting her life, displaying complete confidence in her skill and knowledge, and the seriousness of this wager is not lost on the people. Hi'iaka is of course victorious, and as a result her willingness to gamble her life increases her mana and the level of respect and admiration the people have for her.

Ho'okipa (Hospitality) and Mea 'ai (Food): Preparation, Kānāwai (Etiquette), Ritual, and Abundance

Ho'okipa is an important aspect of Hawaiian culture found throughout the Pele and Hi'iaka mo'olelo. Centuries before this cultural practice was misappropriated by Hawai'i's tourist industry, Kanaka Maoli offered hospitality to one another as a mark of civil conduct. Pukui and Handy note that "inhospitality was so rare that a case would be discussed with horror for years. Nevertheless, there were some who were stingy and avaricious. . . . Being so seldom met with, when a case of inhospitality was found, it was noised abroad and discussed with derision."[47]

Pele and Hi'iaka are just one strand of mo'olelo that includes episodes highlighting hospitable behavior as a positive trait that is rewarded, and inhospitable behavior as very unbecoming and subject to severe punishment. There are many ways that proper etiquette and gracious hospitality are exhibited, complimented, and rewarded within the mo'olelo, including the calling out of a greeting—typically expressed in chant—to the malihini, such as Hi'iaka folks as they are traveling. Entertaining guests is also part of proper etiquette, especially because of Hi'iaka's (and Lohi'au's) high rank, as with the kilu matches held in their honor at various locations. One of the main aspects of ho'okipa, however, revolves around food, including the gathering, preparation, serving, type, and even abundance of food. In some cases, there are kānāwai of eating, dictating what or how certain foods are consumed. Rituals are involved in the preparation of some items, such as 'awa.

Kapihenui's mo'olelo begins with Pele's suggestion to go down to the seashore to gather seafood. The gathering of food is a fun and social activity, and different ocean delicacies are named. Along their journey Hi'iaka mā often see groups of women picking limu or heading to the sea to fish. They occasionally encounter fishermen as well. In each case, when they are recognized or when they ask, fish is provided.

An abundance of food is also a hallmark of proper ho'okipa. When Hi'iaka and Wahine'ōma'o are traveling through Kailua, O'ahu, they stop at the home of Kanahau, a taro farmer devotee of Pele. When he sees the unfamiliar women, he offers ho'okipa. He is captivated by Hi'iaka's beauty and desires her. He tells the women he will bake a pig for them in the morning, but Hi'iaka informs him she eats only lū'au (taro leaves). Kanahau expresses his desire by preparing an incredible quantity of lū'au for Hi'iaka, a laborious task, as lū'au must be thoroughly cooked to be edible, which takes time. In order to accomplish this tedious task, Kanahau must wake up in the middle of the night to begin his preparations. Ho'oulumāhiehie writes:

[Kanahau] arose and went to make a fire to broil lū'au for Hi'iaka. . . . He worked away until the place he had prepared for the cooking was as big as an earth oven. He heaped up the

firewood, and then went to pick young taro leaves. He picked from
the seaward side of the field to the inland side, and from one edge to
the other. There was a huge amount of lūʻau. Then he wrapped the
lūʻau and made piles of lūʻau bundles. When the fire was ready, he
laid the wrapped lūʻau on it. As the first bunch finished cooking, he
placed more on the fire. He worked away at his task until the sun
had fully risen. The cooked lūʻau became a huge pile. . . . When it
was ready, he brought the bundles of lūʻau and put them in front of
Hiʻiaka, saying to her, "Here is your favorite thing, lūʻau. Eat away."

Hiʻiaka began to eat the lūʻau, and while she was eating those
first ones he had cooked, Kaʻanahau was broiling more. This became quite a race between them. Hiʻiaka kept consuming Kaʻanahau's lūʻau but there was always a little more left. It was never gone.
Then Hiʻiaka said to Kaʻanahau, "There have been many places I
have visited in the course of our journey from Hawaiʻi . . . to here,
and I have eaten my favorite food, lūʻau, at all of those places, but
nowhere have I eaten lūʻau as delicious as what I have been served
by you."[48]

Hiʻiaka is flattered by Kaʻanahau's generosity, which moves her to desire him as well: "[Kaʻanahau] made food in such abundance that it left
Hiʻiaka speechless and stirred in her a need and a thirst that could only
be slaked by the droplets of love's own waters."[49]

Food also plays an important role in Lohiʻau's restoration. When
Lohiʻau awakes from death, he is hungry, and requests kalo and lūʻau.
Hiʻiaka dispatches Wahineʻōmaʻo and Pāʻūopalaʻā to fetch poi and lūʻau
for him, which she will cook herself. She tells him, "Truly, getting a bit
of food in you is all that's left to do, and your difficulties will be over. It's
good, though, that you hunger for lūʻau, for that is the staff of life from
ancient times."[50] When Wahineʻōmaʻo asks Lohiʻau's sister Kahuanui for
poi, she desires to send a runner with two large calabashes, worried they
do not have enough to eat. Wahineʻōmaʻo replies, "Do not do that, Chiefess. A small bowl of poi is what I am to get from you . . . that is the order
I was given; I am not to stray from the command. We have no lack of
food, for food from the heavens is what we are eating, and water from the
heavens is our drink. Later, we may indulge in the chief's food."[51] When
the women return, all is speedily prepared:

Just as [Wahineʻōmaʻo returned], Pāʻūopalaʻā was arriving with
her bundles of lūʻau. The small bowl of poi was prepared, and

Hi'iaka held the wrapped lū'au in her hands. [She offered a
prayer] . . . whereupon Lohi'au's lū'au was fully cooked. When
all was ready, Hi'iaka called her man to wake up and eat what
he hungered for. Lohi'au arose and ate. He ate the small bowl
of poi and the lū'au, and then he wanted water. Hi'iaka ordered
Pā'ūopala'ā to get one young coconut, but it had to be niu hiwa,
the dark coconut. Pā'ūopala'ā sped to her task and in no time
the young coconut was delivered. With her teeth [she] husked
the shell clean of its fiber and gave it to Hi'iaka, who then said
to Lohi'au, "Here is the water you shall drink, water that hangs
in the air, or what some refer to as the water of heaven." Lohi'au
drank every bit.[52]

There is a spiritual aspect to the food prepared: poi and lū'au are made
from the root and leaves of kalo, the representation of Hāloa, first ancestor, and a kino lau for Kāne, a god of healing; he is also associated
with the sun and freshwater, necessary elements for life. His name means
male, implying life for Lohi'au, a man. Niu is a kino lau of the god Kū,
another god of healing whose name means upright, erect. Hiwa means
dark-colored; it also means sacred. Thus, hiwa-colored plants and animals are most closely associated with sacred rituals and healing.

Speed ('eleu) and perfection in food preparation is very important, as
is the 'ono (deliciousness) and relishing of it. When Hi'iaka folks arrive
on the Wai'anae coast of O'ahu on their return to Hawai'i island, they
are offered hospitality by the people of Mākua:

The people the[n] asked Hi'iaka to call her companions to land
on the shore and partake in a meal before continuing on the
long journey. It was agreed, and before long, Wahine'ōma'o drew
the canoe near to the shore and the people of Mākua helped to
carry the canoe inland. Looking upon their guests, the people
of Mākua recognized the beauty of their guests, and the most
beautiful among them was . . . Hi'iaka. . . . The people of Mākua
were skilled and quickly had a pig ready for the imu [underground
earth oven], along with chickens, broiled fish, and mixed bowls
of poi 'uwala (sweet potato poi). Others . . . went diving for wana
(urchins), while others went to gather 'opihi (limpets), and 'ina
and hā'uke'uke (other varieties of urchins). The 'inamona (kukui
nut relish) was set out in a bowl, and the people of Mākua had
their welcoming feast prepared.[53]

Aside from the variety and abundance of the food prepared, the paragraph emphasizes the skill and speed at which the food is prepared, as these are also hallmarks of good ho'okipa etiquette.

Ke Lei maila 'o Ka'ula i ke Kai ē (Ka'ula Is Wreathed by the Sea)

The chants "Ke lei maila" and "'O Kalalau pali 'a'ala" are mele aloha 'āina, songs that express love for the land. They also demonstrate 'ike 'āina, knowledge about the land. This knowledge is expressed in eloquent poetry. "Ke lei maila" connects the famed hala groves of Naue in Hā'ena, Kaua'i, with the famed hala groves of Puna, Hawai'i, through Pele and Hi'iaka. It begins in the far west with reference to Ni'ihau and Ka'ula, extending to the far east of Puna, Hawai'i, with mention of Kīlauea.

In Kapihenui, Lohi'au chants "Ke lei maila" during a kilu match at Pele'ula's court. In other mo'olelo, it is chanted by Manamanaiakaluea, the lame fisherwoman spirit of Maui, for Hi'iaka when she is passing through the area. It uses natural imagery, Ka'ula encircled by the sea. Lei are often associated with special occasions, given to special people, symbolic of love and deep emotions. Ka'ula and Ni'ihau are presented as an 'ēko'a, joined by the Inuwai (water sipping) wind of that 'āina. The repetition of mālie (calm) connotes peace and good feelings. The scene then shifts to Naue in Hā'ena on the eastern side of Kaua'i. Like Puna, Hawai'i, Naue is famous for its hala groves, and so it is paired with Puna, Hawai'i, an 'ēko'a linking Lohi'au's homeland of Hā'ena with Pele's homeland of Puna through the image of the hala groves. Naue also means to shake, sway, or tremble, and is a kaona reference to the Pele women and their volcanic activity, to hula, with which they are also associated (naue describes the rotation of the hips in hula), and to the trembling of emotion, particularly when in love. The fragrance of hala, a symbol of lovemaking, is also alluded to. The mele emphatically concludes with the statement that the hala belongs to Naue, and that the woman (Pele) belongs to Puna, to Kīlauea. The mele thus exhibits knowledge of Pele and Hi'iaka, their genealogy and 'āina they belong to. In Kanaka Maoli thought, one is not just "from" someplace (mai), they belong to it (no).

"'O Kalalau pali 'a'ala" is a chanted greeting by Hi'iaka to the 'āina, describing specific wahi pana (Kalalau, Honopū, Waialoha), and the laua'e fern abundant there. Hi'iaka demonstrates proper etiquette by offering an appropriate greeting to the 'āina with the chant, one that simultaneously praises the beauty of that 'āina. Pleasant smells, such as that of laua'e, maile, and so forth, are linked to positive feelings of affection and love. The Nāpali coast is resplendent in the perfume of laua'e ferns, picked by "the woman," once again a metaphoric reference to Pele or Hiʻiaka, who sends her greetings of affection for this ʻāina.

These examples demonstrate how mele are capsules of knowledge, carrying Kanaka Maoli intellectual traditions that are meaningful on their own, with layers of meaning multiplied when viewed within the context of the moʻolelo, and then intertextually within the larger body of moʻolelo. Studying Pele and Hiʻiaka moʻolelo reminds us of the value our kūpuna placed on aloha ʻāina, respect for the land, and can be an impetus to learn and use oli in meaningful ways. Our ʻāina is not just a theme park or a tourist destination. It is our homeland. It is where the bones of our kūpuna lie. It is where the ʻiewe (placenta) and piko (umbilical cord) of our keiki (children) and moʻopuna (grandchildren) are planted. It is where we are woven to the past and the future through moʻolelo.

He Wahi Moʻolelo (A Little Story)

It is summer solstice 2012, and I am on the beach fronting Kahikinaakalā heiau complex at Wailua, Kauaʻi. It is 5 A.M., and I am waiting for sunrise at the place named "The rising of the sun" on the easternmost part of Kauaʻi in the lands where I was raised. As I wait, I imagine Hiʻiaka and Wahineʻōmaʻo centuries before sailing their canoe into these same waters, through the surf of Kaʻōhala in the center of Wailua Bay to the north of me, and Kalehuawehe just offshore. They land their waʻa somewhere along this bank, and Hiʻiaka chants "Kūnihi ka mauna" to the mountain Waiʻaleʻale rising five thousand feet above in the distance, asking permission to enter this island so she can fulfill her kuleana to her sister Pele. One version of the moʻolelo says that the moʻo guardian of Wailua does not respond to Hiʻiaka's call, so she subsequently destroys the moʻo, whose body is divided into large boulders Hiʻiaka scatters across the broad river mouth. Using them as stepping-stones to reach the other side, she makes her way north to Hāʻena, where she will discover that Lohiʻau has died, and she must retrieve him from the moʻo goddesses Aka and Kiliʻoeikapua, who have stolen his body and captured his spirit. Hiʻiaka must revive him so she can return him to her sister Pele at Halemaʻumaʻu on Hawaiʻi on the far eastern edge of the archipelago.

In the east, the sky lightens, and dawn begins to break. I stand alone on the sand facing the rising sun, and oli:

E ala e Kahiki kū
E ala e Kahiki moe
E ala hoʻi mai, ua hiki mai ʻoe

Ua ala ka lani, ua ala ka honua
Ua ala ka uka, ua ala ke kai
A ka lā e hiki mai ai.

Vertical Kahiki awakens
Horizontal Kahiki awakens
Awakening indeed, you are arriving
The heavens wake up, the earth wakes up
The uplands wake up, the sea wakes up
The sun is arriving.

The sight of the huge fireball sun Kānehoalani rising out of the ocean inspires ʻeʻehia, solemn reverence. The surf of Kalehuawehe rumbles offshore, ablaze in the first light of morning. A soft breeze stirs, a flock of wild chickens scratch and peck about the heiau and surround me, the morning traffic buzzes over the bridge behind me, crossing Wailua River to and fro—in modern society, it's off to work everyone goes. A jogger runs along the sands of Wailua on the north side of the river mouth, the rows of windows in the rows of resort buildings reflect the blinding glare of the rising sun. Behind me a tourist couple walk across Lydgate Park from their hotel toward the rising sun, paper coffee cups in hand. I am the only one here today who acknowledges the rising sun in a traditional way. Later I will peruse photos of this sunrise friends post on Facebook from locations across the pae ʻāina. It is easy to wonder if such practices—greeting the rising sun with an oli, remembering moʻolelo handed down mai ka pō mai through ancestors—have any relevance in a society built on global capitalism and foreign technologies. But what is lost in the forgetting of such things?

ʻO ʻOe ia, e Wailua Iki (It Is You, Wailua Iki): Mana Wahine in the Pele and Hiʻiaka Moʻolelo

'O 'oe ia e Wailua iki
E ka lāuli pali o Uli
Ua hele 'ia e Li'awahine
E ka wahine kūhea pali
Kui pua lei o Hoakalei ē
E lei au
E lei ho'i au i nā hala pala 'īloli o Hanakahi
Ua maka 'ele'ele wale i ke anu
Ua 'āha'i 'ia e ke kīna'u i'a o Mahamoku
I Wai'oli
'O ku'u makani Lawalawakua
Kūpani kapa o Wailua iki
Honi pua 'ala Kaiāulu
Kāhea ka luna o Kamae
Ē, he malihini mai ka'u
Mai lalo mai ē, no Kona
Hō mai he leo ē
E uē kāua.[1]

It is you, Wailua Iki
O shaded darkness, cliff of Uli
Traversed by Liʻawahine
By the woman who beckons from the cliffs
String garlands of flowers from Hoakalei
I am adorned
I wear the lei of specked, ripe hala of Hanakahi
With tips gone dark from the cold
Carried along by the kīnaʻu eel of Mahamoku
At Waiʻoli
My gusting wind, the Lawalawakua
Kapa-buffeting wind of Wailua Iki
The Kaiāulu wind bears the scent of fragrant flowers
The heights of Kamae call out
Ah, I have a guest
From the lee side, ah, from Kona
Offer up a voice of welcome, ah
Let us share our tears.[2]

IT IS JUNE 2003 AND I AM STANDING on the edge of the pier at Kawaihae Deep Draft Harbor in the ahupuaʻa of Kawaihae, South Kohala, staring down into the teal green waters. I am here as a kumu for Ka Hoʻi Wai, a Native Hawaiian education teacher training cohort, a part of the College of Education at the University of Hawaiʻi at Mānoa. There are about six other kumu, twenty or so students, and our alakaʻi (leaders) for the next few days, Chad and Pōmaikaʻi Paishon. Uncle Chad is the captain and navigator of *Makaliʻi*, a traditionally designed waʻa kaulua built in 1995 and based at Kawaihae. He is also the executive director of Nā Kālai Waʻa Moku o Hawaiʻi, a nonprofit voyaging and education organization dedicated to protecting and perpetuating Hawaiian culture. We are here for a few days to experience ʻike ʻāina, learning about the land and from the land, through working on and sailing the canoe.

Today we are swimming. Tomorrow we have a "float test." In order to sail on the waʻa, everyone must pass the test by floating in the harbor for forty-five minutes without assistance, and without talking. It is a matter of safety—if we accidentally go overboard while on the open ocean, this training will help us not panic and conserve energy while we wait for the waʻa or the escort boat to pluck us from the water. I am a good swimmer; in fact, I could swim before I could walk. But I am afraid of the deep water that opens up to the sea near Puʻukoholā, Kamehameha's luakini (large heiau where human sacrifices were offered in times of war), near Hale o Kapuni, an underwater heiau where human sacrifices were laid and offered to ʻaumākua manō (shark guardians), a place known for manō who live and spawn off Pelekane Bay nearby. Our family's shark ʻaumākua are not from this place, my ʻohana is not from this place. As if that is not enough, I don't know how I will pull myself out of the harbor. But as a kumu who believes in the Hawaiian philosophy of ma ka hana ka ʻike (knowledge is gained through experience), something I am trying to encourage in these young teachers, how can I *not* get into the water?

Uncle Chad senses my fear. I suspect I'm not the first person he's encountered who has faced this dilemma. He comes over and tells me how to climb onto the back of the escort boat, and from there climb back onto the pier. "Can," he says. Hawaiian leaders don't need to be verbal. Ma ka *hana* ka ʻike—knowledge is in doing, not talking.

I take a deep breath and think. I think about the stories my tūtū told of growing up in Kapaʻahu down in Puna, how they walked for two days to get to Hilo, what kind of toughness that took. I think about Aunty Daisy who lost her home there to a lava flow, and lived in her truck while she rebuilt it herself—when she was in her seventies. I think about the kind of spiritual toughness it took them to endure the racism and sexism they encountered growing up in Hawai'i's territorial years, when they were punished for speaking their native Hawaiian language in school, and discouraged from speaking it in public or passing it on to their children. When few opportunities to be anything but a housewife existed, my tūtū went to Teachers' College and became a special education teacher. Years later when I considered teaching as a career, I asked her why she had chosen it. "I didn't like being called a dummy," she said. At a time when most of my Kanaka Maoli classmates were the first generation in their families to attend college, I had a Hawaiian grandmother who had paved the way. I come from a long line of mana wahine, powerful women. I could do this.

I ignore my fear and jump into the water with my students and colleagues. We laugh and swim and relax at the end of a long hot day. When we are pau, I follow Uncle Chad's instructions to get out of the harbor, no problem. The next day the float test is more a mental challenge than a physical one. At the end of our time Uncle Chad blows a whistle, and we swim to the far end of the harbor, emerge from the water near the small boat ramp, and walk back along the shore. Another kumu gives me a playful whack on the arm. "You made that look so easy!" she admonishes. I smile.

I worry now about my role on the wa'a. I do not have good sea legs, and feel I might be more of a hindrance than a help onboard. Uncle Chad directs me to sit on the navigator's platform at his feet where I document the voyage through photographs. The wa'a exits the harbor, and we pick up speed in the open waters of the 'Alenuihāhā Channel. Under blue skies and a blazing sun, Maui beckons to us across the intensely blue sea. It is twenty-six miles away, but it looks much closer. Makali'i races across the waves, and it feels we could be there in just a few minutes. I imagine Hi'iaka's journey by canoe from Kohala to Maui on her quest to fetch Lohi'au, and their voyage together across these waters on their way back. I imagine Pele's voyage from Kahiki to Hawai'i, crossing this channel from Maui to Hawai'i, the very last stretch of open sea before she finds her home at Kīlauea and settles there. What that was like, traveling over two thousand miles of the vast Pacific and only twenty-six-miles before arriving home, the excitement at seeing the volcanic peaks of the Kohala mountains, Hualalai, Mauna Loa, and Mauna Kea looming ahead, the anticipation of landfall.

Uncle Chad points out various geographic features on the 'āina, some I've never noticed from shore. The green belt of Waikā on the Kohala hillside in the heights of Waimea is the most obvious. The rest of Kawaihae and what is visible of Kohala is dry and barren looking, withered in the hot summer sun. We turn to Maui, Haleakalā rising like a green goddess out of the deep blue sea, ke kai pōpolohua a Kāne. "Let's sail to Maui!" someone says, and we beg Uncle Chad to go. What would it be like to arrive in Honuaʻula on Maui's southeast coast as Hiʻiaka did? Is there a place for us to land there today? Could we sail around to Hāna, home of Kamehameha's favorite wife, Kaʻahumanu? We imagine the looks of surprise, the excitement it would generate. Uncle Chad smiles; I'm sure we're not the first crew of students to ask.

As we turn the waʻa back to Kawaihae, a pod of dolphins rises from the water to greet us and lead the way back. I turn one last time to look at Maui; Haleakalā is a large green woman adorned with a pāʻū of blue sea and white waves, beckoning in the distance.

Mana Wahine (Female Power): Beauty, Intelligence, Sexuality, and Resilience

The previous chapter explored different forms of ʻike—knowledge and recognition and the related skills of ʻaʻapo, ʻeleu, and akamai—adeptness, skill, and intelligence as important cultural values reflected in ʻŌiwi intellectual history and carried by moʻolelo. This chapter continues exploring these themes, specifically focusing on mana wahine, women's power, a primary aspect of Pele and Hiʻiaka moʻolelo, and how they are intertwined.

As I've previously discussed in an article on mana wahine, it is a concept found throughout Oceania, one fundamental to indigenous female identity. Mana is "power," usually referring to the spirit or essence of something living; wahine is "female." Mana wahine is a female-based power, strength, and resilience, the essence of womanhood. It embodies feminist ideas, although "feminism" is a problematic term because mana wahine predates the Western concept.[3]

Within Oceania, mana wahine describes an indigenous, culturally based understanding of female power and empowerment that is rooted in traditional concepts such as moʻokūʻauhau, aloha ʻāina, and kuleana. It is the physical, intellectual, and spiritual (or intuitive) power of women. It is individually embodied, but often employs collaborative strategies with other women for the benefit of the ʻohana or Lāhui, where women are the source of knowledge. Moreover, as Trask explains, it "asserts that women have our own power that is unique to us [and] can't be shared with (or appropriated by) men."[4] Brandy Nālani McDougall argues that mana wahine represents "a force that men must never ignore, for in a world where genealogical ranking [means] everything, the first ancestor [Pō, the female night who gives birth to herself] is the most powerful."[5]

Mana wahine is multiply layered and intertwined within the Pele and Hiʻiaka moʻolelo. In other moʻolelo, Pele's power as a woman and volcanic force of nature is balanced against male kupua, such as the pig–god Kamapuaʻa, who represents the lush windward forests of the northeastern part of the island. The two are rivals and lovers, and their moʻolelo speaks to the sometimes-fickle nature of male–female relationships, and of nature itself. Within the Pele and Hiʻiaka moʻolelo, however, the women are the central characters, and their power is balanced against each other. Their mana wahine also demonstrates the power they have over kāne, both godly and human, over the ʻāina and the (re)shaping of it, as well as the ability to call on elements of the ʻāina (thunder, lightning, wind, rain, and various vegetation), which are also the kino lau of their large ʻohana. McDougall says, "The Hiʻiakaikapoliopele moʻolelo recognizes this power by celebrating procreation, the power of women to bring forth new generations, as well as the power women hold over their sexuality while simultaneously demonstrating a complex view of womanhood as dwelling in the realms of both the sexual and the political, as 'sexual power and political power are very close in the Hawaiian mind.'"[6]

Moʻokūʻauhau, aloha ʻāina, and kuleana root Hiʻiaka's mana wahine in her relationship to her older sister Pele, manifested in several ways: within their moʻokūʻauhau, she is the youngest sister, the pōkiʻi. As the kuaʻana (oldest sibling of the same gender), Pele is responsible for Hiʻiaka, carrying her to Hawaiʻi as an egg, cradling it in her poli (chest, bosom, heart). Their special relationship is embodied by Hiʻiaka's name and the epithet "i ka poli o Pele" (in Pele's heart)—there are as many as forty Hiʻiaka sisters, but Hiʻiakaikapoliopele is special because of the relationship with their older sister. Her status as pōkiʻi prompts her to accept the difficult and dangerous task of fetching Lohiʻau and bringing him back to Hawaiʻi. Hiʻiakaikapoliopele will go because it is her kuleana as Pele's pōkiʻi. Together, Pele and Hiʻiaka represent aloha ʻāina through their symbiotic (pono, ʻēkoʻa) roles as creator and regenerator of the ʻāina. Pele gifts Hiʻiaka with several critical tools: ʻĀwihikalani (a critical eye), ka lima ikaika o Kīlauea (the "strong arm" of Kīlauea), and a pāʻū uila (lightning skirt). ʻĀwihikalani is the power of ʻike pāpālua, the ability to foretell or know ahead of time, to communicate with spirits, to possess supernatural knowledge. Ka lima ikaika o Kīlauea gives Hiʻiaka super strength in battle or in a tough situation when she needs extra assistance.

The power of the pāʻū is important because it is a specifically female garment. Silva argues, "[Hiʻiaka's] skirt is her greatest weapon—a symbol of specifically female power. These supernatural women are related to (but not ruled by) the male gods, Kū, Kāne, Kanaloa, and Lono."[7]

The moʻolelo donʻt specify whether it is the same as the pāʻū provided by her attendant, Pāʻūopalaʻe (Palaʻe skirt) in some moʻolelo, Pāʻūopalaʻā (Palaʻā-fern skirt) in others.

Hiʻiaka is accompanied on her journey by women with their own mana wahine that also falls within the parameters of moʻokūʻauhau, aloha ʻāina, and kuleana. Pāʻūopalaʻe/Pāʻūopalaʻā are the keepers of the sacred pāʻū and assist Hiʻiaka in her healing and reviving of different characters, culminating with Lohiʻauʻs revivification. Pāʻūopalaʻe is able to shield Hiʻiaka with her fern kino lau when the evil moʻo women Kiliʻoeikapua and Kalamainuʻu pelt her with rocks and debris as she scales the sheer cliffs of Makana to reach the cave where they have hidden Lohiʻauʻs corpse. Their moʻokūʻauhau and kuleana are linked to the Pele ʻohana, and they serve as ukali (attendants) to Hiʻiaka on Peleʻs orders. Before Hiʻiaka departs Kīlauea, Pele orders each attendant of a particular kind of pāʻū skirt, beginning with Pāʻūokamaʻo (skirt of maʻo, a Hawaiian variety of cotton), to fit Hiʻiaka with their garment. Once Pele decides that Pāʻūopalaʻe/Pāʻūopalaʻā is the most appropriate, their kuleana is established.[8]

Wahineʻōmaʻo is the "green woman" who becomes Hiʻiakaʻs traveling companion to Kauaʻi. Her personal moʻokūʻauhau is not provided, but her ʻohana are devotees of Pele demonstrating her connection and kuleana. Her name also suggests a relationship to Hiʻiaka through her role of (re)vegetating the ʻāina. She functions as a substitute for Hōpoe who doesnʻt accompany Hiʻiaka on the trip. Wahineʻōmaʻo is an ordinary makaʻāinana, an Everywoman the audience can identify with; Hōpoe cannot fulfill this role because she is also an akua, an element of the ʻāina. Wahineʻōmaʻo is thus a kōkua (helper) in a literal and figurative sense, a vehicle for Hiʻiaka to instruct the audience in history, traditions, moʻolelo, protocol, chants, practices, vocabulary, and other aspects of Kanaka Maoli intellectual tradition.

Hiʻiaka meets Wahineʻōmaʻo in the forests of Puna as she is leaving Kīlauea en route to Kauaʻi, and Wahineʻōmaʻo is on her way to the volcano to sacrifice a pig to Pele on her familyʻs behalf. Hiʻiaka takes a liking to her, and engages her in conversation. When she finds out the purpose of Wahineʻōmaʻoʻs journey, it is her first opportunity to instruct Wahineʻōmaʻo—and the reading audience—in how to recognize Pele, follow protocols that will appeal to Pele, and properly present an offering to her. It is also Hiʻiakaʻs first opportunity to display (to the audience) her mana in "assisting" Wahineʻōmaʻo hurry along and fulfill her kuleana so she can return and accompany Hiʻiaka on her journey. Hiʻiaka is later impressed with Wahineʻōmaʻoʻs keen observation (ʻike) and quickness (ʻeleu) in grasping Hiʻiakaʻs kānāwai and not needing elaborate instruction.

As an Everywoman, Wahineʻōmaʻo has a somewhat comedic role at times, too. This sense of comedy should not be overlooked, as it is part of Hawaiian culture, and thus provides an entertainment factor in the moʻolelo, even when lessons need to be learned. It also allows the reader to be drawn into the joke and enjoy the fun. For example, when Wahineʻōmaʻo is asked to participate in kilu, she is reluctant, because she is not talented in chant:

> It was now Wahineomaoʻs turn to take the kilu, and she was twirling it preparatory to throwing, when Peleʻula stopped her with the remark, "[Y]ou must know the invariable rule of this game, to chant a song before throwing. Why do you omit it now?"
>
> Wahineomao told her that she could never from childhood sing or chant a note. But the hostess, possibly annoyed at her own failure, insisted on Wahineomaoʻs complying with all regulations. It was in vain the latter protested her utter inability to remember or repeat even a few words of couplets of a song.
>
> Finally, in exasperation, she sang out, "Ku-o-ka-o-Wahine-omao" (rough and ready Wahineomao), and threw the kilu, which struck the wand so strong and true that the ringing of the gourds was louder and longer than when Hiʻiaka threw it. When the other side had the throw they again lost. And thus they continued playing till the game ended, Hiʻiaka and her companions winning.
>
> "Ku-o[-]ka," Wahineomaoʻs saying, has ever since been the answer of unpoetical or unmusical people when importuned to chant, sing, or repeat a song.[9]

Because Wahineʻōmaʻo is not a dancer or chanter, her role is relatively nonexistent in hula performances. Ka Palapala thus allows for the expansion of the moʻolelo, providing opportunities to tell other stories outside of performance, which carry ethics, morals, values, and non-performative practices that are just as important and entertaining.

Aikāne (Same-Sex) Relationships

Throughout the moʻolelo, women create and maintain different kinds of relationships; the power and significance of these female relationships exhibit camaraderie in many ways. Hiʻiakaʻs relationship with Hōpoe and Wahineʻōmaʻo are central to the moʻolelo. Hiʻiakaʻs relationship with both of them is described in all of the Hawaiian-language texts as aikāne.

A benign interpretation of aikāne is "friend," although given the kaona built into Hawaiian language, combined with the deeply Christian colonization of Kanaka Maoli beginning in the nineteenth century and its effects on the language, it is difficult to accept such a shallow interpretation of the word, particularly in the context of how it is used to describe particular relationships in moʻolelo kuʻuna such as that between Pele and Hiʻiaka. Pukui and Handy define aikāne as "devoted friends," intimate relationships between men with other men, or women with other women, but not between man and woman; they stress that "the genuine *aikāne* relationship is never sexual," which I believe demonstrates an overtly oppressive Christian influence.[10]

The sexual nature of aikāne relationships is difficult to pinpoint because of the clear Christian condemnation of homosexuality and bisexuality; in light of severe Christian condemnation, Kanaka Maoli quickly learned to suppress, deny, or reinterpret such practices. Charlot argues that sexuality is difficult to define in the moʻolelo because "words like *ipo* [sweetheart] and *aikāne* were losing their *necessarily* sexual implication," also noting several possible pronunciations and origins of the word, which was ultimately a term "used for a man who participated in an intense friendship with another man, a relationship that included sexual relations. The word was applied to lesbian friends as well. The word does not necessarily designate an exclusively homosexual person."[11]

Other words used to describe the intimate aikāne relationships include aloha or pilialoha (aikāne pilialoha), and punahele (favorite); Hiʻiaka also refers to Wahineʻōmaʻo as her hoa pili (close friend). "Kuʻu," the intimate or beloved possessive form of "my" (i.e., kuʻu hoa, my beloved companion), is frequently employed throughout the moʻolelo. Ambiguity surrounding aikāne relationships may be confounding or frustrating to some, but it was a hallmark of Hawaiian poetic expression that continues today, while the blatant exposure of something valuable is considered coarse.

Hiʻiaka and Wahineʻōmaʻo's relationship grows closer as they travel and face many obstacles and hardships together. She is Hiʻiaka's only true emotional support and witness to their trials and tribulations. However, their relationship does not appear to be sexual, adding to the fluidity of the term. In Poepoe, as Hiʻiaka, Pāʻūopalaʻe, and Wahineʻōmaʻo depart from Papalauahi, Hiʻiaka keeps turning around and looking down toward the sea where Hōpoe is, and tears begin streaming down her face. Wahineʻōmaʻo asks her why she is crying. Hiʻiaka responds, "I am thinking about *our* aikāne, the woman stringing lehua blossoms named Hōpoe. Here I am traveling the length and breadth of the land, perhaps going to the sun-snatching island of Kaua'i, the border of our traveling, with you, my close companion of these places, and that aikāne of mine is staying behind without knowing what is going to befall her. That is why I am crying, because of her doom. I know, there is no way that older sister of ours will heed my order to her."[12]

Here Hi'iaka refers to Hōpoe as *"our"* aikāne, even though Wahine'ōma'o has never met her. At first Wahine'ōma'o says she is familiar with the name Hōpoe as Nānāhuki ([To] pull the gaze), the name of the lehua forest at Kea'au. But Hi'iaka tells her the 'āina is named for the woman Hōpoe. Wahine'ōma'o then asks Hi'iaka how she and Hōpoe became aikāne (ho'aikāne), "Is it like how we met?" she asks. Hi'iaka responds, "Yes, it is similar." She then recounts for Wahine'ōma'o how she first met Hōpoe:

> One day some time ago I went down to the sea of Kea'au on an excursion, to the place abundant with limu, 'opihi, he'e pali [young octopus], 'ina and wana. . . . While I was standing there on the point looking for a place for me to step down to the rocks below, there was this beautiful young woman coming from below with her lauhala bag filled with 'opihi kō'ele, he'e pali, limu, 'ina, and wana. She placed them where I was standing and said to me, "Are you a visitor?" I told her I was, that I came down from the mountains and was hungry for fresh delicacies from the sea here, that we lived a life in the mountains where we suffered from hunger for these things of the sea. She then offered the seafood she had gathered, and told me to take as much as I wanted. She gave me a lauhala bag, and I made my selections. I asked her what her name was, and she said, "The name I've been called by my parents since I was young until now is Nānāhuki. But the name everyone calls me is Hōpoe, because I am always picking lehua in the forest named Hōpoe." I said, "I want to you to be an aikāne for me, and your name will forever be Hōpoe. She agreed to my request to be my aikāne, and she accepted the name I said to her, her name. That is how we became friends, and her home became a place for me to visit. For that aikāne my tears fall."[13]

Hi'iaka and Hōpoe's initial meeting demonstrates a few important cultural values: first, the emphasis on malihini and kama'āina, distinctions being made by visitors or newcomers to a place (malihini), and those belonging to a place (kama'āina, *lit.* child of the land). As a kama'āina to

Keaʻau, Hōpoe has a different relationship to and knowledge about that 'āina; as a malihini, Hi'iaka is trying to figure out how to get down to the sea from the rocky coastline; as kama'āina, Hōpoe has already gathered her seafood.

Next, there is an emphasis on beauty throughout the text. While the central female characters are powerful and "beautiful," no specific descriptions of physical traits mark their beauty. This is another kind of ambiguity favored in the text, and it leaves it up to the reader to imagine what u'i (beauty) and 'ōpiopio (youthful) look like. Overtly physical traits, which Amer-European popular culture obsesses over, such as skin, eye, or hair color, height, weight, or hair texture are never mentioned, irrelevant to Kanaka Maoli ideas of attractiveness (for men as much as for women). Descriptions of beauty are references to nature—Hōpoe is the full blooming lehua, attractive people are "pali ke kua, mahina ke alo," backs straight as a cliff (meaning youthful), front (or face) radiant like the moon.

Generosity is a marker of civility and attraction, and Hōpoe immediately exhibits this quality. As soon as Hi'iaka indicates that she is a malihini and hungry for seafood, Hōpoe promptly offers for her to take whatever she wants from what Hōpoe has collected. It doesn't matter that gathering limu, 'opihi, 'ina, wana, and he'epali are time-consuming, dangerous endeavors, particularly along the rocky Puna coastline, with unpredictable crashing waves and surging tides, unprotected by reefs.

Hōpoe's name connects her to her 'āina in another way—while her given name is Nānāhuki, Hōpoe is a name in the region and an inoa kapakapa (nickname) given to her by other kama'āina because of her constant presence in the lehua groves (ulu lehua, moku lehua) of the area, weaving lei lehua. We don't know if she is a devotee of Pele, but lehua are associated with the Pele 'ohana. Considering all these qualities Hōpoe possesses, in Hawaiian thinking, who would not be attracted to such a person? Hi'iaka's attraction to her is unavoidable.

Sexual relations between aikāne in the mo'olelo is embedded in kaona, which heightens the intellectual and emotional enjoyment of the listening or reading audience. Mele shared between the aikāne (composed by one for the other) describe the desire and intimacy of the lovers. Noenoe Silva discusses this in detail with the mele beginning "He ua kui lehua ko Panaewa" (Pana'ewa's lehua-striking rain) composed by Hi'iaka for Hōpoe. Silva explicates the imagery in the mele and how it connotes the closeness of their relationship; the last lines reveal their romantic relationship: "He lei moe ipo / Aloha mai ka ipo / He ipo no e" (A lover's lei / Beloved is the sweetheart / She is a lover).[14]

After Hi'iaka recounts to Wahine'ōma'o how she and Hōpoe first met,

Hiʻiaka chants a mele aloha (love song) for Hōpoe that begins, "E kuu aikane i ke kai hee o Hoeu ma loko" (My beloved in the surfing sea of Hōʻeu inside [Kaimū Bay]). The mele expresses Hiʻiaka's desire for Hōpoe, employing imagery specific to their ʻāina. It details named (and thus familiar) surf spots of their ʻāina (Hōʻeu, ʻĀwili, Kalaloa), named sites Hiʻiaka and Hōpoe have surfed together.

Hiʻiaka recounts (pīnaʻi) the names of ahupuaʻa and familiar ʻāina throughout Puna: Kalapana, Kupahua, Kaunaloa, Kapaʻahu, Kamilo-paekanaka, Kahaualeʻa, Pāhoehoe, Poupoukea, Kamoamoa, Laeapuki, Panauiki, Panaunui, Kealakomo, ʻĀpua, Māwae. There are subtexts embedded in the place names. For example, the line "I ka ʻōpule moe one o ke kai e" ([My beloved] of the "sand sleeping wrasse [ʻōpule, Anampses cuvier, A. godeffroyi]" of the sea) contains sexual imagery, and is related to Kalapana. Fish are often kaona employed for a lover. The "sand sleeping wrasse" is a reference specific to Kalapana, Puna.[15] Several lines address Hōpoe as "kuʻu aikāne," Hiʻiaka's beloved, and the mele concludes with Hiʻiaka's expressed desire for Hōpoe, "Kuu aikane hoi e / Aloha e oe" (My beloved / You are indeed cherished).[16]

Silva argues, and I concur, that imposing Western-constructed categories of sexual identity—heterosexual, homosexual, bisexual, or any others—onto Hawaiian characters is wrong: "In this and other Hawaiian moʻolelo, romantic love between people of the same sex is presented as a normal practice of everyday life rather than as an identity marker. In the stories, such love relationships are cherished by those engaged in them and are supported by others. An understanding of these relationships as valuable in our ancestors' culture assists us in understanding ourselves as healthy when we, too, cherish such relationships."[17]

Despite reticence by some to acknowledge the sexual aspect of aikāne relationships, there is ample evidence to support it. Hawaiian sources such as David Malo's *Hawaiian Antiquities* describe aikāne relationships recorded in moʻolelo that go back in time to the aliʻi nui Līloa in the fifteenth century.[18] Kamakau's *Ruling Chiefs of Hawaiʻi* include various descriptions of aikāne relationships of high-ranking aliʻi kāne such as Kahekili and Kamehameha I. Early haole explorers also documented aikāne relationships among the chiefly men of Kamehameha's court.[19]

Noel Elizabeth Currie closely examines accounts of aikāne described by King, Samwell, Clerke, and Ledyard on Cook's voyage to Kealakekua in 1779. She concludes that what Cook's men observe in describing aikāne relationships between the male chiefs are complex, socially accepted, and significant relationships that indicate social, political, and sexual functions:

[Chief Kalaniʻōpuʻu's aikāne] Palea's interactions with the officers indicate the social and political roles of *aikāne*: he acts as Kalaniopuu's official representative and spokesman. . . . His status and behavior confirm and exemplify the various writers' presentation of *aikāne* as a relationship simultaneously personal (affectionate and sexual: the *aliʻi*'s lover) and official (social and political: the *aliʻi*'s counsellor and confidante), that this relationship was shared by several young men at once, and that it was an accepted part of Hawaiian society, among the chiefly rank at least . . . Hawaiians felt no shame or need to hide these relationships.[20]

As Charlot suggests, aikāne does not necessarily describe an exclusively homosexual relationship; many of the chiefly men described by Malo, Kamakau, Cook's men, and others had children and relationships with women, sometimes with more than one at a time, a cultural practice referred to as punalua (*lit.* "two springs"). Aikāne seems to describe a broad category of intimate, loving relationships between same-sex participants. Bryan Kamaoli Kuwada writes, "Aikāne . . . are those who are in a very intimate relationship/friendship with someone of the same sex. Being an aikāne very often implied a sexual relationship as well, although it was based first and foremost on companionship, with the sex arising more out of that intimacy and closeness than being a requirement of the friendship."[21]

Because aikāne relationships between chiefly men are described as a common, traditional practice, in the Pele and Hiʻiaka moʻolelo, as a Kauaʻi aliʻi, Lohiʻau's aikāne relationship with Kahuakaʻiapaoa is normal and expected. Such an intimate relationship between them also justifies Kahuakaʻiapaoa's intense anger at Pele when he discovers she has killed Lohiʻau, and his determination to avenge Lohiʻau's death. Kahuakaʻiapaoa is also charmed by Pele upon his arrival at the crater, and Hiʻiaka is likewise charmed by Lohiʻau, falling in love with him during the course of their travels together, adding to the fluidity of Hawaiian sexuality and intimate relationships.

While not as explicit as the journals of Cook's men, early missionary papers also refer to chiefly aikāne relationships. The kanikau that begins with the line "He mele kanikau na Kahekili no ka make ana o kana aikane" (A dirge by Kahekili on the death of his aikane) was published in *Ke Kumu Hawaii* in 1835; a death notice for Keawehawaiʻi, described as the aikāne of Hoapili, was published two months later.[22] The missionary papers knew what aikāne referred to. As early as 1834, *Ke Kumu Hawaii* published Paul's letters to the Romans, using the word "aikāne" to describe sodomy.[23] In 1835, *Ka Lama* railed against "puni aikane" (fondness for aikāne relationships) as a sin from the past ('ino kahiko) that needed to stop.[24]

Writing by explorers, missionaries, and scholars has focused on aikāne relationships between chiefly men, with less attention given to aikāne relationships among other social groups, such as maka'āinana, or among women. Ledyard wrote that they never saw any indication that aikāne relationships occurred among the maka'āinana.[25] Anti-aikāne articles and letters printed in the missionary papers did not make such a distinction between classes, and condemned aikāne relationships as a terrible sin that needed to stop, an indication that it was ongoing and more common in daily life than Cook's men observed.

Relationships between female aikāne appear to be as commonplace and normal as do those between men. In *Ruling Chiefs of Hawai'i*, Kamakau describes Ka'ahumanu's strategy with beautiful women who were potential rivals to make them aikāne or punahele.[26] The only other female aikāne relationship mentioned is Kahaumanu, a woman of Kahuwa, Kohala, whose aikāne was a woman named Hinupu; her traveling companion was Mua, wife of Hīna'i, a chief of Waimea.[27] Kamakau describes how ali'i women who have or desire aikāne relationships and women who travel together (as aikāne) are cultural practices that are well reflected in the Pele and Hi'iaka mo'olelo. Aikāne relationships of men and women are prevalent throughout a number of mo'olelo ku'una published in Hawaiian-language newspapers. But perhaps none highlights aikāne relationships between women more prominently than Pele and Hi'iaka mo'olelo.

Rice describes a relationship between Pele and Kaoahi, an ali'i wahine of Ni'ihau whom Pele encounters when she first arrives in Hawai'i, as aikāne. When Pele migrates from Kahiki she lands on Ni'ihau, a smaller island on the northwest side of Kaua'i. Kaoahi's people see Pele and exclaim at her beauty. When Kaoahi hears this, she invites Pele to her home. When Pele arrives, the ali'i woman is startled by Pele's attractive appearance, describing her as "pali ke kua, mahina ke alo" (back straight like a cliff, front radiant like the moon, a common 'ōlelo no'eau praising a fine appearance). The women spend time together while a feast is prepared for them. After their meal, a heap of pāwehe mats is prepared for the two women to relax and pass the time together. Pāwehe refers to the geometric patterns worked into the finely woven mats made from makaloa sedge, a product for which Ni'ihau is renowned. That night, the two women fall asleep together on their mat, and awaken the next morning to the crowing of roosters. Their falling asleep together is described poetically as "ho'oipo loa ana aku me Niolopua," making love with Niolopua, the god of slumber. The kaona of the word hoʻoipo (to make love) suggests sexual intimacy between them.

Once they awaken, Kaoahi sends her kūkini runners to assemble the aloaliʻi (royal court) to pay homage to her companion (kāna aikāne). They then spend the next anahulu (ten days) engaging in the leisure activities of the court—playing kōnane (a board game similar to checkers), kilu, hula, kake (a kind of riddling), olioli (chanting), and heʻe nalu. Without explanation, Pele disappears at the end of the ten-day period, continuing on her journey to Kauaʻi and encountering Lohiʻau.[28]

Women Hiʻiaka encounters in her travels desire to become her aikāne, such as Papanuioleka, a woman from Hilo.[29] She offers hoʻokipa to Hiʻiaka, and joins her when she resumes her journey. But they soon encounter a crazed man, Paikaka, at Hilo Bay. Papanuioleka is so frightened she runs home, abandoning Hiʻiaka. This becomes an etiological point in the moʻolelo: "[Papanuioleka] no sooner arrived [at her home] than she was turned into stone for forsaking Hiʻiaka and breaking her promise. As for . . . Paikaka, he was also turned into stone on the beach to the east of the Waiolama stream, and there he lies to this day. The sandy beach is now known as ʻke one o Paikaka [the sands of Paikaka].' This is just in front of the late Princess Ruth's house in Hilo bay."[30]

Along their journey, Wahineʻōmaʻo desires to become aikāne with Manamanaiakaluhea, the lame fisherwoman spirit they encounter on Maui. When they arrive, Manamana dances a hula for them, "Aloha wale ka iʻa lamalama o kuu aina la" (The vivacious fish of my beloved land is truly loved); iʻa (fish) is a kaona reference to a sweetheart, lover, or potential "catch." It is because of Wahineʻōmaʻo's intense desire to be Manamanaiakaluhea's aikāne that Hiʻiaka agrees to heal her. Wahineʻōmaʻo, stirred by the sexual nature of the hula, declares that she would like Manamanaiakaluhea as "an aikane, an intimate friend."[31] Here a woman dances for the pleasure (and enticement) of another woman, a blatant contrast to the settler colonial representation of hula as women dancing for the pleasure of men.

Hiʻiaka and Wahineʻōmaʻo have an aikāne relationship, although it is different from Hiʻiaka's aikāne relationship with Hōpoe. Various reasons are given in the narratives for how they become aikāne. Kapihenui says it is Pele who asks Wahineʻōmaʻo to become Hiʻiaka's aikāne; Wahineʻōmaʻo tells Hiʻiaka, "Kauoha mai nei iau i aikane oe naʻu" (Pele ordered me to be an aikāne for you).[32] In Paʻaluhi and Bush (1893), Hiʻiaka tells Pele she won't go to Kauaʻi to fetch Lohiʻau without her aikāne Wahineʻōmaʻo.[33] In Hoʻoulumāhiehie it is Wahineʻōmaʻo who desires to be Hiʻiaka's aikāne. When they first meet, she tells Hiʻiaka:

"Tell me your name, for I want you to be my aikāne" . . . [Hiʻiaka replies] . . . "I shall indeed tell you, for we two have struck a bond of intimate friendship. I am Hiʻiaka in the bosom of Pele, and this one's name is Pāʻūopalaʻā." . . .

Wahineʻōmaʻo leaped forth and grasped Hiʻiaka's neck and kissed her by adjoining noses and inhaling deeply, crying out, "Oh my, you have spared me! I would have been in a state of terrible ruin . . . I ask of you to take me as your aikāne. Wherever you go, there, too, shall I."

Hiʻiaka assented to this, saying, "What can I do, but agree to your request, for it is a good one. But to secure our relation as aikāne, let us clap hands and lock fingers."

Then their hands clapped together, and they hooked their fingertips into each other's, and thus was their oath set that they would be together as aikāne, the dearest of friends.[34]

At the end of the moʻolelo, it is Wahineʻōmaʻo who is responsible for bringing Hiʻiaka back from the underworld after Pele kills Lohiʻau, when Hiʻiaka is mourning over the deaths of Hōpoe and Lohiʻau. Hiʻiaka refuses over and over to return to the crater. The only way Wahineʻōmaʻo is able to persuade her to return and ease her grief is through a series of "Kuʻu aikāne" chants that recollect their travels together.[35]

The primary aikāne relationship in the moʻolelo is between Hiʻiaka and Hōpoe. While Hōpoe seems to be a minor character who appears only in the very beginning of the moʻolelo, it is Hiʻiaka's love for her and her association with her birthplace (one hānau) of Puna that motivates Hiʻiaka to have Hōpoe not accompany her to Kauaʻi. Hiʻiaka knows it will be a dangerous trip, and she wants Hōpoe to be safe. She also does not want to be distracted by her feelings for Hōpoe, so she can concentrate on her task and return home as soon as possible. Hiʻiaka's love for Hōpoe prompts her to strike a deal with Pele: she will go to Kauaʻi if Pele agrees to protect Hōpoe. Pele's breaking of that promise is the impetus for Hiʻiaka to seek revenge on her sister, and almost destroy their crater home in the process.

Nā Hoa Aloha a me nā Hoa Paio (Friends and Rivals)

Throughout their travels, Pele and Hiʻiaka encounter a number of women with whom they do not have aikāne relationships. Some of these encounters result in friendships or collaborations, while others are competitions of women's power and knowledge. In Manu, as Kapōʻulakīnaʻu

and her sisters are traveling through Kauaʻi, they save a woman from
domestic abuse:

> They continued on . . . straight to Hanakaʻape. . . . When they
> arrived here, Kapōʻulakīnaʻu saw a woman being beaten by her
> husband. She felt compassion for the woman and sent a part of
> her spirit, called Pua, into the woman, who then was transformed
> into a reddish-brown dog that overpowered the man, his strength
> being reduced to nothing. The dog continued to attack the man
> until the end of his existence under the warmth of the sun. His
> relatives were unsuccessful in their attempts to save him. After
> he died, Kapōʻulakīnaʻu whistled, and the dog ran straight to her
> side. She took a piece of mahiki grass growing next to the stream
> and placed it in the mouth of the supernatural being. The dog
> kino lau quickly transformed, and the woman was changed back
> into her human self.[36]

This incident reveals Kapōʻs power and empathy. Elsewhere in the moʻolelo
she and her sisters transform themselves into whirlwinds and travel on
rainbows. Here she transforms another woman, possibly saving her life.
This informs us that our kūpuna did not value such brutal behavior, and
that we should not either. The kind of violent death that occurs in the
moʻolelo is a sobering reminder of the sanctity of life, the importance of
recognition of the mana of women, of having compassion, and treating
others with respect.

The first major encounter with women who are not friendly to the Pele
clan is in Hāʻena, Kauaʻi, between Pele and two moʻo kupua (supernatural
lizard) women, Kiliʻoeikapua and Kalanamainuʻu. Pele first encounters
them at Lohiʻauʻs hula festival; Hoʻoulumāhiehie, Poepoe, and Desha
present the moʻo women as potential rivals for Lohiʻauʻs affection. Food
is prepared and the gathering eats; afterward the hula festivities begin.
Lohiʻau performs the first hula, which arouses the moʻo women. He calls
on Pele to hula, and she declines, offering instead to chant the history of
the winds of Nihoa, Lehua, and Kauaʻi, a considerable accomplishment.
The moʻo women already admire and are jealous of Peleʻs physical beauty.
Upon hearing her desire to perform an oli makani instead of a hula, they
remark, "Ah! If you can recite all the winds from Nihoa to here, then
you are the native [kamaʻāina] of these islands, and we are all newcomers
[malihini]."[37]

The ability to recall such an extensive list of wind names operates
on multiple levels within the moʻolelo. First, it is a performance of

moʻokūʻauhau. Through such performance, Pele demonstrates her mana and level of ʻike ʻāina, knowledge about the ʻāina; the moʻo women doubt her knowledge, as evidenced by their retort to her. As Silva notes, "Knowledge and ability to call the names of the winds confer the decisive power in the narrative. . . . The winds respond to the calling of their names and accomplish what the caller desires."[38] Pele's mana is displayed in her ʻike ʻāina and chanting of wind names; as an akua associated with the creation of ʻāina, Pele's knowledge of the ʻāina would be part of her kuleana. In this way, Pele is able to defeat her rivals for Lohiʻau's affection, the moʻo women. The oli makani is also a love song to Lohiʻau, reminding him of the kaiʻokia (separating sea) law she has already placed on him, making him kapu (reserved) to her and her alone; it also enables her to "literally blow away her rivals for his affection," as they mysteriously disappear toward the end of the oli.[39] It is also a kind of hoʻopāpā, challenging the audience to listen (or read) carefully, looking for error, and appreciating such skill. It is a performed oli of the most intricate detail, something Hawaiian audiences relish.

As Hiʻiaka travels across the pae ʻāina, many of her encounters with other women are friendly; she is admired for her beauty, and more often than not offered hospitality and friendship, establishing or reestablishing kinship connections with ʻohana or devotees of Pele. Examples include the aliʻi wahine Peleʻula of Kou (Honolulu), Oʻahu, and the aliʻi wahine Mailelauliʻi, Koʻiahi, and Halakaipo of Mākua, Oʻahu. The Mākua women not only befriend Hiʻiaka and offer her hospitality, they collaborate with her to help solve the riddle plaguing the Molokaʻi aliʻi kāne Kaulanakalā. Hiʻiaka and Lohiʻau engage in kilu matches with the chiefly women of Kou and Mākua.

Some women are rude to her along the way, and their lack of recognition of Hiʻiaka as a goddess, combined with their inhospitable behavior, is punished. On Oʻahu, the woman ʻĀpuakehau dares to compare her beauty to Hiʻiaka's, and is punished with death for her impudence.

Hiʻiaka's most notable rival is Waihīnano (alternately Waihīnalo), the wife of ʻOlepau, aliʻi of Maui. Hiʻiaka's encounter with Waihīnano is also an opportunity for Hiʻiaka to exhibit mana wahine and the power of her moʻokūʻauhau. When they arrive on Maui, Hiʻiaka seeks out ʻOlepau's home. When they arrive, preparations are underway for a large feast, but they are not welcomed inside. While ʻOlepau recognizes her, his wives Waihīnano and Kawelokaiʻehuʻehu would not. Even when Hiʻiaka's sister Kapōkūlani (Kapōʻulakīnaʻu) arrives, the women stubbornly refuse to recognize Hiʻiaka's chant requesting permission to enter their home.

Kapō is so upset by their rudeness, she tells the women, "if we're all to

(E nana Helu 42, Buke Mele Hiiaka)

"Kunihi ka mauna i ka lai — e
O Waialeale la — e i Wailua
Huki ae la iluna ka papa o AnoKawai-
    kini (Uaowaikumailani)
Alai ia ae la e Nounou
Nalowale ka ipu-haa
Haa i ka laula
Haa ka ipu, haa makai o Kapaa — e
Haa ka ipu, haa mauka o Kapaa — e
Mai paa i ka leo
He ole ka heahea mai."

A malaila aku ka lakou nei hele ana, a hiki
i na Hala-o-Naue, puana hou ae la o Hiiaka
i Kekahi Mele:

(E nana Helu 23, Buke Mele Hiiaka.)

"A na wai naulu ka uka o Mana
Ke hahai la i ka liu-la o Kaunalewa
Aloha ke kai kui kaa-la
Kai lawe wahine o Nualolo
Ke kuwehu mai la ke ahi o Kalalau
E kuni nei i ka ili — a uli
Uli hewa ka ili i ka ipo ahi e
Moe iki ai la hoi, pono."

A mai laila aku ka lakou nei hele ana a
hoea i Haena, kahi o ke kane a ke kaikuaana
i alualu hele mai ai, ma ke kani o na pahu.
    I ka nana aku auanei ka hana e peahi mai
ana ka uhane o Lohiau ia lakou nei iloko o
kekahi Ana, iwaena o ka pali. O ka lima wale
no nae ka lakou nei i ike aku. Ua lawea ke
uhane e Kilioeikapua ame Kalanaimanu i

sit in this house and let it get . . . sharp and nasty . . . then I, the guest, shall get up and go back home, and you people can do whatever you think is right."[40] Kapō raised Waihīnano, and is horrified by her uncivil behavior. Before she leaves, Kapō warns her, "Listen. It is you I am talking to, the one I raised. Pay attention to the message carried to you like a breeze [in Hi'iaka's chants]. You had best remember that life is in the voice and death is in the voice, as well. Therefore, this beckoning voice should be heeded."[41] When the women continue to insult Hi'iaka and refuse to acknowledge her request, she decides to battle with them over 'Olepau's life. While her decision appears extreme, Hi'iaka is responsible for Lohi'au and Wahine'ōma'o, who are both starving. Hi'iaka feels the women should be punished because 'Olepau is the source of their comfort, and they are overstepping their kuleana in refusing Hi'iaka and company hospitality.

Waihīnano is confident in the mana of her gods, who are akua wahine. It is her confidence, combined with her lack of recognition of Hi'iaka as a powerful akua wahine, that makes her arrogant, and her arrogance that leads to her demise. Hi'iaka begins her series of chants that cause 'Olepau to fall ill. Waihīnano counters with her own series of oli that call on and name the great chiefs of Maui's heritage, a recollection of mo'okū'auhau that also evokes their mana. Hi'iaka then calls on the akua wahine of her mo'okū'auhau, chanting:

Ua make ia
Ke ha'i mai nei nā akua wāhine
I ka hikina o ka lā
Nā wāhine i ka lā o Ha'eha'e
Nā wāhine i ka lā o Kumukahi
Walea wai a Kamiloholu
'Apo lehua o Kuaokalā
'O Pelehonuamea i ka Lua
'O Hi'iaka o ke aka
I ka 'ālawa maka o Ākea
Ke 'ī mai nei Haumea
He kālawa ka ma'i a puni lā
Ua make ia.[42]

[He] is dead
The goddesses have declared it
At the rising of the sun
The women in the [rising] sun at Ha'eha'e
The women in the sun at Kumukahi

Relaxing waters of Kamiloholu
Plucking lehua of Kuaokalā
Red earth Pele of the caldera
Hiʻiaka of the reflection
In the glancing eyes of Ākea
Haumea has declared it
Kālawa is the ensnaring illness
[He] is dead.

In this mele, Hiʻiaka announces that the Pele women (the female deities from the east) have already declared ʻOlepau dead. The life-and-death power of words is thus emphasized: the women have spoken, ʻOlepau's death is enacted. Before Pele, Hiʻiaka, and Haumea are specifically named, their presence is already suggested through the listing (pīnaʻi) of specific place names (inoa ʻāina, wahi pana) they are associated with: Haʻehaʻe and Kumukahi are the easternmost points of Puna, Hawaiʻi, where the sun rises. Kuaokalā and Kamiloholu are also place names in Puna, the latter a tree associated with the fishpond Waiakaʻea. "ʻĀlawa maka" means "to glance," but a secondary meaning is "to diagnose by insight," a knowledge displayed by Hiʻiaka in her proclamation of ʻOlepau's illness, called kālawa, as "intermittent pains in the neck, probably neuritis."[43]

Waihīnano then calls on her own akua wahine:

ʻAʻohe make kuʻu aliʻi iā ʻoe,
Ke hōʻole mai nei nā akua,
Wāhine o ia nei,
ʻO Papa, ʻo Hoʻohōkū,
ʻO Hoʻohōkūkalani, ʻo Mahianuʻu,
ʻO Mahialani, ʻo Kupuwainananuʻu,
ʻO Kupuwaiʻaleʻale akua o ia nei,
E hōʻole mai ana ʻaʻohe e make.[44]

My beloved chief will not die because of you
The gods deny it
[The] female [gods] of this one here
Papa [hānaumoku], Hoʻohōkū [kalani]
Hoʻohōkūikalani, Mahianuʻu
Mahialani, Kupuwainananuʻu
Kupuwaiʻaleʻale, god of this one here
They deny it, he will not die.

Waihīnano calls on the female deities of her genealogy—Papahānaumoku and her daughter Hoʻohōkūkalani are part of the koʻihonua Kumulipo, indicating her different moʻokūʻauhau, and thus different source of mana from the Pele ʻohana.

When Hiʻiaka chants again, she repeats the same opening and closing lines (He is dead / [The] female deities have declared it . . . he is dead). This time, she evokes ʻēkoʻa and calls on the goddesses of the west, "I ke komohana lā o Lehua" (In the west there at Lehua):

ʻO Kaʻehu, wahine a Manua,
ʻO Nuʻakea wahine a Kapōleiʻaikū,
ʻO Kaʻula i ka wēkiu aloha,
ʻO ka makani o Waʻahila wahine,
A Kaʻula o Kaʻulawahine,
A Kūhaimoana . . .[45]

Kaʻehu, wife of Manua
Nuʻakea, wife of Kapōleiʻaikū
Kaʻula at the height of compassion
The wind of the woman Waʻahila
Kaʻula of Kaʻulawahine
And Kūhaimoana.

Later in the chant, Haumea once again announces the illness that will cause ʻOlepau's death, this time lī (chills) and kuni (fever). Nuʻakea is a goddess of wisdom who accompanies Pele from Kahiki, and is named in the oli "Mai Kahiki mai." Waʻahila is the name of a woman who excelled at hula, connects her to Hiʻiaka; Kaʻula is the small islet between Kauaʻi and Niʻihau, named in Pele's oli makani, the island child of Kaʻulawahine (The red woman), where Pele's brother Kūhaimoana resides.

This time Waihīnano responds with a chant that calls upon the moʻo goddesses, the nemesis of the Pele ʻohana, saying they deny Hiʻiaka's power to kill ʻOlepau:

ʻO Kaluahinenui maka ʻaluʻalu
ʻO Kaluahinenui ʻai kanaka
A kini au lā i ka moʻo
A lehu au lā e ka moʻo
O ka moʻo akua o ia nei . . .[46]

Kaluahinenui [The really old woman] with slackened eyes
Kaluahinenui who devours humans
A great legion of lizards
A huge gathering [400,000] by the lizards
The lizard gods of this one here.

For a short period, 'Olepau appears to recover. He is able to eat and drink a bit. But then Hi'iaka calls on the female deities of their locale, Hāna (nā akua wāhine o Hāna nei):

Nā wāhine kaha pu'ewai,
Kui lei lehua o'u 'o Kanileole'a,
'O oki hala lei 'o Kape'a,
'O Kāmeha'ikana akua i ke kukui,
I ka pi'ina i ka 'oi'oina.[47]

The women who cause the fresh water to roil
Lehua-stringing [goddess] Kanileole'a
Kape'a cuts hala for a lei
Kāmeha'ikana, god of the kukui
Ascending the point.

Once more Haumea declares the illness, and once more Waihīnano parries by entreating her multitude of gods. The women who agitate the water reference the mo'o deities for which the region is famous, who live in and around the many freshwater streams and pools. Kāmeha'ikana is a goddess of war, an alternate name for Papahānaumoku; it is also the name of a land area of Hāna. Hi'iaka is thus calling on Waihīnano's akua, not just her own 'ohana, a bold move.

Hi'iaka then calls on her elder sister Kapō'ulakīna'u and her husband Pua, deities of 'anā'anā, life and death dealing. Kapō instantly responds to her sister's request, and 'Olepau dies. The Maui people wail and lament over their chief's death. Hi'iaka reconsiders her decision to kill him, and sets up a process to bring him back to life. However, once recovered, 'Olepau blames Kapō for his death, and takes away her lands, leaving her destitute. Hi'iaka is so upset by his ingratitude that she kills him once more, and then sets out to kill each of his brothers, elevating Kapō and her husband Pua as ali'i nui of Maui.

Ho'opāpā, the verbal dueling between Hi'iaka and Waihīnano, is another opportunity for Hi'iaka to showcase her skills in chant and 'anā'anā. Here she demonstrates the mana of the Pele women once more, and in the end, her mana wahine is superior to the chiefly Maui women and their female akua. Like the contest with the moʻo of the Wailuku River Bridge in Hilo, the repetition of oli, and lines of the oli (He is dead / The female deities have declared it . . . He will not die by you today) also build excitement and anticipation of what is to come. Once again, a male chief is powerless, his life dependent on the generosity of powerful female akua.

Mana i ka Leo, Mana i ka ʻĀina (Power in the Voice, Power in the Land)

In her admonishment to Waihīnano to pay attention to Hiʻiaka's oli, Kapōkūlani reminds her that "life is in the voice and death is in the voice." In mokuna 3, I discussed how oli is closely connected to oral tradition because of its performative aspects, with an emphasis on the verbalization of words—words have power because they are spoken; to Kanaka Maoli, the concept of silent prayer, introduced by the Calvinist missionaries, was ludicrous. How could the prayer have mana if spoken only within one's own head? But with the establishment of Ka Palapala, mele were adapted to print and became an integral genre of Hawaiian literature, the first written poetry. Print gave the oli a new kind of voice, a new life, a new way to be remembered and carried forward to the next generations. Volumes could be written about the oli and mele associated with the Pele and Hiʻiaka moʻolelo. In this section, I will discuss a few examples that relate to mana wahine and the themes of moʻokūʻauhau, aloha ʻāina, and kuleana that also reflect qualities of ʻike, ʻaʻapo, and ʻeleu.

Oli is a vehicle for hoʻopāpā, and an integral part of the moʻolelo, as demonstrated by Hiʻiaka's battle with the moʻo guardians of the Wailuku River Bridge, and with Waihīnano. Handy, Handy, and Pukui write:

> It is logical to suppose that the priests of Pele, who among the native scholars were of course those most versed in the lore of their goddess and her domain, were the ones who evolved the splendid cycle of Pele chants. In the conferences and contests of experts in lore, the word masters (kakaʻōlelo) vied with each other in authority and creative zeal. We may picture those gathered from various localities—from Haʻehaʻe on southeastern Hawaii to Haʻena on northwestern Kauai, the two points most sacred in the hula myth cycle, being, respectively, where the sun rises and sets, out over the sea the southeastward and northwestward extremes of the island chain. In these contests of wits we may conjecture that over a period of some centuries the unity and completeness of the whole cycle of chants was gradually wrought by a cumulative process of

acceptance and sharing between the islands of mele hula describing the events and places on each island reputed to be sacred to Pele and Hiʻiaka.[48]

The proliferation of oli, particularly those chanted by Hiʻiaka, clearly demonstrate ʻaʻapo and akamai in different ways. For example, Hiʻiakaʻs main source of defense is her knowledge (ʻike) and voice (leo); her mana is so powerful that she can kill or bring back to life with the sound of her voice and the mana of her words, demonstrating i ka ʻōlelo ke ola, i ka ʻōlelo ka make, the literal and figurative power of life and death through spoken words. This power is shown in her battle with Waihīnano, Lohiʻau and other charactersʻ revivification, and the destruction of enemies and obstacles in her path, such as the moʻo Panaʻewa, Piliamoʻo and Nohoamoʻo, and the shark guardian of Waipiʻo, Makaʻūkiu. The power of words in Hawaiian culture is thus reflected over and over in the moʻolelo, particularly in the poetic texts.

Through her performance of oli, Hiʻiaka can call on her family members, embodied in the natural elements of the ʻāina and the ʻāina itself. Through oli, Hiʻiaka demonstrates the power of the Pele ʻohana over other moʻokūʻauhau, such as that of Papahānaumoku and Wākea. On this point, Silva explains that the Pele and Hiʻiaka moʻolelo functions as a "counter-narrative to the discourse claiming that the major gods of Hawaiʻi are male[;] . . . [this] counter-narrative is one that celebrates female power."[49] This happens in part because the Papa and Wākea moʻolelo establishes the religious order of the male gods, including ʻAikapu.[50]

The Hawaiian islands are born from Papa and Wākea, their ranking (birth order) of oldest to youngest proceeded from the south (Hawaiʻi) northward (Niʻihau). The Pele migration, however, inaugurates their power over the ʻāina in the exact opposite direction, from the northwest Hawaiian islands down the pae ʻāina to Hawaiʻi. This is significant because origin stories "attempt to establish a hierarchy . . . a social order and are well-springs of authority."[51]

The Pele people do not follow Wākeaʻs ʻAikapu, the worship of male gods centered on the practice of ʻAikapu or "sacred eating." Under ʻAikapu, men and women ate separately, and certain foods were restricted to women. Pele worshippers were ʻAikū, which literally means to eat standing up, "to eat freely; to do as one wishes; to break taboos or transgress."[52] It also means "to eat in an improper manner" or "to take food that is set apart as temporarily or permanently sacred or forbidden to use," and "to act contrary to custom, prescribed rule, or established precedent; to overlook, disregard, or take no notice of a tabu."[53]

In practice, this perhaps meant that Pele followers did not have to follow the ʻAikapu mandated by the kahuna (priest) for the male gods. Kameʻeleihiwa speculates that it "may have been that the Pele *kapu* were not the same as those practices by the *Aliʻi Nui* who lived under the ʻAikapu," particularly since "the political power of the ʻAikapu depended most heavily upon the worship of Kū, or Kūnuiākea, at the *luakini*."[54] ʻAi also means to rule over, so where ʻAikapu suggests a "sanctified leadership" established through Wākea's priest, ʻAikū suggests the "oppositional leadership" of the Pele people, as Pele was an akua who was "noho i ka ʻāhiu" (living in the wild, i.e., she was untamable). The practice of ʻAikū demonstrates another dimension to Pele's godly stature, and reveals the strength of her mana wahine, female power, and the intertwining of mana wahine and political power.

Hoʻoulumāhiehie includes a section of the Kumulipo as part of Pele's oli makani she performs at Hāʻena, Kauaʻi, which is used as a weapon of words against her moʻo rivals, Kiliʻoeikapua and Kalanamainuʻu. Lines 288–317 of Pele's oli makani are extracted from wā ʻehā (the fourth epoch), the birth of crawling things (nā mea kolo), like moʻo. When Pele evokes these lines of the Kumulipo as part of her oli makani, the moʻo women vanish, their moʻokūʻauhau blown away by the power of Pele's. This is another layer of genealogical messaging, of hoʻopāpā, of demonstrating intertextual ʻike on multiple levels.

Oli also communicate deep emotion, the most appropriate vehicle to express love, sadness, or joy, the purpose being to woo or influence other characters' actions or decisions. Examples include Hiʻiaka's expression of affection for Hōpoe, Wahineʻōmaʻo's "Kuʻu aikāne" chants that bring Hiʻiaka back to the crater, and Kahuakaʻiapaoa's "Hulihia" chants expressing his grief over Lohiʻau's death (or in some versions, Lohiʻau's chanting to soften Pele's heart and spare his life). Commenting on the series of hulihia chants in the moʻolelo, Kaʻili writes, "[The hulihia chants] form some of the finest specimens of poetical composition in the Hawaiian language. These are magnificent word-paintings of the actions and effects of volcanic fires, some of the grandest sights of the world; and also tender, loving descriptions of some of the sweetest and most pleasing views of natural scenery. The writer regrets the inability to render a poetical translation of these grand songs that would in any way convey an adequate idea of their beauties."[55] Because of its ability to convey emotion on multiple levels (poetry of the words, and the ability to vocalize the text in different ways), oli is the most appropriate way to convey deep emotion. While hula is often the focus of performance, it is the sequences of oli that eloquently demonstrate the intimacy of the relationships.

The heart of the Pele and Hiʻiaka moʻolelo, both literally and figuratively, is the ʻāina, another political aspect of the narrative. An exhaustive analysis of wahi pana in Pele and Hiʻiaka moʻolelo would be a valuable but tremendous undertaking. Here I will discuss the importance of the connection between the Pele ʻohana and ʻāina, and offer a few selected examples of how oli and wahi pana are interwoven with mana wahine within the moʻolelo.

First and foremost is the direct connection between the Pele ʻohana and the ʻāina; they do not just create land, they are the land *and* the natural elements on the land. Kimura's discussion of wahi pana is relevant to Pele and Hiʻiaka moʻolelo because of their moʻokūʻauhau and kuleana to the ʻāina:

> The abundance of Hawaiian place names is only a hint at their actual number, for there are literally many places where individual boulders are named. Place names are used as displays of wit to express a great deal in a few words, and they are extremely common in Hawaiian poetry and traditional sayings. Perhaps the reason that place names have such evocative power in the Hawaiian language is the emphasis on homeland of *aloha ʻāina* (love of the land, patriotism, pride of place) in the culture . . . to traditional Hawaiians, place names are considered *kupa* (natives) themselves. Place names are like esteemed grandparents linking people to their home, personal past, and their history.[56]

As ancestors, Pele and Hiʻiaka are one strand of our moʻokūʻauhau that links Kanaka Maoli to the ʻāina and our more immediate kūpuna, particularly those of us with roots to Puna and Kaʻū, Hawaiʻi. While the "volcano" may be the common settler colonial and touristic landmark name for Pele's home, for Kanaka Maoli, Mauna Loa, Kīlauea, Halemaʻumaʻu, Mokuʻāweoweo, Papalauahi, and Puʻu ʻŌʻō, specific locations at and surrounding the caldera, are a few descriptive and evocative inoa ʻāina of Pele-related moʻolelo. Even more specific and detailed names that come to us through the narratives and accompanying mele expand this richness of wahi pana: Puʻuoniʻoni (trembling hill) is the point of Hiʻiaka's departure to fetch Lohiʻau; Akanikōlea (plover calling) is the ridge Kamapuaʻa first encounters Pele at the crater; Kapaʻahu (kapa cloak) is the place Pele wrapped herself in kapa cloth and slept, and where her spirit heard the sound of Lohiʻau's pahu drums. Inoa ʻāina evoke story: "Hiʻiaka is a powerful and complementary force to Pele because she is the healer of land: after Pele erupts, destroying the landscape to create new land, Hiʻiaka creates plant life there. Other relatives also exist simultaneously as people and as features of the landscape, such as Pele's father, who is said to be the mountain peak Kānehoalani [Oʻahu]. An unmistakable feeling emerges through the text that people, the gods and the landscape are all members of the same family."[57]

As Keith Basso argues in relation to western Apache place names, "Wisdom sits in places," in part because of the historical connection between the people and their land, demonstrating specific, intimate details of their relationship with it, but also because place names are mnemonic devices that re-create a picture and recall the stories associated with these places.[58]

Connection to the ʻāina demonstrates native status, as exhibited in the oli makani Pele performs. Pele's ability to name nearly three hundred winds and two hundred place names is phenomenal. The difference in number between wind names and place names is because some places have multiple winds: Anahola, for example, has fourteen, while Wainiha has thirty-two. This list is much more significant than the Kauaʻi wind names in the Kūapākaʻa moʻolelo.[59] To even know that the wind of a place has a name is a major shift in consciousness, a more personal way of relating with one's environment. To comprehend that multiple winds inhabit a location, and to be able to identify and name them demonstrates keen observation and familiarity with a place; it is likely that each name reflects a characteristic of a wind or place as much as our personal names reflect or embody our own mana.

As Hiʻiaka travels across the archipelago, she encounters ʻāina as active beings who are both friend and foe. When she arrives on Oʻahu, for example, she sees Makapuʻu and Kauhiʻīmakaokalani, two well-known places on Oʻahu; Makapuʻu (bulging eye) is the moʻo-shaped mountain dividing the Koʻolaupoko and Kona districts of Oʻahu, while Kauhiʻī[lio]makaokalani (The concealed dog eyes of the heavens) is a large dog-shaped rock on the hillside above Kaʻaʻawa who is part of Pele's entourage from Kahiki. He is misnamed and marketed through settler colonial tourist discourse as the "Crouching Lion." Makapuʻu and Kauhi are also Hiʻiaka's relatives with whom she interacts through a series of oli performance. Makapuʻu laments not being able to offer Hiʻiaka any hospitality because of the desolate conditions of the land; Kauhi beseeches Hiʻiaka to take him with her through chanting "ʻO Pele lā koʻu akua" (Pele is my deity).

As she travels, she calls out to the ʻāina who are living beings. In this way, oli is connected to ʻāina and wahi pana. Hiʻiaka demonstrates ʻike ʻāina in the words of her oli. Combined with her performance, it is multiple layers of recognition and affirmation of her knowledge of poetry, of place, and when appropriate, her kinship connections to these places.

This is more evident through a series of uē helu she performs to specific ʻāina; uē helu is a particular kind of chant, "a wailing call of grief and love, recounting deeds of a loved one and shared experiences; to weep and speak thus. *Lit.*, enumerating weeping."[60] Each uē helu begins with a kauoha (command) from Hiʻiaka to the specific ʻāina/character stating "Mai poina ʻoe iaʻu e [mea]" (Don't forget me, [name of place/character]). ʻĀina she performs an uē helu to include Laniloa, Kaʻala, Kamae, Kalalau, and Leinono.[61]

Hiʻiaka also battles characters for whom places are named. These include the moʻo Panaʻewa, Moʻolau, and Mokoliʻi. Panaʻewa is the name of an immense forested area of Hilo, Moʻolau is associated with a damp, boggy region in the uplands of Waimea, and Mokoliʻi is the small islet off of Kualoa, the dividing point between the districts (moku) of Koʻolaupoko and Koʻolauloa on the windward (northeast) side of Oʻahu. The Pele and Hiʻiaka moʻolelo provide the origin of this inoa ʻāina: as Hiʻiaka is traveling, she must slay the moʻo; his tail falls into the sea, only the tip above the ocean's surface, thus the name Mokoliʻi (little lizard). Surrounding place names reflect this moʻolelo: Kualoa is the "long back" of the lizard, the little valley Hakipuʻu is the lizard's "broken back." Renamed through settler colonialism "Chinaman's Hat" (because of its triangular shape) disregards the way the moʻolelo map the ʻāina, demonstrating relationships between specific geological features through their names.[62]

Wahi pana are places made famous through story. Pele and Hiʻiaka are associated with the naming of wahi pana throughout the moʻolelo. For example, in the previously discussed pūhenehene episode with Piʻihonua and Puʻueo, Piʻihonua defeats Puʻueo with Hiʻiaka's assistance, and becomes the winning aliʻi; an area of Hilo on the south side of the Wailuku River is known as Piʻihonua, possibly in commemoration of this aliʻi (and possibly through his victory in this moʻolelo). Puʻueo, on the other hand, is described by Pukui, Elbert, and Mookini as an "elevated place in Hilo ... where Kalani-ʻōpuʻu built the *heiau* of Kanoa."[63] Piʻihonua, Puʻueo, and Punahoa are all ahupuaʻa located near each other in the moku (district) of Hilo; Piʻihonua is "bounded by Punahoa, Waiakea, Humuula, and Puueo."[64] "Eo" can be translated as both "to win, beat; winning, victory" as well as "to lose, be defeated, beaten."[65] Thus Puʻueo can be described as "hill of victory" or "hill of defeat"; the clever double meaning is a classic example of Hawaiian kaona, as viewed in context of the pūhenehene episode in the Pele and Hiʻiaka moʻolelo, it simultaneously implies both. Not only is one side (Piʻihonua) victorious, Puʻueo, prior to Hiʻiaka's intervention on behalf of Piʻihonua, was also victorious before he was defeated.

The moʻo Mokoliʻi (Little Lizard) as viewed from Waikāne looking north. The moʻo battles Hiʻiaka when she travels through Koʻolaupoko, Oʻahu, and loses to her. Its large body is visible on the left with its tail in the water, the tip forming the small islet of Mokoliʻi (*right*). The valley Hakipuʻu (Broken Back) is just out of sight to the left. These geographical features of the ʻāina are related; settler colonial stories that misidentify Mokoliʻi as "Chinaman's Hat" disconnect the island from the surrounding environment, and overrun Kanaka Maoli epistemology of ʻike ʻāina, knowledge about (and from) the land. Photograph by author, 2008.

These examples demonstrate kinship relationships that are recognized and reestablished among the Pele ʻohana and ʻāina, another way of remembering and recounting moʻokūʻauhau. Over five hundred place names are found in Kapihenui, and nearly the same number half a century later in Hoʻoulumāhiehie's text) remain embedded in the moʻolelo. Viewing the moʻolelo as moʻokūʻauhau, the connections made within it between certain wahi pana, such as Hāʻena, Kauaʻi, and Hāʻena, Puna, Hawaiʻi, between the three Kīlauea—on Kauaʻi, at Keawaʻula, Oʻahu, and the volcano on Hawaiʻi island, and between Keaʻau, Waiʻanae, Oʻahu, and Keaʻau, Puna, Hawaiʻi, for example, are seen more clearly. These ʻāina are thus mapped in a kind of genealogical relationship with one another connected through the movement of Pele and Hiʻiaka.

For example, Pele's home is Mauliola, Lohiʻau's is Hālauaola. Mauliola means "breath of life, power of healing."[66] As a primal generative force, Pele is a creator of ʻāina. Hālau is both "long house" and "numerous."[67]

Thus, Hālauaola can mean "house of life" or "many lives"; it poetically suggests Lohiʻauʻs return to life from the dead. It could also refer to the tī leaf–framed structure Hiʻiaka has built to restore Lohiʻauʻs life. The reference to a hālau evokes an association with hula, Lohiʻauʻs favorite activity at which he excels, as a hālau hula is a dance troupe, or hall for dance. For the true ʻōlapa, hula itself is life; Kalākaua is widely quoted as proclaiming hula "the heartbeat of the Hawaiian people."

The abundance of place names contained in the Hawaiian-language versions of the Pele and Hiʻiaka moʻolelo reflects a traditional Hawaiian poetic sensibility that draws from the oral traditions and was firmly kept in place throughout the development of Hawaiian literature; the Kanaka writers focus on inoa ʻāina and wahi pana because they are following traditional cultural protocol expressing aloha ʻāina. This is another reason writers published multiple versions of the moʻolelo, as each writer had island-specific moʻokūʻauhau that highlight the wahi pana of their ʻāina. The more moʻolelo published and circulating, the more knowledge could be collected, debated, remembered, passed on.

Not all inoa ʻāina are found elsewhere. In some cases, they have been left off modern maps, as the specificity of places has been generalized. In other places, they have been overwritten by settler mapping, not always to English: Kaʻōhao in Kailua, Oʻahu, was renamed "Lani Kai" by developers in the 1920s; Puna, Kauaʻi, was renamed "Kawaihau" (ice water) in honor of a glee club started by Prince Leleiōhoku in the late 1800s.[68] The alteration of place names is part of the colonial discourse of power. Houston Wood argues that such transformation changed from "reflecting Hawaiian geographic thought to place names as representing Western control of territory. Simultaneously, the language/order of the Native peoples is displaced and subordinated to that of the Western powers— British, French, and Russian at first, but ultimately and overwhelmingly American. This process is part of the greater economic, political, cultural, and discursive transformation of the Islands since Western contact. Place names provide a means by which this colonization of the Islands can be read . . . [as they] speak of a final twist to this colonization."[69] The renaming, appropriation, and transformation of place is just one aspect of politics contained within the narrative. The politics of place are reflected in multiple ways, including rivalries between different moʻokūʻauhau. As Pele asserts her power over the ʻāina through volcanic eruption or by aiding Hiʻiaka in her battles clearing the land, they simultaneously displacing other akua. Thus the moʻolelo themselves are contested sites within the Hawaiian paradigm of moʻokūʻauhau politics as well as within the colonial discourse of power dynamics.

'O 'Oe ia e Wailua Iki (It Is You, Wailua Iki)

When Hi'iaka mā arrive at the ali'i 'Olepau's home on Maui, 'Olepau's wives rebuff her call seeking permission to enter and receive hospitality; 'Olepau's death is the consequence of their rude behavior. Hi'iaka sees her older sister Kapō there, and chants to her in a recognition of their kinship connection, and aloha for her sister, who lives on Maui. Her oli is a display of her mana wahine—her 'ike, her mana, her aloha, her sense of protocol. It also recognizes Kapō's mana wahine, demonstrating respect and affection for her older sister, a powerful goddess of 'anā'anā, as is Hi'iaka.

There are multiple references to 'āina: Wailua iki, Hoakalei, Hanakahi, Mahamoku, Wai'oli; the winds Lawalawakua, Kaiāulu, Kamae, Kona. The chant ends, "Ho mai he leo e / E ue kaua" (Offer up a voice of welcome / Let the two of us share our tears [of affection]). The oli is a call toward kinship and collaboration, something reflected through the mo'olelo. It is a sharing and celebration of mana wahine—women's knowledge and power.

Noho ka Wahine i ka Mana Wahine
(The Woman Dwells in Her Female Power)

It is 2005 and I have been invited to Hāna, Maui, by the Women's Health Center to discuss the relationship between Pele and Hi'iaka mo'olelo and Hawaiian women's health issues. It is a talk I've given before—to women's addiction support groups in Wai'anae, O'ahu, to kids on Kaua'i in foster care programs, to Kanaka Maoli teens participating in Nā Pua No'eau Kaua'i's gifted and talented summer program. Like women everywhere, Hawaiian women struggle with issues of body image. Some struggle with their sexuality and sexual orientation. Our youth struggle with bullying and social acceptance, trying to find their place in the world. Domestic violence of all kinds pervades our communities; national statistics show that rates of domestic abuse for same-sex couples are equal to those of heterosexual couples, although no such statistics are kept by the state of Hawai'i. For Indigenous communities, these are issues spurred by settler colonialism.

In 1999, a study sponsored by the Harvard Eating Disorder Center showed that within three years of American television being introduced to the island nation of Fiji (one channel), 15 percent of teenage Fijian females reported incidences of bulimia and dissatisfaction with their bodies, something previously unknown in Fijian society. In a 1998 follow-up study, 74 percent of Fijian girls reported feeling "too big or fat," a "shift by young people away from an acceptance of heaviness [that] comes as Fijians and other South Pacific peoples battle problems brought on by high-fat, high-volume diets" introduced by settler colonialism and promoted by television.[70] This is not a problem only in the South Pacific; islands north of the equator and victims of U.S. imperialism, such as Hawaiʻi and Guam, also suffer similar issues.[71]

As our tiny plane flies along the Hāna coastline, I try to pick out Wailua, Keʻanae, the picturesque taro lands for which Maui was once famous. I imagine Kapōʻulakīnaʻu down there somewhere, perhaps weeding her loʻi, or printing a new piece of kapa. If I were traveling along the road to Hāna, I would stop and pick foliage, weave lei from the verdant ferns. If I passed her home, would she call out and invite me in?

A few days later I make my way to Koki beach, located ma kai (seaward) of the cinder cone Ka Iwi o Pele (the bones of Pele). In another moʻolelo, Pele's other sister, the ocean goddess Nāmakaokahaʻi ("Nāmaka"), drives her out of Kahiki for seducing Nāmaka's husband. Nāmaka catches Pele and kills her. It is Pele's spirit that inhabits the crater at Kīlauea, her body is here in Hāna, Maui. The bones of our ancestors are all around us. They are embodied in the names of our ʻāina. They are embodied in our names as well. Their voices are still present in mele and moʻolelo.

In these talks, I always ask, "What would it mean to reclaim our voice?" I recount Hiʻiaka's journey across the pae ʻāina with just a woman or two for company. She has no visible weaponry, and when one is written into the narrative, it is a pāʻū, a woman's skirt that smites her enemies with bolts of lightning. But for the most part, Hiʻiaka must rely solely on her ʻike, her knowledge, and her leo, her voice. Her ʻike is formed in part by her keen observations of her surroundings, and by listening to her naʻau, her "gut" feeling. She calls on her ancestors and family members for assistance on occasion. She is confident and comfortable with her body, her sexuality. She is what we would call today "health conscious," a vegetarian who only consumes lūʻau, but has an occasional craving for ocean delicacies. She is compassionate and powerful, a hula practitioner and a healer, a sister who understands her kuleana, who is self-disciplining to fulfill her obligation to her elder sibling. What would happen, I propose to the women I speak with, if we embraced our mana wahine? What if we discovered we, too, could overcome obstacles and vanquish real and metaphorical moʻo with the power of our voice? What is possible when we, like Kapō and Hiʻiaka, recognize one another's mana and offer up our voices, share our tears?

Hulihia Ka Mauna (The Mountain Is Overturned by Fire): Weaving a Literary Tradition—the Polytexts and Politics of the Pele and Hiʻiaka Moʻolelo

Hulihia ka mauna wela i ke ahi
Wela nopu ka uka o Kūʻia i Hanalei
Ke ʻā pōhaku puʻu lau mai i uka
Kekakoʻiokalā mai i ka lua
ʻO Kamaili kani pololei leo leʻa ā
ʻO ka hinihini kani kua mauna ē
Ke ʻā i kai o Kūkalāʻula
A luna au o Holonēnē
Kū au nānā e maliu mai
ʻO kuʻu ʻike wale aku iā Maukele
I ka papa kahuli lā e ʻĀpua ī
Lā liliʻu he nopu he wela ka wāwae ō
Wela ka papa haʻa ka pāhoehoe
Pau nā niu o Kūlō i ka pō
Hala ka uahi ma ʻō o Kuauli
Pau ʻOmaʻolala i ke ahi
Hiʻa nō ʻeʻe ʻā i ke one ū
Pulupulu i ka lau lāʻau ā
Kū hiʻu ʻia ka lani wili ka pūnohu ʻula
Ke ʻā weo i ka lani
Pōʻele kīkaha ke kua o ka pō
Liʻuliʻu wawaʻu ʻaʻeʻaʻe nā pua mai Kahiki
Hiki ʻo Pele mā i Keahikū, ē
Kahuli Kīlauea me he ama waʻa lā, ī
Haʻahaʻa Puna, kiʻekiʻe Kaʻū, ō
Ka ʻāina i ka ulu o ka makani, ū
He inoa no Hiʻiakaikapoliopele!"

[The mountain is overturned by fire]
The uplands of Kūʻia at Hanalei are burning hot
The many splatter cones of the uplands are ablaze
From Kekakoʻiokalā to the pit
Kamaili rings out with clear voice
Heard indistinctly on the mountain ridges
When it burned below Kūkalāʻula
I was upland at Holonēnē
I stand to watch attentively
Seeing only Maukele
And the twisted lowlands by ʻĀpua
This is a scorching day, the feet are burning hot
The plates of pāhoehoe are burning
The coconut trees of Kūlō were destroyed in the night
The smoke has passed beyond Kuauli
ʻOmaʻolala was destroyed by the fire
The fire plow alights upon the sand
Kindled by the scattered wood
Thrown up to the heavens in a twisted red cloud
Reddish glow lighting up the sky
The god of night soars in the darkness
The travelers from Tahiti slowly wander about
The Pele clan arrives at Keahikū
Kīlauea topples over like the outrigger of a canoe
Puna is depressed, Kaʻū is elevated
Kaʻū, land of increasing winds
A name chant for Hiʻiakaikapoliopele![2]

IT IS MARCH 25, 1990, AND FIFTEEN HUNDRED people representing over thirty Native Hawaiian, environmental, and community groups are marching into the Waokeleopuna rainforest in Puna, Hawai'i, to protest True Geothermal Venture's planned development of a geothermal power plant. Over 140 people are arrested, led by Native Hawaiian kūpuna. There are multiple concerns over the proposed development of geothermal power in Puna, touted by the state as a "renewable" energy source. Some worry about repercussions to health and the environment, others are alarmed over losing a way of life. Kanaka Maoli are upset about these questions. They are also concerned about cultural issues, including the desecration of Pele and her homeland of Puna.

The Campbell Estate, an O'ahu-based company, owned the lands of Kahaualeʻa, an ahupuaʻa in Puna. They had planned to develop a geothermal plant there, but when the lands were covered with yet another lava flow from the eruptions that had begun in 1983, a land swap between the state and the estate was proposed so that the geothermal development could proceed. In 1985, twenty-seven thousand acres of Waokeleopuna's pristine rainforest were traded for twenty-five thousand acres of Campbell Estate's Kahaualeʻa lands. Fifteen thousand acres of Kahaualeʻa was covered with lava, and twelve hundred acres were promised to the National Park Service's Volcanoes National Park, which adjoins the ahupuaʻa. Only thirty-two hundred acres of forested land remained.[3]

One point of Kanaka Maoli protest was that the land the state traded was part of the 1.5 million acres of Hawaiian Kingdom Crown and government lands that had first been confiscated by the provisional government from the kingdom in 1893. These lands were ceded to the United States when annexation occurred in 1898. What wasn't sold off was put under the jurisdiction of the Department of Land and Natural Resources in 1959 when Hawai'i became a state. These "ceded lands" as they are commonly known in Hawai'i are part of the state-controlled public land trust, and are meant, via provision 5f of the Hawai'i Statehood Admissions Act, to benefit Native Hawaiians in perpetuity. Since statehood, this provision has been multiply abused, lands taken for the development of airports, schools, and other public facilities across the archipelago, with no direct benefit to Native Hawaiians. Waokeleopuna was about to suffer the same fate.

Another issue for Kanaka Maoli was the destruction of the rainforest, used to hunt and gather material for cultural practices, including medicinal herbs. Perhaps most important, Kanaka Maoli protest centered on the desecration of the forest as a sacred site to Pele. Led by ʻŌiwi activists with ancestral ties to Pele and the areas of Puna and Kaʻū, the nonprofit

Pele Defense Fund was formed. Several lawsuits followed the land march of 1990.[4]

As a product of a public school system entrenched in a settler colonial version of Hawaiian culture and history, the Waokeleopuna land march is my first major exposure to ʻŌiwi politics and aloha ʻāina activism. Being raised on the other end of the archipelago, Pele and Hiʻiaka were not an obvious presence in my daily environmental experience or practice. It is only through stories my tūtū told of growing up in Puna—days spent visiting family, picking and weaving lauhala, drying fish, tending loʻi, and the stories of "Madame Pele" spun through settler colonial touristic discourse and urban legends (don't take rocks from the volcano, throw gin into the crater as an offering)—that I knew anything about her at all, and such contradictory stories do not resonate with one another.

It isn't until I am in my bachelor's program in Hawaiian studies in 1987 and in hālau hula with Kumu Kaʻimikaua that I am introduced to Pele and Hiʻiaka moʻolelo that are more culturally centered. A new academic discipline, Hawaiian studies is the first academic program to teach Hawaiian moʻolelo outside the narrow frame of the settler colonial gaze of Christianity, tourism, and folklore. It is the first time I am aware of the alternative story, a Kanaka Maoli–centered counter-narrative to the imperial rhetoric about our akua like Pele and Hiʻiaka. This discovery prompts me to study hula and to take ʻōlelo Hawaiʻi more seriously. Studying Pele and Hiʻiaka moʻolelo opened my eyes to the cultural and intellectual history of my kūpuna ʻŌiwi, a history denied by most haole folklorists, about the activism and agency that Kanaka Maoli in the nineteenth and early twentieth centuries employed to strengthen the Lāhui and preserve Hawaiian sovereignty, rally Kanaka Maoli pride, and pass on to future generations of ʻŌiwi—like me.

Hulihia ka Moʻolelo (The Story Is Overturned): Asserting a Kanaka Maoli Politic

The hulihia discourse embodied in the Pele and Hiʻiaka moʻolelo expresses indigenous literary nationalism, presenting and asserting an alternative moʻolelo of Kanaka Maoli and our ʻāina, a counter-narrative to settler colonial religion (Christianity), Western science (like geography and geology), and politics.

In mokuna 3, I outlined four points of discussion in the development of Pele and Hiʻiaka moʻolelo, and examined the first two points—the weaving of oral and written traditions, and the interweaving of oral and literary devices. In this chapter, I explore the next two points:

+ As the practice of literature became more familiar, literary production flourished, with Kanaka Maoli literature adapting (not necessarily adapting *to*) elements of Amer-European writing.
+ The publication of moʻolelo kuʻuna, including Pele and Hiʻiaka, was political, an embodiment of hulihia discourse meant to resist, counter, disrupt, and overturn the settler colonial discourse that infantilized Kanaka Maoli as inferior beings, mythologized Kanaka Maoli history, and denigrated Kanaka Maoli culture, denying the presence of an intellectual history.

Thus, how is the literary tradition of Pele and Hiʻiaka moʻolelo that Kanaka Maoli created different from the oral one? Or from settler colonial writing?

For Kanaka Maoli, literacy did not mean just learning to read and write; it included publishing. Since the first printing press was established at Lāhainā, Maui, in 1831, Kanaka Maoli had been trained in printing and publishing. Kimura notes, "Some have argued that the introduction of writing harmed the Hawaiian people, but there is little evidence to support such an idea and much that contradicts it. Many Hawaiian traditions would be lost today if there was no written Hawaiian language because non-Hawaiians wrote very little about Hawaiian culture, compared to the many writings in Hawaiian on the topic by Hawaiian speakers."[5] Clearly Hawaiian writers were very interested in Hawaiian culture, including moʻolelo kuʻuna. This was particularly true during the period between 1860 and 1948, the period when the independent Hawaiian nationalist press thrived. Silva writes:

> In the nineteenth century . . . Hawaiian literature flourished in the mother tongue. Editors of Hawaiian language newspapers fostered the writing of literature in their papers. . . . Moʻolelo were sometimes said to have been translated from the oral tradition; however, it is important to understand that the written forms of moʻolelo were authored. That is, each of the authors of the many moʻolelo wrote their own versions, using both mnemonic devices from the oral tradition and literary devices that developed over time. They signed their work, usually with their own names, and sometimes with pseudonyms. Moʻolelo appeared in very specific historical contexts as creations of authors who were often also political actors.[6]

It was not coincidental that the Hawaiian-language newspapers moʻolelo kuʻuna, like the Pele and Hiʻiaka moʻolelo, were published in were examples of pro-Hawaiian nationalism. As Silva argues, there was a connection between moʻolelo writers and politics, in part because many papers were owned and edited by Kanaka Maoli active in Hawaiian politics. In other words, the writers, editors, and newspapers had a moʻokūʻauhau and kuleana to publish moʻolelo kuʻuna like Pele and Hiʻiaka. Who were the kanaka behind the newspapers? What is important about the newspapers in which the Pele and Hiʻiaka moʻolelo were published? This section explores these questions.

The second Hawaiian-language Pele and Hiʻiaka moʻolelo to appear in print (and the first after Kaʻili's English-language moʻolelo) was published in *Ka Leo o ka Lahui* (The Voice of the Nation) in 1893. The moʻolelo commenced just two weeks prior to the overthrow (January 17, 1893), and concluded six months later (July 12, 1893): "*Ka Leo o ka Lahui* was formed by Native Hawaiians who sought to organize the Hawaiian race in support of the king and in opposition to the powerful haole business community. Among the newspaper's loyal supporters, that is, those who regularly contributed cash toward its support, were Liliʻuokalani . . . J. Nāwahī and E. Lilikalani, two Hawaiians prominent in political circles, the latter being Kalākaua's genealogist."[7]

Ka Leo o ka Lahui ran from August 19, 1889, to April 13, 1896. It was founded by Honolulu native John Edwin Ailuene Bush, who was also luna hoʻoponopono (editor in chief) in 1891. Bush, considered a powerful orator and political statesman, became involved in newspaper publishing, using the papers to advance his pro-Kanaka Maoli political perspectives. The paper was at the forefront of advocacy of Hawaiian sovereignty. Not surprisingly, missionary forces did not look favorably on the independent Hawaiian newspaper, because of the staff's strong pro-Hawaiian stance that advocated "Hawaiʻi for the Hawaiians." This position highlighted support of cultural practices the missionaries forbade, such as hula, and complementary activities, such as the publication of hula-related texts. Hawaiian nationalist papers were steadfast in their defense and promotion of Kanaka Maoli cultural practices and political rights; the number of Hawaiian-language newspapers increased in the 1880s, when political tensions between Kanaka Maoli and haole began to rise. By 1896, there were fourteen Hawaiian nationalist papers in publication at the same time. The Pele and Hiʻiaka moʻolelo published in *Ka Leo o ka Lahui* was born in this highly charged political era.

The conflict between Kanaka Maoli trying to assert cultural and political autonomy and haole trying to suppress Hawaiian culture, wrest control of the Hawaiian government, and Westernize Hawaiian society culminated in the time period just prior to the overthrow of the

Hawaiian government, when *Ka Leo o ka Lahui* was founded. Kameʻeleihiwa argues that the paper:

> gained fame for its loyal editorials in support of Kalākaua and the
> Hawaiian monarchy. The 1890s were a time of great conflict in
> Honolulu. The haole business and sugar interests had pressed for
> political changes, and with the 1887 Bayonet constitution, took
> power from the Hawaiian king and gave it to a haole cabinet. The
> cabinet . . . was to be comprised of these self-same missionary de-
> scendants and business executives who had also demanded closer
> ties with America in the form of the Reciprocity Treaty or even
> by annexation. . . . Such foreigner settlers had very little concern
> for what they considered a half-witted, backward, and primitive
> race . . . and Hawaiians clearly saw the need to organize politically
> against foreigners who would usurp the Hawaiian crown.[8]

Ka Leo o ka Lahui was originally bilingual, published in both English
and Hawaiian. But by 1892, it deepened its political position of anti-haole
oligarchy and published content only in the Hawaiian language. It did,
in fact, have "a large Native Hawaiian-speaking audience."[9] As staunch
Hawaiian supporters, the paper's staff printed the Queen's protest after
the 1893 overthrow, which the haole-run papers refused to do, keeping
Kanaka Maoli informed about the political struggle over Hawaiian sovereignty. Bush and other editors of Hawaiian nationalist newspapers
continued to criticize the injustices of the provisional government and
the Republic of Hawaiʻi against the deposed queen and Kanaka Maoli
rights in their papers, resulting in arrest, fines, and imprisonment in 1895
for conspiracy and seditious libel. The haole-run publication *The Friend*
commented, "Doubtless there will now be an end to Bush's overflow of
incendiary talk in *Ka Leo [o ka Lahui]*."[10] After his imprisonment, Bush
was able to continue publishing his newspapers for another year before
folding, although it is not clear if their demise was directly linked to his
arrest and imprisonment.

Fluent in Hawaiian and English, Bush was an active public and political figure who was well-known during his lifetime. Dubbed the "Napo-
leon of Printer's Lane," he was born on February 15, 1842, in Honolulu,
Oʻahu.[11] He worked at a number of different jobs before entering publishing. He began his newspaper career at the government paper *Hawaiian Gazette*, and later edited two Hawaiian nationalist newspapers, *Ka
Oiaio* (The Truth) from 1889 to 1896, and *Ka Leo o ka Lahui* from 1891 to
1894.[12] Involved in politics of the Hawaiian kingdom:

he was a member of the Privy Council from 1878 to 1891, commissioner of Crown Lands and president of the Board of Health in 1880; a member of the House of Nobles from 1880 to 1886; minister of finance and minister of the interior in 1882; envoy extraordinary to Sāmoa during Kalākaua's bid for a Pacific empire in 1886; governor of Kauaʻi in 1887; and elected representative from Oʻahu in 1890–1892. In 1888, he became president of Hui Kālaiʻāina. . . . He led many public rallies in support of the king and in opposition to the foreign business–missionary faction. A man dedicated to his nation, he exhorted Hawaiians to guard against foreign manipulation.[13]

At the end of his service to the government, Bush worked as a translator and interpreter for the Oʻahu circuit court.

Unafraid to follow his personal convictions, Bush changed political alliances twice. He was vice president of the Hui Aloha ʻĀina, the patriotic organization dedicated to the restoration of Hawaiian sovereignty formed after the overthrow of the Hawaiian government in 1893. After he was sent to prison in 1895, he supported the Republic for a time, and then switched to the Democratic Party, where his name appeared on the Democratic slate for Congress in 1900. Bush was not successful in his bid for Congress, and when the Home Rule Party formed in 1900, he joined them. Home Rule was considered a viable alternative to the Republican and Democratic parties, which Hawaiians such as Bush felt were inadequate in supporting their concerns. While Bush staunchly supported Kanaka Maoli rights, he was not appointed to a cabinet position during Kalākaua's reign. Unhappy with Liliʻuokalani's ascension to the throne after Kalākaua's death in 1891, Bush helped form the Liberal Party, which he advocated for and publicized in his newspaper, using it to criticize Liliʻuokalani. The loss by the Liberal Party to the queen's supporters in the 1892 election prompted Bush to editorialize, "The practical defeat of the Liberal Party is the lost opportunity of the Hawaiians to regain a political footing in their own country, and they will now continue to be trampled upon as they have been since 1887. . . . It looks now as though the only hope for equal rights in this country lies in—shall we say it—annexation."[14] Bush later reversed his opinion toward annexation to the United States, saying that after the overthrow of the monarchy, "the United States with all its vices was not fit to annex Hawaii."[15]

Bush died in Honolulu on July 5, 1906, at the age of sixty-five. Throughout his life he worked on behalf of the Hawaiian people and the nation of Hawaiʻi. His obituary described him as "He kanaka oia i hoopihaia kona puuwai i ke aloha no kona aina hanau a me na'lii o Hawaii, a pela me ka lahui oiwi o Hawaii" (a man whose heart was filled with compassion for his birthplace and the chiefs of Hawai'i, and the Hawaiian people).[16]

The Pele and Hi'iaka mo'olelo published in *Ka Leo o ka Lahui* was co-signed by Simeona Pa'aluhi. Pa'aluhi was born on September 25, 1844, to Kauewa (w) and Paaluhi (k) of Kamalō, Moloka'i.[17] Around 1867 he left Moloka'i to attend Reverend W. P. Alexander's seminary in Wailuku, Maui.[18] In 1870, Pa'aluhi became the kahu (pastor) of the Kalihi to Moanalua region for the O'ahu Evangelical Association (OEA).[19] Pa'aluhi served as a Kākau 'Ōlelo (secretary) for the 'Ahahui, as well as a member of the Pa'i Mo'olelo (Committee to Publish History).[20] In 1907 Pa'aluhi relocated to Kaua'i, where he was the kahu hope (associate pastor) of the church at Ko'olau, East Kaua'i, serving with Kahu R. P. Puuki.[21] He remained in this position until May 2, 1913, when he died of heart failure at the age of sixty-eight.

Kame'eleihiwa suggests that Bush and Pa'aluhi wrote another lengthy traditional mo'olelo published in *Ka Leo o ka Lahui*, "He Mo'olelo Ka'ao o Kamapua'a" (A Story of the [Pig–God] Kamapua'a). While the Kamapua'a mo'olelo was unsigned, she notes the similarity between the opening remarks of that mo'olelo and Pele and Hi'iaka as nearly identical. Pa'aluhi's position on the Pa'i Mo'olelo committee for the OEA indicates his knowledge of Hawaiian literary traditions, so it isn't surprising he would be associated with the publication of these mo'olelo ku'una.

Pa'aluhi and Bush began publishing a Pele and Hi'iaka mo'olelo not previously set to print. However, by the end of January 1893, only seventeen installments into their narrative, they stopped it, citing knowledge of a previously printed version—Kapihenui's. They apologize to their readers for starting over, and begin the next issue with a near word-for-word reprint of Kapihenui with this introduction: "The Hi'iaka story, which was first published here, lacked a proper conclusion. We have received another version with a more complete ending. Therefore, forgive us dear readers for beginning the mo'olelo anew. This one will run straight to the conclusion for your enjoyment because this mo'olelo is full of good mele of the past, something for the people now to carry on."[22] Charlot laments the unfortunate loss of another independent tradition; this is particularly true when there are elements in this version of the mo'olelo that resonate with versions by Ka'ili, Ho'oulumāhiehie, Poepoe, and Desha. Pa'aluhi and Bush's abandoned narrative could have provided additional details not included in other versions, leading to new insights into the mo'olelo.

The newspaper *Ka Loea Kalaiaina* (The Political Expert) published Moses Manu's "Pelekeahi'āloa" in 1899. The paper was associated with the

Hui Kālaiʻāina (Hawaiian Political Association), which was formed by makaʻāinana in 1888 after the Bayonet Constitution was forcibly enacted. The Hui was stalwart in its support of Queen Liliʻuokalani, and after the overthrow, resolute in their determination to restore the monarchy. The paper ran between 1897 and 1900. It was published by T. C. Pokipala and edited by D. W. Kamaliʻikāne, and maintained a political, pro–Kanaka Maoli focus that was staunchly anti-annexationist. Little is known about Pokipala or Kamaliʻikāne. Pokipala owned a publishing house (hale paʻi), and he was the president of the Hui Moʻolelo Hawaiʻi Lani Honua (Hawaiʻi Heaven [and] Earth Historical Society) in 1905. Similarly, no additional information about the association is known at this time, other than that they collected and published moʻolelo kuʻuna.

Moses Manu was born in Kīpahulu near Hāna, East Maui. He was a prolific writer of moʻolelo, both Hawaiian and foreign. Between 1866 and 1899, Manu published thirty-four stories in Hawaiian-language newspapers. He worked in publishing in Honolulu for a time, for the newspaper *Ke Au Okoa*. He was involved in both the Hui Kālaiʻāina and the Hui Aloha ʻĀina; in 1896 he was a delegate to the Hui Aloha ʻĀina convention, representing the Kīpahulu–Hāna districts. His "Pelekeahiʻāloa" version published in *Ka Loea Kalaiaina* explicitly describes the Pele and Hiʻiaka moʻolelo as political (moʻolelo kālaiʻāina) in his referencing of Kapihenui.

In 1905, the short-lived periodical *Hawaii Aloha* (Beloved Hawaiʻi) (July 15–November 24, 1905) began publishing what would become the longest and most elaborate of the Pele and Hiʻiaka moʻolelo, "Ka Moolelo o Hiiaka-i-ka-poli-o-pele, ka Wahine i ka Hikina a ka La, a o ka Ui Palekoki Uwila o Halemaʻumaʻu" (The Legend of Hiʻiakaikapoliopele, the Woman from the East, and the Lightning-Skirted Beauty of Halemaʻumaʻu), or "Ka Uʻi Pelekoki Uila." Published weekly, the periodical was edited by Joseph Mokuʻōhai Poepoe. "Ka Uʻi Pelekoki Uila" is attributed to Hoʻoulumāhiehie, a possible pseudonym for Poepoe. The connection between the two is unclear, but Laiana Wong, Silva, and Nogelmeier have discussed it in separate works. Nogelmeier writes:

> It seems likely that Hoʻoulumāhiehie is a fiction, a pen name for Poepoe himself, or one he used when collaborating with others, for Poepoe acknowledged that the work was his own . . . [writing] "The Hiiaka story, I negotiated on my own with another, then combined it with the original material I already had, along with what I obtained through research, as well as through the assistance of Mr. Pokipala, President of the ʻHawaii Lani-Honuaʻ Hawaiian Historical Association, and G. M. Keone."[23]

Poepoe was the son of Poepoe (k) and Keawehiku (w), and was born in Kohala, Hawai'i, in 1852. He was well educated and multilingual, fluent in English and knowledgeable in French, Latin, and Hebrew. He worked as a teacher for a time before receiving his license to practice law. Changing careers once again to become a newspaperman and editor, he was one of the most prolific Hawaiian editors, associated with a number of prominent newspapers, and a highly accomplished writer. He was a well-respected author, educator, and scholar, who was "knowledgeable about rare words and deeper meanings. He was an unequalled editor, fine story-teller, and unforgettable translator."[24] Poepoe edited a number of Hawaiian-language newspapers, including *Ka Hoku o ke Kai* (1883–1884), *Kuokoa Home Rula* (1901–1912), *Ka Na'i Aupuni* (1905–1908), and *Ke Aloha Aina* (1911–1912). Poepoe's association with *Ka Elele Evanelio* (The Evangelical Messenger) suggests he was Mormon.

Edited by Poepoe, *Hawaii Holomua* (Hawai'i Progress) was one of only two newspapers (the other being Bush's *Ka Leo o ka Lahui*) that printed the queen's protest after the overthrow. This demonstrates Bush and Poepoe's bravery, because under the provisional government editors were regularly arrested, fined, or jailed for supporting the Hawaiian government or criticizing the provisional government, the Republic of Hawai'i, and annexationists. Like Bush, Poepoe also changed political affiliations several times. After the Kaua Kūloko (rebellion) of 1895, Poepoe became the editor of *Ka Nupepa Kuokoa*, switching his political affiliation from anti- to pro-annexation. Like Bush, he later joined the Home Rule Party.

In its relatively short four-month run, *Hawaii Aloha* published at least thirteen installments of the Pele and Hi'iaka mo'olelo.[25] The periodical folded before the conclusion of the mo'olelo; fortunately, it was soon picked up by another publication, *Ka Na'i Aupuni* (To Conquer the Nation).

Ka Na'i Aupuni (November 27, 1905–April 24, 1908) was a daily Hawaiian-language newspaper published in Honolulu owned by Charles Kahiliaulani Notley and edited by Poepoe. The two teamed up again in 1908 with *Kuokoa Home Rula*. Both newspapers and both men were associated with the Home Rule Party. Notley was the president of the Home Rule Party in 1905 and its candidate for United States Congress, a position he ran for several times but never won. Like Bush, Notley and Poepoe continued to advocate a pro-Hawaiian position in their papers after the overthrow and annexation through their continued involvement in newspaper publishing, keeping traditional Hawaiian literature and other important Hawaiian issues at the forefront of public discussion.

One of only two known photographs of Joseph Moku'ōhai Poepoe. This photograph appeared in the newspaper *Ka Nupepa Kuokoa* on April 18, 1913, accompanying an article on his passing.

Poepoe also worked with Pokipala in the Hui Mo'olelo Hawai'i Lani Honua as their chairperson in 1905.

Poepoe's political and professional careers were intertwined with the history of these papers. When he later became editor of another Home Rule paper, *Ke Aloha Aina* (The Patriot), Poepoe was elected to the Territorial Legislature, five months before he died. Like Bush, Poepoe was a strong political figure who was not afraid to speak his mind and support the Hawaiian kingdom. Mookini states:

> [Poepoe] was an intimate friend of the royal family . . . and had opposed the constitution of 1887 which limited the power of the monarchy. He described it as "very similar to the Constitution of the United States, where they had no nobility and every man was as good as his neighbor. Now, in Hawaii, we have had chiefs from time immemorial, and it is our duty to support them." He argued that "The aim of the constitution was to make Hawaii a republic. The Americans have no respect for royalty, for they have no King. . . . It will not be long before Hawaii becomes an entire republic. We who cherish our King ought not to allow this to be done."[26]

Poepoe is credited with writing and publishing a number of mo'olelo that appeared as serialized newspaper articles and independently published books, including *Ka Moolelo o ka Moi Kalakaua* (The History of King Kalākaua) (1891), "Moolelo o Kamehameha I" (The History of Kamehameha I) (*Ka Na'i Aupuni*, 1905–1906), "Moolelo Hawaii Kahiko" (History of Old Hawai'i) (*Ka Na'i Aupuni*, 1906), and "Ka Moolelo Hiwa- hiwa o Kawelo" (The Esteemed History of Kawelo) (*Kuokoa Home Rula*, 1909–1910). Poepoe is associated with two Pele and Hi'iaka mo'olelo, "Moolelo o Hiiakaikapoliopele" (Story of Hi'iakaikapoliopele) (*Ka Na'i Aupuni*, 1905–1906) and "Ka Moolelo Kaao o Hiiaka-i-ka-poli-o-pele" (Legend of Hi'iakaikapoliopele) (*Kuokoa Home Rula*, 1908–1911).[27] An English translation, "Battle of the Owls: A Hawaiian Legend" (*Thrum's Hawaiian Annual*, 1891), is attributed to him. He also published a legal guidebook for Kanaka Maoli, *Ke Alakai o ke Kanaka Hawaii: He Buke no na Olelo Hooholo o ka Aha Kiekie* (The Leader of the Hawaiian People: A Book for the Judgments of the [Hawai'i] Supreme Court) (*Hawaiian Gazette*, 1891).[28]

Ho'oulumāhiehie's mo'olelo in *Ka Na'i Aupuni* picked up where it had left off in *Hawaii Aloha*. Under pressure from their readership, the *Ka Na'i Aupuni* editors began concurrently reprinting the beginning of the mo'olelo, 105 installments into the story. Although challenging to read at times, this created a more complete record of the mo'olelo within one newspaper.

The Hilo-based *Ka Hoku o Hawaii* (The Star of Hawai'i) is the longest-running Hawaiian-language newspaper (1906–1948). It was published by the Star of Hawai'i Publishing Company, which was founded by the Reverend Stephen Langhern Desha Sr., who served as its president as well as the luna ho'oponopono and luna nui (chief officer) for the major-ity of the paper's run (1906–1932). Despite being founded after Hawai'i's annexation to the United States, it remained loyal to Queen Lili'uokalani and retained a royalist perspective.

Desha was born on July 11, 1859, in Lāhainā, Maui. His parents were John Rollin Langhern Desha and Eliza "Laika" Hoa (Brewer) Desha. Educated in Hawaiian at a Maui public school, Desha was sent to Hono-lulu at the age of eleven by his father to attend the Royal School, where he was educated, for the first time, in English. Desha graduated from the North Pacific Missionary Institute in Honolulu, run by the Hawaiian Evangelical Association, in 1883. He spent two months in San Francisco before returning home to Hawai'i, where he was first assigned the pastor-ate of Nāpo'opo'o Church, a position he held until 1889. In 1889, Desha and his family left South Kona for Hilo, where he became the pastor of Haili Church; he served that congregation until his death on July 22, 1934.

Like his publishing predecessors, Desha was also committed to pub-lic service. He was a member of various community groups and boards in Hilo and Kona. In 1905 and again in 1909 he was elected to Hawai'i County's initial Board of Supervisors. He became a territorial senator in 1913, running as a Republican, a position he held for over twenty years. Desha was close to Prince Jonah Kūhiō Kalaniana'ole, and supported his vision of establishing the Hawaiian Homes Commission, which he did in 1920.[29]

Desha was married four times. His first three wives died from different illnesses. In 1913 he married Julia H. Keonaona, whom he credits in his Pele and Hi'iaka mo'olelo. Within the pages of his history of Kamehameha I, Desha relates a story about how niuhi (tiger) sharks were caught by his wife Keonaona's grandfather.[30] Keonaona is perhaps a source for his Pele and Hi'iaka mo'olelo.

Founder, president, and editor of *Ka Hoku o Hawaii*, Desha was noted for his eloquent speeches and knowledge of Hawaiian mo'olelo. In a eulogy that appeared in the August 1934 *Friend*, Reverend Henry P. Judd wrote, "[Desha] had a remarkable gift of oratory in his native tongue, in which he was a master. He was saturated with the spirit of ancient *mele*, folklore, traditions, and stories of the Hawaiian people. It was easy for him to make his point by introducing some apt story or telling illustrations from Hawaiian history or mythology."[31]

In the introduction to *Kamehameha and His Warrior Kekūhaupi'o*, originally published, like his Pele and Hi'iaka mo'olelo, during his tenure as editor of *Ka Hoku o Hawaii*, the editors wrote:

> In large part, the recording of the traditions told here was motivated by Desha's proud advocacy of the Hawaiian people. Desha, newspaper editor and territorial senator from Hilo as well as pastor, saw this serial as a way to inform younger generations of Hawaiians of their culture and their past. He wrote not only of the exploits of two famous warriors but also of the traditions and values which guided them and other Hawaiians in earlier times. Desha hoped, through sharing his knowledge of his ancestors and their ways, to instill within his Hawaiian readers a greater sense of pride in themselves. Today his message continues to inspire.[32]

Desha was the last Kanaka Maoli writer to publish an epic-length Pele and Hi'iaka mo'olelo, and one of the last writers and publishers of a Hawaiian-language newspaper; *Ka Hoku o Hawaii* went out of business in 1948, when the numbers of Hawaiian-language speakers began to severely decline.

Ka Hoku o Hawaii, September 18, 1924. Desha and Keonaona's "Hiiakaikapoli-opele" ran on the front page alongside two foreign stories, "Elevaira Alava Resa" and the more familiar "Tarzan."

Ka Hoku o Hawaii is the only newspaper that printed two separately authored and different versions of the Pele and Hiʻiaka moʻolelo. The first, "He Moolelo no Pele ame kona Kaikaina Hiiaka i ka Poli o Pele" (Pele and Her Younger Sister Hiʻiakaikapoliopele), is a Kauaʻi account attributed to William Hyde Rice that ran from May 21 to September 10, 1908. It is unfortunate that only nine installments of the moʻolelo still survive on microfilm. Gaps in dates of publication indicate that conceivably up to eight installments, or nearly half of the story, is missing from the microfilm.

Rice was the son of William Harrison and Mary Sophia Rice, the first ABCFM missionaries to permanently settle on the island of Kauaʻi. Rice was born in Honolulu in 1846 during his parents' tenure at Punahou School. In 1854, the senior Rice resigned his position with the ABCFM and moved his family to Kauaʻi, where he became manager of the Līhuʻe sugar plantation.

The younger Rice married Mary Waterhouse, and together they had eight children. From 1867 to 1869 he managed the ranch portion of Līhuʻe plantation operations before starting his own enterprise in 1872, when he purchased thousands of acres of land in the Kīpū area from Princess Ruth, establishing Kīpū Ranch. Rice was also granted lands from Kōloa to Hanamāʻulu through Kekūanāoʻa, the governor of Oʻahu and husband of one of Kamehameha I's daughters.

Rice is a problematic figure who was actively involved in kingdom politics. He was a member of the House of Representatives (1870–1890), and appointed governor of Kauaʻi by Queen Liliʻuokalani in 1891, a position he held until 1894. Between 1895 and 1898 he was a member of the Senate under the Republic of Hawaiʻi. While Rice was not in Honolulu when the overthrow occurred in 1893, he was one of the architects of the 1887 Bayonet Constitution, which reduced Kalākaua's powers and politically disenfranchised Kanaka Maoli.

Aside from the economic and social impact of his ranching business and his involvement in Hawaiʻi politics, Rice also had a cultural impact on Hawaiian society through his collection and publication of Hawaiian folklore, history, and literature. Rice spoke fluent Hawaiian; raised by Hawaiian caregivers, he acquired an added depth of understanding of the language.

In *Kauaʻi: The Separate Kingdom*, Edward Joesting gushes over Rice's contributions to Hawaiian literature, writing, "Many believe his book *Hawaiian Legends* is the closest written expression of the ancient legends."[33] Written from a settler perspective, Joesting overstates Rice's contribution; while he did have an excellent command of the Hawaiian language, *Hawaiian Legends*, as with most writing in the area of Hawaiian culture and literature, ignored or dismissed Hawaiian-language sources (including his own Pele and Hiʻiaka moʻolelo), reframing the English-language "translations" of the moʻolelo to fit a Western paradigm. Rice acknowledges no Kanaka Maoli sources for Hawaiian moʻolelo, although he certainly had some.

One example is Paul Puhiʻula Kanoa (1832–1895), a prominent, well-respected Kanaka Maoli. Joesting calls Kanoa a "close friend" of Rice who "had an understanding of the history and legends of the Islands and over the years the two had long talks, of assistance in Rice's writing of *Hawaiian Legends*."[34] If this is true, he is an uncredited source for Rice's *Legends*. There are actually two Paul Kanoas, and Rice was likely friends with both. Both served as governor of Kauaʻi before Rice did, and both served with Rice in the legislature of the kingdom. The elder Kanoa (1802–1885) was born in South Kona, Hawaiʻi. In his youth, he served as an assistant to missionaries Gerrit P. Judd and Hiram Bingham, and later served as a clerk to Oʻahu governor Mataio Kekūanāoʻa. He was elected to the Hawaiian legislature, where he served in many legislative sessions between 1845 and 1882. Paul Puhiʻula Kanoa was the elder Kanoa's hānai son. Following his father into politics, he served as governor of Kauaʻi in 1881; in 1883, King Kalākaua appointed him to the Privy Council. He served in the legislature between 1886 and 1887 with John E. Bush. In 1886 he was appointed to the position of minister of finance by Kalākaua, and to the Board of Education for the Kawaihau district of Kauaʻi in 1888. He was voted into the House of Nobles for a four-year term in 1890 as a member of the Reform Party. In 1891 he was reappointed to the Privy Council by Queen Liliʻuokalani, along with Bush and E. Lilikalani.

Nearly twenty years later, the same editors of *Ka Hoku o Hawaii* published another Pele and Hiʻiaka epic, "He Moolelo Kaao no Hiiaka-i-ka-poli-o-Pele, ka Wahine i ka Hikina a ka La a o ka Uʻi Palekoki Uwila o Halemaumau" (The Story of Hiʻiakaikapoliopele, the Woman at the Rising of the Sun, and the Beautiful Lightning Skirt of Halemaʻumaʻu), which ran for 151 installments from September 18, 1924, to July 17, 1928. Credited to Julia Keonaona and Stephen Desha, it is an almost exact reprint of the 1905–1906 Hoʻoulumāhiehie moʻolelo published in *Hawaii Aloha* and *Ka Naʻi Aupuni*. One hundred and fifty-five installments of this lengthy series are available on microfilm. In the four years that the moʻolelo was printed in the newspaper, there are only twelve dates available on microfilm in which installments of the moʻolelo did not occur.[35]

Around the time Rice's Pele and Hiʻiaka moʻolelo appeared in *Ka Hoku o Hawaii*, the Home Rule newspaper *Kuokoa Home Rula* (Independent Home Rule) published a version by Poepoe. Located in Honolulu, *Kuokoa Home Rula* was a weekly newspaper published between 1901 and 1912. It was owned by Notley and edited by Poepoe from 1903 to 1912, who had previously worked together on *Ka Naʻi Aupuni*. The paper was printed mostly in Hawaiian, with some English. As a home rule newspaper, it was staunchly pro–Native Hawaiian. Like other Hawaiian newspapers of the time, *Kuokoa Home Rula* featured news from abroad, foreign stories in serial form, and Hawaiian legends.

Poepoe's "Ka Moolelo Kaao o Hiiaka-i-ka-poli-o-pele" (The Legend of Hiʻiakaikapoliopele) ran from January 10, 1908, through January 20, 1911. During the course of its publication, Poepoe referred to manuscripts he was using that provided Maui and Hawaiʻi island versions of the moʻolelo. Between Rice and Poepoe, readers had the rare opportunity to enjoy and compare two completely different versions of the Pele and Hiʻiaka moʻolelo being published almost simultaneously. As with other newspapers lost over time, it is regrettable that not all issues of the paper containing installments of the moʻolelo are preserved on microfilm, rendering the moʻolelo available to readers and scholars today incomplete.[36]

This brief overview of the Kanaka Maoli writers, newspaper publishers, editors, and their newspaper demonstrates a clear interweaving of art and politics, moʻolelo kuʻuna, Hawaiian language, and the importance of moʻolelo such as Pele and Hiʻiaka as vehicles carrying the political message of hulihia by the poʻe aloha ʻāina, the patriots of the times. It is another layering of moʻokūʻauhau, demonstrating how it is not just linear, but multidimensional, an expression of makawalu.

As I discuss in the next section, the writers and editors didn't just publish moʻolelo kuʻuna as oral traditions captured in writing. They're moʻolelo developed as literature, incorporating traditional oral meiwi, adapting them to writing, and weaving Western literary meiwi into their literature. Perhaps most important, they made their cultural–political purpose clear as they developed literature as an expression of Hawaiian mana.

He Mana nō ka Moʻolelo Palapala (Literature as Mana)

As I discussed in mokuna 3, earlier Pele and Hiʻiaka moʻolelo such as Kapihenui retained a more oral style in their presentation in print. Moʻolelo published in the 1880s–1920s were more literature-based, incorporating prose descriptions and authorial asides (kōkua) meant to elucidate their purpose for publishing the moʻolelo and educate their reading audiences, pointing out unique or important vocabulary words, for example, or providing intertextual readings, comparing their moʻolelo to other versions, and other moʻolelo from Hawaiʻi and abroad. In this way writing became a repository of memory and led to the flourishing of a national literature at a level unknown in other indigenous communities in the Pacific and Americas, and perhaps around the world.

There is no introduction or exposition in Kapihenui to explain the writer's or editor's purpose for printing it. Kaʻili's "A Hawaiian Legend by a Hawaiian Native" (1883) is the first to explain its publication. After the moʻolelo concludes, a short paragraph justifies the value of publishing it:

> Legends of all countries are the predecessors of history. At a time when *no authentic narrative of events existed in Hawaii* actual events were handed down from generation to generation by word of mouth suffering certain changes, and with the lapse of time, being exaggerated and exalted into the dignity of something

supernatural. But still, after passing through all the change, which must inevitably be made in a record that is kept solely in the mind and handed down from remote ages for many generations orally there will be something of truth, a shadow of fact, in the traditional story, which may aid the student to form tolerably correct ideas of what life was in those ancient days among the people who originated it. As a legend of ancient Hawaii "Hiiaka" has a value which students of ancient Hawaiian history will most highly appreciate, although as an interesting and well written narrative it will be highly prized by the general reader. From another point of view the story has also an attraction; it was written by a Hawaiian native, and to some extent shows the degree of *culture* that has given the Hawaii of to-day *a high rank* among the civilized peoples of the earth.[37]

It isn't clear if Kaʻili or the newspaper editors wrote the paragraph, although referring to the author as "a Hawaiian native" and rationalizing the publication of a traditional Hawaiian moʻolelo suggest the newspaper editors. The inclusion of the editorial is important as the English newspapers of the time were geared toward haole readers, who for the most part did not support Kanaka Maoli and their insistence of self-determination and resistance against foreign intrusion into government affairs. This is particularly true of the *Pacific Commercial Advertiser (PCA)*, an establishment settler newspaper that was anti–Hawaiian government. As Chapin notes:

> Establishment papers (or the mainstream, commercial press) need not represent the majority of the people. Rather, establishment papers . . . are part of a power structure that formulates the policies and practices to which everyone is expected to adhere.
>
> The American Protestant Mission introduced an establishment press to Hawaiʻi. Mission editors in the Hawaiian and English languages promoted American culture and values. . . . As the English language gained dominance through the [nineteenth] century, so, too, did establishment papers in English gain even greater power. By the end of the century, an alliance of missionary descendants and haole . . . American business interests, operating as an oligarchy, backed by the American military, and aided and abetted by the oligarchy's newspapers, overthrew the queen and the Hawaiian government representing the majority population [of Kanaka Maoli].[38]

The *PCA* is the result of the Protestant mission (ABCFM), and strongly endorsed American culture and values, marking the publication of a traditional Hawaiian moʻolelo as somewhat strange for the paper.

The editorial acknowledges moʻolelo as oral tradition, and thereby a precursor or foundation of history (writing). It also states a purpose of educating its modern nineteenth-century readers, who would have been Americans. It pointedly mentions that the moʻolelo demonstrates Kanaka Maoli are educated and civilized at an international level. This emphasis can be read as a counter-narrative to haole discourse continually insisting that Kanaka Maoli were backward, ignorant, and incapable of self-determination (which justified the eventual overthrow of the government). The moʻolelo was published just after Kalākaua's coronation (February of that year), which featured hula, including hula Pele, against which the haole community strongly reacted. Kalākaua's promotion and support of Kanaka Maoli cultural practice such as hula is surprisingly supported by this commentary—surprising only in that it was published in an English-language newspaper generally forwarding haole perspectives and politics and read predominantly by haole.

What may factor into the timing of Kaʻili's moʻolelo is that it appears two years after Princess Ruth Keʻelikōlani successfully stopped the 1880–1881 lava flow from destroying Hilo, by offering traditional hoʻokupu and oli to Pele. Moreover, Keʻelikōlani passed away in May 1883, three months prior to Kaʻili's moʻolelo appearing in print in the *Advertiser*. Keʻelikōlani is specifically alluded to by Kaʻili, her home on Hilo Bay mentioned as a wahi pana connected to an episode in the moʻolelo, a place Hiʻiaka and her companions travel to and through, an intersection of mana wahine—regal, powerful Hawaiian women who were and remain strong symbols of Hawaiian culture, each staunchly upholding traditional practices, living on and traversing the same ʻāina, connected through moʻolelo across time periods. As a powerful, mana-full Kanaka Maoli wahine herself, was Kaʻili perhaps evoking a subtle (or not so subtle) message of cultural and gendered hulihia discourse?

A decade later, Paʻaluhi and Bush published a version of "Hiiakaikapoliopele" in the nationalist paper *Ka Leo o ka Lahui* (January 5–July 12, 1893). The introduction to the moʻolelo, signed by Bush, was so long it took two issues to publish it. It provides an overview of the moʻolelo, but more important, it outlines the purpose for its printing. Bush acknowledges that literature is a treasured part of every nation:

> As always the stories and tales of the ancient times of our land were indeed very beautiful and truly enjoyable, something of

Hawaiʻi that needs to be cherished like the delights of every nation in their stories, tales, and songs of their lands. Regarding this loss of the stories, it is an omen [ʻōuli] of the seer [kilo] to see with the gut [naʻau] filled with the anxious thoughts continuing with his nation on the land of his ancestors, therefore, we must continue to publish the true stories of the lands written about in the stories.[39]

He then expresses the concern over the disappearance of oral traditions (hoopaa waha ia) recorded in the Hawaiian language, suggesting the disappearance of the Hawaiian language as well. Bush explains the role of the moʻolelo in forming connections to the past as a vital part of aloha ʻāina—evoking Kanaka love for the land as an important part of nineteenth-century patriotism, a political message not lost on an audience living through the struggle over political sovereignty, culminating just two weeks later with the overthrow of the Hawaiian kingdom. Bush stresses that it was important to "continue speaking to the youth to perpetuate the positive emotion of the people who love the land through the stirring stories and songs of the 'birth sands,' the 'storied places' and the famous deeds of the ancestors."[40]

As Marie Alohalani Brown points out in her research on Kanaka Maoli perspectives on variation in moʻolelo, while writers such as Paʻaluhi and Bush were well aware of the oral traditions, they were also aware of the transformation of oral tradition to written, authored narratives: "As always with the moʻolelo of old, transmitted orally from one generation to the next, the moʻolelo constantly evolved, altered each time [it was told] by the people who preserved the continuity of the moʻolelo. . . . And from the time that the actual moʻolelo of this family was transformed into a kaʻao until this day, so were the exploits associated with the man-seeking voyage on which Hiʻiaka went transformed into wondrous acts."[41] The development of a literary tradition was one that was vigorously discussed. Paʻaluhi and Bush and other writers of the time wrestled with defining and distinguishing the relationship between moʻolelo (history and story) and kaʻao (fiction, legend), which were sometimes combined as one term, moʻolelo kaʻao. Brown writes, "Moʻolelo can be transformed over time by multiple re-tellings into kaʻao, which, as Bush and Paʻaluhi's statement seems to imply, is a genre that transforms historical figures into heroes (or even anti-heroes) whose exploits *may* take on heroic proportions."[42] Brown also discusses the fluidity between the terms with S. N. Haleʻole's explanation of his moʻolelo *Lāʻieikawai*:

Another example of the interrelation between ka'ao and mo'olelo pertains to [Hale'ole's] . . . "Ka Moolelo o Laieikawai," which was first published in *Kuokoa* on November 29, 1862, and reached its conclusion on April 4 of the same year. . . . In his preface of the first installment, Hale'ole explains that, "He umikumamawalu makahiki me ekolu malama ka malamaia'na o keia Moolelo Kaao, e ka mea nana e hoopuka nei keia moolelo maloko o kana Buke Moolelo, e hoomaka ana ma ka malama o Augate, M. H. 1844" (Hale'ole 1862). It has been eighteen years and three months that this Mo'olelo Ka'ao has been kept by the person [Hale'ole] who will publish this mo'olelo in his Book of Mo'olelo, beginning in the month of August, M. H. 1844." . . . From his comment, it appears that mo'olelo and ka'ao, at least in this case, are interchangeable genres, or that Lā'ieikawai fits into both categories. The owner and editor of the *Kuokoa*, Henry M. Whitney, republished Hale'ole's mo'olelo as a book the next year, but the title was changed to "Ke Kaao o Laieikawai." . . . It is clear by the title that this book was assigned the genre of ka'ao; however, the front matter of the book notes, "Kakauia mailoko mai o na Moolelo Kahiko o Hawaii nei" (Hale'ole) [Written from ancient mo'olelo of Hawai'i]. What to say of this account first published by the writer as a mo'olelo and later as a ka'ao?[43]

By 1899, when Manu's "Pelekeahi'āloa" appeared in print, the Hawaiian government had been overthrown, replaced by the provisional government, despite vehement protests by Queen Lili'uokalani and her supporters that had continued through the rest of the 1890s. The subsequent Republic of Hawai'i established in 1894 was replaced by annexation to the United States in 1898. Hawaiian had been banned as a language of public instruction by the Republic in 1896, contributing to the erosion of Hawaiian language and culture. By 1899, the Kanaka Maoli population was down to less than forty thousand, and the foreign population was up to two hundred thousand.

From Manu forward, Kanaka Maoli writers and editors were no longer content with brief introductions or conclusions explaining the mo'olelo or their reasons for their publication. The erosion of Hawaiian-language fluency and cultural knowledge was rising, so writers and editors began to intersperse mo'olelo with asides to readers. At the beginning of "Pelekeahi'āloa" Kapō'ulakīna'u asks her mother, Haumea, for permission to travel from Kahiki and explore the world. Haumea agrees to her request, saying:

I give my consent for your departure, and if your younger sisters wish to accompany you, care for them and let them serve you, as "children are easily obtained, but younger siblings are not" [aole e loaa ana ia oe ka pokii ke imi ia, o ke keiki o ia ka mea loaa ia oe].

When Haumea was finished speaking, tears filled Kapōʻulakī-naʻu's eyes because of the kind instructions their mother Haumea provided. Thus, dear reader, you have learned that it was Haumea who first said, "A younger brother or sister is not easily found" [o ka pokii, aole ia e loaa ke imi ia]. These words spoken by Haumea are true, and should be remembered by the younger generation today who are learning to speak English.[44]

Like Paʻaluhi and Bush before him, Manu directs his kōkua (authorial asides) to the younger generations who are (apparently) not as fluent in Hawaiian language, a great concern of the writers, who were also businessmen and political leaders. It would be difficult if not impossible to have a full functioning government and vibrant society if people were deficient in language and literacy. Manu also takes more time to explain the significance of important cultural knowledge, making sure readers wouldn't miss it. One example is his discussion of the practice of spiritual possession (haka, noho), as always directly addressing the reader, making his intentions clear: "Remember, dear reader, Kapōʻulakīnaʻu first began this work of human spiritual possession with the chief Halāliʻi on the island of Niʻihau. This was accomplished before she made a circuit of all the Hawaiian islands. Since that time, many people have been possessed by this wondrous daughter of Haumea, as well as by her brother and sister, just as the author has told here."[45]

Such asides didn't just explain archaic vocabulary or aspects of the moʻolelo. They also commented on events of the day, weaving the moʻolelo of the past with their present situation, a politicized move. In concluding Kapōʻulakīnaʻu's time on Niʻihau, Manu directly addresses his readers again, writing, "Dear reader, let us leave the land of the patterned [pāwehe] mats that is now possessed by haole owners, of whom it has been said, 'The owners formed a company, and now Niʻihau is gone' [E ka mea heluhelu, e haalele kaua i ka mokupuni no na ka moena pawehe, e noho onia nei e na haole i olelo ia, 'Hui ai na ona, lilo Niihau']."[46] In another example, also unrelated to the course of the narrative, he digresses to recount the moʻolelo of Boki, an aliʻi who was governor of Oʻahu for a time in the 1820s, and a nemesis of Kaʻahumanu, as he was anti-Christian. After discussing Boki's ill-fated voyage to the South Pacific in search of sandalwood in 1829, Manu remarks, "From that time to this, nothing more has ever been heard of Boki or the others, except the saying called out by this crazed man, which remains in the memory from this generation to the next. This is why the author thought about relaying it to the readers of this legend, to benefit the modern readers of this new time. Let us now set this aside for there is more to come; let us catch up and travel together with the procession of godly women."⁴⁷ Authorial asides added supplementary, sometimes tangential information to the ongoing narrative, weaving contemporary wahi moʻolelo (bits of story) into the larger narrative, braiding new strands into the lei moʻolelo. Elsewhere, Manu boldly invites the readers to participate in the moʻolelo, as when he says, "Dear reader, let us recite together Kānemilohaiʻs prayer [E pule kaua e ka mea heluhelu]."⁴⁸

Whereas Kapihenuiʻs moʻolelo abruptly ends in 1861, and Paʻaluhi and Bush lament a "proper" ending in 1893, by 1899 Manuʻs moʻolelo concludes, summarizing his final thoughts: "Pele had many great adventures and accomplished many incredible things across the Hawaiian archipelago; these amazing feats have never been forgotten by the ancient legends of our ancestors, and they continue to be embedded in the hearts of true Hawaiians. This moʻolelo recounting Peleʻs arrival in the Hawaiian islands and her legendary status is thus passed down to this new era, and is truly ours."⁴⁹ Again, the thoughts on the minds of the writers were remembering and honoring the ancestors and the moʻolelo, and challenges readers when he says *true* Hawaiians will value and internalize the moʻolelo because they are part of Hawaiian identity. This is a radically different construction of Hawaiian identity than what would occur in subsequent decades, when the establishment of Hawaiian Home Lands and blood quantum requirements would thereafter legally and, sadly, politically divide the Lāhui. Manu is essentially arguing that it is the internalization of Kanaka Maoli intellectual tradition passed down mai ka pō mai, mai nā kūpuna mai that shaped Kanaka Maoli and belonged to them (pili maoli).

From the introduction to the story, Hoʻoulumāhiehie makes clear there are various versions, and some people are still knowledgeable about the moʻolelo. After listing (helu) the names of eight Hiʻiaka sisters, he writes, "Wahi hoi a kekahi poe paa moolelo Hiiaka, he lehulehu loa ka nei poe Hiiaka, ua piha ke kanaha a oi. A ma ka mahele hoi a kekahi poe, he ewalu no Hiiaka e like aela no me ia i hoike ia aela." (According to some who are knowledgeable in the lore of Hiʻiaka, there are many of these Hiʻiaka, some forty or more. And in versions known by others, there are but eight Hiʻiaka, the same number shown above.)⁵⁰ Hoʻoulumāhiehie then lists these other eight Hiʻiaka sisters and their hōʻailona.

He also thanks S. L. Peleiōhōlani as one of his sources who helped provide specific details and information. Similarly, Poepoe thanks J. W.
Naihe of Kohala and D. K. Waiʻaleʻale for sharing their ledgers of hand-
written moʻolelo for the purpose of comparison.[51] His version is perhaps
the most comparative, and he tells his readers he has two versions in
his possession, a Maui version and a Hawaiʻi version. Throughout the
moʻolelo he compares and contrasts them whenever they diverge, saying,
"The Maui version says this . . . and the Hawaiʻi version says that . . . ," a
direct indication of the comparative literary studies in which the Hawaiian intellectuals of the period were engaged.

The last Hawaiian-language Pele and Hiʻiaka was published by Desha
and Keonaona. Desha introduces the moʻolelo by writing:

> This famous story was first published many years ago, however,
> the current of time has crept forward; new generations of the
> Hawaiian nation have come, and it is a good thing for them to
> read for themselves the stories of their land, the grandchildren of
> the people who first read this famous story of Hawaiʻi nei. There
> are a number of famous stories of our beloved land that stir the
> heart and awaken the cherishing thoughts of remembrance of the
> times past of our beloved land, and the cherished thoughts grow
> for our land and our beloved nation.
>
> We offer this famous ancient story of Hawaiʻi nei to bless our
> *Ka Hoku o Hawaiʻi* readers, and with hope this version of this
> famous story of our beloved land will be something that educates
> everyone about the ancient ways of our beloved ancestors.[52]

Collectively the Kanaka Maoli writers and editors displayed a consistent message of knowledge preservation, always with an eye to the future.
Their literary traditions were created from oral traditions because it was
a way to preserve and perpetuate those stories. Writing allowed for the
continuity of makawalu, or variation in tradition by providing multiple
opportunities for printing the range of moʻolelo. Moʻolelo are important, because, as Brown notes, "Moʻolelo are vehicles for teaching the next
generation about Hawaiian culture, they impart important lessons, and
they preserve knowledge about gods, chiefs, genealogy, places, and other
valued elements of Hawaiian knowledge. Therefore, it is not surprising
that Native Hawaiian writers used authorial asides in various ways as
storytelling strategies. Undoubtedly, these same storytelling strategies
are a legacy of oral tradition."[53] Brown points out here the importance
of the writer's own voice and thoughts as a storytelling strategy. Not

just a legacy of oral tradition, such storytelling strategies demonstrated Kanaka Maoli agency and intellectualism, weaving the thoughts, values, ethics, and poetry of the ancestors with their own, a literary lei they could hand down to us, which we in turn can cherish, a tangible, artistic gift of Hawaiian nationalism that we, too, perhaps can add to with an eye toward the future as well.

Kanaka Maoli Literary Nationalism

Perhaps the most important aspect of Hawaiian literary nationalism in the period between 1860 and 1928 is the vibrant intellectual community that developed between readers and writers. Writers, readers, and, to an extent, editors were also literary critics. They conversed with one another, and acknowledged differing and sometimes competing versions and traditions. They critiqued one another as well, sometimes getting into heated public debates recorded in the pages of the newspapers, an amazing record of their intellectual arguments. Always, they had preservation of knowledge and perpetuation for future generations in mind. By the time the first epic moʻolelo was published in 1861, anti-Hawaiian haole rhetoric had been firmly in print for three decades, and Kanaka Maoli had had enough. The publication of the moʻolelo kuʻuna, including Pele and Hiʻiaka moʻolelo, was a hulihia, an overturning with a purpose of returning, a re-genesis of Hawaiian cultural knowledge in order to continue the intellectual tradition handed down mai ka pō mai, mai nā kūpuna mai.

Kanaka Maoli were not content to record just one version. Recording multiple versions is an exercise in makawalu. Brown writes, "Establishing that the writer has collaborated, or conferred, with others who know different versions of the moʻolelo is yet another way to promote the reader's acceptance of variants and variations, and thus, foster a favorable reception of the writer's own moʻolelo."[54]

Interaction between audience and performer in an oral context was reformulated within the pages of the newspapers, creating a critical literary tradition; readers wrote in to praise, criticize, or condemn writers and their moʻolelo, and writers wrote to the newspapers to ask their readers, who represented the collective memory of the people, to respond to their stories, asking for comments, additions, or corrections.[55] They also wrote their own complaints about how their moʻolelo were edited.

Six months after "He Moolelo no Hiiakaikapoliopele" concluded, Kapihenui wrote to rival paper *Ka Nupepa Kuokoa* to complain that several important chants were shortened in *Ka Hoku o ka Pakipika*, and the moʻolelo as printed by them was "not the same as the copy" he provided. He asked editors of *Kuokoa* to "please . . . republish this moʻolelo, because . . . the *Pakipika* is lazy"; in part because *Ka Hoku o ka Pakipika* was "shortening the lengthy chants [and] not following the manuscript I gave them."[56] *Ka Nupepa Kuokoa*'s editors did not respond to Kapihenui's plea, and never reprinted the hulihia chants or republished "Hiiakaikapoliopele."

Writers also exhibited a great deal of intertextuality, referencing foreign literature and texts, such as the Bible, as much as other Hawaiian moʻolelo. Hoʻoulumāhiehie includes a particularly detailed analysis of Pele and Hiʻiaka's names and how they relate to the Hebrew names Pele (amazing, wondrous) and Heylel (a sparkling or bright thing). He cites the sixth and seventh books of Moses and Isaiah 9:6 to support his analysis, concluding, "In the story of Hiʻiaka that we, dear reader, are seeing now, Hiʻiaka lived in the bosom of Pele, just like the noted account of Lazarus in Abraham's bosom."[57] Pele's knowledge expressed in the oli makani is also intertextual, referring to Laʻamaomao, a wind goddess associated with the moʻolelo kuʻuna Kūapakaʻa, and a section of the chant interweaving lines from the Kumulipo, which is discussed further in mokuna 5.

Such a high degree of literary criticism and literary activism was important during a time when Kanaka Maoli saw the publication of moʻolelo kuʻuna as a political strategy for strengthening and preserving cultural knowledge. Moʻolelo kuʻuna were a vital part of literary nationalism meant to support political nationalism. Their publication asserted pride in cultural identity, presented an intellectual history, and expressed Hawaiian creativity. As such, the moʻolelo demonstrated a deft interweaving of the old and new, the oral and written, the Native and Western, and created a new, dynamic lei moʻolelo that carried Kanaka ʻŌiwi cultural thought, belief, and practice forward. In this way it was an integral part of the literary nationalism that flourished in the Hawaiian kingdom between 1860 and 1893, and asserted a culturally based nationalism.

These literary depictions of a vibrant and healthy Kanaka society alone is a political assertion of identity: Kanaka Maoli were not helpless Natives in need of paternalistic intervention that could "save" them from "heathen barbarism," as they were characterized by missionaries. These were a robust people who had achieved a high level of civilization centuries prior to Western invasion. They were an intellectual, artistic society who worked hard, played hard, and who demonstrated pride in their heritage and ʻāina.

The interactive critique of published moʻolelo was an early formation of indigenous literary criticism that was an integral part of Hawaiian literary nationalism, one that began with the nationalist papers in the 1860s. The most vigorous critics were recognized, respected writers such as Samuel Kamakau, S. N. Haleʻole, John Bush, Joseph Poepoe, Stephen Desha, and Emma Nakuina (who also published under the name Kaʻili).

In response to a criticism of Kamehameha I's moʻokūʻauhau he published in *Ka Nupepa Kuokoa* in 1865, S. N. Haleʻole provides a detailed account of the years he spent meticulously researching it, interviewing knowledgeable people about it, and traveling around the islands, including spending nine months in North Kohala, Kamehameha's birthplace, to verify it. He stresses the need to provide an accurate Hawaiian history for the future, stating that if he and others did not work so hard to collect, verify, and publish Hawaiian moʻolelo:

> How will the future generations know our history? How indeed? . . .
>
> Our studying and researching the history of Hawaiʻi nei is of great importance because it will soon disappear, along with the original language of Hawaiʻi. Therefore, we must wake up, take a stand, and study and research as well the history of the Hawaiian islands of our ancestors before the dim memory of the past and the heart [mauli] of the language and the faint glimpse of knowledge from those days is but a hazy trace of memory for today's generations. . . . Our research . . . isn't meant to be reduced to something that is just entertainment and just for play, something that is just fiction, no; we study these things for the generations after us. Because soon the people today who truly know and understand the history of this nation will disappear. Therefore, the stories that we are researching, sharing, and editing are . . . a great treasure . . . for this generation and the generations to come. And for these reasons, we have begun to publish the stories of these islands over the past few weeks, and we will continue to do so.[58]

Kamakau stresses similar points in his critique of moʻolelo being published in 1867–1868. In a letter to the editors of *Ka Nupepa Kuokoa*, Kamakau praises the moʻolelo writers for "speaking the wisdom of our entire Nation; they are becoming the leaders of the Nation and the youth, the ones who will enlighten the generations to come."[59] He then corrects some of the details in the moʻolelo of Kana and Niheu, Keoloewa and Pākaʻa, which were being published in *Ka Nupepa Kuokoa* and *Ke Au Okoa* at the time. Kamakau is supportive, but also critical, stating that "the writers should first correct the genealogies and the Hawaiian history," because "they are the ones who are leading the Nation in knowledge and truth. The writers of history and stories are the people of importance in Hawaiian history, in the genealogies, and the ancient legends of Hawai'i nei."[60]

Collectively the writers and editors of mo'olelo ku'una were acutely aware of the importance of publishing mo'olelo, doing their best to gather as many versions as possible, and being as meticulous as they could in verifying facts and details, always with an eye to educate the current generations of their time and beyond.

Hulihia ka Mauna, Wela i ke Ahi
(The Mountain Is Overturned by Fire)

The Pele and Hi'iaka mo'olelo climaxes or concludes, depending on the version, with a series of hulihia chants performed by Paoa, Lohi'au, and/ or Hi'iaka at the rim of Halema'uma'u, Pele's home. Mokuna 3 includes a definition of hulihia as "overturned." A second meaning of huli, the root word, is "to look for, search, explore, seek, study; search, investigation, scholarship."[61] Both definitions of huli/hia are integral to the study of Pele and Hi'iaka mo'olelo. The first overthrows, reverses, or at least turns the prevailing thought or argument of previous Amer-European-centric framing and understanding of the literature within the context of the second, the study and scholarship on Pele and Hi'iaka mo'olelo from a Kanaka Maoli perspective.

"Hulihia ka mauna" literally means "the mountain is overturned." Figuratively, it can refer to the overturning of the established order, sovereignty, or genealogy of other godly or chiefly rule, such as those of Papahānaumoku and Wākea (where the islands are born in an order that differs from how Pele travels across them), or Kāne (an important male god who cannot dominate Pele; one of the male gods of the 'Aikapu, which the Pele people do not follow). The mo'olelo describes Pele's physical transformation of the landscape through forceful eruptions that destroy Hi'iaka's beloved companion Hōpoe and her lehua groves of Puna, and the destruction of her love Lohi'au. Metaphorically, at the point in the narrative the hulihia chant opening this chapter occurs, Pele's anger toward Hi'iaka and Lohi'au has "overturned" or subsided, allowing for a healing process of the 'āina and of Pele and Hi'iaka's relationship to begin. This chapter extends the metaphor by asserting that the metaphoric "mountain" of Western scholarship is also being overturned with the commencement of an indigenous literary analysis of this mo'olelo, one framed within the context of indigenous discourses, such as moʻokūʻau-hau and literary nationalism.

ʻAuʻa ʻia e Tama i Tona Moku (Child Hold Fast to Your Land): Puna Today

It is 2014: gasoline in Hawaiʻi is nearly five dollars a gallon, home electricity bills have skyrocketed, food and consumer goods prices are obscenely high (blamed on fuel and transportation costs), and interest in geothermal energy development in Puna, Hawaiʻi, has resurfaced. So have protests against it.

The state of Hawaiʻi has mandated a goal of 70 percent clean energy by 2030, 40 percent of which is designated as locally generated renewable sources. While geothermal wells have a finite lifespan, it is oddly considered a renewable, sustainable energy source that will free Hawaiʻi from dependence on foreign oil. Tūtū Pele and the ʻāina of Puna are once more under threat.

Hawaiʻi has long been known as the most fossil-fuel dependent of the U.S. states. The Hawaiʻi Clean Energy Initiative Web site admits that "this can be explained in large part because of our dependence on tourism and the military—together, they make up roughly *50% of our total economy*."[62] The link between settler colonial institutions such as tourism and the military, and the continued destruction of ʻāina, is clearly acknowledged, even by the state. In testimonies to the Hawaiʻi County Council on April 25, 2012, amid concerns for health and safety, Pele and Hiʻiaka moʻolelo were evoked in testimonies against geothermal, by Kanaka Maoli and settlers.

In 2014, Kanaka Maoli feel the economic pinch even more than before. Prominent cultural and political leaders who once helped lead the protests against geothermal development in Puna in the 1980s and 1990s are now supporting it, citing the importance of controlling the resource and making money—despite continued concerns over environmental and health issues still not adequately resolved. As principal partners of the Innovation Development Group (IDG), internationally known indigenous rights attorney Mililani Trask and respected kumu hula Cy Bridges have publicly supported geothermal, claiming, as cultural practitioners, that geothermal development does not desecrate Pele, and does not deny Kanaka Maoli cultural practices, or cultural practitioners. IDG supporters boldly claim that geothermal energy is "a gift from Pele" for the Hawaiian people. Both point to Māori development of geothermal resources in Aotearoa (New Zealand) as evidence that indigenous peoples can benefit from geothermal development. While Kanaka Maoli of Hawai'i and Māori of Aotearoa acknowledge and maintain long-standing relationships, cultural differences and differences in geology make seamless comparisons between each land base regarding geothermal development problematic. Moreover, geothermal development in Aotearoa is not problem-free. Environmental issues, particularly the pollution of air and freshwater sources (such as the Waikato river) are ongoing concerns.[63]

Only time will tell if or how geothermal development will occur in Puna, and what effect it will have. Perhaps the Pele and Hi'iaka mo'olelo will continue to play a role in protecting the 'āina from further geothermal development, perhaps these mo'olelo will be evoked to support it. Perhaps they will educate more people on the importance of these godly sisters, how they represent nature, their homeland of Puna, and the importance of aloha 'āina. Perhaps it can help hulihia the discourse of settler colonial development and desecration, or geothermal development will hulihia cultural conceptions of who Pele and Hi'iaka are. Perhaps Pele herself will hulihia ka mauna i ke ahi and halt such desecration herself once more.

Aloha Kīlauea, ka ʻĀina Aloha (Cherished Is Kīlauea, the Beloved Land): Remembering, Reclaiming, Recovering, and Retelling—Pele and Hiʻiaka Moʻolelo as Hawaiian Literary Nationalism

'O Puna lehua 'ula i ka hāpapa
I 'ula i ka papa ka lehua o Puna
Ke kui 'ia maila e nā wāhine o ka Lua ē
Mai ka Lua au i hele mai nei, mai Kīlauea
Aloha Kīlauea, ka 'āina a ke aloha.[1]

Puna with red lehua on the plain
The foundation is reddened by these lehua of Puna
The women of the crater string lei
From the crater I've come, from Kīlauea
Cherished is Kīlauea, the beloved land.[2]

IT IS JANUARY 1992, AND I AM ASLEEP on the floor of a rented house in Pāhoa, a small town in rural Puna, Hawai'i. There are twenty of us scattered throughout the home, mostly students from Leeward Community College's Hawaiian Theater and hula classes. I am here to assist the kumu, and the students are here to research the topic of their next production on the history of Kalapana, an ahupua'a down the road, next to Kapa'ahu and Poupou, lands where my kūpuna lived before the Volcanoes National Park took them, before economic hardships forced them off the land and into the cities, before developers bought it up and renamed it Royal Gardens, and before Tūtū Pele's relentless lava flows reclaimed her domain for herself.

The alarm beeps at 3:30 A.M., jolting us from our dreams. The pō is pitch black outside and silent. Our group is quietly donning sweatshirts and jackets over jeans and T-shirts, grabbing slippers and tennis shoes, piling into our rented caravan of vehicles to drive nearly forty miles from Pāhoa near the ocean to Halema'uma'u crater rising approximately four thousand feet above sea level. The geographic distance between here and there is really only about twenty miles. But the volcano has been active since 1983, and over the years, a series of eruptions and lava flows have consumed major portions of the highways and roads through Kaimū, Kalapana, and Kapa'ahu so many times that the county, state, and federal governments have given in to Pele, abandoning all attempts at reopening the thoroughfares, almost doubling the driving time from here to Halema'uma'u. But we don't mind. The tires hum on the dark road, the headlights illuminating the blackness of pō. No one else is on the road.

We arrive at Halema'uma'u and are greeted by an empty parking area; it is hours before throngs of tour buses and rental cars will invade the park. This time of pō is ours alone. Someone opens the van door and we stumble out into the night, where we are quickly enveloped by the frigid predawn mountain air, which is so cold it makes us gasp. I can't recall ever being this cold before in my life as I pull my sweatshirt tighter around me. There is not even a hint of the impending sunrise in the sky, and a few dim flashlights help light our path to the crater's edge. No one needs to tell us to be quiet. We wait in reverent silence for the lightening of the sky in the east that will announce Kāne's expected arrival.

Once we've carefully picked our way across the rugged, uneven ground to a spot near the lip of the caldera, the flashlights silently click off one by one, and soon we are plunged once again into the black pō of night. It feels like forever in the blackness, cocooned by the chilly swirls of sulfurous mist that dissolve on our cheeks, waiting for a new day, and ourselves, to be reborn. The blackness is meditative, the cold transformative; I feel like

I am alone on the mountain, at the beginning of time and the birth of the universe, awaiting the spark of creation that will propel the earth's life forces through Pele's magmatic fires.

The eastern sky transforms from black, to aubergine, to deep blue, to a fiery orange. Quietly we gather into two makeshift lines facing east, as Kumu Victoria Holt Takamine settles onto the hard, cold ground with her ipu heke, preparing to launch us into honoring Pele at the breaking of day.

"E hoʻomākaukau!" she commands. Are you ready! It is not a question, but an expectation.

"ʻAe! Lapakū ka wahine aʻo Pele i Kahiki!" Yes, we respond with the first line of the oli, the woman Pele is active in Kahiki. As the rising sun begins to transform the sky, we dance:

> Lapakū ka wahine aʻo Pele i Kahiki
> ʻOaka e ka lani noke nō
> ʻEliʻeli kau mai
> ʻOaka e ka lani noke nō
> ʻEliʻeli kau mai
> ʻUhī a ʻuhā mai ana ʻo Pele
> I ka lua aʻo Halemaʻumaʻu
> ʻOaka e ka lani noke nō.

> Pele is active in Tahiti
> Continuously flashing in the heavens
> May profound reverence alight
> Continuously flashing in the heavens
> May profound reverence alight indeed
> Rumbling, puffing, Pele comes
> To the crater at Halemaʻumaʻu.

As the last ipu beat subsides, we pause, breathless in the cold thin air, arms stretched out, one palm resting over the back of the other hand, right leg forward at a slight angle, the ball of our right foot firm on the hard cold earth, pointing east with a hela. Our voices proclaim as one, "He inoa no Pele!" This dance is dedicated to Pele.

Kumu Vicky taps two final beats to release us from our hula. The kapu of night, the realm of akua, has broken, and we look around, smiling, bodies warmed by our hoʻokupu of hula, the brightening sky suggesting warmth as well. Several of us take lei haku of lehua made the night before and place it on the rim of the caldera, a simple hoʻokupu to acknowledge Tūtū Pele, as the steam rises from below.

Mai ka Lua aʻu i hele mai nei, mai Kīlauea,
Ke kui ʻia maila e nā wāhine o ka Lua ē
ʻO Puna lehua ʻula i ka papa
I ʻula i ka papa ka lehua o Puna.

From the crater I've come, from Kīlauea,
The women of the caldera have strung leis
The foundation of Puna is crimson, covered in lehua blossoms.
Sacred is the fountain covered with the lehua blossoms of Puna.

I can't help but hulihia the oli and remember it backward.

We drink in our surroundings—the cloudless sky, the sharp profile of Mauna Loa high in the distance, the jagged, ancient cliffs of Halemaʻemaʻu, puffs of silvery steam rising lazily from a vent on the crater wall to the west, Uēkahuna, home of Pele's shark brother Kamohoaliʻi. Standing here on the precipice of the caldera at the dawn of day, I truly understand, Aloha Kīlauea, ka ʻāina a ke aloha—Kīlauea is cherished, the land of the beloved.

Weaving a Lei of Poetics and Politics

The construction of a moʻolelo is similar to that of a lei. In each process, the crafter selects the material and then carefully places it in a desired order for a particular effect. Lei, like moʻolelo, are sometimes kapu to or representative of specific occasions, places, or kanaka. Examples of such symbolism include the use of hala, lehua, maile, palapalai, palaʻā, and other hula-related forest plants mentioned throughout the Pele and Hiʻiaka moʻolelo. In this context, they often represent the beauty of the women or their association with hula, and evoke the beauty and power of the ʻāina. As the opening mele demonstrates, lehua is primarily associated with Puna, a key symbol of the Pele ʻohana from their ʻāina.

Like lei makers, writers and editors carefully select and place their materials. Both work within a context of multiple possibilities with nearly endless choices. Why did the nineteenth- and early twentieth-century writers and editors choose to remember, write, and publish the moʻolelo they did? What was important in these moʻolelo? Why was it so important to them to preserve mele and moʻolelo in print for future generations? How are we to understand the layers of knowledge contained within these culture treasures, moʻolelo such as Pele and Hiʻiaka? An ʻōlelo noʻeau queries, "Ka hohonu i hiki ʻole ke ana ʻia, akā, ua ʻike ʻia nō kahi mau papa" (The depth is unfathomable, but several strata have indeed been seen). What are some of the strata of Hawaiian culture revealed in Pele and Hiʻiaka moʻolelo?

Moʻolelo reflect how Kanaka Maoli imagined themselves as a Lāhui. In *Red on Red: Native American Literary Separatism,* Craig Womack (Creek) argues that "a key component of nationhood is a people's idea of themselves, their imaginings of who they are. The ongoing expression of a tribal voice, through imagination, language, and literature, contributes to keeping sovereignty alive in the citizens of a nation and gives sovereignty a meaning that is defined within the tribe rather than by external sources."[3] The Pele and Hiʻiaka moʻolelo and its expression of aloha ʻāina (simultaneously love for the physical presence of the *land* as well as the political governance of the people) was a key component in how Kanaka ʻŌiwi in the mid-nineteenth to early twentieth centuries imagined themselves as a nation.

Moʻolelo ʻŌiwi—individual, collective, cultural, communal—express the core of who Kanaka Maoli are as kanaka, individuals who make up larger communities and the Lāhui. Stories can be many things—encouraging, inspiring, uplifting. Stories can also be dangerous because of their ability to influence individuals, communities, and whole societies. How we tell stories is perhaps the most vital aspect of how art is creative, innovative, inspiring. At their core, the stories we choose to tell are political because of their inherent power of transformation, something at the center of all art.

Kanaka Maoli of the late nineteenth to early twentieth centuries imagined themselves as poʻe aloha ʻāina, nationalists for whom the publication of moʻolelo kuʻuna was a strategy to support efforts of building and maintaining the Lāhui. Between 1860 and 1928, the publication of Pele and Hiʻiaka moʻolelo contributed to the development of Hawaiian literary nationalism and Kanaka Maoli identity as a Lāhui.

Moʻolelo provided a counter-narrative to the dominant discourses of settler colonialism, which imagined (constructed) Kanaka Maoli differently from how they imagined themselves. The publication of Pele and Hiʻiaka moʻolelo between 1860 and 1928 reflected and upheld Hawaiian cultural values, language, and identity, demonstrating the depth of knowledge, civility, and intellectual thought and history contained within these traditions. Written primarily in Hawaiian (and one text in English), these texts were penned for a Kanaka Maoli audience to instruct and encourage the retention and valuing of cultural knowledge and practices. This occurred even after—or especially after—the loss of Hawaiian sovereignty in 1893 and annexation to the United States in 1898. In contrast, texts published by settler colonial authors such as Emerson, Thrum, and Westervelt, for example, reflect settler colonialism and Western literary aesthetics.[4] Instead of upholding Hawaiian cultural values in a way meant to exhibit cultural artistic achievement, these settler texts justified the settlement and imagining of Hawai'i by others (non-'Ōiwi), an ongoing colonial project. Penned for an English-speaking, primarily American audience, just after annexation, these texts provided a carefully constructed glimpse into the Indigenous people of the Hawaiian islands, the newly acquired U.S. possession. The differences between them speak to the different ways Kanaka Maoli and haole imagined the Hawaiian nation.

Ka'ili's "A Hawaiian Legend by a Hawaiian Native" is the only English-language Pele and Hi'iaka mo'olelo that appears to be written in and not translated into English, and by a Kanaka Maoli author well versed in Hawaiian culture, Hawaiian poetics, and the tradition of Pele and Hi'iaka. Throughout her mo'olelo, Ka'ili provides insightful interpretations of vocabulary, practices, and tradition in a way that settler writers such as Emerson, Thrum, and Westervelt ignored or could only speculate about. Ka'ili was also keenly aware of cultural differences in literary practices, summarizing chants, detailed episodes, and genealogical information in a manner similar to settler writers such as Rice (English text) and Emerson do, to suit the preferences of a haole audience. Yet when compared side by side with the Hawaiian texts of writers after her, such as Poepoe, Ho'o-ulumāhiehie, and Desha, the presentation of Ka'ili's mo'olelo is in line with the strand of the Pele and Hi'iaka mo'olelo they present.

Thus, in tracing the history of Pele and Hi'iaka mo'olelo as an assertion of Hawaiian literary nationalism, a literature firmly and vocally resisting haole colonization, it is important to see the politicized intertextuality of the various mo'olelo. The narratives of Kanaka Maoli writers such as Kapihenui, Pa'aluhi and Bush, Ka'ili, Ho'oulumāhiehie, Poepoe, and Desha are counter-narratives to settler colonial "myths" penned by Emerson, Thrum, Westervelt, Rice, and many others. Kanaka Maoli writers actively sought to disrupt and "unwrite" the colonial misappropriation of our traditional mo'olelo. This is why Kanaka 'Ōiwi–produced texts can be read as political strategies embodying resistance, especially as they involve cultural and linguistic coding in multiple ways, including the use of mele, kaona, and so forth. This strategy of resistance worked because it was well executed, playing to dismissive colonial attitudes that wrote off mo'olelo as "pagan" myths and "harmless" folktales. Conversely, haole misunderstanding of the cultural and linguistic codes embodied in these mo'olelo resulted in misappropriations of the texts. More specifically, the presentation of Pele and Hi'iaka mo'olelo as myths and legends by armchair scholars such as Westervelt, Emerson, and Thrum enabled the transformation of the mo'olelo into nontraditional Hawaiian genres, such as children's literature, which functioned as an indoctrination into settler colonial views.

One way to understand this is through kaona and the way the Pele and Hiʻiaka moʻolelo were and are culturally encoded for a Hawaiian audience. Kaona is reflected in the poetics of a hulihia discourse that expressed Hawaiian literary nationalism in multiple ways. The literature itself is evidence for differentiating between Pele and Hiʻiaka moʻolelo composed by Kanaka ʻŌiwi for our own cultural inspiration and invigoration, and haole-created narratives that centered around a colonial discourse of empire-building and oppression and advanced the project of settler colonialism. Haole first misunderstood, later mistranslated, and subsequently appropriated Pele and Hiʻiaka for their own agenda.[5] Most important, the differences in representation and understanding for audiences were, and still are, mediated through colonialism. This understanding is further complicated because as Kanaka ʻŌiwi have been cut off from our ʻōlelo makuahine (mother tongue) and increasingly influenced by global popular culture, many today have lost sight of our genealogical and cultural connections to Pele and Hiʻiaka, moʻolelo, and Hawaiian culture in general. As Womack writes, "The construction of a [national literary identity] reaffirms the real truth about our place in history—we are not mere victims but active agents in history, innovators of new ways, of Indian ways, of thinking and being and speaking and authoring in this world created by colonial contact."[6] The vast collection of Hawaiian moʻolelo in the Hawaiian-language newspapers and the literary criticism that surround them demonstrate the active agency of Kanaka Maoli of the late nineteenth to early twentieth centuries as they built a national literature with the intention of raising a culturally centered national consciousness, one that refuted the agenda of settler colonialism.

Moʻolelo contain cultural values passed down mai ka pō mai, mai nā kūpuna mai. These reflect an indigenous intellectual history that wove writing into oral traditions. Ka Palapala became another site of cultural memory, a vehicle to record and transport Kanaka Maoli values to future generations of the Lāhui. Pele and Hiʻiaka moʻolelo are laden with core cultural concepts such as moʻokūʻauhau and aloha ʻāina that are multiply layered throughout the corpus of the moʻolelo. Writing about aloha ʻāina, Silva explains:

> Aloha ʻāina is an old Kanaka concept based on the family relationship of the people to the land, and on the idea that people actually were born of the material of the land. According to traditional Hawaiian cosmologies, all things on the earth are alive and are the kinolau—the many physical bodies—of gods, who are themselves physically related to people in genealogies. . . . The islands, the

taro, and the people are thus conceived of as members of the same family who love and sustain each other. In the struggle against annexation, Joseph Nāwahī, John Ailuene Bush, and others developed "aloha 'āina" as a discourse of resistance, and simultaneously as a particularly Kanaka style of defensive nationalism.[7]

As Silva points out, aloha 'āina is a discourse of resistance (and nationalism), one informed by a discourse of mo'okū'auhau, as Kanaka pride in heritage is rooted on the 'āina. These concepts are particularly relevant in the study of this mo'olelo about Pele and Hi'iaka, akua who are physical manifestations of 'āina and elements of nature. A better vehicle to present and enact literary aloha 'āina than Pele and Hi'iaka mo'olelo, ancestors who embody the 'āina itself, is difficult to conceive.

The power of Pele and Hi'iaka is ultimately linked to the 'āina; they are simultaneously land and ancestor, and to recall their mo'olelo is to recount the mo'okū'auhau of the Hawaiian people, which are inextricably linked. Kanaka Maoli continue to honor our ancestors by following traditional naming practices of bestowing ancestral names from within one's genealogy, including those of the gods, goddesses, and 'āina. Hawaiian family names still reflect those of previous eras—Poepoe and Ka'awaloa, Punahoa and Kamohoali'i, Kalawakua and Desha, are just some of the many families who are named for the 'āina and who are still a part of the Hawaiian nation. We continue to celebrate and honor these places, these ancestors. Similarly, while some other family names may have changed, interwoven with new genealogies, Pele's descendants and those of the nineteenth-century writers and editors are still part of the living Lāhui today.

For Kanaka 'Ōiwi, Pele was and is revered as a god and ancestor whose spiritual presence is still felt and whose physical power cannot be denied. As with the taro child Hāloanaka, the elder sibling of the Hawaiian people, Kanaka 'Ōiwi are genealogically connected with Pele. As Pelehonuamea, she is an incarnation of Papahānaumoku, the Hawaiian Earth Mother, or closely linked to her because she is the creator of new land. Pele is associated with the birth and growth of land in other ways, including through her relationship with her numerous Hi'iaka sisters, particularly the youngest, Hi'iakaikapoliopele, with whom Pele is particularly close. They metaphorically represent the healing of the land through revegetation after it is devoured or created by their elder sister, Pele. Thus, Pele and Hi'iaka work in tandem. This balance appropriately reflects two cultural thoughts: the reciprocally supportive relationship between older and younger sibling, an important Hawaiian value on which traditional society was based, and the balance of opposing principles as represented by the Hawaiian value of pono.

Mana wahine is celebrated throughout the moʻolelo, reinforcing the power of the Pele women. Pele is also an important symbol for Kanaka Maoli in part because she is the only female volcano deity in the Pacific. Her mana wahine is manifested in her power to create and destroy land. Her followers are ʻAikū, able to disregard the religious system of ʻAikapu that regulated society and the worship of the male deities Kāne, Kū, Lono, and Kanaloa. Hiʻiaka is an important representation of mana wahine through her practices of hula, ʻanāʻanā, poetic composition, and her aikāne relationships with other women. Thus, their moʻolelo raises issues of power, gender, sexuality, and desire, themes presented throughout.

As deities, Pele and her sisters embody a spiritual element in the dynamics of gender and power politics. The establishment of Christianity suppressed Pele worship. But religious practices are interwoven throughout the moʻolelo, providing a guide of sorts showing rituals, offerings, and prayers. Hiʻiaka instructs Wahineʻōmaʻo on her kānāwai to eat fish from head to tail and not waste anything. She instructs her on the proper way to approach Pele and the chants used in supplication to her. ʻAnāʻanā embodies the two sides of the healing arts: the power to give or restore life through prayer and supplication (via Hiʻiakaikapoliopele), and the power to take life through similar means (via Kapōʻulakīnaʻu). The healing ritual for Lohiʻau is described with prayer chants, and after each prayer, Hiʻiaka asks Wahineʻōmaʻo if it is correct, emphasizing preciseness for the words to be effective. Thus, where open worship of Pele was frowned on in Christianized society, the worshipping, honoring, and admiration for the goddesses remained alive on paper, dancing across the pages for Kanaka Maoli education and enjoyment.

The complexity of a makawalu discourse is demonstrated in the corpus of Pele and Hiʻiaka moʻolelo in the intricate interweaving between writers, editors, texts, publications, and even language. As previously mentioned, Rice, a haole missionary descendant, wrote in Hawaiian, and Kaʻili (Emma Nakuina), a prominent Kanaka Maoli woman, wrote in English. Rice also published his own English "translation," the only writer to do so. *Ka Hoku o ka Pakipika* and *Ka Leo o ka Lahui* printed the same version (with variations) of one strand of the Pele and Hiʻiaka moʻolelo, *Hawaii Aloha*, *Ka Naʻi Aupuni*, and *Ka Hoku o Hawaii* printed the same version of another. Writers such as Bush and Poepoe were also editors at Hawaiian nationalist newspapers that published Pele and Hiʻiaka and other moʻolelo kuʻuna, and were heavily involved in politics before and after the overthrow. Hoʻoulumāhiehie and Poepoe are possibly the same person, and if not, their work was often published in the same newspapers at the same time.

Meiwi are poetic devices that demonstrate intellectual and aesthetic traditions that bridge oral performance and literature. Meiwi are integral to Kanaka Maoli poetics. They are woven throughout the moʻolelo in multiple ways, although the inclusion of beautifully wrought mele are perhaps the pua (blossoms) that highlight Hawaiian poetics. Hawaiian language is integral to the development of meiwi, and the more knowledge one has of Hawaiian language, the more depth of understanding the multiple layers and nuances is possible.

Hawaiian literary nationalism demonstrates moʻolelo as social and political action. For Kanaka ʻŌiwi, moʻolelo is story *and* history. Moʻolelo in all its forms—remembering, experiencing, creating, telling, and retelling story (or "talk story")—is social and political action. It is proactive decolonization, which takes many forms, as well as assertion of individual, political, and cultural identity. When we compose or perform oli, when we sing or recite mele as song or poem, or when we choreograph these into hula, all core elements of our culture as Kanaka ʻŌiwi, we are actively engaged in decolonial poetics. We are, in essence, simultaneously choosing to remember, retell, re-create, reclaim, and revalue the traditions, beliefs, and practices of our kūpuna and our Lāhui. Simultaneously, as poʻe aloha ʻāina we are engaging in new expressions of Hawaiian nationalism, one that still includes literary production, as we make conscious choices *not* to forget, as settler colonialism pressures us to do. We continue to assert a kuleana consciousness that compels us *not* to be constrained by Western practices or attitudes that tell us *not* to engage or carry forward our traditions or culture, *not* to remember our ancestors or their creative and intellectual skills, *not* to be Kanaka ʻŌiwi.

ʻŌiwi poet, scholar, and nationalist Haunani-Kay Trask is inspired by African American writer and scholar Toni Morrison's thought that "the best art is political," and that one "ought to make it unquestionably political and irrevocably beautiful at the same time."[8] Discussing her own work, Trask concurs, arguing that "resistance to the strangulation of our people and culture is interwoven with a celebration of the magnificence of our nation: the lavish beauty of our delicate islands; the intricate relationship between our emotional ties to one another and our ties to the land; the centuries-old ways of caring for the ʻaina (land), the kai (sea), and, of course, the mana (spiritual power) that is generated by human beings in love with, and dependent on, the natural world . . . [it] is both decolonization and recreation."[9]

In the period 1860–1928, Kanaka Maoli published numerous versions of Pele and Hiʻiaka moʻolelo as part of the development of a Hawaiian national literature meant to support the Lāhui, the Hawaiian nation in fact (pre-1893) and feeling (post-1893). Perhaps Pele and Hiʻiaka were metaphors of decolonization and re-creation for Kanaka Maoli writers and editors in the nineteenth and early twentieth centuries, their powerful, beautiful history evoked, voices of fire to inspire and encourage the poʻe aloha ʻāina. They employed writing as a tool to assert a cultural and political identity meant to build the nation in a culturally conscious way, understanding the idea that history is embedded in story, as the word "moʻolelo" communicates. Perhaps the best literary vehicle showcasing their efforts is the multiple versions of the Pele and Hiʻiaka moʻolelo.

After Kalākaua was forced to sign the Bayonet Constitution in 1887, he published a large collection of traditional moʻolelo in English, *Legends and Myths of Hawaii*. Tiffany Ing cautions that although that the volume "cannot be interpreted exclusively as a response to that event," it is part of a much longer, much more extensive royal political strategy to preserve Hawaiian culture, "part of the Hawaiian monarch's efforts to maintain sovereignty by preventing Hawaiʻi's haole politicians from turning the kingdom over to the United States."[10] Kalākaua's efforts were not in isolation, as a large number of Kanaka Maoli writers were contributing to the strategy of strengthening Kanaka culture and politics through publishing moʻolelo, creating a body of national Hawaiian literature that was intentional. While moʻolelo kuʻuna were distinct from other literatures, these other literatures from around the globe were published alongside moʻolelo Hawaiʻi, which supported a well-read, well-educated, literate Native population. The writers who published Pele and Hiʻiaka moʻolelo were just as political and determined in their efforts to uphold and promote ʻŌiwi sovereignty as they were in promoting cultural knowledge, language, and values embodied in the moʻolelo. Thomas King (Cherokee) writes that "the magic of Native literature . . . is not in the themes of the stories—identity, isolation, loss, ceremony, community, maturation, home—it is in the way meaning is refracted by cosmology, the way understanding is shaped by cultural paradigms."[11] These moʻolelo were meant to reflect cosmology and cultural paradigms with the intent to shape Kanaka Maoli political identity. Silva discusses the intertwining of Pele and Hiʻiaka moʻolelo with the political resistance of the Lāhui: "Reading the historical and political intertextually with literature allows us to see how some of these processes work and gives us a fuller understanding and appreciation of who the Kanaka Maoli of the time were. It should also add to our collective understanding of the immense variety of possible modes of resistance to colonialism."[12]

Publishing Pele and Hiʻiaka moʻolelo was a political act. In the independent national press of the 1860s, moʻolelo kuʻuna and moʻokūʻauhau were published alongside political commentary, launching "a tradition of counter-hegemonic action through newspaper writing and publication that lasted well into the twentieth century.... It was in and through these newspapers that Kānaka Maoli articulated the concept of ʻaloha ʻāina.'"[13] Charlot discusses the political aspect of the publishing of the moʻolelo, stating that "*Ka Hoku o ka Pakipika* was the first newspaper to be published entirely by Hawaiians without foreign, church, or government support. This caused a public controversy in which the nationalist, nativist tendency of the paper was made explicit. David Kalākaua, later king of Hawaiʻi, was one of the editors.... The publication of the first Pele and Hiʻiaka series can therefore be considered part of the newspaper's politico-cultural program."[14]

A closer examination of the text, however, reveals additional layers of political messaging. The Pele and Hiʻiaka moʻolelo live on, surviving in a literary era in part because of the numerous mele contained within the moʻolelo. This link to a performative aspect of culture allowed the knowledge to survive during a time when the actual practice of hula (in a sacred or culturally meaningful context) was publicly outlawed, forced underground because of settler colonialism. Publishing mele in the context of a moʻolelo achieved several outcomes: it kept the knowledge alive in a public forum, which asserted a cultural discourse of identity; and it did so in a way that haole did not identify as political, a kaona-laden veiling of a hulihia discourse—one that sought to uphold Hawaiian culture and politics and resist (and later overturn) haole colonization.

Pele and Hiʻiaka moʻolelo embody a hulihia discourse that demonstrates Kanaka Maoli intellectual history and promotes cultural values. It also expresses a makawalu discourse of multiplicity, a spectrum of perspectives integral for the development and maintenance of a robust lāhui. Writers publishing Pele and Hiʻiaka moʻolelo were well aware of the different traditions, and were not bothered by it. Hoʻoulumāhiehie notes, "There are many versions of the story of Hiʻiaka held by different people, and it is because of them that the portion of chants by and for Hiʻiaka has grown.... The writer does not boast that his is the definitive story of Hiʻiaka, and that those of others are flawed and distorted. That is not the case."[15] The different strands of moʻolelo that offer alternative narratives reflect the mind-set of a generation, a blossoming of knowledge, rather than competition, and does not appear to conflict with or create any sense of anxiety for Kanaka. Rather, as Silva notes, Pukui acknowledges that "several versions of the story seem to coexist peacefully in the shared consciousness of the people."[16] Written moʻolelo became a site of cultural memory, alongside the performance of hula, as Stillman discusses, and sometimes in place of hula performance when it was not possible under the surveillance of settler colonialism.[17] Multiple versions of moʻolelo allowed for more sites to record and evoke memory, more acknowledgement of moʻokūʻauhau, more expression of aloha ʻāina, more opportunity to solidify Kanaka Maoli tradition mai ka pō mai, mai nā kūpuna mai.

The Pele and Hiʻiaka moʻolelo (1860–1928) laid the foundation for Hawaiian literary nationalism today. Hawaiian literary production in the later twentieth and early twenty-first centuries is strongly woven from the intellectual traditions of our nineteenth- and early twentieth-century literary production, which were themselves woven together with oral traditions of the past and of their generations. Collectively they inform expressions of Hawaiian literary nationalism by contemporary Kanaka Maoli cultural practitioners, including our writers, visual and multimedia performers, and artists.

Unfortunately, many of the concerns expressed by Kanaka Maoli over a century ago are still with us. Like our kūpuna writers of the past, we, too, are concerned about the longevity of the moʻolelo and their application for future generations. They were concerned about the loss and misinterpretation of Hawaiian moʻolelo and the erosion of Hawaiian language, which led to eroded understanding of meiwi and the nuances of expression. Despite the resurgence in the Hawaiian language and availability of Hawaiian-language resources over the past thirty years, we must remain vigilant; our language and culture is constantly threatened by global homogenization, the dominance of English, and misappropriation of our knowledge in settler colonial discourse, particularly in the realms of tourism, science, and New Age spirituality. Such abuse is even more rampant with the advent of the World Wide Web. Websites such as Sacred-Texts.com, for example, make settler colonial texts such as Emerson and Westervelt globally available and present them as ahistorical, decontextualized, but somehow authoritative interpretations of Hawaiian history, culture, thought, and practice. New Age "goddess" sites proliferate on the Internet, literally displacing ʻāina-rooted ancestors such as Pele and Hiʻiaka, whose function and role in Kanaka Maoli culture is misappropriated, destroying their mana.

Hawaiian culture, including Pele and Hiʻiaka moʻolelo, are reinterpreted by multinational media such as Disney (e.g., *Rip Girls, Lilo & Stitch*), continuing settler colonial strands of knowledge production about

Kanaka Maoli that began with Cook's journals, missionary writings, and the mythologizing of moʻolelo by armchair folklorists.

While we must compete with an onslaught of foreign-centered video games and DVDs for the attention of our ʻōpio, our nineteenth-century kūpuna would marvel at the speed and ease of modern computer and digital technology, which makes the preservation of and accessibility to the moʻolelo much easier than anything they might have dreamed. In a globalized, digitally connected world, the Internet is a waʻa that carries moʻolelo through cyberspace; but who are its navigators? What is their source of knowledge? Abuse of Hawaiian knowledge and misappropriation of Hawaiian moʻolelo is even more rampant, reminding us that technology does not come without danger or cost.[18]

The Pele and Hiʻiaka moʻolelo is also a foundation for resistance inspired by the discourse of hulihia, the overturning of settler colonialism, and the silencing of ʻŌiwi voices.[19] In a critique of Disney's *Lilo & Stitch 2: Stitch Has a Glitch*, for example, Kīhei de Silva explains one way the Pele and Hiʻiaka moʻolelo can be used to overturn the yoke of settler oppression, in a move described by Waziyatawin (Dakota) as "Indigenous truth-telling":[20]

> [Hiiakaikapoliopele] is a story in which relationships and their priorities are examined, tested, broken, redefined, and rebuilt. It is a story of chaos, order, and identity; it provides us with a world view on which we, like Hiʻiaka, can surf the dialectic. A famous Pele chant asks "I hea kāua e laʻi ai[?]" and answers, "Ma ke ʻale nui a e liʻa nei." Where do we find peace in times of instability? On the big waves that we hold so dear. *Hiiakaikapoliopele* poses the same question and offers the same answer: little is stable, know your board, learn to ride.
>
> . . . So where do we find harmony in these unstable times? It starts with our own careful learning of *Hiiakaikapoliopele*. Of plot, character, and kaona. And it absolutely requires the reintroduction of this moʻolelo into the bosoms of our families. We turn off the DVD players, we gather the kids and grandkids at our feet, and we haʻi moʻolelo. It's a long story. It takes years of bedtimes to tell and retell. When told and retold, it will again become part of us. As familiar as breathing. A board for surfing anything the world throws our way.[21]

Kanaka ʻŌiwi continue to remember, reclaim, retell, perform, and read Pele and Hiʻiaka moʻolelo. We continue to create compositions that honor them. In this way, we continue to disrupt settler colonial appropriations, culminating in the reemergence of the Kanaka strand today in multiple media as a consequence of the Hawaiian cultural renaissance that began in the 1960s and the sovereignty movement that gained momentum in the 1990s. Pele and Hiʻiaka remained alive in newly composed mele. Hula hālau continued to perform traditional compositions passed down mai ka pō mai, mai nā kūpuna mai. In the period of cultural renaissance, Kanaka Maoli artists in multiple genres continued to pay tribute to Pele via new documentation technologies that help preserve and perpetuate Hawaiian culture and values.[22] In this era of cultural regeneration, some traditional chants have been transformed into contemporary mele.[23]

De Silva offers important insights into the adaptation of "Aia lā ʻo Pele" from a traditional oli to a modern mele. He describes how it had been set to music by respected kumu hula Mae Loebenstein, from whom Kawai Cockett learned it: "Aunty Mae's work belongs to the tradition of late 19th and early 20th century *hula kuʻi*, wherein older, chanted compositions were tastefully set to Western music—to guitar and ʻukulele in particular—in a manner that complemented the content, phrasing, and rhythms of the original. . . . It serves, as do the best musical compositions of the genre, to revitalize chants that might otherwise be forgotten or taken for granted."[24] Such adaptation of traditional mele from older styles of performance to newer ones are similar to how oral traditions were adapted to writing. In both cases, the new style or technology became a vehicle to carry the thought and message of the composition forward to be remembered, retold, and appreciated by new audiences and new generations.

Pele and Hiʻiaka continue to inspire our contemporary leaders, thinkers, scholars, and writers who remember and memorialize them in our own academic and creative work; myriad examples abound, but I'd like to highlight a few selected ones that represent different ways Pele and Hiʻiaka are represented by contemporary Kanaka Maoli writers.

Haunani Trask's "Night Is a Sharkskin Drum" is a contemporary poem that draws on traditional imagery:

Night is a sharkskin drum
      sounding our bodies black
        and gold.

     All is aflame
   the uplands a *shush*
      of wind.

From Halemaʻumaʻu
    our fiery Akua comes:

E, Pele e,

    E, Pele e,

        E, Pele e.[25]

The sharkskin drum is the pahu, used in specific traditional hula, including some associated with Pele and Hiʻiaka. The reference to the wind suggests Pele's vast oli makani and her relationship with the ʻāina. It is a reminder that the ʻāina does not just refer to what is visible, but the invisible or spiritual elements as well. The *shush* of wind is onomatopoeia that gives voice to the wind, another kind of personification demonstrating it is a living entity. The fiery Akua of Halemaʻumaʻu is of course Pele, who responds to the call of the chanter addressing her, "E, Pele e." These lines suggest traditional oli and supplication to Pele, which call her by name. When we call, even now, Pele responds; all is aflame in the uplands of Halemaʻumaʻu because she is alive.

Jeanne Kawelo Kinney's "Pele at the KTA" imagines Pele as a modern Hawaiian woman shopping in the iconic local Big Island grocery store. Most of the poem describes Pele breezing through the aisles, alternately ignoring or selecting different items associated with modernity:

She ignores the cans of Spam and tuna
brushes past the stocked aisles of pasta and rice.

Each of these are manufactured food items that represent settler colonialism. She is in search of matches,

the largest box she can find.
Her hair sweeps the ground as
she swoops the matches into her cart.
And lighter fluid—not a big bottle
but a smaller, daintier one.

Kinney's humorous approach to Pele comes through—why would a volcano goddess need matches, or lighter fluid? The description of her long hair sweeping the ground is a visual image that evokes volcanic lava flows that sweep the land (here the store's floor). It connotes the description of Pele as untamed ('āhi'u)—she is a woman who does not bother to cut or otherwise contain her hair. It is also a somewhat stereotyped (or iconic) image of a Hawaiian woman. Other descriptive language builds on this representation of Pele: she

> hisses past the bottles of dressings
> finding them sweet and useless

and makes her way to the beer cooler, reaching

> for a six-pack of Bud, on sale,
> the cool cans nearly sizzle against her skin.

The "s" sounds throughout—sweep, swoop, sweet, six-pack, sale, sizzle— all build on the hiss of the first line, the sound of molten lava covering the land, also suggesting her impatience and temperamental nature. Then,

> People step back as she
> approaches the check-out line,
> *What,* her eyes practically hiss,
> *You neva saw one woman made of fire?*

Pele's irritable temperament is clearly demonstrated, visibly represented by her literally being on fire, a shocking sight to the other customers in the market, but a humorous one to the reader. While her words are not vocalized to the other customers, her thoughts are written in Hawai'i Creole English (HCE), the modern vernacular in Hawai'i created from Hawaiian and multiple immigrant languages that developed during the sugar plantation era, and became widespread after the banning of Hawaiian language by the Republic of Hawai'i in 1896, and which is used in resistance to "standard" American English.

The poem concludes when

> Someone clears his throat.
> "Looks like you're next,"
> a calm voice says, a smooth
> mellow voice, like an ocean.

Annoyed, Pele turns, her eyes flashing:

"Lohiau!" she says in surprise.
Lohiau, she murmurs to herself,
as she straightens her pareu,
adjusts her posture. Good thing
she has her six-pack of Bud.
Who knows where things might lead,
outside the doors of KTA.[26]

Knowledge of the moʻolelo and the passionate relationship between Pele and Lohiʻau is helpful in understanding what is implied in Pele's words and body language. The beer reference draws from both Hawaiian and Western images. ʻAwa is a traditional drink with a relaxing, narcotic-like effect. It grew abundantly in Puna, and was used as an offering to Pele. Touristic discourse of settler colonialism invented a ritual of offering alcohol, nonexistent in traditional times in Hawaiʻi, specifically bottles of gin, as a replacement offering for Pele, one that tourists could easily accomplish. The beer and the pareu (sarong) wrapped around Pele's body are symbols of makaʻāinana or working-class status. Kinney's imagining of Pele and Lohiʻau meeting by happenstance in a local market reflects the Kanaka Maoli philosophy that our akua are all around us, and that while some might think, in modern times, that there is a vast separation between moʻolelo from the past and our lives today, in fact they are not so separate.

Alohi Aeʻa's poem "The Road to Kēʻē" also references the Pele and Hiʻiaka moʻolelo:

There is no magic hand.
There is no magic skirt.

We are left to scale
this mountain alone.

We are left only
with what we can find:

A trail marked with blood
Stones whose names

lie forgotten.[27]

The "magic hand" and "magic skirt" reference Pele's gifts to Hiʻiaka to help her along the journey to Kēʻē, Lohiʻau's home, Kīlauea, the lima ikaika (strong arm) and the pāʻū uila (lightning skirt). Metaphorically, the mountain represents a large obstacle; combined with "the trail marked with blood" it implies colonialism, and the process of decolonization. Stones (pōhaku) are very traditional, important symbols with multiple meanings and kaona. Here they represent the Pele clan and ʻāina simultaneously. They also represent resistance, a powerful image evoked in protest mele against the overthrow and annexation, including Ellen Kekoaohiwaikalani Wright Prendergast's "Mele ʻAi Pōhaku" (Rock-Eating Song), which emphatically stated that Hawaiians would rather eat stones, the "wondrous food of the land," than submit to annexation to the United States.[28]

The ideas of naming and forgetting are equally powerful images. Personal names for ʻāina, and the smallest elements of ʻāina, such as stones, were not uncommon in Hawaiian culture, in part because naming something both gives it mana, and recognizes its inherent mana. It demonstrates a more intimate connection with ʻāina, as wind names do. The concept of forgetting is linked to memory and remembering. When everything is forgotten, even the name of something—which is a capsule of knowledge and history, connections to the past, to the culture, to the Lāhui, and to one's own identity—is equally forgotten, a process of erasure facilitated by settler colonialism and its preference for assimilation into the dominant culture.

My poem "Pele's Appeal" imagines Pele addressing a contemporary audience, and is written in her voice. It begins with the opening lines of the mele "Holo mai Pele" (Pele comes [from Kahiki]) in Hawaiian, and then transitions into English:

Perhaps you've heard about me on a tour bus, or seen my story danced
    on stage—
Everyone wants to tell it, but few of them get it right.
So let me set the record straight—not that I have to:

Esteemed daughter of Haumea, I am Haumea when I so choose
Red the sacred color:
        blood-colored,
        lehua-colored,
        eternal-raging-fires-colored
A malihini woman traveling from the shores of Kahiki.

Contrary to popular belief I was not chased out by my older sister
    Nāmakaokahaʻi
for sleeping with her man—

(Okay, maybe I did)—
But it was my decision to go, no other, carrying the egg-shaped sister close
to my heart.
Kū and Lono bailed the canoe Honuaiākea while Kamohoaliʻi steered.

The poem intentionally weaves lines of traditional mele from the Pele and Hiʻiaka moʻolelo between sections, braiding Hawaiian with English, traditional poetry mai ka pō mai, mai nā kūpuna mai with contemporary writing that retells the epic, which Pele occasionally comments on throughout the poem. Pele's voice is allowed to speak back to settler colonialism in the poem, commenting on its impact on her, on her ʻāina:

Some claim to know me:
give her gin it's her favorite,
burn incense on the lip,
channel her mana standing on Birkenstocks—
it's Stonehenge with a view of the Pacific!

Scientists poke and prod my belly like obstetricians
geologists tell tales of lithospheres and tectonic plates, magma and
basaltic strata
as they chip and pick away at my skin
looking for secrets to unlock the mysteries of this woman,
seeking to become real men.

…

Some claim me as an ancestor, while others deny me,
some see me only as a means to their own ends:
tourist trinkets sold for cash,
scientific exploration as entertainment on the Discovery channel,
a Lemurian goddess to restore their soul,
giving faith to the faithless,
answers to the unknowable,
seekers of a destiny not their own.

Nakeke, nākulukulu, nakeke, nākulukulu—
I crave ʻopihi picked fresh from the shores of Puna,
while sisters surf the waves of Hōʻeu in the sea of Kaimū,
brothers dive for hāʻukeʻuke and other delectable reef-found treasures,
Hōpoe and Hiʻiaka entrance me with their dance in the sea of Nānāhuki.

I destroyed them all just to make a point: I will not be tamed.
No scientist can explain that.[29]

Spoken word poet Jamaica Heolimeleikalani Osorio's unpublished poem "What They Cannot See: A Mele from Hiʻiaka to Hōpoe" is written in Hiʻiaka's voice, a modern mele aloha that reflects the deep love Hiʻiaka felt for Hōpoe, imbued with a sensuality only a lover could convey. Osorio describes the poem as being "inspired by her own Hōpoe."[30] It begins with Hiʻiaka describing seeing Hōpoe for the first time, "Pulling my glance with the diction of your dance." Hiʻiaka is entranced by Hōpoe's beauty, enhanced through the fluid motions of her body, "Gliding over the land like water over itself." Hōpoe's given name, Nānāhuki, is embedded in the first line; because of her mana reflected in her name, Hiʻiaka cannot look away.

In a passage in the middle of the poem, Hiʻiaka criticizes how she and Hōpoe are portrayed by white male settler colonial writers:

Can you see those strange men
Watching us from beyond the page
From under this breath
Can you see the way they have drawn us naked and grown
How they have missed your skin feathered with yellow lehua
How they have done you no justice
How they have written us into stillness
Into silence
How it seems through them,
We have been forgotten
How we have barely existed
I wonder how it is they cannot see
I wonder what has made them so blind.

Osorio's Hiʻiaka refuses to be silenced by the haole men who misrepresent them in their myths. While written in English, like the other examples of poetry above it contains kaona images that add depth to the poem. For example, the "strange" men aren't just odd, they are strangers, malihini, and thus do not have the same familiarity with this "place" (Hōpoe, the woman, Hōpoe, the forest) as a kamaʻāina; Hiʻiaka has intimate knowledge of Hōpoe that the men do not possess.

Her description of Hōpoe as having skin "feathered with lehua" provides an ʻāina-based, alternative visualization of the "naked and grown" woman imagined by the haole male writers. The yellow lehua blossom is a richly layered sensual image—lehua are soft, delicate; it alludes to the Waikoʻolihilihi, a freshwater pool in Puna where lehua blossoms were floated on the water, so that when one bent down to sip from the pool, the delicate stamens of the lehua softly brushed the face. It is a kaona image of oral sex performed on a female, represented by the freshwater pool. Yellow is a color associated with the aliʻi class, the most sacred, in part, because it is the most rare and thus most precious. The yellow feathers of the mamo bird are alluded to in the feathering of Hōpoe's skin; mamo were found only on Hawaiʻi island, and were used in the choicest feather work for the highest-ranking aliʻi, thus symbolizing someone highly cherished and beloved. In contrast, the men's image is coarse and pornographic, not at all capturing the mana wahine of Hiʻiaka, Hōpoe, or their relationship.

The relationship between settler colonialism and forgetting is asserted—the men misrepresent the women, whose moʻolelo mai ka pō mai, mai nā kūpuna mai is thus disrupted, the waʻa of myth incapable of carrying the story forward, leading to a loss of cultural memory, a forgetting of moʻokūʻauhau and moʻolelo. The final two lines of this passage reference blindness; vision, to see, is ʻike, and ʻike also means knowledge, to know. Thus one who is ʻike ʻole, blind, is also one who is ignorant.

The final section of the poem asks Hōpoe to remember, to embody ancestral memory of Hiʻiaka and the love they share so it may be carried forward mai ka pō mai, mai nā kūpuna mai. Osorio does this by asserting a different kind of forgetting, asking Hōpoe to "forget that I am leaving," which means to remember Hiʻiaka:

> forget that i am leaving
> forget that there is more beyond the walls of this ʻāina
> this ahu
> extending into sky
> remember the calm of this movement
> the forever of this voice
> and know
> that i will return
> either in body
> spirit
> or song
> so that our dance
> shall never end.

Their dance is their relationship, it is also "Ke haʻa lā Puna," the first hula of the moʻolelo, the one that establishes Hiʻiaka as a practitioner of hula, her relationship with Hōpoe, and the tradition of Pele and Hiʻiaka moʻolelo. It is the dance that sets into motion all the natural elements of Puna, called to life through the verbalization of the words of the mele as much as the winds of Kauaʻi respond to Pele's call in her oli makani.

In other mele, Hiʻiaka humbly says all she has to offer is her voice, which is in actuality her most powerful gift—i ka ʻōlelo ke ola, i ka ʻōlelo ka make, in the language is the power of life and death. She asks Hōpoe to remember "the forever of this voice" that will continue to regenerate as the flora on the ʻāina, fulfilling her kuleana to Hōpoe, to the Lāhui. Outside the context of the poem, these final lines can be read as a metaphoric message of Hawaiian literary nationalism, that as long as we continue to remember our moʻolelo, to keep them alive, they shall inspire us for all generations to come.

The recovering, reclaiming, and retelling of our moʻolelo kuʻuna includes incorporation of new forms of storytelling and story performance, such as slam and written poetry, which help us weave the lei of Hawaiian literary nationalism strong and firm, a vibrant cultural practice of the past that is resilient, able to guide and inform us as we work toward growing a healthy Lāhui that includes advocacy for a politically sovereign future.

Strands of oral and written moʻolelo of Pele and Hiʻiaka are still being woven by Kanaka Maoli.[31] In Hawaiian, English, and HCE, in print, multimedia, and performance, the lei moʻolelo spirals through time, mai ka pō mai, mai nā kūpuna mai, into the future. Contemporary expressions of traditional moʻolelo allow us to be waʻa, carrying the meanings of these moʻolelo into the future, in a way reminiscent of how Pele carried Hiʻiaka close to her heart on their voyage to Hawaiʻi.

Aloha Kīlauea, ka ʻĀina a ke Aloha
(Cherished Is Kīlauea, the Beloved Land)

The previous chapters opened with an oli from within the Pele and Hiʻiaka moʻolelo that reflected the main ideas presented in each. Mokuna 6 began with a hulihia, an oli demonstrating the overturning of the pre-established order of things. Thus, it seems fitting to huli (flip) the heading of this concluding chapter, named not for the first line of an oli, but the last. I do this for several reasons. First, the central imagery is the plucking and stringing or weaving of lei. "ʻO Puna lehua ʻula i ka papa" (Puna, the red lehua on the foundation) describes Puna, Hawaiʻi, Pele's home. It strongly conveys aloha ʻāina, love for the land. In the time it was published, it would have immediately evoked a sense of patriotic nationalism among Kanaka Maoli, something it can do for us today as well as we continue to fight on multiple fronts to love, cherish, protect, nurture, and revive our ʻāina, our ea, and our lāhui. "Aloha Kīlauea ka ʻāina a ke aloha" can be translated as both greetings to and love expressed to Kīlauea, the land where love is found, or the land of the beloved (Pele and/or Hiʻiaka).

Ultimately, the oli demonstrates what Womack reminds us, that "Native artistry is not pure aesthetics, or art for art's sake: as often as not, Indian writers are trying to *invoke* as much as *evoke*. The idea behind ceremonial chant is that language, spoken in the appropriate ritual context, will actually cause a change in the physical universe."[32] In *The Common Pot*, Lisa Brooks (Abenaki) argues that Womack "is speaking not just of mystical 'invocation' but of the power of words to bring about practical and political change."[33] The Hawaiian proverb "I ka ʻōlelo ke ola, i ka ʻōlelo ka make" (In words are the power of life and death) reflect these diverse applications and simultaneous meanings as well.

Haʻina ʻia mai ana ka Puana (The Story Is Told)

Haʻina ʻia mai ana ka puana is a common refrain at the end of mele that signals to the audience that the performance is ending, "the story is told." The discussions of Pele and Hiʻiaka moʻolelo throughout this book are individual pua—blossoms carefully selected and woven into lei, small samples of the enormous body of moʻolelo that illustrate the larger wealth of cultural knowledge contained within it. Collectively, these examples highlight some of the values, as represented by practices, skills, and themes specific to Kanaka ʻŌiwi culture, and not just in the traditional time period in which they are set. Charlot notes that:

> the vast Pele literature is clearly an important resource for the study of Hawaiian culture, containing a wealth of details on such subjects as household customs, hula, rituals, and the life of the separated soul. Moreover the history of Hawaiian thinking can be followed on important subjects from classical times until those of the composition of the series. Most important, the Pele literature attests to the fundamentally religious and esthetic character of Hawaiian culture: Pele has constantly inspired great works of music, dance, and literature. The quality of the art attests to the power of the god.[34]

The multiple publication of these moʻolelo in the nineteenth- and early twentieth-century Hawaiian-language newspapers by multiple authors demonstrates their cultural, literary, and political value to our more immediate Kanaka ʻŌiwi ancestors of that historical period. Because moʻolelo inherently implies both story and history, there is an entertainment and educational value built into these moʻolelo for a Kanaka audience. It is through the moʻolelo that they—and we—can learn about cultural practices and values in a way that is also enjoyable, and this is why the writers and editors took the time to present and explain different actions, elements, cultural practices, vocabulary words, place names, and so forth contained within the moʻolelo, as well as why they presented multiple scholarly and comparative versions of it. Their political value was recognized by nineteenth-century Hawaiian intellectuals and writers, such as Moses Manu, who calls Kapihenui's moʻolelo a "moʻolelo kālaiʻāina," a political story as relevant and recognized to Kanaka ʻŌiwi of his time as it was to generations before him, and to us today. Edward Said reminds us of the political importance of such stories when he writes, "[Stories are] the method colonized people use to assert their own identity and the existence of their own history. The main battle in imperialism is over land, of course; but when it came to who owned the land, who had the right to settle and work on it, who kept it going, who won it back, and who now plans its future—these issues were reflected, contested, and even for a time, decided in narrative."[35] From a Native American perspective, King states that "the truth about stories is that that's all we are."[36] He quotes Okanagan storyteller Jeannette Armstrong, who says, "Through my language I understand I am being spoken to, I'm not the one speaking. The words are coming from many tongues and mouths of Okanagan people and the land around them. I am a listener to the language's stories, and when my words form I am merely retelling the same stories in different patterns."[37] The multiple telling and retelling of Pele and Hiʻiaka moʻolelo in many forms—through the performance of mele and hula, or through being recorded on the page—are analogous. These literary and cultural treasures were and still are meaningful to Kanaka Maoli. We still recall, reclaim, and retell them. They form the foundation of our contemporary arts, both performative and literary.

The disappearance of long, serialized epics after the last Hawaiian-language newspapers folded speaks to the change in power dynamics. How did colonization affect the production of Hawaiian literature? From 1861 through the 1920s, there was a great flowering of Hawaiian literature that ended in part because of the ban on the Hawaiian language in the schools. With a sharp decline in readership, Hawaiian manaʻo—expressed so eloquently and passionately for the century prior ma ka ʻōlelo Hawaiʻi (in the Hawaiian language)—no longer flourished.

Around the 1930s, Hawaiian literature in any form literally vanished for approximately three decades. It wasn't until the Hawaiian renaissance of the 1960s—inspired in part by the civil rights movement across the United States and as part of the Hawaiian sovereignty movement—that Hawaiian literature, in a new contemporary form, emerged. While the long-serialized Pele and Hiʻiaka epic seemed lost to antiquity, it still influenced contemporary poets and writers, like Trask, whose creative and academic work draws on the images of these illustrious ancestors, as well as from their ancestral strength. As Daniel Heath Justice (Cherokee) writes of his intellectual and cultural history, "Our literature is the textual testament to our endurance; just as our oral traditions reflect the living realities and concerns of those who share them, so too do our literary traditions."[38]

While most Hawaiian writers today compose in English, HCE, and Hawaiian, Pele and Hiʻiaka's presence is most felt in a return to the performative origins of hula. From backyard hula to the Merrie Monarch stage to venues around the world, Pele and Hiʻiaka moʻolelo live through the performance of selected mele and hula choreographed, practiced, and presented by hālau hula.

This happened, in part, because for Kanaka, Pele and Hiʻiaka are ancestors, a connection to the ancient past and our deeply held cultural traditions still with us, evident all around us today in our ʻāina, elements of nature, and cultural practice such as hula. They are the epitome of hope. They inspire.

Charlot argues that Pele is not a role model for human behavior: "A number of women activists have spoken of Pele as a model for their conduct ... human beings are not permitted to act like gods."[39] Kanaka Maoli women leaders, cultural practitioners, and scholars, however, view Pele and Hiʻiaka through a framework of kinship. Mary Kawena Pukui and Pualani Kanakaʻole Kanahele acknowledge their genealogical lineage to Pele and Hiʻiaka, as do I. They are kūpuna who are honored and admired, and perhaps in that capacity serve as role models, as ancestors who set a foundation for nā pulapula (the descendants) to uphold, honor, protect, and defend our kūpuna and the culture they created and embodied; it is a matter of moʻokūʻauhau, aloha ʻāina, and kuleana that motivates us, not the false desire to "act like gods." Stories are guides for human behavior and social structure (as is religion, and by extension, stories about gods of that religion), and moʻolelo, particularly of akua and aliʻi, provide inspiration for kanaka conduct. Silva addresses how this aspect of the moʻolelo is one reason publishing moʻolelo kuʻuna such as the Pele and Hiʻiaka moʻolelo was important:

Both *Hiʻiaka* and *Kawelo* are stories filled with details of the ancient religion: prayers to the ancient gods and details of appropriate ceremonies and sacrifices. It is not an accident that these same
two epics had also appeared in 1861 in *Ka Hoku o ka Pakipika* . . .
because they are both particularly inspiring hero epics. Both
1861 and 1893–1913 were times when the Hawaiian culture and
language were under serious attack. Hiʻiaka is a hero: when moʻo,
sharks, or anything threatens human beings, she dispatches them
mercilessly; she also heals people of illnesses and injuries. . . .
Both hero stories are inspiring for the people—one for women,
and the other for men.[40]

In an article on Mana Wahine Week celebrating the strengths and
accomplishments of Māori women, Glenis Philip-Barbara (Ngati Rangi)
writes, "Is it any wonder that having come from such [strong] women
that Tairawhiti[41] women are leaders, creators and innovators well worth
celebrating and acknowledging?"[42] Kanaka ʻŌiwi women, too, come from
such strong women, sometimes named by them, sometimes named in
honor of their memories. Even today, "Pele and Hiʻiaka and many other
ʻaumakua . . . have their namesakes amongst living descendants of their
lineage."[43]

A central metaphor of Māori literature is the spiral, where past, present, and future are interwoven throughout the moʻolelo in a very indigenous way, one that counters the linear timelines imposed by settler colonialism that delineate physical, psychological, spiritual, and cultural
separation between past, present, and future constructs of time and
identity.[44] It is an Oceanic concept applicable to Kanaka Maoli literature
and culture as well. Brandy Nālani McDougall's poem "Pele" reflects this
perspective:

> I was born in red, a fire call beneath
> the water, lava shooting from the earth,
> blood spilled over like a river calling
> forth kuʻu puʻu in the waiting sea.
> I was born beneath, before sound, restless
> for the kupukupu in its quiet
> breath, falling to the black basalt in sleep,
> for the tide and its lei of salted steam.
> I was born in red, the incendiary bloom
> of the waiting sun turning in my womb,
> its ʻiewe spun in fire, blackened

in the heat of my throat's vibration—
The first word is mine.
The last word is mine.[45]

McDougall's poem speaks to Pele's eternal nature; she is lava, creation from the beginning. She is still creating, active at Kīlauea, uninterrupted for three decades now; the formation of Lōʻihi, a new island off the southeast coast of Hawaiʻi island, will continue long after we are gone. Hiʻiaka will grace the ʻāina with her healing presence, causing the stark lava landscape to flourish with vegetative life once again. The spiral of time and interweaving of elements continues.

I have deployed Kanaka ʻŌiwi metaphors of the haku lei and the waʻa as appropriate to discussing Hawaiian literature, with the Pele and Hiʻiaka moʻolelo as a selected example. The haku lei functions metaphorically in a way that is similar to the spiral image; once the lei is complete, it is typically turned back on itself, forming a complete and unbroken circle. The haku lei is also composed of different strands that are tightly woven in an intricate pattern; any material may be used, because what gives the lei beauty, value, and strength is the regular pattern and tight weave of the lei.

When a lei is complete, the end is joined to its point of origin—the spiral re-created. In *The Polynesian Family System in Kaʻu, Hawaii*, Pukui shares the following prayer for Pele, which speaks of how Pele's canoe has weathered the storms of Puna. As we discuss the spiraling of moʻolelo through time, it feels appropriate to end with the waʻa metaphor. Waʻa carried Pele as she traveled from Kahiki to Hawaiʻi. Waʻa carried Hiʻiaka from Hawaiʻi to Kauaʻi and home again. Similarly, moʻolelo function as waʻa, transporting cultural knowledge across the ocean of space and time, mai ka pō mai—from the distant past originating in night with Kumulipo, mai Kahiki mai—from the homelands by our kūpuna, mai nā kūpuna mai—from our ancestors to ka Lāhui Hawaiʻi o kēia ao, the Hawaiian nation today:

Kuʻu waʻa ē, holo kuʻu waʻa
Holo kuʻu waʻa palolo i ka ʻino o Puna ē
ʻO Puna ka ʻāina noho a ka wahine,
Wahine i ka ʻiu o nā mauna.
Nona ka waʻa i ʻike ia,
I hoʻokele kapu ʻia e ke kaikunane,
Ua ʻike a.

My canoe—my canoe sails on,
It sails and weathers the storms of Puna
Puna is the land where the Woman dwells,
The Woman who dwells on the summit of the mountains.
Her canoe is very well known,
It was steered with kapu by her brother.
This is so.[46]

In discussing this chant, Pukui notes that her kumu Keahi Luahine, who was from Kauaʻi, told her this story about this mele, "One of her *tutu*, a very large man, always used this *mele pule*. When her brother went out to catch turtles at Wanini, he used to stand to one side of the door of the house and chant this until the boys returned. It was an old, old *mele* for Pele."[47]

Moʻolelo demonstrating the continued connection between Pele and Hiʻiaka and Kanaka Maoli today are woven throughout each chapter; my own lei moʻolelo woven within, among, between other stories. For Kanaka Maoli, our lei of stories are woven from strands handed down mai ka pō mai, mai nā kūpuna mai. Strands of oral tradition—mele, hula, haʻi moʻolelo are remembered and retold through continued performance and practice of these ancient art forms, now interwoven with newer genres of performance art, such as spoken word poetry, stage plays, and film. Strands of written traditions—Ka Palapala that emerged in the Hawaiian language in the nineteenth century—are interwoven with oral traditions, and are also interwoven with new expressions of Ka Palapala in Hawaiian, in English, in HCE; in poetry, prose, drama, screenplays, texts, blogs, and social media. Collectively, our lei moʻolelo continues, as Trask says of her own political work and poetry, to weave a "rope of resistance" for unborn generations.[48]

Once again, two opposite ends of the lei meet, a spiral through space and time, connecting older moʻolelo and moʻokūʻauhau with new ones. Pukui was from Kaʻū, Hawaiʻi, as was my grandfather's ʻohana, yet there is a connection to Wanini, Kauaʻi—for Pukui, it was through her kumu, Keahi Luahine; for me, it is through my grandmother's family and Tūtū Enoka Kāwika, ʻāina where our family has lived for generations, land located in the moku of Haleleʻa, just beyond the reaches of Hāʻena, Lohiʻau's home. Like Pele, Hiʻiaka, and Lohiʻau, Hawaiian families continue to traverse these beloved islands.

When I first came across this chant, there was something about it that seemed familiar, although I couldn't place it. Not remembering honu (turtles) being abundant at Wanini when I was growing up in the 1970s, I asked my dad, who confirmed that yes, they were around when he was raised there in the 1940s–1960s; he then showed me the photo below, of my kupunahine kuakahi (great-grandmother), Louise Akeao Apo, born in Kapaʻahu in 1895, two years after the independent kingdom of Hawaiʻi was illegally overthrown and occupied with U.S. assistance, an occupation that continues still, despite its illegality. Tūtū Akeao was raised in Kapaʻahu, Puna, the place Pele first laid her head to rest when her spirit traveled to Kauaʻi and met with the handsome hula-dancing chief Lohiʻau.

Here she was, sitting in the calm waters at Wanini, just in front of the family home, bathing my dad's younger brother in a turtle shell, from a honu caught by my grandfather, his own moʻokūʻauhau tracing back to Kaʻū, the ʻāina bordering Pele's homeland.

It is not clear in this photo, but the beaches at Wanini (as with many other places) were strewn with barbed wire in 1942; martial law had been declared after Japan attacked Pearl Harbor on Oʻahu, December 7, 1941, drawing the United States and Hawaiʻi into war. My dad recalls growing up at that time, how the barbed wire was meant to "protect" Hawaiʻi from Japanese invasion. In reality, it was just a nuisance for Kanaka Maoli trying to access the ocean for recreation and sustenance. But keeping Kanaka Maoli away from the ocean—our source of life—was impractical and impossible.

This photo represents a link in my moʻokūʻauhau, a succession of story and history. It represents ʻāina intimately known by multiple generations of my ʻohana, including my own. I can tell you that just beyond the left frame of the photo, only yards away from the sandy strip of beach, is the old house, the one that was over a hundred years old when it was torn down and rebuilt in the 1970s when my Aunty Kaui (Tūtū Akeao's oldest daughter) chose to escape the hectic city life of Honolulu and live there full time once again. The house sits on two acres of flat sandy land with a hill that rises sharply behind it for approximately two hundred feet to the expansive plateau above that is now the Princeville Ranch, the old representative of settler colonialism slowly being devoured by the new—the luxury Princeville Resort (a current photo would show the opulent condominiums and homes on the hillside behind Tūtū Akeao's head in the photo). There is a punawai, a freshwater spring, near the base of the hillside that fed a series of ʻauwai (irrigation ditches) dug back and forth in a zigzag pattern across the hillside before returning the water to the small stream that led to a sandbar just behind where the photographer was standing. My kūpuna planted kalo all across the hillside

My kupunahine kuakahi (great-grandmother), Louise Akeao Apo, bathing my uncle in a honu shell in front of our family home at Wanini, Kaua'i, circa 1945. Sarah P. Meyer collection, courtesy of the author.

because the sandy flats could not hold the freshwater as well; it is a lo'i technique that is rare today, one new generations of farmers could study. They also planted watercress in the 'auwai, and it was not uncommon when my grandmother was young for her brothers to hike up the hill to the ranch and buy 'ōpū pipi (beef tripe) and fix a pot with watercress picked fresh from the 'auwai. The nutrient-laden water would flow to the sandbar, which flourished with limu 'ele'ele, a particular type of seaweed that was delicious in beef stew. The limu 'ele'ele is no longer there because of excessive nutrients from the fertilizers used on the resort's golf courses on the plateau above, the needs of leisure for wealthy tourists outweighing cultural practice, sustainability, food sovereignty, and mālama 'āina for Kanaka Maoli and others.

When Kaua'i was struck by Hurricane 'Iniki in 1992, most of the island was devastated—many had no electricity, food, water, or shelter for months; parts of the island have still not recovered. But the hillside protected the Wanini homes from the brunt of the winds. In the months we stayed there after the hurricane, we had freshwater to drink, cook, and bathe with, to keep our food cold, and to share with neighbors. We still have a small lo'i kalo, and the patch of fresh watercress that helped sustain us is smaller. But it is still there, along with the grove of banana, massive mango trees on the hillside, papaya "planted" by birds, and a massive grapefruit tree Aunty loved, a gift from my dad. All was shared and exchanged with others. The broad reef still protects the 'āina from high waves and rough seas common in the winter months. It is not as abundant with fish now as it was before, as no traditional fishing kapu regulates what and what size and how much people take, and too many people—tourists, settlers, and new Pacific Island immigrants displaced from their own homelands because of U.S. imperialism—do not know, understand, or care about the sustainable ocean management practices mālama 'āina entails.

It is impossible for me to not read this photo as an act of resistance, a Kanaka Maoli kūpuna determined to enjoy a moment in the sea bathing her youngest mo'opuna, despite the beach being strewn with barbed wire and orders from the U.S. military to keep out. It is a personal inspiration of mana wahine—to visibly see a woman I never had the privilege of meeting except through stories, mo'olelo carried by my grandmother and her siblings, my dad and his. It is a reminder that despite every effort at cultural genocide and forced assimilation Kanaka Maoli of her and previous generations endured, my Tūtū Akeao would only speak 'ōlelo Hawai'i, and refused to learn English. Ua holo pipi ka'ao (And the stories continue).

E huahua'i, e huahua'i ē!
He inoa no Hi'iakaikapoliopele

KA HOPENA

Ka Pule Pani
He Pule no Hiʻiakaikapoliopele

E aloha aʻe ana au i kuʻu haku
E kalokalo aʻe ana au i kuʻu akua
E kala aku ana au i kuʻu hewa
E wehe mai hoʻi ʻoe i ka paʻa i hemo
He aha lā kaʻu hewa nui iā ʻoe e kuʻu akua?
He hala ʻai paha?
He hala iʻa paha?
He hala kapa paha?
He hala malo paha?
He hala kānāwai hoʻohiki paha?
He ʻōlelo a he hua paha na ka waha?
He aha ka hala?
Inā ʻo ka hala ia
Wehe ʻia i ke kua
Wehe ʻia i ke alo
Wehe ʻia i pau ka pōʻino me ka haumia
E ola hoʻi au kāu pulapula
E Kāne i luna, e Kāne i lalo
ʻO Kāne loa, ʻo Kāne poko
ʻO Kāne, kū i ka ʻueke
ʻO Kāne kū i ke kala
E kala i ka make ʻanāʻanā
E kala i nā make a pau
E ola hoʻi au.[1]

The Closing Prayer
Hiʻiakaikapoliopele's Prayer

I offer my affection to my guardian
I appeal to my deity
Forgive my wrongs
Open that which is held fast, to release it
How have I wronged you, my deity?
A sin of food?
A sin of fish?
A sin of kapa cloth?
A sin of the loincloth?
A sin of a law or an oath?
A wrong statement or word from the mouth?
What is the wrong?
If wrong it is
Open up the back of it
Open up the front of it
Open it up, that misfortune and defilement be ended
Grant life to me, your descendant
O Kāne above, O Kāne below
O long Kāne, O short Kāne
O Kāne, filled with release
O Kāne, filled with absolution
Absolve the sorcerer's curse
Dismiss death of every kind
Grant life to me.[2]

'Ōlelo Wehewehe Hope / Notes

Ka Pule Wehe / The Opening Prayer

   1. Unless otherwise stated, all translations are my own.

'Ōlelo Ha'i Mua / Preface

   1. Courtesy of composer Makana Garma.

Ka Pane / The Response

   1. The terms Kanaka Maoli, Kanaka 'Ōiwi, Kanaka Hawai'i, Kanaka, Native Hawaiian, and Hawaiian refer to the indigenous people of the Hawaiian islands and their descendants, and will be used interchangeably throughout this book.

   2. Trask, *From a Native Daughter*, 147.

Nā Mahalo / Acknowledgments

   1. Handy and Pukui, *The Polynesian Family System in Ka'u, Hawaii*, 206.

'Ōlelo Mua / Introduction

   1. Kapihenui's text is clearly printed *kai'kua*, which can be interpreted multiple ways, including *kaikua*, a sparsely inhabited place, or *kai 'kua* (a contraction of *akua*), sea of gods, spirits. Emerson presents the line as *kai kuwā*, and Kanahele translates the line as "Puna's sea resounds [kuwā] in the hala," which most closely reflects the thought in the surrounding lines and throughout the oli. Kanahele's *Ka Honua Ola* also contains extensive notes on these and other lines, and alternate translations. She states, and I concur, "When translating, all definitions must be considered." Kanahele, *Ka Honua Ola*, 117.

   2. Kapihenui, "He Moolelo no Hiiakaikapoliopele," December 26, 1861, 1.

   3. Mai ka pō mai and mai nā kūpuna mai are two phrases that represent key concepts of the Hawaiian worldview that acknowledge the beginnings of time and the wisdom of the ancestors passed down through the generations. Such key concepts transcend time, and knowledge contained in information and practices handed down across generations from the ancestors are considered very valuable and worth preserving and emulating. It recognizes the importance of humility, a culturally desirable trait, in that it reminds us that we are not the source of knowledge, nor did time begin with us; we are the recipients of such gifts, and

descend from such wise forebearers. Mai ka pō mai and mai nā kūpuna mai thus remind us to acknowledge, respect, and appreciate such knowledge.

4. Mele means song, poem, or a chant of any kind, including those used as hula or performance texts; to sing or chant. Each of these meanings is suggested when using mele throughout this book.

5. Kanahele and Wise, *Ka Honua Ola*, i.

6. For a more in-depth discussion on hula and colonialism, see Imada, *Aloha America*.

7. Haole is often translated as a Caucasian or white person of American or European descent. I am adopting Jace Weaver's term Amer-European (which he acknowledges borrowing from John Joseph Matthews) because of the connotation of the term, which Weaver explains is different from the more familiar "Euroamerican." Amer-European, Weaver argues, "connotes something very different. They are Europeans who happen to live in America. Matthew's terminology reflects the difference in worldviews between the two peoples, Native and non-Native. Born of and shaped by a different continent, Amer-Europeans will never truly be of this continent, never truly belong here, no matter how many generations they may dwell here." Weaver, *That the People Might Live*, xiii–xiv. Hawaiʻi is not part of the North American continent, and arguably not even a part of the United States. However, the term is appropriate to define haole under the rubric of settler colonialism.

8. Indian folklorist Sadhana Naithani discusses this point more in depth in "Prefaced Space."

9. Nogelmeier, *Mai Paʻa i ka Leo*, 1.

10. Kimura, "Native Hawaiian Culture," 173.

11. Shanley, "Writing Indian," 141, quoted in Brooks, "Digging at the Roots," 236.

12. Lyons, "Rhetorical Sovereignty," 452.

13. Nakuina published the moʻolelo under the name "Kaili," which is part of her Hawaiian name. It is common and culturally acceptable for longer Hawaiian names (such as Kaʻilikapuolono) to be shortened in a similar way. Therefore, it is not a pseudonym of any sort. But because Nakuina also published under her surname, I will refer to her by both names (one or the other) where appropriate.

14. Silva, "Pele, Hiʻiaka, Haumea," 160.

15. Kanahele, *Ka Honua Ola*, xv.

16. Manu, "He Moolelo Kaao Hawaii no ke Kaua Nui Weliweli ma waena o Pele-Keahialoa me Waka-Keakaikawai: He mau kupua Wahine Kaʻeaeʻa," May 13, 1899, 4.

17. Justice, "Indigenous Literary Nationalism."

18. See Fagan et al., "Canadian Indian Literary Nationalism?"

19. Warrior, *Tribal Secrets*, xviii–xix.

20. Justice in Fagan et al., "Canadian Indian Literary Nationalism?" 21.

21. Ibid., 24.

22. Ibid., 19–44; Justice, "Indigenous Literary Nationalism."

23. Brooks, "Digging at the Roots," 234–235.

24. Ibid., 235.

25. Allen, *Trans-Indigenous*.

26. Tengan, *Native Men Remade*, 10.

27. Brooks, "Digging at the Roots," 235.

28. Charlot, "Pele and Hiʻiaka"; Silva, "Talking Back to Law and Empire."

29. Multiple reprints have been published by a number of publishers since the original 1915 edition; Emerson's text is also widely available on the Internet.

30. No standard orthography for Hawaiian language was in place until the creation of the ʻAhahui ʻŌlelo Hawaiʻi (Hawaiian Language Association) in 1977, which began a process to discuss the standardization of written Hawaiian. Written Hawaiian was created in 1822 by a cadre of American missionaries who spoke English as a first language; English is one of the few languages with no diacritical marks. Their inability to create an acceptable and comprehensive system to mark Hawaiian words carried over into the twentieth century, resulting in inconsistent rendering of words, names, and phrases.

31. Kimura, "Native Hawaiian Culture," 182.

32. wa Thiongʻo, *Decolonising the Mind*; Kimura, "Native Hawaiian Culture."

33. Womack, *Red on Red*, 16.

34. Elbert and Pukui, *Hawaiian Dictionary*, 254; Silva, "Talking Back to Law and Empire," 101.

35. Charlot, "Pele and Hiʻiaka," 59.

36. Silva, *Aloha Betrayed*, 25.

37. Kanahele, *Ka Honua Ola*, xiv.

38. Elbert and Pukui, *Hawaiian Dictionary*, 31, 167.

39. This concept is discussed within a Māori, creative context by Māori scholar and poet Robert Sullivan in *Star Waka*.

40. Elbert and Pukui, *Hawaiian Dictionary*, 375.

41. See hoʻomanawanui, "He Lei Hoʻoheno no nā Kau a Kau."

42. Pukui, "Aspects of the Word Lei."

43. Elbert and Pukui, *Hawaiian Dictionary*, 186.

44. See Wolfe, "Settler Colonialism and the Elimination of the Native."

45. Tengan, *Native Men Remade*, 25.

46. Silva, personal communication.

47. McNicoll, "Graphic Artist's Note," 13.

48. Brooks, "Digging at the Roots," 241.

49. Stillman, "Re-membering the History of the Hawaiian Hula," 187.

50. Ibid., 188.

51. See Stillman, "Re-membering the History of the Hawaiian Hula"; Tengan, *Native Men Remade*; Osorio, *Dismembering Lāhui* and "On Being Hawaiian."

52. I have written extensively on ʻike ʻāina; see "ʻIke ʻĀina" and "Hanohano Wailuanuiahoʻāno."

53. Kanahele, *Holo Mai Pele*, xxvii.

54. Kanahele, *Ka Honua Ola*, 109.

55. Ibid., 112.

56. McGregor, *Nā Kuaʻāina*, 143–44.

57. Nakuina, *Wind Gourd of La'amaomao*, 138, 140.

58. Elbert and Pukui, *Hawaiian Dictionary*, 33–34. PH indicates Emerson's *Pele and Hiiaka*.

59. Hau'ofa, "Our Sea of Islands," 152.

60. See Silva, "E Lawe i ke Ō."

61. Kanahele, *Ka Honua Ola*, 114.

62. Ibid.

63. Ibid.

64. Ibid., 115.

65. Ibid., 117.

66. Kimura, "Native Hawaiian Culture"; Basso, *Wisdom Sits in Places*; Shanley "Writing Indian"; and Brooks, "Digging at the Roots."

67. Kanahele, *Ka Honua Ola*, 115.

68. Kanahele interview in Mugge, *Kumu Hula*.

69. Kanahele, *Holo Mai Pele*, xxvii.

70. Kanahele, *Ka Honua Ola*, 109.

71. Silva, "He Kānāwai e Ho'opau i na Hula Kuolo Hawai'i"; Kamahele, "Hula as Resistance." In 2009, kumu hula and cultural activist Victoria Holt Takamine traveled to Bogotá, Colombia, with her hālau and spoken word poet Jamaica Heolimeleikalani Osorio to participate in the Hemispheric Institute Encuentro at the Universidad Nacional de Bogotá. Her performance, titled "Hula as Resistance," addressed hula as a political practice and tool of resisting imperialism. See http://hemisphericinstitute.org/.

Mokuna / Chapter 1

1. Nogelmeier, *Epic Tale of Hi'iakaikapoliopele*, 55, 57. Original versions can be found in *Ka Na'i Aupuni*, March 12, 1906, 4; and the Kuluwaimaka Collection (HI.M. 51, book II, 57–58), the Henriques-Peabody Collection (HI.M. 77, 14), and MS SC Roberts 4.3 and 4.4, 9–10, Bishop Museum Archives.

2. Nogelmeier, *Epic Tale of Hi'iakaikapoliopele*, 55.

3. Merrie Monarch is the preeminent hula competition in the world. A four-day event dedicated to the "Merrie Monarch" King David Kalākaua, credited with reviving the hula (including traditional hula Pele) through his patronage, disregarding a previously imposed ban on hula implemented by Calvinist missionaries who viewed the hula as degrading and "barbarous." The festival, held in Hilo, Hawai'i, began in 1964 under the direction of the Hawai'i Chamber of Commerce and kumu hula George Naope. The hula competition is the highlight of the weeklong festivities honoring Kalākaua. The primary purpose of the festival is "the perpetuation, preservation, and promotion of the art of hula and the Hawaiian culture through education." See http://www.merriemonarch .com/. The festival is credited with playing a major role in the revival of hula and other traditional cultural practices during the cultural renaissance of the 1960s and 1970s.

4. Notley and Poepoe, "What Is Poi?"; Halai, "He Mele." Some traditions

name Papa and Wākea's daughter Hoʻohōkūikalani (to generate stars in the heavens) as the mother of the Hāloa brothers. See "Moolelo Hawaii," 79; Kepelino, *Kepelino's Traditions of Hawaii*, 60–62; Handy, Handy, and Pukui, *Native Planters in Old Hawaiʻi*, 74. Others do not name their mother, but identify Hāloa or Hāloa and Hāloanaka simply as sons of Wākea. See Kalama, "He Mele," 52; Malo, *Hawaiian Antiquities*, 244. Kamakau cites the 1838 *Moolelo Hawaii* as one source for the Wākea and Hoʻohōkūkalani parentage of Hāloa (*Tales and Traditions of the People of Old*, 162n9), but also acknowledges the different versions of the tradition when stating, "Those of Hawaiʻi [island] rely on the genealogy of Hāloa; however, Oʻahu and Maui were the true origin of the genealogy of Hāloa" (37). The various accounts of Hāloa's lineage are within the scope of makawalu, multiple perspectives reflecting different islands and genealogies. The examples from *Ka Hae Hawaii* above are just two different mele koʻihonua (genealogical or origin chants) published in the Hawaiian-language newspapers, demonstrating an intellectual discourse on Hawaiian moʻolelo by Kanaka Maoli.

5. Trask, *From a Native Daughter*, n.p.

6. Young, *Rethinking the Native Hawaiian Past*, 66.

7. Kameʻeleihiwa, *Legendary Tradition of Kamapuaʻa*, xii.

8. Kameʻeleihiwa, "Synopsis of Traditional Hawaiian Culture," 1–2.

9. Kimura, "Native Hawaiian Culture," 183. See also Pukui, *ʻŌlelo Noʻeau*, 206.

10. Kameʻeleihiwa discusses this at length in her book *Native Lands and Foreign Desires*.

11. See Kameʻeleihiwa, *Nā Wāhine Kapu*, 27–28. As previously noted, there are multiple ways to interpret these names. For example, Haumea may be a contraction of "hānau mea" referring to the birthing process. Hau is also a contraction of hahau, "to lay before; to offer, as a sacrifice or prayer" (Elbert and Pukui, *Hawaiian Dictionary*, 60). Ioane Hoʻomanawanui recalls growing up in Hilo learning from culturally knowledgeable kūpuna that Haumea means "gatherer." Multiple layers and interpretations of meanings reflect makawalu practices.

12. See Kameʻeleihiwa, *Native Lands, Foreign Desires*.

13. Stannard, *Before the Horror*, 74.

14. Kameʻeleihiwa, "Synopsis of Traditional Hawaiian Culture," 3.

15. For a more in-depth discussion on the impact of foreign diseases on the population collapse of Kanaka Maoli, see Stannard, *Before the Horror*.

16. Osorio, *Dismembering Lāhui*, 30.

17. Kameʻeleihiwa, "Synopsis of Traditional Hawaiian Culture," 4.

18. Bingham, *Residence of Twenty-One Years in the Sandwich Islands*, 6.

19. Steward, *Journal of a Residence in the Sandwich Islands*, 88.

20. Kameʻeleihiwa, "Synopsis of Traditional Hawaiian Culture," 5.

21. Silva, "He Kānāwai e Hoʻopau i na Hula Kuolo Hawaiʻi," 29.

22. Burlin, *Imperial Maine and Hawaiʻi*, 64.

23. Phillips, *Protestant American and the Pagan World*, 93–94.

24. Kimura, "Native Hawaiian Culture," 187.

25. "Hawaiian Education," 1.

26. Osorio, *Dismembering Lāhui*, 31.

27. *The Friend*, August 1845, 119.

28. See Birkett, "French Perspective on the Laplace Affair."

29. The mōʻī's proclamation was co-opted as the motto of the state of Hawaiʻi when statehood was conferred in 1959. For further discussion, see Silva, "Early Struggles with the Foreigners," in *Aloha Betrayed*; and Sai, "Political History."

30. Kameʻeleihiwa discusses the land awards in detail; see *Native Lands and Foreign Desires*.

31. Kameʻeleihiwa, "Synopsis of Traditional Hawaiian Culture," 10.

32. Osorio, *Dismembering Lāhui*, 47.

33. Ibid., 56.

34. Ibid., 18.

35. Silva, "He Kānāwai e Hoʻopau i na Hula Kuolo Hawaiʻi," 31.

36. Ibid., 31–32.

37. Kent, *Hawaii*, 31.

38. See Silva, "*Ka Hoku o ka Pakipika*: Emergence of the Native Voice in Print," in *Aloha Betrayed*.

39. See Mookini, *Hawaiian Newspapers*; Chapin, *Guide to Newspapers of Hawaiʻi*.

40. Kuykendall, *Hawaiian Kingdom*, 256.

41. Osorio, *Dismembering Lāhui*, 150.

42. Ibid., 225.

43. See Silva, "The Merrie Monarch: Genealogy, Cosmology, Mele, and Performance as Resistance," in *Aloha Betrayed*.

44. Bacchilega, *Legendary Hawaiʻi and the Politics of Place*, 64.

45. Alexander, *History of the Later Years of the Hawaiian Monarchy*, 1.

46. Elbert and Pukui, *Hawaiian Dictionary*, 21.

47. Translated from Kamakau, "Ka Moolelo Hawaii" (August 26, 1869), 1. The original text reads: "O ke aupuni o Hawaii nei, he aupuni aloha alii, he aloha ka leo i ka pane mai, he aloha ka olelo, he aloha ke kamailio pu ana, he malama i ka leo o haule wale iho ilalo, aole no ke kuai, aole no ka hoolimalima, aole no ka hoopilimeaai wale, aka, no ke aloha oiaio maoli. Ua pili keia aloha i na Moi a me naʻlii aloha maikai i na makaainana a me ka lahui holookoa."

48. Silva, *Aloha Betrayed*, 11.

49. Elbert and Pukui, *Hawaiian Dictionary*, 121. Kameʻeleihiwa discusses the process of traditional kālaiʻāina in detail; see *Native Lands and Foreign Desires*, 83–110.

50. Liliʻuokalani, *Hawaii's Story by Hawaii's Queen*, 229, 231.

51. Ibid., 387–388.

52. Silva, "Introduction," 34. Silva discusses this period in depth in "The Anti-annexation Struggle," in *Aloha Betrayed*.

53. Silva, "Introduction," 35–36.

54. The Hawaiian Homes Commission Act was introduced in 1920, signed into law in 1921, and enacted in 1922.

55. This is discussed in detail in J. Kēhaulani Kauanui's *Hawaiian Blood*.

56. Ben Finney has written extensively on *Hōkūle'a* and the Polynesian Voyaging Society; see *Sailing in the Wake of the Ancestors*. More information on the history of *Hōkūle'a* and the early voyages is available at the archived Polynesian Voyaging Society Web site, http://pvs.kcc.hawaii.edu/, and on the current Web site, http://www.hokulea.org/.

57. See McGregor, "Kaho'olawe: Rebirth of the Sacred," in *Nā Kua'āina*; and the Kaho'olawe Island Reserve Commission Web site, http://www.kahoolawe.hawaii.gov/.

58. Apology Bill of 1993, Pub. L. No. 103-150, 107 Stat. 1510 (1993).

59. Goodhue, "From Resistance to Affirmation," 36.

60. Ibid.

61. Silva, "Introduction," 47–48.

62. Kirch, *On the Road of the Winds*, 80.

63. Elbert and Pukui, *Hawaiian Dictionary*, 69.

64. The first mo'olelo to name Kū[w]ahailo as Pele's father is Pa'aluhi and Bush ("Ka Moolelo o Hiiakaikapoliopele," January 5, 1893). Rice's "He Moolelo no Pele ame Kona Kaikaina Hiiaka i ka poli o Pele" is the only mo'olelo to name Moemoea'ali'i as her father (May 21, 1908).

65. Elbert and Pukui, *Hawaiian Dictionary*, 1, 99, 249. *A'a* figuratively refers to the womb and offspring, referencing the fertile birthing process of land; alternative words are also suggested, such as 'a'a, to venture, especially with bravery, and 'a'ā, to burn, blaze, or glow, like molten lava.

66. Andrews, *A Dictionary of the Hawaiian Language*, 110–111. Hau is also another name for the hula 'āla'apapa, described by Elbert and Pukui as a "type of ancient dramatic hula" (*Hawaiian Dictionary*). Andrews describes it as an ancient hula as well (46). As such, it suggests Hi'iaka's connection to hula may be genealogical. Other alternative interpretations of Haumea's name are provided earlier in this chapter.

67. Polapola is a Hawaiian rendering of what is often called Bora Bora, an island in the Tahitian group. When in Tahiti in 2006, I was repeatedly told by indigenous Tahitians that Bora Bora is a foreign rendering, and that the actual place name is Porapora, which is closer to the Hawaiian pronunciation.

68. Pā'ūopala'e is often described as a kahu (caretaker) of ferns surrounding the volcanic region. The native fern palai or palapalai (*Microplepio setosa*) is a homonym (palae, palai); it grows in the Hawaiian rainforest, including the volcanic uplands of Pele's home. It is also closely associated with hula, used in lei and kūpe'e (wrist and ankle adornments) in hula, to decorate the hula kuahu (altar) and represents Hi'iakaikapoliopele. Neal describes it as a synonym for the pala'ā or lace fern (*Sphenomeis chinensis*) (*In Gardens of Hawaii*, 15, 16). Valier notes its use to decorate the hula kuahu and its association with Hi'iaka (*Ferns of Hawai'i*, 56).

69. There are different ways to interpret this; paoa is a strong smell, good or bad, also unlucky, especially at fishing or sex (fishing is also used as a metaphor

for sexual encounters); or to have a taste or craving for (Elbert and Pukui, *Hawaiian Dictionary*, 315). It also alludes to Pāoa, the name of Pele's digging stick.

70. See Kalmijn, "Electric and Magnetic Field Detection in Elasmobranch Fishes"; MacIver, "Shark's Sixth Sense"; Meyer, Holland, and Papastamatiou, "Sharks Can Detect Changes in the Geomagnetic Field," 129–130.

71. Kimura, "Native Hawaiian Culture," 180.

Mokuna / Chapter 2

1. Manu, "He Moolelo Kaao Hawaii no ke Kaua Nui Weliweli ma waena o Pele-Keahialoa me Waka-Keakaikawai," August 12, 1899, 1.

2. "Pelekeahiʻāloa" (Pele of the eternal fires) is a shortened, modernized title I use throughout the book to reference the longer, more cumbersome (and incorrectly marked) original title, "He Moolelo Kaao Hawaii no ke Kaua Nui Weliweli ma waena o Pele-Keahialoa me Waka-Keakaikawai: He mau kupua Wahine Kaʻeaeʻa" (A Hawaiian Legend of the Great and Terrible War between [Pelekeahiʻāloa] and Waka-the shadow in the water [Wakakeakaikawai]: The Supernatural Heroines).

3. See Basham, "Ka Lāhui Hawaiʻi, He Moʻolelo, He ʻĀina, He Loina, a He Ea Kākou."

4. Kimura, "Native Hawaiian Culture," 187, 189.

5. Kameʻeleihiwa, *Legendary Tradition of Kamapuaʻa*, xiv.

6. Silva, "E Lawe i ke Ō," 234.

7. Kamakau, *Ruling Chiefs of Hawaiʻi*, 241.

8. Hale Kuamoʻo, *Mamaka Kaiao*.

9. Perreira, "He Haʻiʻōlelo Kuʻuna," xv, xvi, 324–325.

10. Elbert, "Hawaiian Literary Style and Culture," 350, 353.

11. Elbert, "Symbolism in Hawaiian Poetry," 390.

12. Charlot, *Classical Hawaiian Education*, 226.

13. Silva, "E Lawe i ke Ō," 241.

14. Pukui, "How Legends Were Taught," n.p.; Elbert, "Hawaiian Literary Style," 347.

15. Elbert, "Hawaiian Literary Style," 347, 349; Kameʻeleihiwa, *Legendary Tradition of Kamapuaʻa*, viii–ix; Silva, *Aloha Betrayed*, 67.

16. Pukui, "How Legends Were Taught," n.p.

17. Ibid.; Elbert, "Hawaiian Literary Style," 347.

18. Kimura, "Native Hawaiian Culture," 188–189.

19. Ibid.

20. Stillman, "Re-membering the History of the Hawaiian Hula," 191.

21. See Chapin, *Shaping History*, 2–4.

22. Ibid., 3.

23. Mookini, *Hawaiian Newspapers*, xiv.

24. Silva, *Aloha Betrayed*, 54–55.

25. Silva, "Talking Back to Law and Empire," 105.

26. Ibid., 106.

27. Nogelmeier, *Mai Pa'a i ka Leo*, 2.

28. In a general survey of the Hawaiian-language newspapers as a whole, very few American stories are found. It is possible that the United States was overlooked because it was a relatively new country with a "young" literature. It is also possible that U.S. literature was ignored because of anti-American sentiment due to the country's mishandling of Hawai'i. It is also possible that because England was a dominant world power with a rich literary history—and Hawai'i respected this—Hawai'i publishers followed their lead, snubbing American authors and writing.

29. Simpson and Roud, *English Folklore*, 254.

30. Ibid.

31. Bacchilega, *Legendary Hawai'i*, 9.

32. Brooks, "Digging at the Roots," 236.

33. Stillman, "Re-membering the History of the Hawaiian Hula," 188.

34. Ibid., 187, 188.

35. Lyons, "Rhetorical Sovereignty," 453.

36. Brooks, "Digging at the Roots," 250.

37. Ibid., 257.

38. Kanahele, *Ka Honua Ola*, chapter 1.

39. Kimura, "Native Hawaiian Culture," 188.

40. Kuwada, "Finding Mana in the Mundane," 109.

41. Kimura, "Native Hawaiian Culture," 188.

42. [Poepoe], "Ka Moolelo Kaao o Hiiaka-i-ka-poli-o-pele," April 24, 1908, 1.

43. Manu, "Pelekeahi'āloa," May 13, 1899, 1.

44. Brooks, "Digging at the Roots," 236, 255.

45. Kimura, "Native Hawaiian Culture," 178.

46. Ibid., 179.

47. Elbert and Pukui, *Hawaiian Dictionary*, 338. See also Pukui, *'Ōlelo No'eau*, 294.

48. See Kame'eleihiwa, *Legendary Tradition of Kamapua'a*, ix–xii.

49. Mo'olelo by Ho'oulumāhiehie, Poepoe, and Desha closely overlap, and each names eight Hi'iaka sisters and their hō'ailona (symbols): Hi'iakamākolewāwahiwa'a ("Red-eyed Hi'iaka who smashes canoes," lei hala and rainbows), Hi'iakawāwahilani or Hi'iakawāhilani ("Hi'iaka heaven destroyer," saturating rain clouds that arrive off the ocean), Hi'iakanoholani ("Hi'iaka dwelling in the heavens," pieces of bright rainbow and the lying rainbow), Hi'iakaka'alawamaka ("Hi'iaka with glancing eyes," long-eyed 'ōhiki sand crab), Hi'iakaikapoliopele ("Hi'iaka in the heart of Pele," pala'ā fern in the forest, her kānāwai or etiquette law is eating fish from head to tail), Hi'iakakapua'ena'ena ("Hi'iaka the sacred red-hot glowing"), possibly Hi'iakakapuaaneane ("Extremely aged Hi'iaka," red glowing heat or flushed feeling a person feels when she approaches them), Hi'iakalei'ia ("The lei-adorned Hi'iaka," all lei except lei hala), and Hi'iaka'ōpio ("The young Hi'iaka") (Ho'oulumāhiehie, "Ka Moolelo o Hiiakaikapoliopele," June 1, 1906, 3).

50. Shanley, "Writing Indian," 141.

51. Stillman, "Re-membering the History of the Hawaiian Hula."

52. Kānepuʻu, "Ka Poe Kakau Moolelo a Kaao Paha," 1.

53. Translated from Manu, "Pelekeahiʻāloa," August 12, 1899, 1.

54. Ibid.

55. Pukui, ʻŌlelo Noʻeau, 156.

56. Ibid.

57. Translated from Kamakau, "He Wahi Manao Paipai," January 5, 1867, 3; and "Ka Moʻolelo Hawaiʻi," October 6, 1870, 1.

58. Translated from Manu, "Pelekeahiʻāloa," August 12, 1899, 1.

59. Ibid. A translation by Pukui in the BMA's Hawaiian Ethnological Notes (HEN) collection indicates mokulehua as the "cut lehua," although it is also a "solemn feast after the cutting (moku) of an ʻōhiʻa log for a temple image" and a "cluster of lehua trees." It also implies mōkū, "remaining long in one place," suggesting both intimate familiarity with a specific location or practice; lehua also means "expert," furthering the metaphor. Elbert and Pukui, Hawaiian Dictionary, 252.

60. Hawaiʻi Forestry Association, "Dryland Forest Restoration Forum," 10.

61. Over the years, Molokaʻi has been particularly vulnerable to transnational global capitalism in multiple forms, despite its relatively small geographic size and small population. Aside from Molokaʻi Ranch, other commercial entities have been seeking ways to exploit Molokaʻi's natural resources, from cruise ships to wind farm developments, to transnational agribusiness. For example, despite heavy political lobbying to get genetically modified organisms (GMOs) labeled in Hawaiʻi, and to halt GMO farms, transnational entities such as Monsanto have heavily invested in Molokaʻi, and on other islands, resulting in divided communities who must weigh the economic benefits of employment with potentially irreversible destruction to the environment, Hawaiian culture, and community-based, rural lifestyles.

62. Silva's article "E Lawe i ke Ō" contains an excellent catalog of wind metaphors and different applications in Hawaiian culture and literature. She also cites Sydney Iaukea's "makani discourse" as a Hawaiian way of knowing. See Iaukea, "Land Agendas vis à vis Wind Discourse."

63. Silva, "E Lawe i ke Ō," 240.

Mokuna / Chapter 3

1. Kapihenui, "He Moolelo no Hiiakaikapoliopele" (February 20, 1862), 4.

2. Hoʻoilo is the rainy or "winter" season. "Kāpeku ka leo o ke kai, ʻo [H]oʻoilo ka malama" (When the voice of the sea is harsh, the winter months have come) is noted by Pukui as an ʻōlelo noʻeau "first uttered by Hiʻiaka" (Pukui, ʻŌlelo Noʻeau, 166). See also Elbert and Pukui, Hawaiian Dictionary, 81.

3. Wawalu does not exist on any modern maps; it is a more intense form of walu, "to claw, scratch, rub, grate, rasp, scrape, [pinch]" (Elbert and Pukui, Hawaiian Dictionary, 381, 383).

4. Makaliʻi is the name of a month, and collectively "the six summer months" (Elbert and Pukui, *Hawaiian Dictionary*, 226). It is also the name of the constellation Pleiades, which rises in October and marks the beginning of the Makahiki, a four-month season of peace and rest from warfare and hard labor similar to a harvest festival in other cultures; it also marks the beginning of the rainy season.

5. Wendt, "Towards a New Oceania," 49.

6. Ibid., 50.

7. One example is the Hawaiian creation chant Kumulipo. Scholars such as Martha Beckwith and John Charlot have theorized that the appearance of fish and birds during the first two wā (time periods, chapters) denote that these species hold a place of rank within the ordering of species as the first to appear or be "born." This concept is as culturally rooted for Kanaka Maoli as Darwin's theory of evolution is for Western scientists. I discuss this in more detail in my article "He Lei Hoʻoheno no nā Kau a Kau."

8. This refers to the Kapihenui strand of the Pele and Hiʻiaka moʻolelo.

9. An article accompanying the mele notes it is reprinted from the newspaper *Nu Hou* in 1854. "No na Mele," March 21, 1860, 4.

10. The mele was accompanied by a short article, "Ka lua o ko Kaleiopaoa mau mele" (The second of Kaleiopaoa's songs). Reprinted from the newspaper *Nu Hou*, June 24, 1854.

11. Translated from "No na Mele," 204.

12. Chapin, *Shaping History*, 29.

13. Ibid., 31.

14. "No na Mele," 204.

15. Ibid.

16. See G. W. Kahiolo, *He Moʻolelo no Kamapuaʻa* (The Legend of [the Pig–God] Kamapuaʻa).

17. Kimura, "Native Hawaiian Culture," 181.

18. See Paʻaluhi and Bush, "Ka Moolelo o Hiiakaikapoliopele"; Emerson, *Pele and Hiiaka*; and the BMA manuscript "Ka Moolelo no Hiiakaikapoliopele" (HI.L.23). Stillman describes the BMA "souvenir books" in part as part of the "poets' responsibility to preserve poetic repertoire" where "poets and honorees collected poetic texts along with other traditions that can be conveniently glossed . . . as antiquarian. These materials were written down in ledger books that were kept as personal souvenirs. By the 1920s, many of the surviving souvenir books eventually passed into the care of the Bishop Museum. . . . In terms of poetic repertoire, it appears that the vast majority of these souvenir books were compiled by people who were either poets themselves or who, as members or close associates of nobility, enjoyed access to these traditions" (Stillman, "Re-membering the Hawaiian Hula," 191).

19. Translated from Manu, "Pelekeahiʻāloa," August 19, 1899, 1.

20. Chapin, *Shaping History*, 59.

21. Ibid., 61.

22. Chapin says J. K. Kaunamano and G. W. Mila were the editors (ibid., 59). Silva discusses Kalākaua's involvement much more in depth in chapter 3 of *Aloha Betrayed*, "The Merrie Monarch: Genealogy, Cosmology, Mele, and Performance Art as Resistance."

23. There was a free pilot issue on September 9, 1861.

24. Examples include, but are not limited to, "Mooolelo no Keaniniulaokalani" (October 3, 1861) and "Ka Moolelo o Kapakohano" (October 31–November 7, 1861) by S. N. Haleʻole, and "He Moolelo no Kaililauokekoa" (October 31, 1861) by S. Hinau.

25. Kapihenui's name is printed as J. N. in the first installment (December 26, 1861) and M. J. at the end (July 17, 1862). A letter to the editor of *Ka Nupepa Kuokoa* dated February 28, 1862, was signed J. M. Kapihenui. It is unclear which set of initials is correct, and where there may be typographical errors. Later references to the moʻolelo exclude any first initials.

26. Interior Department letter, January 11, 1858, to John Cummins. Hawaiʻi State Archives. I follow this letter and refer to Kapihenui as a male.

27. Charlot, "Pele and Hiʻiaka," 62.

28. Kapihenui, "He Moolelo no Hiiakaikapoliopele," April 24, 1862, 4.

29. Ibid., February 6, 1862, 4.

30. Ibid., February 20, 1862, 4.

31. The BMA Mele Index began as a card index around the 1980s that "was compiled of poetic repertoire by first lines . . . [that] did not inventory the contents of all the manuscript sources" available (Stillman, "Re-membering the Hawaiian Hula," 193). It has since been updated to an online system that allows users to search the extensive collection of oli, mele, and hula texts, which are catalogued by the first two lines of each. It still does not contain many notes on individual mele or collections.

There are hundreds of hula texts catalogued in the BMA Mele Index related to the Pele and Hiʻiaka moʻolelo, many of which end with the formulaic line "He inoa no Hiʻiakaikapoliopele" ([Dedicated] in the name of [or to the goddess of hula] Hiʻiakaikapoliopele). This tag line is not usually included in the Pele and Hiʻiaka moʻolelo published in the newspapers, indicating a transition of oli or mele from performance to literary text.

32. Translated from Kapihenui, "He Moolelo no Hiiakaikapoliopele," July 10, 1862, 4.

33. Ibid., July 17, 1862, 1.

34. Ibid., July 10, 1862, 4.

35. Ibid., July 17, 1862, 1. Kūkeʻeilani can be interpreted as "standing crooked in the heavens." Nei refers to a rumbling sound like an earthquake, or the tumultuous sound of strong winds. Hoʻoilo is the rainy winter season that often includes strong winds.

36. "Hiiakaikapoliopela," BMA manuscript (HI.L.23, 160).

37. Ibid.

38. Ibid.

39. Ibid.

40. Ibid.

41. Ibid.

42. See Silva, "He Kanawai e Hoʻopau i na Hula Kuolo Hawaiʻi." A variety of hula, including hula kahiko (traditional hula), was prominently featured at Kalākaua's coronation, including twelve hula ʻai haʻa dedicated to Pele, one of which was a hulihia ("Hulihia ka mauna wela i ke ahi"). The program also featured ten hula kilu dedicated to Hiʻiaka and Lohiʻau. See "Papa Kuhikuhi o na Hula Poni Moi, February 12, 1883," 8–9.

An editorial in *Ka Nupepa Kuokoa* negatively described the hula performance as ʻino (sinful) because "weheia ae la na hula pegana kahiko o ka wa pouli loa o keia lahui kanaka" (the ancient pagan hulas of the time of deepest darkness of the people were displayed). What was particularly egregious, according to the article, was that the printed program was proof the hula were "ua hoomakaukau mua ia me ke akahele loa" (carefully preplanned). "Ka Lapuwale o ka Poaono Nei," 2.

Missionary descendant and attorney William Richard Castle (who would soon become a member of the Committee of Safety, responsible for the overthrow of the Hawaiian government) went so far as to charge the printer R. Grieve with obscenity through "the *printing* of objectionable matter" because of the hula titles that Castle wasn't even able to understand himself. See "A Celebrated Case," 3.

43. In other texts, such as [Poepoe's] "Ka Moolelo Kaao o Hiiaka-i-ka-poli-o-pele," Nohoamoʻo is replaced by Kuaua.

44. Kapihenui, "He Moolelo no Hiiakaikapoliopele," January 23, 1862, 1.

45. Ibid., December 26, 1861, 1; March 6, 1862, 4; July 10, 1862, 4.

46. Pukui, Elbert, and Mookini, *Place Names of Hawaiʻi*, 13.

47. "Hulihia ka mauna" is found in Kapihenui, Rice, and Emerson; "Hulihia Kīlauea" is found in Kapihenui and Emerson.

48. The other four chants, which are not as well known or found in multiple texts, are "Po Puna i ka uahi kui maka lehua" (Kapihenui, "He Moolelo no Hiiakaikapoliopele," April 3, 1862, 4), "O Puna aina lehua ula i ka papa" (ibid., May 15, 1862, 4), "E kuu aikane i ke kai hee o Hoeu maloko" ([Poepoe], "Ka Moolelo Kaao o Hiiaka-i-ka-poli-o-pele," July 31, 1908, 1), and "Kua loloa Keaau i ka nahele hala" (Emerson, *Pele and Hiiaka*, 34). The "Kua Loloa" chant is not found in any of the other Hawaiian newspaper sources; however, it is included in Kanahele, *Holo Mai Pele*, who describes it as "an account of Hiʻiaka's battle with the dragon lizard, Panaʻewa" (15). Line 9 states, "Momoku ahi Puna hala i ʻApua" (All of Puna is charred wood as far as ʻApua), indicating great devastation.

49. Elbert and Pukui, *Hawaiian Dictionary*, 29.

50. Pukui, Elbert, and Mookini, *Place Names of Hawaiʻi*, 148, 13.

51. Elbert and Pukui, *Hawaiian Dictionary*, 242. Kanahele (2011) identifies Maukele (not Maʻukele) as "a common name for a lush rainforest" (19n25).

52. Pukui, Elbert, and Mookini, *Place Names of Hawaiʻi*, 106; ʻĪʻī, *Fragments of Hawaiian History*, 109.

53. Pukui, 'Ōlelo No'eau, 271.

54. Kamakau, Ruling Chiefs of Hawai'i, 118, 231.

55. Elbert and Pukui, Hawaiian Dictionary, 110.

56. Kimura, "Native Hawaiian Culture," 177.

57. Bishop Museum Archives HEN, 1602–1606.

58. Elbert and Pukui, Hawaiian Dictionary, 134.

59. Bishop Museum Archives HEN, 1602–1606.

60. Kimura, "Native Hawaiian Culture," 180.

61. Kapihenui, "No ka Moolelo o Pele," 1.

62. In 1980 Congress enacted the Comprehensive Environmental Response, Compensation, and Liability Act (CERCLA), which was a response to the discovery of toxic waste dump sites. A Superfund environmental program was established to identify and address abandoned hazardous waste sites; it is administered by the Environmental Protection Agency. Pearl Harbor has been a Superfund site since the program began in the 1980s. While not geographically connected to Pu'uloa, Lualualei is considered part of the Pearl Harbor Naval Complex.

Mokuna / Chapter 4

1. Kapihenui, "He Moolelo no Hiiakaikapoliopele," March 13, 1862, 4.

2. The 1958 movie was adapted from the 1949 Rogers and Hammerstein musical, which was based on the 1947 publication by James Michener, an American writer noted for sweeping historical epics of American states, including *Hawaii*, which was published in 1959, the year Hawai'i became a state. Both *South Pacific* and *Hawaii* have influenced global perceptions of Hawai'i as a place of settler colonial conflict, paternalism, and power, continuing the erasure of Native agency within a native articulated space.

3. Andrade, Hā'ena, 15.

4. Tuhiwai Smith, Decolonizing Methodologies, 2.

5. Ka'ili, "A Hawaiian Legend by a Hawaiian Native," September 1, 1883, 2.

6. Bacchilega, Legendary Hawai'i and the Politics of Place, 109–110.

7. Ibid.

8. Kapihenui, "He Moolelo no Hiiakaikapoliopele," January 2, 1862, 1.

9. Ka'ili, "A Hawaiian Legend by a Hawaiian Native," August 25, 1883, 3. Pa'aluhi and Bush reference the same scene; see "Ka Moolelo o Hiiakaikapoliopele," January 17, 1893, 1. So does Emerson, but he does not refer to the type of wave (a detail that would be interesting and educational to a Kanaka Maoli audience, but perhaps not to a Western, non-surfing one). See Emerson, Pele and Hiiaka, 13.

10. Walker, Waves of Resistance, 2, 4–5.

11. Ka'ili, "A Hawaiian Legend by a Hawaiian Native," September 1, 1883, 2; also found in Pa'aluhi and Bush, Ho'oulumāhiehie, and Poepoe. The issues of Ka Hoku o Hawaii that may contain this episode in Desha are missing from the microfilm reels.

12. The original Hawaiian text is from Kapihenui, "He Moolelo no Hiia-kaikapoliopele," February 13, 1862, 4. Another version of this scene is found in Pa'aluhi and Bush, "Ka Moolelo o Hiiakaikapoliopele," and [Ho'oulumāhiehie], "Ka Moolelo o Hiiaka-i-ka-poli-o-pele," although in this version Hi'iaka's encounter with Palani and 'Iewale appears later in the narrative.

13. Pukui and Elbert, *Hawaiian Dictionary*, 309.

14. Ibid.

15. Sterling and Summers, *Sites of Oahu*, 171.

16. Pukui and Elbert, *Hawaiian Dictionary*, 94.

17. Ho'oulumāhiehie initially describes Kalehualoa as "a place in the upland of Kahana, according to some people," but cites the noted ali'i S. L. Peleiōhōlani who "says that the sandy beach running across the front of Kahana is actually Kalehualoa. It was named because the chiefs of Kahana, the men and the women, wore lei woven from lehua blossoms when they embarked on the canoes. Then their retainers gathered on both sides of the vessel and pulled it back and forth across the bay" ("Ka Moolelo o Hiiaka-i-ka-poli-o-pele," January 30, 1906, 4). Desha adds that "this [specific] place was called the 'alo one o Kahana, 'o Kalehualoa (sandy stretch of Kalehualoa)" ("He Moolelo Kaao o Hiiakaikapoliopele," January 26, 1926, 1).

18. Employing kaona, there are multiple ways to translate this name. The most literal translation might be "the open lehua," the lehua being a blossom closely associated with the Pele sisters, their volcanic home, and hula. Wehe also means to loosen, untie, or tip, as well as to depart, while lehua is also a "rainbow-colored mother-of-pearl shell used for a fishing lure" or an expert (Elbert and Pukui, *Hawaiian Dictionary*, 199, 383). Thus it could easily refer to the expert way Kapō'ulakīna'u raises the surf and expertly causes the men to fall off their boards and perish; it could also refer to the mother-of-pearl shells used to create eyes on ki'i (tiki) images, hence the name pae ki'i, row of images, which also connects to the name of the second surf break, Makaīwa, meaning "mother-of-pearl eyes, as in an image, especially of the god Lono" (ibid., 226).

19. Translated from Manu, "Pelekeahi'āloa," July 1, 1899, 4, and July 8, 1899, 4.

20. Mention of the petroglyph stones in other scholarship refer to them as pae ki'i or Paemāhū (Wichman, *Kaua'i*, 72; Dickey, "Stories of Wailua," 14, Pukui, Elbert, and Mookini, *Place Names of Hawai'i*, 173). Dickey includes an alternate tradition of the images associated with the mo'olelo of the kupua figure Maui (15). Pukui, Elbert, and Mookini identify the stones as paemāhū, "rocks at mouth of Wai-lua River, Kaua'i, believed to have been men turned to stone by Kapō. *lit.* homosexual row" (*Place Names of Hawai'i*, 173). Wichman follows this highly problematic translation. Māhū is a "homosexual, of either sex; hermaphrodite; a man who assimilates his manners and dresses his person like a woman." There is no indication in the mo'olelo that the men were māhū. The surfing scene is firmly heterosexual, particularly with the men inviting the women to surf in tandem on the same board with them, a highly suggestive, sexual metaphor. Alternative translations include māhu, "steam, vapor, fumes; to steam; same

as 'ōlapa trees," connoting being wet or dampened, and mahū, "weak, flat, as diluted kava or stale beer; insipid; quiet, peaceful, undisturbed."

Pae ki'i literally means "a row of images," although it refers to "rows of clouds, as on the horizon." Pae (row) also means "cluster, group, margin or bank, as of a taro patch; level, as of a platform; to land, disembark, come ashore; to mount or catch a wave, as of a surf rider, washed or drifted ashore." Thus, the grouping of the petroglyph-marked stones on the riverbank also connotes being the landing place of the surfers after being drowned in the huge surf; the stones sit so close to the ocean on the riverbank that they are regularly dampened by the sea spray. Wailua is a place where famous ali'i and voyagers land when traveling to Kaua'i, including Hi'iaka, and ki'i (statues, carved images) are associated with the state religion of the ali'i; several important heiau are also located in the vicinity, with the paeki'imahūowailua just steps away from Hikinaakalā heiau and the pu'uhonua (refuge) of Hauola. All of these layers of important connotations related to the mo'olelo, the paemahū, and Wailua are literally lost in translation. I suggest an alternative translation, "The cluster of petroglyph stones [representing the defeated men] resting peacefully at Wailua." See Elbert and Pukui, *Hawaiian Dictionary*, 220.

21. Walker, *Waves of Resistance*, 18.

22. Ka'ili, "Tauhi vā," quoted in Walker, *Waves of Resistance*, 18–19.

23. Translated from Kapihenui, "He Moolelo no Hiiakaikapoliopele," March 13, 1862, 4.

24. Ka'ili, "A Hawaiian Legend by a Hawaiian Native," September 21, 1883, 3.

25. This is discussed in more detail in Silva, "E Lawe i ke Ō."

26. Walker, *Waves of Resistance*, 29.

27. Silva, "Talking Back to Law and Empire," 101. A more in-depth discussion and analysis of hula and the Pele mo'olelo is found in Barrere, Pukui, and Kelly, *Hula Historic Perspectives*; Kanahele and Wise, *Ka Honua Ola*; Charlot, "Pele and Hi'iaka"; and Silva, "I Kū Maumau."

28. Silva, "Talking Back to Law and Empire." Variations of the five scenes identified by Silva are found in most of the Pele and Hi'iaka mo'olelo. The function of the hula is described by Charlot in "Pele and Hi'iaka" and closely examined in Silva.

29. Silva, "Talking Back to Law and Empire," 119.

30. Ibid., 120.

31. Andrews, *A Dictionary of the Hawaiian Language*, 293.

32. Rice, "He Moolelo no Pele ame kona Kaikaina Hiiaka i ka Poli o Pele," August 6, 1908, 1. Koananai is an chiefly woman of Keālia, who is noted for her Haumea-like supernatural and unusual births to her children. See "He Moolelo no o Aahoaka, ke Koa a me Kona Hanau Kupaianaha ana." In Ka'ili, they participate in a kilu game at Pele'ula's court in Kou (now Honolulu), O'ahu ("A Hawaiian Legend by a Hawaiian Native," September 21, 1883, 3). In [Poepoe], Hi'iaka and Lohi'au are invited to play kilu with the chiefly women of Mākua, O'ahu ("Ka Moolelo Kaao o Hiiaka-i-ka-poli-o-pele," December 9, 1910, 2).

33. Nogelmeier, *Epic Tale of Hiʻiakaikapoliopele*, 255–257. Original Hawaiian text by [Hoʻoulumāhiehie], "Ka Moolelo o Hiiaka-i-ka-poli-o-pele," May 21 and 22, 1906, 4. See also Desha [and Keonaona], "He Moolelo Kaao no Hiiaka-i-ka-poli-o-pele, ka Wahine i ka Hikina a ka La, a o ka Ui Palekoki Uwila o Halemaʻumaʻu," January 4, 1927, 1.

34. ʻĪʻī, *Fragments of Hawaiian History*, 46.

35. *Ka Hoku o ka Pakipika*, February 5, 1863, 2. It was a common practice for Christian churches, beginning in the nineteenth century, to be built on the foundations of heiau, the traditional places of worship (terminated in 1819 with the overthrow of the ʻAikapu), or for heiau to be dismantled and the large stones used in their walls and platforms repurposed to build the foundation and walls of churches.

36. Elbert and Pukui, *Hawaiian Dictionary*, 152.

37. Kaʻili, "A Hawaiian Legend by a Hawaiian Native," September 1 and 10, 1883, 3. See also Paʻaluhi and Bush, "Ka Moolelo o Hiiakaikapoliopele," January 25, 1893, 4; [Poepoe], "Ka Moolelo Kaao o Hiiaka-i-ka-poli-o-pele," December 25, 1908, 1, 3; January 1, 1909, 1. The issues of *Ka Hoku o Hawaii* that may contain this episode in [Desha and Keonaona], "He Moolelo Kaao no Hiiakaikapoliopele, ka wahine i ka hikina ka la a o ka ui palekoki uwila o Halemaumau," are missing from the microfilm reels, so it is unknown if it is included in the narrative.

38. Kaʻili, "A Hawaiian Legend by a Hawaiian Native," September 11, 1883, 3. Found with variations in Hoʻoulumāhiehie, "Ka Moolelo o Hiiaka-i-ka-poli-o-pele," and [Poepoe], "Ka Moolelo Kaao o Hiiaka-i-ka-poli-o-pele."

39. Emerson, *Pele and Hiiaka*, 51.

40. Nogelmeier, *Epic Tale of Hiʻiakaikapoliopele*, 252. The original Hawaiian text is found in Hoʻoulumāhiehie, "Ka Moolelo o Hiiaka-i-ka-poli-o-pele, ka Wahine i ka Hikina a ka La, a o ka Ui Palekoki Uwila o Halemaʻumaʻu," May 15–19, 1906, 4.

41. Ibid.

42. Ibid.

43. Ibid., 254.

44. See Silva, *Aloha Betrayed*.

45. Translated from Kapihenui, "He Moolelo no Hiiakaikapoliopele," January 23, 1862, 1.

46. Ibid.

47. Handy and Pukui, *Polynesian Family System in Kaʻu, Hawaii*, 191.

48. Nogelmeier, *Epic Tale of Hiʻiakaikapoliopele*, 140. Original Hawaiian text for notes 46–50 by Hoʻoulumāhiehie, "Ka Moolelo o Hiiaka-i-ka-poli-o-pele, ka Wahine i ka Hikina a ka La, a o ka Ui Palekoki Uwila o Halemaʻumaʻu," January 17, 1906, 4.

49. Nogelmeier, *Epic Tale of Hiʻiakaikapoliopele*, 141.

50. Ibid., 213.

51. Ibid.

52. Ibid., 213–214.

53. Maly, "He Moʻolelo Kaʻao no Hiʻiaka-i-ka-poli-o-Pele," A6. Original Hawaiian text by Desha [and Keonaona], "He Moolelo Kaao no Hiiaka-i-ka-poli-o-pele, ka Wahine i ka Hikina a ka La, a o ka Ui Palekoki Uwila o Halemaʻumaʻu," January 4, 1927, 1.

Mokuna / Chapter 5

1. Hawaiian text originally published in Hoʻoulumāhiehie, "Ka Moolelo o Hiiaka-i-ka-poli-o-pele, ka Wahine i ka Hikina a ka La, a o ka Ui Palekoki Uwila o Halemaʻumaʻu," July 2, 1906, 4. Nogelmeier, *Ka Moʻolelo o Hiʻiakaikapoliopele*, 321.

2. Nogelmeier, *Epic Tale of Hiʻiakaikapoliopele*, 298–299.

3. See hoʻomanawanui, "Mana Wahine."

4. Trask, *From a Native Daughter*, 263–264.

5. McDougall, "Laugh of the Goddess," 1.

6. Ibid., quoting Kameʻeleihiwa.

7. Silva, "Talking Back to Law and Empire," 25.

8. Kaʻili, "A Hawaiian Legend by a Hawaiian Native," September 21, 1883, 3.

9. Ibid.

10. Handy and Pukui, *Polynesian Family System in Kaʻu, Hawaii*, 73.

11. Charlot, "Pele and Hiʻiaka," 93, 70n38.

12. Original Hawaiian text by [Poepoe], "Ka Moolelo Kaao o Hiiaka-i-ka-poli-o-pele," July 31, 1908, 1.

13. Ibid.

14. Silva, "Pele, Hiʻiaka, and Haumea," 166.

15. Titcomb, *Native Use of Fish in Hawaii*, 19; Fornander, "Na Akua Oopu," 511.

16. [Poepoe], "Ka Moolelo Kaao o Hiiaka-i-ka-poli-o-pele," July 31, 1908, 1.

17. Silva, "Pele, Hiʻiaka, and Haumea," 166.

18. Malo, *Hawaiian Antiquities*, 256.

19. See Morris, "Aikāne."

20. Currie, *Constructing Colonial Discourse*, 120, 129.

21. Kuwada, "How Blue Is His Beard?" 28.

22. "He mele kanikau," 64; "Make," 87.

23. "Ka Episetole a Paulo i ko Roma, Mokuna 1, pauku 22–28," 22.

24. "No ka hewa o ka manao nui ma ke kino," 4; Haʻanio, "Elua ano nui ma keia manao elua," *Ke Kumu Hawaii*, March 14, 1838, 84.

25. Ledyard, *John Ledyard's Journal of Captain Cook's Last Voyage*, 132–133.

26. Kamakau, *Ruling Chiefs of Hawaiʻi*, 314.

27. Ibid., 112.

28. Rice, "He Moolelo no Pele ame kona Kaikaina Hiiaka-i-ka-Poli-o-Pele."

29. Kaʻili, "A Hawaiian Legend by a Hawaiian Native," September 1, 1883, 3.

30. Ibid. Ruth Keʻelikōlani was the daughter of the high chief Kekūanāoʻa

and Kalanipauahi; when Keʻelikōlani's mother died in childbirth, she was hānai (raised) by Kaʻahumanu, high-ranking wife of Kamehameha I. She was educated at the Chiefs' Children's School. As an adult she served on the Privy Council, and in 1855 was appointed governor of Hawaiʻi island. When a lava flow threatened Hilo in 1881, the people asked for her to intercede, and she was successful. The dire circumstances are described in a letter to the editor of the Hawaiian newspaper *Ko Hawaii Paeaina* by one of the editors, J. U. Kawainui, titled "Ka Pele ai Honua ma Hilo" (The lava consuming the land at Hilo), 3.

While much is made in haole sources of Queen Kapiʻolani's defiance of Pele on a trip to the volcano in 1824, bolstering missionary views that Iehova was more powerful than Pele, little discussion of Keʻelikōlani's successful intercession with Pele was made. She offered hoʻokupu (tribute, gifts) to Pele, including traditional oli, and the lava flow ceased just outside of Hilo. Keʻelikōlani was a hero greatly beloved by the people. She was a staunch Hawaiian-language advocate, refusing to speak English, even though she knew the language.

While her primary residence was on the opposite side of the island in Kailua, Kona, the home Nakuina describes was situated on a parcel of land traditionally associated with the Kamehameha family, which is approximately where the soccer field of Wailoa Park in Hilo is located today, in the area of the Kamehameha statue.

31. Emerson, *Pele and Hiiaka*, 69.

32. Kapihenui, "He Moolelo no Hiiakaikapoliopele," January 16, 1862, 1.

33. Paʻaluhi and Bush, "Ka Moolelo o Hiiakaikapoliopele," January 17, 1893, 1.

34. Nogelmeier, *Epic Tale of Hiʻiakaikapoliopele*, 40. Original Hawaiian text by Hoʻoulumāhiehie, "Ka Moolelo o Hiiaka-i-ka-poli-o-pele, ka Wahine i ka Hikina a ka La, a o ka Ui Palekoki Uwila o Halemaʻumaʻu," September 1, 1905.

35. The best examples of the "kuʻu aikāne" mele series are found in Kapihenui, "He Moolelo no Hiiakaikapoliopele"; and Rice, "Pele ame Kana Kaikaina Hiiaka i ka Poli o Pele."

36. Translated from Manu, "Pelekeahiʻāloa," June 24, 1899, 4.

37. Nogelmeier, *Epic Tale of Hiʻiakaikapoliopele*, 13. Silva's "E Lawe i ke Ō" provides an in-depth analysis of a fairly identical scene from Poepoe, detailing the different levels of importance of the oli makani, the multiple layers of cultural information contained within them, and how they are linked to the larger cultural context surrounding the moʻolelo.

38. Silva, "E Lawe i ke Ō," 242.

39. Ibid., 248.

40. Nogelmeier, *Epic Tale of Hiʻiakaikapoliopele*, 300.

41. Ibid.

42. Kapihenui, "He Moolelo no Hiiakaikapoliopele," April 24, 1862, 4.

43. Pukui and Elbert, *Hawaiian Dictionary*, 19, 488.

44. Kapihenui, "He Moolelo no Hiiakaikapoliopele," April 24, 1862, 4.

45. Ibid.

46. Ibid.

47. Ibid.

48. Handy, Handy, and Pukui, *Native Planters in Old Hawaiʻi*, 335.

49. Silva, "Talking Back to Law and Empire," 117.

50. Kameʻeleihiwa, *Native Lands and Foreign Desires*, 23.

51. Mageo, "On Memory Genres," 26.

52. Elbert and Pukui, *Hawaiian Dictionary*, 10.

53. Kameʻeleihiwa, *Legendary Tradition of Kamapuaʻa*, 145.

54. Ibid.

55. Kaʻili, "A Hawaiian Legend by a Hawaiian Native," September 21, 1883, 3.

56. Kimura, "Native Hawaiian Culture," 178.

57. Silva, "Talking Back to Law and Empire," 111.

58. Basso, *Wisdom Sits in Places*, 47, 105.

59. For comparative purposes, see Nakuina, *Wind Gourd of Laʻamaomao*.

60. Elbert and Pukui, *Hawaiian Dictionary*, 363.

61. Kapihenui, "He Moolelo no Hiiakaikapoliopele," February 13, 1862, 4.

62. hoʻomanawanui, "This Land Is Your Land, This Land Was My Land," 133.

63. Elbert, Pukui, and Mookini, *Place Names of Hawaiʻi*, 196.

64. Kumu Pono Associates, *Mauna Kea*, 281.

65. Elbert and Pukui, *Hawaiian Dictionary*, 42.

66. Ibid., 242.

67. Ibid., 52.

68. Elbert, Pukui, and Mookini, *Place Names of Hawaiʻi*, 129, 98; Dole, "Hui Kawaihau," 8.

69. Wood, *Displacing Natives*, 6–7.

70. "Eating Disorders Rise after Fiji Gets TV," A1, A5; Becker, "Television, Disordered Eating, and Young Women in Fiji."

71. "Eating Disorders Rise after Fiji Gets TV," A5.

Mokuna / Chapter 6

1. Kanahele, *Holo Mai Pele*, 18–21.

2. Ibid.

3. McGregor, *Nā Kuaʻāina*, 188.

4. McGregor discusses this in more depth. See "Puna" in *Nā Kuaʻāina*; for a more detailed history and recent updates; see also the Pele Defense Web site, http://www.peledefensefund.org/.

5. Kimura, "Native Hawaiian Culture," 20n, 221.

6. Silva, "Pele, Hiʻiaka, and Haumea," 160.

7. Kameʻeleihiwa, *Legendary Tradition of Kamapuaʻa*, xvii.

8. Ibid., xvi.

9. Ibid., xvii.

10. "Bush's Conspiracy," 5.

11. "Ua Hala o John E. Bush," 2; "Died," 7.

12. Kameʻeleihiwa, *Legendary Tradition of Kamapuaʻa*, xviii.

13. Ibid.

14. Kuykendall, *Hawaiian Kingdom*, 522.

15. Mookini, *Hawaiian Newspapers*, xi.

16. "Ua Hala o John E. Bush," 2.

17. Kamau, "Hoalohaloha no Rev. S. Paaluhi," 3. (w) and (k) refer to wahine (woman) and kāne (man), and are commonly used in Hawaiian writing to designate the mother (w) and father (k) in a genealogy.

18. Kalani, "No ke Kula Kahuna o Wailuku," 2; Kamau, "Hoalohaloha no Rev. S. Paaluhi," 3.

19. "Moolelo o ka Ahahui Euanelio o ka Mokupuni o Oahu," 5; Kamau, "Hoalohaloha no Rev. S. Paaluhi," 3.

20. "Moolelo o ka Ahahui Euanelio o ka Mokupuni o Oahu," 5.

21. Kamau, "Hoalohaloha no Rev. S. Paaluhi," 3.

22. Translated from Paʻaluhi and Bush, "Ka Moolelo o Hiiakaikapoliopele," January 17, 1893, 1.

23. Nogelmeier, *Epic Tale of Hiʻiakaikapoliopele*, 432. See also Poepoe, "He Hoakaka," December 18, 1905, 2.

24. Translated from "Hala ka Mea Hanohano Joseph Mokuohai Poepoe," 1.

25. There are eight issues missing from microfilm, with at least three obvious gaps in the moʻolelo during the month of September. The missing dates are September 8, 15, and 22; October 2, 12, and 27; and November 3, 1905.

26. Mookini, *Hawaiian Newspapers*, xiii.

27. Silva discusses Poepoe's work in more depth in "E Lawe i ke Ō," 244. Both "Ka Moolelo Hiwahiwa o Kawelo" and the *Ka Naʻi Aupuni* version of "Hiʻiaka" were signed by "Hoʻoulumāhiehie."

28. Forbes, *Hawaiian National Bibliography*, 407.

29. When Desha's son John graduated from Harvard, he served for several years as Kūhiō's secretary. Later, when Kūhiō passed away, Desha, along with Reverend Akaiko Akana, conducted Kūhiō's service at Kawaiahaʻo Church. See Hibbard, McEldowney, and Napoka, "Introduction," xix.

30. Desha, *Kamehameha and His Warrior Kekūhaupiʻo*, 11–13.

31. Judd, "Stephen L. Desha," 362–363.

32. Hibbard, McEldowney, and Napoka, "Introduction," xiii. Desha's work with Hawaiian moʻolelo was acknowledged by others such as Martha Beckwith, who thanked him in her introduction of her translation of the epic romance *Lāʻieikawai*.

33. Joesting, *Kauaʻi*, 145.

34. Ibid., 155.

35. These dates are October 2, 1924, April 27, May 25, June 1, June 8, June 15, June 22, June 29, and July 6, 1926; March 13, June 5, and July 3, 1928. Unfortunately, there are a number of periods where significant portions of the newspapers are missing from microfilm, and no hard copies are available. These include a nine-month period from November 20, 1924, to August 20, 1925. As

a weekly publication, over a nine-month period, there are possibly as many as forty issues—and as many installments of the moʻolelo—missing from microfilm and no longer accessible to us today. In the remaining time period in which the moʻolelo was printed, ten additional issues of the newspaper are not on microfilm and otherwise not available. These dates are July 20, 1926; April 26, July 5, July 26, August 30, September 6, October 6, 1927; February 28, March 27, and April 10, 1928.

36. No installments are available for fifteen issues from 1910: May 27, June 10, June 24, July 8, July 15, August 12, August 26, September 2, September 9, September 16, October 7, October 21, October 27, November 3, or November 10.

37. "The Legend of Hiiaka," *Pacific Commercial Advertiser*, October 13, 1883, 3; my emphasis.

38. Chapin, *Shaping History*, 2–3.

39. Translated from Paʻaluhi and Bush, "Ka Moolelo o Hiiakaikapoliopele," January 5, 1893, 1.

40. Ibid.

41. Brown, "Native Hawaiian Perspectives on Variation in Moʻolelo," 6, 7.

42. Ibid., 7.

43. Ibid., 7–8.

44. Translated from Manu, "Pelekeahiʻāloa," May 20, 1899, 4.

45. Ibid.

46. Ibid., June 10, 1899, 1.

47. Ibid., July 1, 1899, 4. Manu's account of the ill-fated voyage differs from other writers; see Kamakau, *Ruling Chiefs of Hawaiʻi*; and ʻĪʻī, *Fragments of Hawaiian History*.

48. Ibid., August 19, 1899, 1.

49. Ibid., December 30, 1899, 1.

50. Hawaiian text from Hoʻoulumāhiehie, "Ka Moolelo o Hiiaka-i-ka-poli-o-pele, ka wahine i ka Hikina a ka la, a o ka Ui Palekoki Uwila o Halemaʻumaʻu," July 15, 1905, 2; Nogelmeier, *Epic Tale of Hiʻiakaikapoliopele*, 1.

51. Poepoe, "Ka Moolelo Kaao o Hiiaka-i-ka-poli-o-pele," April 24, 1908, 1.

52. Desha [and Keonaona], "Olelo Hoakaka Mua [Introduction]," "He Moolelo Kaao no Hiiakaikapoliopele, ka wahine i ka hikina ka la a o ka ui palekoki uwila o Halemaumau," September 18, 1924, 1.

53. Brown, "Native Hawaiian Perspectives on Variation in Moʻolelo," 16.

54. Ibid., 13.

55. These are discussed in the work of Charlot, "Pele and Hiʻiaka"; Silva, *Aloha Betrayed*; and Nogelmeier, *Mai Paʻa i ka Leo*.

56. The original Hawaiian text reads, "Ke oluolu ka Luna o ke *Kuokoa*, e hoopuka hou ia ia moolelo, no ka mea, ua hoopuka au i ka moolelo o Hiiakaikapoliopele ma ka *Hoku o ka Pakipika*, aole i pololei ka hoopuka ana a ka *Pakipika*, ua molowa no. A o na mele loloa ua hoopokoleia, aole like me ke kope." Translated from Kapihenui, "No ka Moolelo o Pele," 1.

57. Nogelmeier, *Epic Tale of Hiʻiakaikapoliopele*, 29.

58. Translated from Haleʻole, "Na Manao o S. N. Haleole," 3.

59. Translated from Kamakau, "He Mau Mea i Hoolaha ia no na mea i loko o na kaao Hawaii," 3.

60. Ibid.

61. Elbert and Pukui, *Hawaiian Dictionary*, 89.

62. Hawaiʻi Clean Energy Initiative Web site, http://www.hawaiicleanenergy initiative.org/.

63. Stewart, "Geothermal Energy."

Mokuna / Chapter 7

1. Manu, "Pelekeahiʻāloa," September 23, 1899, 1.

2. Translated from Kapihenui, "He Moolelo no Hiiakaikapoliopele," May 15, 1861, 4.

3. Womack, *Red on Red*, 14.

4. Thomas G. Thrum and William Drake Westervelt published a number of traditional Hawaiian moʻolelo in translation.

5. This is discussed more extensively by Silva in *Aloha Betrayed*; and Wood in *Displacing Natives*.

6. Womack, *Red on Red*, 6.

7. Silva, "I Kū Maumau," 18.

8. "Toni Morrison," 2094.

9. Trask, "Writing in Captivity," 19.

10. Ing, "'To Be or Not to Be,' That Was Not the Question," 2.

11. King, *Truth about Stories*, 112.

12. Silva, "I Kū Maumau," 21, 28.

13. Ibid., 17–18.

14. Charlot, "Pele and Hiʻiaka," 61–62.

15. Nogelmeier, *Epic of Hiʻiakaikapoliopele*, 34.

16. Silva, "Talking Back to Law and Empire," 110.

17. See Stillman, "Re-membering the History of the Hawaiian Hula."

18. See hoʻomanawanui, "Moʻolelo as Social and Political Action."

19. Benham and Heck discuss this in *Cultural and Educational Policy in Hawaiʻi*.

20. See Waziyatawin, "Maka Cokaya Kin."

21. De Silva, "Stitch Has a Glitch."

22. Examples include musical albums such as *The Pele Legends in Authentic Hawaiian Chants* by Keliʻi Tauʻā, *Haʻakuʻi Pele i Hawaiʻi* by Edith Kanakaʻole, and *Pele* by Roland Cazimero, visual art by Herb Kawainui Kāne, including *Pele, Goddess of Hawaii's Volcanoes*, and video documentaries by Nā Maka o ka ʻĀina, including *Pele's Appeal*.

23. Examples of traditional chants recorded as contemporary mele include the Makaha Sons of Niʻihau, "ʻO Kalalau [Pali ʻAʻala]" (The Fragrant Kalalau

Cliffs), Kawai Cockett, "Aia lā o Pele" (There Is Pele), and the Brothers Cazimero, "Noʻenoʻe Maikaʻi ke Aloha" (Love Is Nicely Tranquil).

24. De Silva, *He Aloha Moku o Keawe*, 22.

25. Trask, *Night Is a Sharkskin Drum*, 5.

26. Kinney, "Pele at the KTA," 44.

27. Aeʻa, "Road to Kēʻē," 93.

28. The mele is more commonly known by its first line, "Kaulana nā pua" (Famous are the children [of Hawaiʻi]). It was composed by Prendergast as a mele aloha ʻaina (nationalist anthem, *lit.* patriot song, or song expressing love for the land) in 1893 within weeks following the illegal overthrow of the Hawaiian kingdom. It was published many times in the Hawaiian newspapers during this period; *Ka Leo o ka Lahui* reprinted the mele under the title "He Lei no ka Poe Aloha Aina" (A Lei for the People Who Love the Land) because they received many requests for it (May 16, 1893, 3).

29. hoʻomanawanui, "Pele's Appeal," 80–90.

30. Jamaica Osorio, personal communication, July 12, 2012.

31. Pualani Kanakaʻole Kanahele and Nālani Kanakaʻole Zane's Hālau o Kekuhi stage production, publication, and DVD *Holo Mai Pele*, and Pacific Resources for Education and Learning's (PREL) DVD and graphic novel *Pele Searches for a Home*, are just a few examples of new media productions. *Pele Searches for a Home* can be accessed online via ʻŌiwi TV, http://www.oiwi.tv /live/channels/keiki/pele-searches-for-a-home/. The graphic novel and more information about the video and the Hoʻomau series it is a part of can be accessed online via PREL's Web site, http://ehoomau.prel.org/pele-searches-for-a-home/.

32. Womack, *Red on Red*, 16–17.

33. Brooks, *Common Pot*, Kindle edition, 169.

34. Charlot, "Pele and Hiʻiaka," 73.

35. Said, *Culture and Imperialism*, xii–xiii.

36. King, *Truth about Stories*, 2.

37. Armstrong, in Ortiz, *Speaking for the Generations*, 181, quoted in King, *Truth about Stories*, 2.

38. Justice, *Our Fire Survives the Storm*, 7.

39. Charlot, "Pele and Hiʻiaka," 58.

40. Silva, "I Kū Maumau," 26.

41. Tairawhiti is a region of Aotearoa (New Zealand) located on the east coast of the North Island; the main town is Gisborne.

42. Philip-Barbara, "Mana Wahine Week a Winner."

43. Pukui and Handy, *Polynesian Family System in Kaʻu, Hawaii*, 35.

44. Sullivan, "English Moko," 12–13.

45. McDougall, "Pele," 13.

46. *Ua ʻike a* is explained by Pukui as "like the *amama ua noa* of the *pule*; it is like the period at the end of a sentence, and a *mele* is not complete without it." Pukui and Handy, *Polynesian Family System in Kaʻu, Hawaii*, 130–131.

47. Ibid., 138.

48. Trask, *Light in a Crevice*, 56.

Closing Prayer

1. Nogelmeier, *Ka Moʻolelo o Hiʻiakaikapoliopele*, 106; [Hoʻoulumāhiehie], "Ka Moolelo o Hiiaka-i-ka-poli-o-pele," December 9, 1905, 1.

2. Nogelmeier, *Epic of Hiʻiakaikapoliopele*, 100–101.

Papa Wehewehe ʻŌlelo / Glossary

ABCFM—American Board of Commissioners for Foreign Missions.

aikāne—intimate, often sexual relationship with someone of the same gender.

ʻAikapu—*lit.* "sacred eating." The traditional, religiously rooted system dictating social order until it was abolished in 1819 just prior to the arrival of ABCFM missionaries. It was based on the primacy of four male gods, Kāne, Kū, Kanaloa, and Lono.

ʻAikū—*lit.* "[to] eat standing." The ʻAikū was the antithesis of the ʻAikapu, which was not followed by the Pele people.

ʻAinoa—*lit.* "free eating." The period following the abolition of the ʻAikapu.

ʻāina—*lit.* "that which feeds." The Hawaiian term for land, an important symbol and metaphor in Hawaiian consciousness often expressed poetically in oral and written poetry.

akua—deity, god, spirit, supernatural (superhuman) spiritual entity.

aliʻi (aliʻi nui, aliʻi ʻaimoku, kaukau aliʻi, etc.)—general term for the chiefs, royalty, ruling class; different terms indicate status level; aliʻi nui is literally the "important leader," aliʻi ʻaimoku is "the leader of the land," kaukau aliʻi is a lesser-ranking chief.

aloha ʻāina—*lit.* "love for the land," the term represents consciousness of the importance of Hawaiian land and our connection to it. In the nineteenth century it took on an expressly political meaning of nationalism and patriotism.

ʻāwihikalani—*lit.* "the chief's discerning eye." The "critical eye" Pele endowed Hiʻiaka with in some versions of the epic (along with a lightning skirt and a strong arm) as she commenced on her journey to Kauaʻi to fetch Pele's mortal chiefly love, Lohiʻau.

ʻēkoʻa—a Hawaiian literary device of oppositional pairings that often connote balance and symmetry within Hawaiian speech and writing.

haʻi moʻolelo—*lit.* "to tell a story." Haʻi moʻolelo refers to storytelling, oral performance of traditional epics or literature.

haku moʻolelo—*lit.* "to compose a story." The haku moʻolelo is one who compiles and edits a version or variant of a traditional story or historical account of events, as well as a creative writer who composes his or her own fictional narrative. Similarly, a "haku mele" is one who composes songs or poetry.

helu—*lit.* "to count, recount, list, enumerate." A common Hawaiian literary device.

hōʻailona—a sign or symbol. A common Hawaiian literary device.

hoʻoulu lāhui—*lit.* "to increase, reinvigorate the Hawaiian nation." A motto of King David Kalākaua, who ruled in the later nineteenth century, as a way to rally and encourage the Hawaiian people suffering the dire effects of colonialism, including massive depopulation from foreign-introduced diseases, and dispossession from traditional lands by sugar planters and foreign land owners.

hulihia—*lit.* "to overturn." An important series of critical chants in the Pele and Hiʻiaka literature that document volcanic eruptions at the Halema'uma'u crater. Metaphorically, hulihia implies an overturning of settler colonialism and the growing influence of foreigners in the nineteenth century through the publication of the Pele and Hiʻiaka literature. It has been used politically in the modern era within the context of the Hawaiian independence movement.

Kahiki—*lit.* "the arriving." It is the homeland of Hawaiians, often directly associated with Tahiti.

kaiʻokia kānāwai—*lit.* "sea-separating law." When Pele left Lohiʻau to return to the crater at Halema'uma'u, she imposed a kānāwai (restriction) over him until he was safely returned to her.

kālaiʻāina—*lit.* "to carve the land." In general, it means politics. The term comes from the action of reappropriating the lands when a new chief came to power in traditional times to his loyal followers.

kamaʻāina—*lit.* "child of the land." One native to a specific location, or one very familiar with an area because of living in that place for a long time, often generations of a family.

Kanaka Maoli, Kanaka ʻŌiwi, ʻŌiwi Maoli—synonymous terms meaning indigenous Hawaiian.

kaona—metaphor, underlying, poetic, symbolic, or connotative meaning, considered the hallmark of Hawaiian poetic devices, and Hawaiian poetic thought.

Ka Palapala—*lit.* "the printing." Hawaiian literature, Hawaiian literary tradition commencing with the introduction of printing in Hawaiʻi in the 1830s.

kapu—sacred, restriction, private.

kuleana—simultaneously one's rights or privilege and one's responsibilities. This is an important concept in Hawaiian culture, and people often carry multiple kuleana in myriad ways (personal, familial, cultural, professional, etc.).

kupuna—elders, ancestors; plural, kūpuna.

lāhui, lāhui Hawai'i—*lit.* "nation, Hawaiian nation." The lāhui is both the nation in a political sense, particularly during the period of the Hawaiian monarchy (1840–1893), but also applied to those who trace genealogy to the aboriginal people of the Hawaiian islands prior to Western contact in 1778 (the federal and state standard defining the term Native Hawaiian).

mahalo—thanks, appreciation; mahalo nui, mahalo nui loa are common variations that mean many thanks, with great appreciation.

mai ka pō mai—*lit.* "from the night forth." Poetically, pō refers to the ancient past and the time of the gods (before humans). Refers to traditions coming down to the present from the time of creation.

mai nā kūpuna mai—*lit.* "from the ancestors forth." Refers to traditions, practices, thoughts, and worldview that privileges knowledge from the ancestors and its continuity into the present.

maka'āinana—the working-class people who supported the chiefly class through fishing, farming, and other trades and professions.

makawalu—*lit.* "eight eyes." Reference to multiple perspectives based on traditional concepts of knowledge.

mālama 'āina—*lit.* "to care for the land." Similar to aloha 'āina.

mana—spiritual power, charisma.

mana wahine—a kind of indigenous feminism; the power of women.

mele—song, poem.

meiwi, meiwi mo'okalaleo—Hawaiian literary and poetic devices.

mo'okū'auhau—genealogy.

mo'olelo (mo'olelo ha'i waha, mo'olelo ku'una)—narrative, story, history. Mo'olelo ha'i waha are stories that are told (versus stories that are written); mo'olelo ku'una are traditional stories (oral and written).

oli—chant, to chant.

pā'ū uila—*lit.* "lightning skirt." One of the gifts Pele bestows on Hi'iaka to embark on her long and dangerous journey across the islands to fetch Lohi'au.

po'e aloha 'āina—*lit.* "the people who love the land."

pono—Hawaiian concept of justice, balance, harmony. A very important cultural practice.

wahi pana—*lit.* "places made famous through stories about them." A term used to describe legendary places that distinguish how they are special and why they are remembered and celebrated over time.

Papa Kuhikuhi o nā Mea Kūmole ʻia / Works Cited

Aeʻa, Alohi. "The Road to Kēʻē." *ʻŌiwi: A Native Hawaiian Journal* 1 (2010): 92–93.

Alexander, W. D. *History of the Later Years of the Hawaiian Monarchy, and the Revolution of 1893.* Honolulu: Hawaiian Gazette, 1896.

Allen, Chadwick. *Trans-Indigenous: Methodologies for Global Native Literary Studies.* Minneapolis: University of Minnesota Press, 2012.

Allen, Paula Gunn. "Introduction." In *Spiderwoman's Granddaughters: Traditional Tales and Contemporary Writing by Native American Women*, ed. Paula Gunn Allen. New York: Fawcett Columbie, 1989.

Andrade, Carlos. *Hāʻena: Through the Eyes of the Ancestors.* Honolulu: University of Hawaiʻi Press, 2008.

Andrews, Lorrin. *A Dictionary of the Hawaiian Language.* Honolulu: Board of Commissioners of Public Archives of the Territory of Hawaiʻi, 1922.

Bacchilega, Cristina. *Legendary Hawaiʻi and the Politics of Place: Tradition, Translation, and Tourism.* Philadelphia: University of Pennsylvania Press, 2007.

Barrere, Dorothy, Mary Kawena Pukui, and Marion Kelly. *Hula Historical Perspectives.* Honolulu: Bishop Museum Press, 1980.

Basham, Leilani. "Ka Lāhui Hawaiʻi, He Moʻolelo, He ʻĀina, He Loina, a He Ea Kākou." *Hūlili: Multidisciplinary Research on Hawaiian Well-Being* 6 (2010): 37–72.

Basso, Keith H. *Wisdom Sits in Places: Landscape and Language among the Western Apache.* Albuquerque: University of New Mexico Press, 1996.

Becker, Anne E. "Television, Disordered Eating, and Young Women in Fiji: Negotiating Body Image and Identity during Rapid Social Change." *Culture, Medicine, and Psychiatry* 28 (2004): 533–559.

Beckwith, Martha Warren. *Hawaiian Mythology.* Honolulu: University of Hawaiʻi Press, 1976.

Benham, Maenette K. P., and Ronald Heck. *Cultural and Educational Policy in Hawaiʻi: The Silencing of Native Voices.* Mahwah, N.J.: Lawrence Erlbaum Associates, 1998.

Bingham, Hiram. *A Residence of Twenty-One Years in the Sandwich Islands.* Hartford, Conn.: Hezekiah Huntington, 1848.

Birkett, Mary Ellen. "French Perspective on the Laplace Affair." *Hawaiian Journal of History* 32, no. 15 (1998): 67–99.

Brandt, Patricia K. "Making a Case for Geothermal." *Big Island Chronicle* (April 30, 2013). Available at http://www.bigislandchronicle.com/2013/04/30/guest-column-from-idg-making-a-case-for-geothermal/.

Brooks, Lisa. *The Common Pot: The Recovery of Native Space in the Northeast.* Minneapolis: University of Minnesota Press, 2008.

———. "Digging at the Roots: Locating an Ethical, Native Criticism." In *Reasoning Together: The Native Critics Collective,* ed. Craig S. Womack, Daniel Heath Justice, and Christopher B. Teuton, 234–264. Norman: University of Oklahoma Press, 2008.

Brothers Cazimero. *Follow Me.* Honolulu: Mountain Apple Records, 1991.

Brown, Marie Alohalani. "Native Hawaiian Perspectives on Variation in Moʻolelo." Unpublished paper, 2011.

Burlin, Paul T. *Imperial Maine and Hawaiʻi: Interpretive Essays in the History of Nineteenth-Century American Expansion.* Lanham, Md.: Lexington Books, 2008.

"Bush's Conspiracy." *The Friend* 53, no. 1 (January 1895).

Cazimero, Roland. *Pele.* Honolulu: Mountain Apple Records, 1979.

"A Celebrated Case." *Hawaiian Gazette* 18, no. 10 (March 7, 1883).

Chapin, Helen G. *Guide to Newspapers of Hawaiʻi, 1834–2000.* Honolulu: Hawaiian Historical Society, 2000.

———. *Shaping History: The Role of Newspapers in Hawaiʻi.* Honolulu: University of Hawaiʻi Press, 1996.

Charlot, John P. *Classical Hawaiian Education: Generations of Hawaiian Culture.* Lāʻie: Pacific Institute, Brigham Young University, 2005.

———. "Pele and Hiʻiaka: The Hawaiian-Language Newspaper Series." *Anthropos* 93 (1998): 55–75.

Cockett, Kawai. *ʻO Kaʻōhao Kuʻu ʻĀina Nani.* Honolulu: Hoʻolōkahi/Nani Mau Records, 1993.

Currie, Noel Elizabeth. *Constructing Colonial Discourse: Captain Cook at Nootka Sound.* Montreal: McGill-Queen's University Press, 2005.

Desha, Stephen L., Sr. *Kamehameha and His Warrior Kekūhaupiʻo.* Trans. Frances Frazier. Honolulu: Kamehameha Schools Press, 2000.

[Desha, Stephen L., and Julia Keonaona]. "He Moolelo Kaao no Hiiaka-i-ka-poli-o-Pele, ka wahine i ka hikinaa ka la a o ka uʻi palekoki uwila o Halemaumau." *Ka Hoku o Hawaii,* vol. 18, no. 17 (September 18, 1924)–vol. 22, no. 8 (July 17, 1928).

———. "Olelo Hoakaka Mua." In "He Moolelo Kaao no Hiiaka-i-ka-poli-o-Pele, ka wahine i ka hikina a ka la a o ka uʻi palekoki uwila o Halemaumau." *Ka Hoku o Hawaii* 18, no. 17 (September 18, 1924).

de Silva, Kīhei. *He Aloha Moku o Keawe: A Collection of Songs for Hawaiʻi, Island of Keawe.* Kailua: Kīhei de Silva, 1999.

———. "Stitch Has a Glitch." Kaʻiwakīloumoku Hawaiian Culture Center, Kamehameha Schools. Available at http://kaiwakiloumoku.ksbe.edu/.

Dickey, Lyle. "Stories of Wailua, Kauaʻi." In *The Twenty-Fifth Annual Report of the Hawaiian Historical Society for the Year 1916,* 14–36. Honolulu: Paradise of the Pacific Press, 1917.

"Died." *Hawaiian Star* 14, no. 4452 (June 29, 1906).

Dole, Charles. "The Hui Kawaihau." *Kauai Historical Society Papers*. No. 16. Līhuʻe: Kauaʻi Historical Society, 1929.

"Eating Disorders Rise after Fiji Gets TV." *Honolulu Advertiser* (May 20, 1999).

Edith Kanakaʻole Foundation, and Hālau o Kekuhi. *Holo Mai Pele*. Stage production program. Honolulu: Edith Kanakaʻole Foundation and Hālau o Kekuhi, 1996.

Elbert, Samuel H. "Hawaiian Literary Style and Culture." *American Anthropologist* 53, no. 3 (1951): 345–354.

———. "Symbolism in Hawaiian Poetry." *Etc.* 18 (1962): 389–400.

Elbert, Samuel H., and Mary Kawena Pukui. *Hawaiian Dictionary*. Rev. ed. Honolulu: University of Hawaiʻi Press, 1986.

Elbert, Samuel H., Mary Kawena Pukui, and Esther T. Mookini. *Place Names of Hawaiʻi*. Honolulu: University of Hawaiʻi Press, 1986.

Emerson, Nathaniel B. *Pele and Hiiaka: A Myth from Hawaii*. Honolulu: ʻAi Pōhaku Press, 1998.

———. *Unwritten Literature: The Sacred Songs of the Hula*. Honolulu: ʻAi Pōhaku Press, 1997.

Fagan, Kristina, et al. "Canadian Indian Literary Nationalism? Critical Approaches in Canadian Indigenous Contexts—a Collaborative Interlogue." In *Cultural Grammars of Nation, Diaspora, and Indigeneity in Canada*, ed. Christine Kim, Sophie McCall, and Melina Baum Singer. Special issue of *Canadian Journal of Native Studies* 29, nos. 1/2 (2009): 19–44.

Finney, Ben. *Sailing in the Wake of the Ancestors: Reviving Polynesian Voyaging*. Honolulu: Bishop Museum Press, 2004.

Forbes, David. *Hawaiian National Bibliography, 1780–1900*. Vol. 4. Honolulu: University of Hawaiʻi Press, 2003.

Fornander, Abraham. "Na Akua Oopu." In *Fornander Collection of Hawaiian Antiquities and Folk-lore*, ed. Abraham Fornander, 510–511. Vol. 5. Honolulu: Bishop Museum Press, 1918.

Friend 3, no. 15 (August 1845).

Goodhue, Kauʻi. "From Resistance to Affirmation: We Are Who We Were." *ʻŌiwi: A Native Hawaiian Journal* 1 (1998): 36–39.

Haʻanio, Samuela. Untitled letter. *Ke Kumu Hawaii* 3, no. 24 (April 25, 1838).

Halai, J. D. K. "He Mele." *Ka Hae Hawaii* 5, no. 5 (May 2, 1860).

"Hala ka Mea Hanohano Joseph Mokuohai Poepoe." *Ka Nupepa Kuokoa* 51, no. 15 (April 18, 1913).

Hale Kuamoʻo. *Mamaka Kaiao: Modern Hawaiian Vocabulary*. Honolulu: University of Hawaiʻi Press, 2003. Available at http://www.wehewehe.org/.

Haleʻole, S. N. "Ka Moolelo o Kapakohano." *Ka Hoku o ka Pakipika*, vol. 1, no. 6 (October 31, 1861)–vol. 1, no. 7 (November 7, 1861).

———. *Ke Kaao o Laieikawai*. Honolulu: Henry Whitney, 1863.

———. "Mooolelo no Keaniniulaokalani." *Ka Hoku o ka Pakipika* 1, no. 2 (October 3, 1861).

———. "Na Manao o S. N. Haleole." *Ka Nupepa Kuokoa* 4, no. 22 (June 1, 1865).

Handy, E. S. Craighill, Elizabeth Green Handy, and Mary Kawena Pukui. *Native Planters in Old Hawai'i: Their Life, Lore, and Environment*. Honolulu: Bishop Museum Press, 1991.

Handy, E. S. Craighill, and Mary Kawena Pukui. *The Polynesian Family System in Ka'u, Hawaii*. Honolulu: Mutual Publishing, 2006.

Hau'ofa, Epeli. "Our Sea of Islands." *Contemporary Pacific* 6 no. 1 (1994): 148–161.

Hauola, B. K. [B. Kalaiohauola]. "He Wahi Kaao a me Kekahi Mele Pu." *Ka Hae Hawai'i*, vol. 5, no. 14 (July 4, 1860), vol. 5, no. 20 (August 15, 1860).

"Hawaiian Education." *Pacific Commercial Daily Advertiser* 1, no. 247 (February 23, 1883).

Hawai'i Forestry Association. "Dryland Forest Restoration Forum" (November 14, 1997). Available at http://www.hawaiistateassessment.info /library/Dryland_Forest_Restoration_Forum_Minutes_%201997Forum Proceedings.pdf.

"He Lei no ka Poe Aloha Aina." *Ka Leo o ka Lahui* 2, no. 706 (May 16, 1893).

"He Mele Kanikau." *Ke Kumu Hawaii* 1, no. 8 (February 18, 1835).

"He Moolelo no o Aahoaka, ke Koa a me Kona Hanau Kupaianaha ana." *Ka Nupepa Kuokoa*, vol. 15, no. 53 (December 30, 1876)–vol. 16, no. 9 (March 3, 1877).

Hibbard, Don, Holly McEldowney, and Nathan Napoka. "Introduction." In *Kamehameha and His Warrior Kekūhaupi'o*, by Stephen L. Desha, Sr., trans. Frances Frazier, xiii–xx. Honolulu: Kamehameha Schools Press, 2000.

Hinau, S. "He Moolelo no Kaililauokekoa." *Ka Hoku o ka Pakipika*, vol. 1, no. 6 (October 31, 1861)–vol. 1, no. 18 (January 23, 1862).

ho'omanawanui, ku'ualoha. "Hanohano Wailuanuiaho'ano: Remembering, Recovering, and Writing Place." *Hūlili: Multidisciplinary Research on Hawaiian Well-Being* 8 (2012): 187–243.

———. "He Lei Ho'oheno no nā Kau a Kau: Language, Performance, and Form in Contemporary Hawaiian Poetry." *Contemporary Pacific* 17, no. 1 (2005): 29–81.

———. "He Mo'olelo mai nā Kūpuna mai: 'O ka Wehewehe 'ana o ka Mo'olelo "'O Pelekeahi'āloa a me Wakakeakaikawai" (A Story from the Ancestors: An Interpretive Analysis of the "Pele-of-the-eternal-fires and Waka-of-the-shadowy-waters" Myth Cycle). M.A. thesis, University of Hawai'i at Mānoa, 1997.

———. "'Ike 'Āina: Native Hawaiian Culturally Based Literacy." *Hūlili: Multidisciplinary Research on Hawaiian Well-Being* 5 (2009): 203–244.

———. "Mana Wahine: Feminism and Nationalism in Hawaiian Literature." *Anglistica* 14, no. 2 (2010): 27–43.

———. "Mo'olelo as Social and Political Action: Responding to Jack Zipes (De-Disneyfying Disney) and Waziyatawin (From the Clay We Rise)." Paper presented at the University of Hawai'i at Mānoa International Symposium "Folktales and Fairy Tales: Translation, Colonialism, and Cinema," Honolulu, September 23–26, 2008. Available at http://scholarspace.manoa .hawaii.edu/handle/10125/16458.

———. "Pele's Appeal." *Acoma: The Italian Journal of American Studies* 29–30 (2004): 80–90.

———. "This Land Is Your Land, This Land Was My Land: Kanaka Maoli versus Settler Representations of ʻĀina in Contemporary Literature of Hawaiʻi." In *Asian Settler Colonialism: From Local Governance to the Habits of Everyday Life in Hawaiʻi*, ed. Candace Fujikane and Jonathan Okamura, 116–154. Honolulu: University of Hawaiʻi Press, 2008.

[Hoʻoulumāhiehie]. "Ka Moolelo o Hiiaka-i-ka-poli-o-pele, ka Wahine i ka Hikina a ka La, a o ka Ui Palekoki Uwila o Halemaʻumaʻu." *Ka Naʻi Aupuni*, vol. 1, no. 5 (December 1, 1905)–vol. 2, no. 155 (January 15, 1906).

———. "Ka Moolelo o Hiiaka-i-ka-poli-o-pele, ka Wahine i ka Hikina a ka La, a o ka Ui Palekoki Uwila o Halemaʻumaʻu." *Ka Naʻi Aupuni*, vol. 2, no. 1 (June 1, 1906)–vol. 2, no. 116 (October 17, 1906).

———. "Ka Moolelo o Hiiaka-i-ka-poli-o-pele, ka Wahine i ka Hikina a ka La, a o ka Ui Palekoki Uwila o Halemaʻumaʻu." *Hawaii Aloha* (July 15–November 24, 1905).

Iaukea, Sydney L. "Land Agendas vis à vis Wind Discourse: Deconstructing Space/Place Political Agendas in Hawaiʻi and the Pacific." *Pacific Studies* 32, no. 1 (2009): 48–72.

ʻĪʻī, John Papa. *Fragments of Hawaiian History*. Honolulu: Bishop Museum Press, 1959.

Imada, Adria L. *Aloha America: Hula Circuits through the U.S. Empire*. Durham: Duke University Press, 2012.

Ing, Tiffany. "ʻTo Be or Not to Be,' That Was Not the Question: A Rhetorical Study of Kalākaua's *Legends and Myths of Hawaii: The Fables and Folk-Lore of a Strange People*." M.A. thesis, University of Hawaiʻi at Mānoa, 2003.

Interior Department letter to John Cummins (January 11, 1858). Trans. E. H. Hart. Honolulu: Hawaiʻi State Archives.

Joesting, Edward. *Kauaʻi: The Separate Kingdom*. Honolulu: University of Hawaiʻi Press, 1984.

Johnson, Rubellite Kawena. "Essays in Hawaiian Literature: Hawaiian 261 Reader." Unpublished paper, 2001.

Judd, Henry P. "Stephen L. Desha." *Friend* 104, no. 8 (August 1934).

Justice, Daniel Heath. "Indigenous Literary Nationalism." Available at http://www.danielheathjustice.com/scholarship.html.

———. *Our Fire Survives the Storm: A Cherokee Literary History*. Minneapolis: University of Minnesota Press, 2006.

"Ka Episetole a Paulo i ko Roma, Mokuna 1, pauku 22–28." *Ke Kumu Hawaii* 1, no. 3 (December 10, 1834).

Kaʻili [Emma Nakuina]. "A Hawaiian Legend by a Hawaiian Native." *Pacific Commercial Advertiser*, vol. 28, no. 9 (August 25, 1883)–vol. 28, no. 16 (October 13, 1883).

Kaʻili, Tēvita. "Tauhi vā: Nurturing Tongan Sociospacial Ties in Maui and Beyond." *Contemporary Pacific* 17, no. 1 (2005): 83–114.

Kalākaua, David. *Legends and Myths of Hawaii: The Fables and Folk-Lore of a Strange People.* New York: C. L. Webster and Co., 1888.

Kalama, L. S. "He Mele." *Ka Hae Hawai'i* 5, no. 12 (June 20, 1860).

Kalani, J. "No ke Kula Kahuna o Wailuku." *Ka Nupepa Kuokoa* 6, no. 46 (November 16, 1867).

"Ka Lapuwale o ka Poaono Nei." *Ka Nupepa Kuokoa* 22, no. 9 (March 3, 1883).

Kalmijn, A. J. "Electric and Magnetic Field Detection in Elasmobranch Fishes." *Science* 218, no. 4575 (1982): 916–918.

Kamahele, Momi. "Hula as Resistance." *Forward Motion* 2, no. 3 (1992): 40–46.

Kamakau, Samuel Manaiakalani. "He Mau Mea i Hoolaha ia no na Mea i loko o na Kaao Hawaii." *Ka Nupepa Kuokoa* 7, no. 7 (February 15, 1868).

———. "He Mele i Kilauea." *Ka Hae Hawaii* 4, no. 51 (March 21, 1860).

———. "He Wahi Manao Paipai." *Ka Nupepa Kuokoa* 6, no. 1 (January 5, 1867).

———. "Ka Lua o ko Kaleiopaoa mau Mele." *Ka Hae Hawaii* 4, no. 52 (March 28, 1860).

———. "Ka Moolelo Hawaii." *Ke Au Okoa* 5, no. 19 (August 26, 1869).

———. "Ka Moolelo Hawaii." *Ke Au Okoa* 6, no. 25 (October 6, 1870).

———. *Ruling Chiefs of Hawai'i.* Honolulu: Kamehameha Schools Press, 1992.

———. *Tales and Traditions of the People of Old: Nā Mo'olelo a ka Po'e Kahiko.* Honolulu: Bishop Museum Press, 1991.

Kamau, William. "Hoalohaloha no Rev. S. Paaluhi." *Ka Nupepa Kuokoa* 51, no. 19 (May 16, 1913).

Kame'eleihiwa, Lilikalā. *A Legendary Tradition of Kamapua'a: The Hawaiian Pig–God.* Honolulu: Bishop Museum Press, 1996.

———. *Nā Wāhine Kapu: Divine Hawaiian Women.* Honolulu: 'Ai Pōhaku Press, 1999.

———. *Native Lands and Foreign Desires: Pehea La e Pono ai?* Honolulu: Bishop Museum Press, 1992.

———. "A Synopsis of Traditional Hawaiian Culture: The Events Leading to the 1887 Bayonet Constitution and the Overthrow of the Hawaiian Government, 1 AD–1898." Unpublished paper originally prepared for the Department of Education, Hawaiian Immersion Program, State of Hawai'i, 1992.

"Ka Moolelo o Hiiakaikapoliopele." Manuscript. Bishop Museum Archives, Henriques-Peabody Collection, HI.L23.

Kanahele, Pualani Kanaka'ole. *Holo Mai Pele.* Honolulu: Pacific Islanders in Communications and Edith Kanaka'ole Foundation, 2001.

———. *Ka Honua Ola: The Living Earth.* Honolulu: Kamehameha Publishing, 2011.

Kanahele, Pualani Kanaka'ole, and Kalani Wise. *Ka Honua Ola: The Living Earth.* Honolulu: Center for Hawaiian Studies, University of Hawai'i at Mānoa, 1989.

Kanahele, Pualani Kanaka'ole, and Nālani Kanaka'ole Zane. *Holo Mai Pele: The Epic Hula Myth.* New York: Pacific Islanders in Communications and International Cultural Programming, 2004.

Kanakaʻole, Edith. *Haʻakuʻi Pele i Hawaiʻi*. Honolulu: Hula Records, 1978.

Kane, Herb Kawainui. *Pele, Goddess of Hawaii's Volcanoes*. Captain Cook, Hawaiʻi: Kawainui Press, 1987.

Kānepuʻu, J. H. "Ka Poe Kakau Moolelo a Kaao Paha." *Ka Hoku o ka Pakipika* 2, no. 3 (October 30, 1862).

Kapihenui, M. J. "He Moolelo no Hiiakaikapoliopele." *Ka Hoku o ka Pakipika*, vol. 1, no. 14 (December 26, 1861)–no. 43 (July 17, 1862).

———. "No ka Moolelo o Pele." *Ka Nupepa Kuokoa* 4, no. 8 (February 23, 1865).

Kauanui, J. Kēhaulani. *Hawaiian Blood: Colonialism and the Politics of Sovereignty and Indigeneity*. Durham: Duke University Press, 2008.

Kawailīʻulā, S. K. "Mooolelo o Kawelo." *Ka Hoku o ka Pakipika*, vol. 1, no. 1 (September 26, 1861)–vol. 1, no. 11 (December 5, 1861).

Kawainui, J. U. "Ka Pele ai Honua ma Hilo." *Ko Hawaii Paeaina* 4, no. 33 (August 15, 1881).

Kelly, Anne Keala. *Noho Hewa: The Wrongful Occupation of Hawaiʻi*. DVD. Kailua: Kuleana Works, 2009.

Kent, Noel. *Hawaii: Islands under the Influence*. Honolulu: University of Hawaiʻi Press, 1993.

Kepelino. *Kepelino's Traditions of Hawaii*. Ed. Martha Warren Beckwith. Honolulu: Bishop Museum Press, 2007.

Kimura, Larry Kauanoe. "Native Hawaiian Culture." In *Native Hawaiian Study Commission Report on the Culture, Needs, and Concerns of Native Hawaiians*, 173–224. Vol. 1. Washington, D.C.: Government Printing Office, 1985.

King, Thomas. *The Truth about Stories*. Minneapolis: University of Minnesota Press, 2003.

Kinney, Jeanne Kawelo. "Pele at the KTA." *ʻŌiwi: A Native Hawaiian Journal* 3 (2005): 44.

Kirch, Patrick. *On the Road of the Winds: An Archaeological History of the Pacific Islands before European Contact*. Los Angeles: University of California Press, 2002.

Kumu Pono Associates, *Mauna Kea: Ka Piko Kaulana o ka ʻĀina (Mauna Kea: The Famous Summit of the Land): A Collection of Native Traditions, Historical Accounts, and Oral History Interviews for: Mauna Kea, the Lands of Kaʻohe, Humuʻula, and the ʻĀina Mauna on the Island of Hawaiʻi*. Hilo: Kumu Pono Associates, 2005.

Kuwada, Bryan Kamaoli. "Finding Mana in the Mundane: Telling Hawaiian Moʻolelo in Comics." *Anglistica* 14, no. 2 (2007): 107–117.

———. "How Blue Is His Beard? An Examination of the 1862 Hawaiian-Language Translation of 'Bluebeard.'" *Marvels and Tales: Journal of Fairy-Tale Studies* 23, no. 1 (2009): 17–39.

Kuykendall, Ralph. *The Hawaiian Kingdom*. Vol. 2. Honolulu: University of Hawaiʻi Press, 1938.

Ledyard, John. *John Ledyard's Journal of Captain Cook's Last Voyage*. Edited by

James Kenneth Munford et al. Oregon State Monographs: Studies in History #3. Corvallis: Oregon State University Press, 1963.

"The Legend of Hiiaka." *Pacific Commercial Advertiser* 28, no. 16 (October 13, 1883).

Liliʻuokalani. *Hawaiʻi's Story by Hawaiʻi's Queen.* Honolulu: Mutual Publishing, 1990.

Lyons, Scott Richard. "Rhetorical Sovereignty: What Do American Indians Want from Writing?" *CCC* 51, no. 3 (2000): 447–468.

MacIver, Malcolm. "A Shark's Sixth Sense." *Science in Society* (July 31, 2009). Available at http://scienceinsociety.northwestern.edu/content/articles/2009/research-digest/sharks/a-sharks-sixth-sense.

Mageo, Jeannette Marie. "On Memory Genres: Tendencies in Cultural Remembering." In *Cultural Memory*, ed. Jeannette Marie Mageo, 11–33. Honolulu: University of Hawaiʻi Press, 2001.

Makaha Sons of Niʻihau. *Nā Mele Henoheno nā Makahiki Mua, Helu ʻElua.* Honolulu: Poki Records, Tropical Music, 1999.

"Make." *Ke Kumu Hawaii* 1, no. 11 (April 1, 1835).

Malo, David. *Hawaiian Antiquities (Moolelo Hawaii).* Translated from the Hawaiian by Nathaniel B. Emerson. Honolulu: Bishop Museum Press, 1951.

Maly, Kepa. "He Moʻolelo Kaʻao no Hiʻiaka-i-ka-poli-o-Pele: A Legendary Tale of Hiʻiaka Who Is Held in the Bosom of Pele." In *Oral History Study: Ahupuaʻa of Mākua and Kahanahāiki, District of Waiʻanae, Island of Oʻahu*, A1–13. San Francisco: Institute for Sustainable Development, 1998.

Manu, Moses. "He Moolelo Kaao Hawaii no ke Kaua Nui Weliweli ma waena o Pele-Keahialoa me Waka-Keakaikawai: He mau kupua Wahine Kaʻeaeʻa." *Ka Loea Kalaiaina*, vol. 3, no. 18 (May 13, 1899)–vol. 3, no. 50 (December 30, 1899).

McDougall, Brandy Nālani. "Laugh of the Goddess: Humor as Mana Wahine in the Moʻolelo of Hiʻiakaikapoliopele." Unpublished paper, 2006.

———. "Pele." In *The Salt Wind: Ka Makani Paʻakai*, 13. Honolulu: Kuleana ʻŌiwi Press, 2007.

McGregor, Davianna Pōmaikaʻi. *Nā Kuaʻāina: Living Hawaiian Culture.* Honolulu: University of Hawaiʻi Press, 2007.

McNicoll, ʻAlika. "Graphic Artist's Note: Alter(native) Perspectives, a Hawaiian Approach to Book Design." *ʻŌiwi: A Native Hawaiian Journal* 2 (2002): 11–18.

Meyer, C. G., K. N. Holland, and Y. P. Papastamatiou. "Sharks Can Detect Changes in the Geomagnetic Field." *Journal of the Royal Society: Interface* 2, no. 2 (2004): 129–130.

Mookini, Esther T. *The Hawaiian Newspapers.* Honolulu: Topgallant, 1974.

"Moolelo Hawaii." *Ka Hae Hawaiʻi* 3, no. 18 (August 4, 1858).

"Moolelo o ka Ahahui Euanelio o ka Mokupuni o Oahu." *Ka Nupepa Kuokoa* 18, no. 16 (April 19, 1879).

Morris, Robert J. "Aikāne: Accounts of Hawaiian Same-Sex Relationships in the Journals of Captain Cook's Third Voyage, 1776–80." *Journal of Homosexuality* 19, no. 4 (1990): 21–54.

Mugge, Robert, dir. *Kumu Hula: Keepers of a Culture*. VHS. Secane, Pa.: MugShot Productions, 1989.

Naithani, Sadhana. "Prefaced Space: Tales of the Colonial British Collectors of Indian Folklore." In *Imagined States: Nationalism, Utopia, and Longing in Oral Culture*, ed. Luisa Del Giudice and Gerald Porter, 64–79. Logan: Utah State University Press, 2001.

Nakuina, Moses. *The Wind Gourd of La'amaomao*. Trans. Sarah Nākoa and Esther T. Mookini. Honolulu: Kalamakū Press, 2005.

Nā Maka o ka 'Āina, or *Pele's Appeal*. Honolulu: Nā Maka o ka 'Āina, 1989.

Neal, Marie C. *In Gardens of Hawaii*. Honolulu: Bishop Museum Press, 1965.

Nimmo, H. Arlo. *Pele, Volcano Goddess of Hawai'i: A History*. Jefferson, N.C.: McFarland, 2011.

———. *The Pele Literature, an Annotated Bibliography of the English-Language Literature on Pele, Volcano Goddess of Hawai'i*. Honolulu: Bishop Museum Press, 1992.

Nogelmeier, M. Puakea, ed., trans. *The Epic Tale of Hi'iakaikapoliopele*. Honolulu: Awaiaulu Press, 2006.

———. ed., trans. *Ka Mo'olelo o Hi'iakaikapoliopele*. Honolulu: Awaiaulu Press, 2006.

———. *Mai Pa'a i ka Leo: Historical Voice in Hawaiian Primary Materials, Looking Forward and Listening Back*. Honolulu: Bishop Museum Press, 2010.

"No ka Hewa o ka Manao Nui ma ke Kino." *Ka Lama Hawaii* 1, no. 12 (May 2, 1834).

"No Na Mele." *Ka Hae Hawaii* 4, no. 51 (March 21, 1860).

Notley, Charles Kahiliaulani, and Joseph Moku'ōhai Poepoe. "What Is Poi?" *Kuokoa Home Rula* 46, no. 1 (1909).

Ortiz, Simon, ed. *Speaking for the Generations: Native Writers on Writing*. Tucson: University of Arizona Press, 1998.

Osorio, Jonathan Kay Kamakawiwo'ole. *Dismembering Lāhui: A History of the Hawaiian Nation to 1887*. Honolulu: University of Hawai'i Press, 2002.

———. "On Being Hawaiian." *Hūlili: Multidisciplinary Research on Hawaiian Well-Being* 3, no. 1 (2006): 19–26.

Pa'aluhi, Simeon, and John Edwin Ailuene Bush. "He Mo[o]lelo Kaao no Kamapuaa." *Ka Leo o ka Lahui*, vol. 2, no. 220 (June 22, 1891)–vol. 2, no. 290 (September 28, 1891).

———. "Ka Moolelo o Hiiakaikapoliopele." *Ka Leo o ka Lahui*, vol. 2, no. 616 (January 5, 1893)–vol. 2, no. 724 (July 12, 1893).

Pacific Resources for Education and Learning. *E Ho'omau! Pele Searches for a Home*. DVD and graphic novel. Honolulu: Pacific Resources for Education and Learning, 2011.

"Papa Kuhikuhi o na Hula Poni Moi, February 12, 1883." Bishop Museum Archives, Honolulu.

Perreira, Hiapokeikikāne. "He Haʻiʻōlelo Kuʻuna: Nā Hiʻohiʻona me nā Kiʻina Hoʻāla Hou i ke Kākāʻōlelo." Ph.D. diss., University of Hawaiʻi at Hilo, 2011.

Philip-Barbara, Glenis. "Mana Wahine Week a Winner." *Gisborne Herald* (April 28, 2007). Available at http://mal3ficent.livejournal.com/171358.html.

Phillips, Clifton Jackson. *Protestant America and the Pagan World: The First Half Century of the American Board of Commissioners for Foreign Missions, 1810–1860.* Cambridge: East Asian Research Center, Harvard University, 1969.

[Poepoe, Joseph]. "Battle of the Owls: A Hawaiian Legend." In *Thrum's Hawaiian Almanac and Annual for 1892*, 86–87. Honolulu: Press Publishing Co. Steam Print, 1891.

———. "He Hoakaka Aku." *Ka Naʻi Aupuni* 1, no. 19 (December 18, 1905).

———. [Hoʻoulumāhiehie]. "Ka Moolelo Hiwahiwa o Kawelo." *Kuokoa Home Rula*, vol. 7, no. 1 (January 1, 1909)–vol. 8, no. 13 (April 1, 1910).

———. "Ka Moolelo Kaao o Hiiaka-i-ka-poli-o-pele." *Kuokoa Home Rula*, vol. 6, no. 2 (January 10, 1908)–vol. 9, no. 2 (January 13, 1911).

———. "Ka Moolelo o Hiiakaikapoliopele." *Ka Naʻi Aupuni* 1, no. 4 (November 30, 1905).

———. *Ka Moolelo o ka Moi Kalakaua.* Honolulu: n.p., 1891.

———. "Ka Moolelo o Kamehameha I, Ka Na-i Aupuni o Hawaii, ka Liona o ka Moana Pakipika." *Ka Naʻi Aupuni*, vol. 1, no. 1 (November 27, 1905)–vol. 2, no. 143 (November 16, 1906).

———. *Ke Alakai o ke Kanaka Hawaii: He Buke no na Olelo Hooholo o ka Aha Kiekie.* Honolulu: Hawaiian Gazette, 1891.

———. "Moolelo Hawaii Kahiko." *Ka Naʻi Aupuni*, vol. 1, no. 57 (February 1, 1906)–vol. 2, no. 154 (November 29, 1906).

Pukui, Mary Kawena. "Aspects of the Word Lei." In *Directions in Pacific Literature: Essays in Honor of Katharine Luomala*, ed. Adrienne L. Kaeppler and H. Arlo Nimmo, 103–115. Honolulu: Bishop Museum Press, 1976.

———. "How Legends Were Taught." Hawaiian Ethnological Notes, Bishop Museum Archives, Honolulu.

———. *ʻŌlelo Noʻeau: Hawaiian Proverbs and Poetical Sayings.* Honolulu: Bishop Museum Press, 1983.

Rice, William Hyde. "He Moolelo no Pele ame kona Kaikaina Hiiaka i ka Poli o Pele." *Ka Hoku o Hawaii*, vol. 3, no. 4 (May 21, 1908)–vol. 3, no. 20 (September 10, 1908).

Sai, Keanu. "Political History." Available at http://www.hawaiiankingdom.org/political-history.shtml.

Said, Edward. *Culture and Imperialism.* New York: Vintage Books, 1993.

Shanley, Kathryn. "'Writing Indian': American Indian Literature and the Future of Native American Studies." In *Studying Native America: Problems and Prospects*, ed. Russell Thornton, 130–151. Madison: University of Wisconsin Press, 1998.

Silva, Noenoe K. *Aloha Betrayed: Native Hawaiian Resistance to American Colonialism.* Durham: Duke University Press, 2004.

———. "E Lawe i ke Ō: An Analysis of Joseph Mokuohai Poepoe's Account of Pele Calling the Winds." *Hūlili: Multidisciplinary Research on Hawaiian Well-Being* 6 (2010): 233–261.

———. "He Kānāwai e Hoʻopau i na Hula Kuolo Hawaiʻi: The Political Economy of Banning the Hula." *Hawaiian Journal of History* 34 (2000): 29–48.

———. "I Kū Maumau: How Kānaka Maoli Tried to Sustain National Identity within the United States Political System." *American Studies* 45, no. 3 (2004): 9–31.

———. "Introduction." In *Kūʻē: The Hui Aloha ʻĀina Anti-Annexation Petitions, 1897–1898*, comp. Nalani Minton and Noenoe K. Silva. Photocopy. 1998. Available at http://libweb.hawaii.edu/digicoll/annexation/pet-intro.html#1.

———. "Pele, Hiʻiaka, and Haumea: Women and Power in Hawaiian Language Literature." In *Women Writing Oceania*, ed. Caroline Sinavaiana and Kēhaulani Kauanui. Special issue of *Pacific Studies* 30, nos. 1/2 (2007): 159–181.

———. "Talking Back to Law and Empire: Hula in Hawaiian-Language Literature in 1861." In *Law and Empire in the Pacific: Fiji and Hawaiʻi*, ed. Sally Engle Merry and Donald Brenneis, 101–121. Santa Fe: School of American Research Press, 2004.

Simpson, Jacqueline, and Steve Roud. *A Dictionary of English Folklore*. New York: Oxford University Press, 2000.

Smith, Linda Tuhiwai. *Decolonizing Methodologies: Research and Indigenous Peoples*. Dunedin: Otago University Press, 2003.

Stannard, David. *Before the Horror: The Population of Hawaii on the Eve of Western Contact*. Honolulu: Social Services Research Institute, 1989.

Sterling, Elspeth, and Catherine Summers. *Sites of Oahu*. Honolulu: Bishop Museum Press, 1978.

Steward, Charles Samuel. *Journal of a Residence in the Sandwich Isles, during the Years 1823, 1824, and 1825*. New York: John P. Haven, 1828.

Stewart, Carlo. "Geothermal Energy." *Te Ara: The Encyclopedia of New Zealand*. Available at http://www.teara.govt.nz/en/geothermal-energy.

Stillman, Amy Kuʻuleialoha. "Re-membering the History of the Hawaiian Hula." In *Cultural Memory: Reconfiguring History and Identity in the Postcolonial Pacific*, ed. Jeannette Marie Mageo, 187–204. Honolulu: University of Hawaiʻi Press, 2001.

Sullivan, Robert. "The English Moko: Exploring a Spiral." In *Figuring the Pacific: Aotearoa New Zealand Cultural Studies*, ed. Howard McNaughton and John Newton, 12–28. Christchurch: Canterbury University Press, 2005.

———. *Star Waka*. Auckland: Auckland University Press, 1999.

Tauʻā, Keliʻi. *The Pele Legends in Authentic Hawaiian Chants*. Honolulu: Pumehana Records, 1977.

Tengan, Ty P. Kāwika. *Native Men Remade: Gender and Nation in Contemporary Hawaiʻi*. Durham: Duke University Press, 2008.

Thrum, Thomas G. *Hawaiian Folk Tales: A Collection of Native Legends*. Chicago: A. C. McClurg and Co., 1907.

———. *More Hawaiian Folk Tales: A Collection of Native Legends and Traditions*. Chicago: A. C. McClurg and Co., 1923.

Titcomb, Margaret. *Native Use of Fish in Hawaii*. Honolulu: University of Hawai'i Press, 1982.

"Toni Morrison." In *Norton Anthology of African American Literature*, ed. Henry Louis Gates and Nellie McKay, 2094–2098. New York: Norton, 1997.

Trask, Haunani-Kay. *From a Native Daughter: Colonialism and Sovereignty in Hawai'i*. Monroe, Maine: Common Courage Press, 1993.

———. *Light in a Crevice Never Seen*. Corvallis, Ore.: Calyx Books, 1994.

———. *Night Is a Sharkskin Drum*. Honolulu: University of Hawai'i Press, 2002.

———. "Writing in Captivity: Poetry in a Time of Decolonization." In *Inside Out: Literature, Cultural Politics, and Identity in the New Pacific*, ed. Vilsoni Hereniko and Rob Wilson, 17–26. Lanham, Md.: Rowman and Littlefield, 1999.

"Ua Hala o John E. Bush." *Ka Na'i Aupuni* 2, no. 30 (July 7, 1906).

Valier, Kathy. *Ferns of Hawai'i*. Honolulu: University of Hawai'i Press, 1995.

Walker, Isaiah Helekunihi. *Waves of Resistance: Surfing and History in Twentieth-Century Hawai'i*. Honolulu: University of Hawai'i Press, 2011.

Warrior, Robert. *Tribal Secrets: Recovering Native American Intellectual Traditions*. Minneapolis: University of Minnesota Press, 1995.

wa Thiong'o, Ngũgĩ. *Decolonising the Mind: The Politics of Language in African Literature*. Portsmouth, N.H.: Heinemann, 1986.

Waziyatawin, "Maka Cokaya Kin (The Center of the Earth): From the Clay We Rise." Paper presented at the University of Hawai'i at Mānoa International Symposium "Folktales and Fairy Tales: Translation, Colonialism, and Cinema," Honolulu, September 23–26, 2008. Available at http://scholarspace.manoa.hawaii.edu/handle/10125/16456.

Weaver, Jace. *That the People Might Live: Native American Literature and Native American Community*. New York: Oxford University Press, 1997.

Wendt, Albert. "Towards a New Oceania." *Mana Review: A South Pacific Journal of Language and Literature* 1, no. 1 (1976): 49–60.

Westervelt, William Drake. *Hawaiian Legends of Volcanoes: Collected and Translated from the Hawaiian*. Boston: Ellis Press, 1916.

Wichman, Frederick. *Kaua'i: Ancient Place Names and Their Stories*. Honolulu: University of Hawai'i Press, 1998.

Winduo, Steven Edmund. "Unwriting Oceania: The Repositioning of the Pacific Writer Scholars within a Folk Narrative Space." *New Literary History* 31, no. 3 (2000): 599–614.

Wolfe, Patrick. "Settler Colonialism and the Elimination of the Native." *Journal of Genocide Research* 8, no. 4 (2006): 387–409.

Womack, Craig. *Red on Red: Native American Literary Separatism*. Minnesota: University of Minnesota Press, 1999.

Wood, Houston. *Displacing Natives: The Rhetorical Production of Hawai'i*. Lanham, Md.: Rowman and Littlefield, 1999.

Young, Kanalu G. Terry. *Rethinking the Native Hawaiian Past*. New York: Garland, 1998.

Papa Kuhikuhi Hōʻike / Index

Kanaka ʻŌiwi nationalist, poet, artist, scholar, and aloha ʻāina advocate **kuʻualoha hoʻomanawanui** is associate professor of English at the University of Hawaiʻi at Mānoa specializing in Oceanic literatures and indigenous literacy, with a focus on traditional moʻolelo and place-based learning. She is a founding and chief editor of *ʻŌiwi: A Native Hawaiian Journal*.